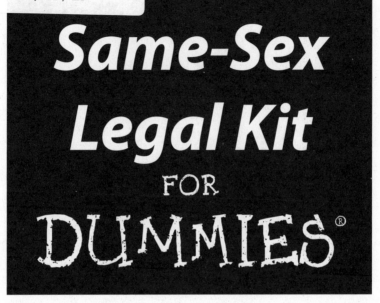

Same-Sex Legal Kit
FOR
DUMMIES®

by Carrie Stone, JD
Co-owner and operator of Rainbow Law

John G. Culhane, JD
Professor of Law and Director of the Health Law Institute at
Widener University School of Law

WILEY

John Wiley & Sons, Inc

Same-Sex Legal Kit For Dummies®

Published by
John Wiley & Sons, Inc.
111 River St.
Hoboken, NJ 07030-5774
www.wiley.com

For general information on our other products and services, please contact our Customer Care Department within the U.S. at 877-762-2974, outside the U.S. at 317-572-3993, or fax 317-572-4002.

For technical support, please visit www.wiley.com/techsupport.

Wiley publishes in a variety of print and electronic formats and by print-on-demand. Some material included with standard print versions of this book may not be included in e-books or in print-on-demand. If this book refers to media such as a CD or DVD that is not included in the version you purchased, you may download this material at http://booksupport.wiley.com. For more information about Wiley products, visit www.wiley.com.

Library of Congress Control Number: 2012949800

ISBN 978-1-118-39521-9 (pbk); ISBN 978-1-118-43526-7 (ePub); ISBN 978-1-118-43528-1 (ePDF); ISBN 978-1-118-43530-4 (eMobi)

Manufactured in the United States of America

10 9 8 7 6 5 4 3 2 1

WILEY

About the Authors

Carrie Stone, JD, is an LGBT legal rights activist and co-owner/operator of Rainbow Law (www.rainbowlaw.com), the first and only online legal information and document preparation resource designed specifically for the LGBT community. She's also a freelance writer, blogger, and podcaster on LGBT legal issues.

Carrie received her Doctor of Jurisprudence (JD) at West Virginia University (WVU) College of Law where she was awarded a public interest law scholarship. She's been a guest lecturer at WVU, teaching courses in women's studies, LGBT legal rights, and comparative law. Carrie is also a frequent speaker on LGBT legal and civil rights at college campuses, churches, community centers, and LGBT events across the country.

In 2004, Carrie (along with her life partner, Elisia Ross), journeyed more than 3,000 miles on bicycles — from San Francisco to New York City — to advocate for marriage equality. A documentary about their ride, *A Time to Ride*, was produced by award-winning filmmaker Keith Wilson. Along the route, Carrie spoke to politicians, to the media, at churches, and on the steps of city halls about the need for equal legal rights for LGBT families.

OUT Magazine recognized Carrie's efforts by presenting her with the *OUT 100 Award* for her contributions to LGBT society and culture. Carrie's also been featured in the *Advocate, Girlfriends,* and *Curve* magazines, and on a variety of radio shows and online magazines.

Carrie and Elisia were married in 2003 in Ontario, Canada. For the past eight years, they've been building a sustainable house out of recycled materials on 6 acres in rural West Virginia. In 2010, Carrie gave a presentation on their house-building experience at the Mother Earth News Fair. The couple created a website (www.builtfromtrash.com) with details and photos of the build, and they are currently writing a book on the subject, tentatively titled *Recyclabuilt*.

Carrie has three grown children, two grandchildren, a couple of dogs and cats, a few chickens, and several goats. She's an avid bicyclist, yoga enthusiast, and organic gardener.

John G. Culhane, JD, is a leading academic and popular authority on LGBT and many other issues. He is Professor of Law and Director of the Health Law Institute at Widener University School of Law, a contributing writer to *Slate Magazine*, and a columnist for *The New Civil Rights Movement*. He has also written for *The New York Times,* the *Huffington Post, Dissent Magazine,* the *Philadelphia Inquirer, 365gay.com* (where he was a columnist), and many other publications. He has been seen or heard on shows including *All*

Things Considered, Radio Times, Midday with Dan Rodricks (all on National Public Radio), *Voice of America,* and *The American Law Journal.* He also was featured in the award-winning documentary film *America Betrayed.* An avid blogger, he maintains his own site (Word in Edgewise), and has done guest blogging for a number of sites, including *Family Scholars, The Courage Campaign,* and *Prop 8 and the Right to Marry.* His posts have generated interest and response across the political spectrum, from bloggers ranging from Andrew Sullivan to Maggie Gallagher. He is a frequent speaker at LGBT-themed conferences, including Lavender Law.

He is the author of more than 30 law review articles on a wide range of topics, including marriage equality; the relationship between tort law and the recognition of same-sex relationships; HIV and blood donation policy; public health law; the intersection of sports and law (including articles on the NFL concussion litigation and the Penn State sex abuse case); compensating victims of disasters; gun policy; and product liability. He wrote a chapter for *Reconsidering Law and Policy Debates: A Public Health Perspective* (Cambridge) and edited the book.

He received his BA with high honors from the College of William and Mary and his JD from Fordham Law School, where he was an associate editor of the Law Review. He has taught at the Yale School of Public Health (where he holds the title of Lecturer) and at Southern Methodist University.

Among his awards are the Outstanding Faculty Award (three times) and the Douglas E. Ray Award for Faculty Scholarship (twice). The *National Jurist* also recognized him as one of "23 Law Professors to Take Before You Die." An avid swimmer, John Culhane lives in Philadelphia with his partner David and their twin daughters.

Dedication

Carrie Stone, JD: Because LGBT legal equity remains one of the last unresolved civil rights issues, I dedicate this book to the countless victims of legal discrimination and to the activists who struggle to bring about equal rights for all.

John G. Culhane, JD: dedicates this book to those in the LGBT advocacy community who fight so tirelessly to eliminate the need for books like this, and to his family for indulging him in his endless hours of writing.

Authors' Acknowledgments

Carrie Stone, JD: I want to thank my life partner, Elisia Ross, for her encouragement, patience, and editorial insights, and for providing me with a never-ending supply of hot coffee. I also express my sincere appreciation to my editors, Chad Sievers and Michael Lewis, for their guidance and enthusiasm for the book's subject matter. And finally, a heartfelt thanks to my children and grandchildren, for their love, patience, and support.

John G. Culhane, JD: acknowledges Chad Sievers and Michael Lewis, the editors at Wiley. Chad's reminders about the importance of this book kept me going during this whole process. Thanks also to my co-author, Carrie Stone, for making collaborating on a tight schedule more than bearable!

Thanks also to my many colleagues at my law school and in the legal and political opinion fields for encouraging me, and in so much more than the writing of this book. In particular: Jean Eggen (always), Alan Garfield, Erin Daly, Andy Strauss, Linda Ammons, Jay Vanasco, and John Corvino. And thanks to Daniel Connelly for his brisk and spot-on assistance with several areas of the book.

And to David, for encouraging me to write this book in the first place, and for his constant support, love, and encouragement.

Publisher's Acknowledgments

We're proud of this book; please send us your comments at http://dummies.custhelp.com. For other comments, please contact our Customer Care Department within the U.S. at 877-762-2974, outside the U.S. at 317-572-3993, or fax 317-572-4002.

Some of the people who helped bring this book to market include the following:

Acquisitions, Editorial, and Vertical Websites

Project Editor: Chad R. Sievers

Acquisitions Editor: Michael Lewis

Copy Editor: Chad R. Sievers

Assistant Editor: David Lutton

Editorial Program Coordinator: Joe Niesen

Technical Editor: Sean Lemieux, JD

Vertical Websites: Melanie Orr

Editorial Manager: Carmen Krikorian

Editorial Assistant: Alexa Koschier

Art Coordinator: Alicia B. South

Cover Photos: © kostas koutsoukos / iStockphoto.com and© Ricardo Infante Alvarez / iStockphoto.com

Cartoons: Rich Tennant (www.the5thwave.com)

Composition Services

Project Coordinator: Patrick Redmond

Layout and Graphics: Laura Westhuis

Proofreaders: Lauren Mandelbaum, Christine Sabooni

Indexer: Valerie Haynes Perry

Publishing and Editorial for Consumer Dummies

    Kathleen Nebenhaus, Vice President and Executive Publisher

    David Palmer, Associate Publisher

    Kristin Ferguson-Wagstaffe, Product Development Director

Publishing for Technology Dummies

    Andy Cummings, Vice President and Publisher

Composition Services

    Debbie Stailey, Director of Composition Services

Contents at a Glance

Table of Contents

Introduction

*U*ntil a few decades ago, there would have been no reason to write *Same-Sex Legal Kits For Dummies* — a legal kit for gay, lesbian, and bisexual people trying to protect their rights, their relationships, and their expectations. Consider the obstacles that would have existed.

Although same-sex couples obviously have been in committed relationships, they were largely invisible. Even the few who may have been courageous enough to venture out and buy such a book would have had good reason not to do so. No laws protected LGBT folks from discrimination or recognized their relationships. Indeed, in many states even their most basic acts of sexual intimacy branded them as criminals, outside the law's protection. Nor could couples take advantage of private agreements to protect themselves, because in many cases hostile courts didn't enforced such agreements. So the book would have had few readers, and little reason even to exist.

And even if such a book had been written, no respectable publisher would have gone anywhere near it. No bookstore would have wanted to stock it, and few people would have purchased it.

Today, of course, the landscape is completely different. LGBT people, single and in couples, are everywhere, and highly visible — from celebrity lesbian and gay couples like Ellen DeGeneres and Portia de Rossi, Elton John and David Furnish, and Neil Patrick Harris and David Burtka, to gay dads and lesbian moms pushing their kids in strollers. But all this visibility hasn't yet led to legal equality.

However, for many same-sex couples, the law in most states doesn't recognize their relationship. And even where it does, the federal Defense of Marriage Act (DOMA) cripples the legal status of married gay and lesbian couples by roping off all *federally* granted rights, benefits, and obligations, keeping them on the wrong side of the velvet rope.

In this book, we steer a course through the roiling legal waters that you (and your partner) must navigate in order to protect yourself and your family — to the still-incomplete extent that you can. We look at the law of marriage, civil unions, and domestic partnerships, and then provide you with the tools you need to safeguard your property, make sure you and your partner can make decisions for each other, and help to cement your relationship to each other and to your kids. And because the law is always changing on these topics, you'll want to check out this book's website (www.dummies.com/go/samesexlegalkit) as they happen. We have so much to discuss, some of which is complicated when you first encounter it. But this kit can break the issues down into manageable chunks and provide you with peace of mind.

About This Book

In writing *Same-Sex Legal Kit For Dummies,* we have a few related purposes in mind. The first is to provide a user-friendly guide to the law, relating to LBGT people and same-sex relationships. As anyone who follows these developments knows, the situation today is a confused mess. Some states grant full marriage equality to same-sex couples. Others grant civil unions, a novel status that tries to replicate marriage but withholds the *word* "marriage" from gay and lesbian couples. Then there are domestic partnerships, which (unfortunately) mean different things in different states and localities. And a majority of states flatly ban same-sex unions. Picking through the legal debris also requires an understanding of DOMA, the federal law that swamps states' efforts to grant their gay and lesbian residents equality under the law.

Against this backdrop, the book offers sound legal and practical advice for you and your partner in your effort to secure for your family the rights and benefits — and to accept the obligations, too — that opposite-sex couples often take for granted. Much of the advice we offer is especially important for couples that can't marry, but not all of it: Straight or gay, even many married couples don't take the steps they should to protect themselves and their families in the cases where such protections are most needed: a breakup, illness or disability, and death. You can take some practical steps, both legal and simple, that can go a long way toward mooring your family's ship in a safe harbor.

Sometimes, unfortunately, you can do little or nothing, and we discuss cases (such as immigration and personal injury law) where that's so — in part to inspire you to become the kind of legal activist who can work to change the status quo. We even offer unsolicited advice about how to "get your activist on."

Conventions Used in This Book

For the sake of consistency and readability, we use the following conventions throughout the text:

- ✔ When we first introduce a new term, we *italicize* it and provide an everyday definition close at hand.
- ✔ We **bold** important keywords.
- ✔ We format all website addresses in `monofont`, and for the ebook versions, we make those URLs active. If a website has a line break, you can ignore it when typing in the address.

In addition, many different terms are used to refer to people who have a same-sex orientation. To simplify matters, we use the following terms:

- **LGBT** refers to the entire lesbian, gay, bisexual, and transgendered community. Sometimes this is the appropriate term.

- **Same-sex couples** or **gay and lesbian couples** interchangeably, unless we have a reason to distinguish between same-sex male and female couples (as with surrogacy for male couples versus sperm donation for female couples).

Because the law in so many areas is unsettled or unclear, we hedge on many of our statements. Words or phrases like "usually" or "not often" are sometimes necessary. We present the law as best we can, but we remind you throughout the book that you sometimes need to proceed without complete confidence that the result will turn out as intended — again, because things aren't always clear.

What You're Not to Read

Like all *For Dummies* books, this one is organized so that you can find the information that matters to you and ignore the stuff you don't care about. You don't even have to read the chapters in any particular order; each chapter contains the information you need for that chapter's topic, and we provide cross-references if you want to read more about a specific subject. You don't even have to read the entire book — but gosh, don't you want to?

Occasionally, you'll see sidebars, which are shaded boxes of text that go into detail on a particular area of the law or an interesting case. You don't have to read these unless you're interested; skipping them won't hamper you in understanding the rest of the text. (But we think you'll find them fascinating!)

Foolish Assumptions

In researching and writing this book, we've made some assumptions about you, the reader. We assume the following:

- You are in a same-sex relationship, or are considering getting into one, or need some help in figuring out how to get out of one.

- You want to understand how the law affects you, your partner, and (if you have them or are considering having them) your child(ren).

✔ You need useful, clearly explained guidance to help you understand and deal with the legal problems that confront you and your family.

✔ You want a convenient, comprehensive, and easy-to-understand resource that covers all this information without making you feel like . . . a dummy.

How This Book Is Organized

For Dummies books are known for breaking a topic down into broad categories so you can find what you need without having to pore over a lot of information that isn't important to you. In this complex and ever-changing legal realm, we break your kit down into several parts.

Part 1: How the Law Views Marriage and Same-Sex Relationships

This part of the book provides you with the legal information you'll need to get started on figuring out what you should do to protect your rights. Marriage is the most reliable way of doing that, but the legal landscape that same-sex couples encounter is rocky indeed. We work through the different forms of legal relationship that are available to some couples, in some states, and explain how they're alike and different.

We also feature a discussion of other social and legal impediments that gay and lesbian single people and couples face every day and offer some suggestions on how to deal with them.

Part II: Everyday Law and Your Family

Despite the challenging legal context in which gay and lesbian couples must operate, there's no stopping life from happening. In this part, we deal with some of the most important issues that you'll face in the "everydayness" of living together. First, how (and when) do you decide to move in together? And if you do, how are you going to handle your financial arrangements, including your taxes? What will you do when one of you becomes ill? While we're on the subject of sad news, how will you handle a breakup, if that day ever comes?

This part also includes a discussion of one of the most important decisions any couple — or single person, for that matter — ever makes: whether to bring children into the family. For gay and lesbian couples, the choices are even tougher.

Part III: Planning Ahead to Protect Your Loved Ones

Estate planning is vital for any couple. But for same-sex couples who are less protected (if at all) by the law than their straight counterparts, attending to the many big decisions and small details that will determine what happens to your stuff after you become incapacitated or die is especially important. In this part we explain wills and trusts and why the living revocable trust is such an important estate planning tool for you and your partner. We also highlight employment benefits, another important source of support for the person you leave behind.

This part also deals with a little-noticed but potentially important problem: how the law treats your relationship when one of you is injured or killed through a third person's wrongful conduct and what you can do (not much, often) to try and recover the damages that a legally married couple would always be eligible to seek.

Part IV: Handling Other Relevant Issues

Because of DOMA, certain areas of the law that only sometimes affect gay and lesbian couples are much more difficult to navigate. In this part, we consider two of them: immigration law (which makes it much, much harder for you to get your same-sex partner into the country than it is for opposite-sex couples) and military law (which, in spite of the welcome repeal of Don't Ask, Don't Tell, still disadvantages you).

This part closes with an invitation to activism. We offer some suggestions on how to tap into your passion, strengths, and interests in order to effect real changes in the law — the law that you can see treats you and your family unfairly in so many different ways.

Part V: The Part of Tens

The Part of Tens is one of the most popular features of *For Dummies* books because it condenses lots of information into small, easily digested nuggets. In this part, we set forth a list of suggestions for dealing with disgruntled relatives. We also point out the ways in which the law harms the entire LGBT community.

On the CD

This book comes with your very own CD, which contains a number of useful categories of information. In Appendix A (at the end of the book), you can find a guide that lists all the helpful documents and forms that appear on the CD.

Icons Used in This Book

Throughout the text, we place icons in the margins that alert you to certain types of information. Here's a glossary of those terms and what they mean:

This icon points you to practical suggestions for implementing the recommendations offered on a given subject.

This icon reminds you of important things to think about or do when considering the material that we discuss.

This icon may point out a landmine that, if not avoided, can frustrate your efforts. Or it may remind you to consult a lawyer for specific legal advice on a complex topic or where state laws differ.

Not surprisingly, this icon refers you to forms or laws that are on the CD.

Where to Go from Here

The beauty of this *For Dummies* book is that, unlike a textbook, you don't have to read the chapters in order to unpack your legal kit. Where you start is up to you and depends on where your greatest legal or practical need lies.

If you want to get grounded and up-to-date on the marriage equality issues, start with Chapter 2. If you're reading this book to find out more about estate planning, start with Chapter 11. If you're considering bringing kids into your family, Chapter 7 is your launching site. If you want to understand the tax law, proceed to Chapter 8. And if you need to figure out immigration law, flip to Chapter 17.

Because the law is constantly changing and evolving, there is no way we could write a completely updated book. By the time we finish the writing and have the book printed and shipped, courts, state legislatures, and the voting public may have changed policy. As a result, we use www.dummies.com/go/samesexlegalkit to provide updates. Refer to this website to see what changes have been made.

Part I

How the Law Views Marriage and Same-Sex Relationships

The 5th Wave   By Rich Tennant

"It's not just me suggesting we get married; it's also the State of New Hampshire."

In this part...

*O*ne of the toughest things about organizing your life together as a same-sex couple is just in figuring out where you stand under the law. You have many complexities to navigate, and even in the best case — where you can be legally married under your state's law — your relationship doesn't have the same legal currency as your opposite-sex counterpart's does.

In this part, we demystify the law. We explain the twists of gay and lesbian relationship recognition, laying out the various statutes the law has created for couples (like you) that it hasn't quite figured out how to handle. Marriage, civil unions, domestic partnerships, and the suffocating overlay to all these laws that goes by the name of the Defense of Marriage Act (DOMA) are here. We also discuss other legal and social challenges that your family will likely have to face, and address different forms of discrimination that you may face and how to deal with it.

Chapter 1

Being Aware of Same-Sex Legal Issues

In This Chapter

▶ Explaining the need for a legal kit for LGBT people

▶ Outlining the areas of the law where same-sex couples are treated differently

*L*ife isn't always fair, but the law should be.

If you're in a gay or lesbian relationship, though, you have more than likely figured that the law *isn't* fair. Do you want to cement your commitment to your partner by getting legally married? In most states, you can't. And even if you can marry, the law treats you differently in many ways.

First, because of a federal law called the Defense of Marriage Act (DOMA), your marriage isn't worth as much as a straight union (in the eyes of the law). And in many places, you can still be discriminated in other ways, too, such as in employment, adoption, tax liability, inheritance, immigration, and even in your ability to recover damages in tort law. And this isn't even a complete list.

This book is the legal kit you need to deal with these inequities — if you assemble the pieces in the ways we're going to lay out, you can work around the barriers the law has placed in your path. This chapter serves as a jumping-off point to this book. Here we briefly explain why having this legal kit is necessary and how the law treats you and your partner. We explain what the law does, and how private agreements can help you achieve some of the most important goals for you and your partner.

Unfortunately, we can't say that you can solve *all* the problems that discriminatory laws create for you and your same-sex partner. Here and in the following chapters we try to make clear the distinctions between what you can accomplish and what you can't and when a legal route isn't the best one.

Recognizing Why a Same-Sex Legal Kit Is Essential

The law has a substantial impact on many broad areas of human experience. For couples in same-sex relationships, that impact is often painful, confusing, and simply unfair. If you're single, you may encounter similar painful circumstances. In the following sections, we identify the broad legal disabilities that confront you and your partner, if you have one, every day. We can then use this information to help you work through to the solutions.

Lack of marriage equality

No single legal problem has anywhere near the impact of the denial of the right to marry. In Chapter 2, we explore this problem in detail. It's healthy to question whether the law should tie so many rights and benefits to marriage in the first place, but it surely does. And as of this writing, only a very few states (six, plus the District of Columbia, with a couple others probably on the way) recognize the right of gay and lesbian couples to marry. Several others confer virtual equality through civil union and domestic partnership laws.

Married couples inherit each other's property, can jointly adopt children, are often eligible for partner health benefits, enjoy tax advantages, can bring their spouses into the country as permanent residents, are eligible for government benefits, and . . . well, the list is extensive. Unmarried couples, by contrast, are shut out of most of these goodies. The good news: Even if you can't legally marry, you can cobble together some of these benefits by creating or signing the right legal documents — wills, trusts, co-parenting agreements, designation of partner as beneficiary under eligible pension plans, and so on. We explain these options in detail throughout this book.

DOMA further muddles the marriage mess. This law, enacted by Congress in 1996, states that even when gay and lesbian couples are legally wed within their own state, for federal purposes their marriages don't count. This law means that the government withholds from same-sex couples most of the weightiest benefits that married couples enjoy: the right to file joint income taxes; the ability to sponsor their spouses to receive a green card; the right to collect Social Security death benefits; and, for those in the military, the right to many of the benefits available to their married fellow soldiers. As we point out, DOMA's effect on same-sex couples is both pervasive and pernicious — in other words, it's bad!

Children and family challenges

Your inability to marry your partner spills over into the rest of your family, creating problems that we explore in Chapter 3. The law's refusal to recognize you and your partner as spouses can cost your family plenty — financially, legally, and practically. Check out just a few instances:

✔ Married couples receive many financial advantages over unmarried folks. Therefore, families headed by legally unmarried parents suffer financially compared to those with married parents.

✔ Unmarried couples have a harder time adopting children in many states. As a practical matter, this may mean that your child only has one legal parent. The other parent can therefore be excluded from making important decisions about the child, no matter the contrary wishes of the family.

✔ On the everyday level, your family may not be treated with the respect that families headed by opposite-sex couples take for granted. School officials may be clueless, and encounters with people ranging from store clerks to total strangers can be needlessly stressful.

Other forms of discrimination

In many different arenas, members of the LGBT community are discriminated against — sometimes individually and sometimes because they're in a same-sex relationship. In Chapter 4, we address these issues.

How do you know when you've been discriminated against? And after you know you have been, what (if anything) can you do about it? Some of the questions importantly addressed in this chapter include the following:

✔ In what setting has the discrimination occurred? Were you denied a place to live? A job? Did a business refuse to deal with you, or your family, or did an employee treat you poorly?

✔ If you were discriminated against, what can you do about it? Does the law protect you against this type of discrimination based on sexual orientation?

✔ Even if you can prove actionable discrimination, what do you want to do about it? We explore the advantages and disadvantages of bringing a lawsuit, and discuss the alternatives.

Identifying How the Law Affects You Every Day

The big-picture legal questions draw a great deal of the public's attention, but you have a lot more to consider from the viewpoint of the life you and your partner share. Some of the issues you need to consider are directly affected by the law, others, less so. In Part II, we survey the most important issues that you need to deal with in structuring your life together with your partner. Doing so isn't easy, but you can do plenty, which we discuss in the following sections.

Eyeing issues of living together

The focus on marriage and the legal recognition of your relationship can crowd out discussion of one of the most important decisions that a couple makes: whether to move in together and how to deal with the consequences of that decision. In Chapter 5, we explore these broad issues.

Does living together make sense for you and your partner? Not all couples in love can live together (at least not all the time!), and living together often brings about unexpected and unpleasant surprises. We provide practical suggestions for how to make this vital decision and give advice on drawing up an agreement that outlines how you can divide expenses and assign the chores and other duties that householders need to do.

Chapter 5 also explores whether you should buy or rent your dwelling and provides food for thought on the details of home purchase, including:

- ✔ How to finance the purchase
- ✔ Whether to own the property jointly
- ✔ How to deal with legal issues relating to home ownership, as an unmarried couple

Joining assets: Yes or no?

If you and your partner decide to live together, you'll face another practical question: Should you and your partner join assets? Chapter 6 begins by encouraging a frank discussion about money issues — almost never the easiest conversation for a couple to have.

We then sketch out some of the considerations that should go into your decision about whether to mingle (in this sense), and how to divide assets and liabilities if you do go that route. We also explore the possibility of going halfway: Merging some of your assets, but maintaining some financial autonomy.

Grasping adoption and family issues

For some couples, bringing children into the family follows moving in together and getting your financial house in order. So Chapter 7 explores — and, we hope, simplifies — the knotty issues that same-sex couples face in trying to become parents, and the challenges of raising those children in an environment that only inconsistently recognizes the family as an intact unit.

We start with some practical advice for deciding on whether you even want to raise kids and relate that to the important decisions you have to make on whether you want to adopt or to use the services of third parties (sperm donors, egg donors, and surrogates) to maintain some biological connection to at least one of you. We explore the pros and cons of each course of action, and we explain the legal and practical issues that arise in both contexts. We also discuss the virtues of bringing foster children into your home.

Because the law in many states offers incomplete (or worse) protection to same-sex parents and their children, we explore ways of dealing with the fallout from these legal stumbling blocks. From birth certificates, to parenting agreements, to nominating your partner as guardian of your child, this discussion should help you navigate the problems that arise when only one parent can legally adopt the child. We also discuss ways to financially protect the kid.

Your relationship may not last forever. As much as everyone hates hearing this, everyone also knows it to be true. And for gay and lesbian couples, figuring out what you're going to do about your child(ren) if and when that sad day ever dawns is important. You need to have a frank discussion of how to plan for the assignment of rights and responsibilities, for visitation, and for custody, if and when the relationship ends.

Considering potential tax issues

You don't need anyone to tell you that tax law and policy is complicated — so much so that even many well-educated people throw up their hands and hire someone to prepare their income tax returns. For many gay and lesbian couples, though, it's even worse.

If you and your partner are lucky enough to live in a state that sees you as a couple entitled to the same rights as a married couple — through outright marriage equality, civil unions, or domestic partnerships — you should be able to file a joint *state* tax return. But because of DOMA, you can't file a joint *federal* return. For federal purposes, you aren't married!

Wait. It gets worse. Because your state return depends on your federal return, the practical result is that you have to create two federal state tax returns:

- ✔ The real one that you'll file
- ✔ A mock (fake) return that you'll work off in order to create your joint state return

If you think that sounds both unfair and annoying, you're right. Having to create two returns also drives up the cost of your tax preparation. There's no help for it, at least not while DOMA remains law. There are other problems, too — having to do with property and estate taxes. Exemptions that legally married couples enjoy just aren't available to same-sex couples, at least not at the federal level.

In sickness and in health

Serious physical or mental illness creates a confusing welter of problems not only for the sick person but for those in close legal or emotional proximity to him or her. Everyone should take the time to create the legal documents needed to deal with medical and financial decision making for when illness falls. Doing so is especially important for same-sex couples, because

- ✔ In most states, your partner won't be the default person to make decisions for you when you become sick.
- ✔ Even in states where you're the default person, hostility among family members and hospital and long-term care healthcare providers can make an already-stressful situation worse.

We also address the many issues relating to the agonizing decision whether and when one partner needs long-term medical assistance. Check out Chapter 9 for a complete discussion.

When relationships end

Breaking up is tough whether or not you're legally married. That's in part because the dissolution of your relationship isn't just a legal issue, although that aspect of the matter tends to assume the greatest importance. When a couple (same-sex or opposite-sex) splits, all sorts of other matters are affected, such as the following: the circle of friends is fractured, with people often forced to choose between one partner and the other; financial realities change, usually for both partners, and often quite dramatically; and the lives of children, if any, are thrown into upheaval.

Chapter 10 tells you what you need to know and do to deal with these wrenching events. You can possibly make the whole thing less painful if you follow a few steps, which we lay out. We divide the issue between marriage equality (and equivalent) states and those where you and your partner are legal strangers to each other. We also provide clear advice as to how to make the cleanest break possible:

✔ Revoking your legal documents

✔ Getting a mediator

✔ Being fair to each other (no matter how hard that can be!);

✔ Refraining from using your kids as pawns

✔ Splitting property

Protecting Your Loved Ones

As hard as the law and society make it for you and your partner to live together as a couple in the everydayness of life, you can often easily overlook the need for long-range financial planning. Making long-term financial planning is important for all people, unmarried and married couples and single folks. What may differ, though, are the steps you need to take (and how you can take them) — they vary to an extent depending on your legal status.

Estate planning

The most basic document of estate planning is the will. Whether or not your relationship is recognized under state law, you need to create a will in order to avoid the default rules about the distribution of your estate. Making sure your will is valid and thinking about the probate process (and why you want to avoid the uncertainty that it creates) are important. Chapter 11 discusses these points in greater depth.

But for many same-sex couples, the best strategy is to create a trust to protect your assets and to make sure that your assets both avoid probate and go to the person of your choosing. Because many people don't know how to create a trust, they often don't consider this option. We provide a detailed road map and define the trust and then explain how it works. We then discuss considerations when drafting a trust and preparing for some of the contingencies that may arise in Chapter 13. We also discuss how to actually fund the trust in Chapter 14.

Making sure your loved one gets employment benefits

Another issue that poses needless difficulty for many gay and lesbian couples is employee benefits. You can often pass these benefits on to your partner, but only with thoughtful planning. Chapter 15 explains how to do so.

Trying to collect damages after an injury to your partner

Probably one of the least often considered issues confronting gay and lesbian couples is how the law treats, and usually denies, the right to collect damages in tort law when someone's negligent (or worse) behavior ends up causing the harm or outright destruction of your relationship.

Because this issue is a state-law matter, your success or failure often turns on whether your relationship is legally recognized. If so, you're generally eligible to recover the emotional distress or loss of consortium you experience from your partner's serious personal injury or under wrongful death statutes. But if you can't marry, civilly unite, or enter into a domestic partnership, you're generally out of luck. Chapter 16 gives you a few suggestions on how you may be able to get around these strict legal rules, and consider whether it's worth your effort to try.

Dealing with Other Issues

Some issues don't fit into the categories that we discuss earlier in this chapter. You may have encountered the following problems in your life:

- ✔ Because of DOMA, immigration law favors opposite-sex married couples over their same-sex counterparts. Chapter 17 explores how immigration works, and we suggest some alternatives that might be available to some couples, at least sometimes.

- ✔ The repeal of *Don't Ask, Don't Tell* (the policy that allowed gays and lesbians to serve in the military as long as they didn't tell anyone about their sexual orientation) was a milestone. But the repeal didn't make married same-sex couples the equivalent of opposite-sex ones. And the repeal didn't solve other problems confronting gay and lesbian soldiers. Chapter 18 guides you through these problems and what you can do to address them.

- ✔ Want to do something about all this inequality? Then become an activist! There's no one-size-fits-all rule for how to do this, but we provide some suggestions in Chapter 19.

Chapter 2

Living in a Same-Sex Marriage or Relationship

*U*nless you follow developments in LGBT legal issues with the obsession Ahab once reserved for Moby Dick, you're not likely to have a clear idea of where the law stands on same-sex relationships. The situation is confusing indeed, because states are all over the lot, and the law is constantly changing. Many states ban same-sex marriages (and sometimes even *substantially equivalent* relationships). A growing but still small number allow full marriage equality. And others confuse the situation further by affording more limited recognition to same-sex couples, through odd legal creatures like *civil unions, domestic partnerships,* and even something called a *designated beneficiary.*

This inconsistency among the states can create huge headaches for couples trying to figure out where they stand, especially if they move from one state to another or try to dissolve their relationship. Add in a federal law called the Defense of Marriage Act (DOMA), which is also a huge inconsistency between marriage recognition for state law purposes and under federal law. In this chapter, we break down these complexities and hazard a guess as to what the future might hold.

Marriage equality 101: A very brief history of the movement

Although the political and legal push for full marriage equality for lesbian and gay couples has exploded during the past 20 years, the movement is much older. In 1953, a provocative — and much cited — letter appeared in a publication called "One," suggesting that marriage was the natural endpoint of what was then called the *homophile* movement. But not until shortly after the Stonewall riots of 1969 when a trio of gay couples who challenged their exclusion from marriage to state courts did the movement receive a jolt of energy. These suits, brought in the early 1970s — in Kentucky, Minnesota, and Washington — all failed spectacularly. Worse, a few of these courageous people even lost their jobs for trying. But they had previewed the national debate.

In the 1990s, the debate took a different turn, beginning in Hawaii. By 1996, the Hawaii Supreme Court likely was going to find that the state couldn't lawfully keep same-sex couples from obtaining marriage licenses. Gripped by a panic that same-sex marriages would then join pineapples among the state's principal exports, the US Congress in 1996 enacted the Defense of Marriage Act (DOMA), and many states followed suit with their own mini-DOMAs. These smaller versions of the law were designed to prevent the recognition of same-sex marriages, whether performed in the home state or elsewhere.

At the same time, though, cases seeking full marriage equality began to percolate through state courts — this time with greater success. In 1999, the Vermont Supreme Court led the charge with its decision in *Baker v. State*, requiring the state legislature to afford the rights and benefits of marriage to same-sex couples, but not mandating that the lawmakers call this package of rights "marriage." Thus was born the civil union. And in 2003, the Massachusetts Supreme Judicial Court took the final step. *Goodridge v. Department of Public Health* required full marriage equality, including the name — no substitutions, please.

This mix of one-step forward movement toward equality and one-step back laws (and state constitutional amendments) banning same-sex marriages continues to this day. Recently the focus has shifted to *popular referendums*, people who oppose same-sex unions gather signatures in order to put the right of gay and lesbian couples to marry to a popular vote. The result has been confusion for both the same-sex couples who could use clarity and for the general public trying to make sense of the issues and legal rules.

Understanding What Marriage Really Is

Before launching into a discussion of how the marriage equality movement has progressed, we need to step back for a moment and think about what marriage *is*, in the first place.

A lively debate is going on about the purposes of marriage and the incentives that the state is trying to create or support by recognizing these unions. But for purposes of this book, we can limit our discussion to the difference between civil and religious marriage. To some extent, confusion over that crucial distinction is at the bottom of the whole controversy over whether to recognize same-sex unions.

As the Massachusetts Supreme Judicial Court pointed out in *Goodridge v. Department of Public Health,* the state's role in marriage is purely civil. It issues marriage licenses, and these licenses confer a set of rights, benefits, and obligations. According to the *Goodridge* court, recognizing civil marriage is a way for the state to support stable relationships over transient ones and to provide a sturdy foundation for raising children.

Note the absence of the religious meaning of marriage from the foregoing description. Yet for many, marriage and religion are intimately connected. To an extent, this connection is the state's fault: Religious officials are deputized by the state to solemnize marriages, and solemnization is required for the marriage to become valid. But marriages can also be solemnized by state officials — usually, a justice of the peace — and states can't require couples to involve religion as a condition of getting married.

Despite this (probably ill-advised) state involvement in religion, and no matter how closely associated marriage and religion are for many people, the fact remains that the marriage rights under discussion in this book (and at the center of the public debate currently being conducted) are *civil* rights. In fact, any religion that didn't want to solemnize same-sex marriages wouldn't be required to even if marriage equality became the law of the land.

Moving Toward Marriage Equality

Less than ten years ago, no state gave same-sex couples the right to marry. And opinion polls were in agreement with the law — consistently strong majorities agreed with the statement that marriages should be restricted to the union of a man and a woman.

What a difference a decade makes. As of this writing, six states and the District of Columbia allow gay and lesbian couples to marry on the same basis as straight ones, and two more states (Washington and Maryland) are poised to join them within a few months (if the laws permitting same-sex marriages survive ballot initiatives seeking to repeal them). In those states that allow same-sex couples to marry, gay and lesbian couples that choose to do so are entitled to all the same rights and benefits — and are under the same obligations — as every other married couples, but only under *state* law, and only if they remain a resident in their home state.

An additional nine states (including, for now, Washington) grant all the benefits of marriage under some other name — either civil unions or domestic partnerships. And three states provide a more limited set of rights.

These developments are not surprising when you consider the sharp shift in public opinion during the past ten years. A number of recent polls show a majority of Americans in favor of full marriage equality. The details behind those numbers show even better news: support for equality correlates directly with age. The younger the person, the likelier he or she is to vote for same-sex equality. In the not-too-long run, full marriage equality will probably be achieved.

But it's much too soon to celebrate. This book is needed, in part, because in most states same-sex couples still don't enjoy the rights and benefits (nor are they subject to the obligations, though) of marriage. A majority of states still ban same-sex unions of any kind, and some have done so by amending their state constitutions. Federal law also continues not to recognize same-sex marriages.

The following sections help put the marriage debate into perspective. We provide an overview of what states are doing, how some states have handled the debate (civil unions and domestic partnerships), and a frank discussion of whether marriage is even right for you and your partner. We also discuss DOMA and how it affects your marriage even when your state fully recognizes it.

A quickly changing landscape: How different states handle marriage

All this discussion about seven states doing this, three states doing that, and so on clearly indicates that this area of the law is in flux — and will probably continue to be for at least a few more years. That's why figuring out exactly where your state stands on *your* relationship is important.

The easiest situation to understand is also the worst. If you live in one of the many states that doesn't recognize same-sex relationships, you and your partner are legal strangers to each other. (Even in such a state, though, you may live in a city or town that allows you to register as domestic partners. You can acquire some limited rights that way. We discuss that status in the next section.)

In other states, your situation will be less clear. Sometimes you'll be in a legal limbo: your legislature may have enacted a marriage equality law, but its effective date is delayed while opponents try to repeal it through a ballot measure. Such a measure was successful in Maine and is currently being tried in both Maryland and Washington. Taking steps forward while you're waiting out possible changes in the law is difficult. If you can, wait until the legal dust settles.

And then several states have moved toward marriage equality in stages. California is the most dramatic example, having gotten there through a series of steps over a period of more than two decades, culminating with full marriage equality in 2008 — only to take a step back with the passage of Proposition 8, which outlawed same-sex marriages but left the statewide domestic partnership law intact. And same-sex partners who wed during that brief window of opportunity are still legally married in California, thereby creating a weird minority class of gay and lesbian married couples.

Other states, such as Vermont, New Hampshire, and Connecticut, have gone from civil unions to full marriage equality. If you live in states that have moved in stages, you need to keep track of how the state looks at your relationship. Sometimes your civil union converts to marriage automatically, and sometimes it doesn't. Welcome to the wacky world of same-sex relationship recognition.

Before you do anything as a committed (or even sort of committed) gay or lesbian couple, make sure you know exactly where your state stands on relationship recognition. The website that we're maintaining for this book (www. dummies.com/go/samesexlegalkit) helps you keep track of developments as they occur. Appendix B on the CD also contains a state-by-state list of marriage laws.

Understanding what civil unions and domestic partnerships mean

Some states have created civil unions in an effort to confer equality on same-sex couples. Other states have done the same via domestic partnerships, but this term is more ambiguous, because it also refers to local laws that can't and don't do as much. And some states have even created some other designations. This section defines these statuses to help you determine whether they are right for you.

Civil unions (sort of) resemble marriage, but they're separate and not equal

Civil unions are a statewide status intended to confer the same rights and benefits as marriage but without using the word "marriage." Entering into a civil union requires the same legal formalities as entering into a marriage:

✔ You first obtain a license.

✔ You then have an authorized official (who may be a civil servant or a clergy member, just as with marriages) solemnize it.

Civil unions are just as hard to *get out of* as marriages because the same divorce laws apply (refer to Chapter 10 for more info).

Most states that recognize civil unions make them available only to same-sex couples. Two states — Illinois and Hawaii — also allow opposite-sex couples to enter into civil unions.

For many committed gay and lesbian couples, civil unions are a great advance because they allow the couples to use the same default rules that married couples enjoy under state law. Civil union status can dispense with the need to spend lots of time and money hiring lawyers and creating documents in an only partially successful effort to mimic the rights that straight couples have long been able to access just by walking down that aisle.

Despite the advantages the civil unions bring gay and lesbian couples, civil unions are a poor substitute for marriage in at least three ways:

- ✔ **People don't really understand civil unions.** Ask ten random people what a civil union is, and you're likely to get ten different answers. New Jersey and Vermont created civil union commissions to assess whether civil unions were doing their job of making same-sex couples equal under state law, and both found that they weren't. For example, third parties, such as hospital staff, sometimes refused to recognize civil unions in dealing with gay and lesbian couples, which is one reason Vermont moved to full marriage equality.

- ✔ **Marriage isn't just about the legal rights, as important and necessary as those rights are.** Marriage is also about a certain social status and membership in an institution that is widely understood and supported. Giving same-sex couples the benefits without the label is promoting a "separate but equal" regime. Separate can't be equal when the purpose of creating the civil union status is to reserve the preferred label for opposite-sex couples.

- ✔ **Many of the most important rights that marriage confers are federal rights, not state rights.** Federal law doesn't recognize civil unions, so same-sex couples can't file federal joint income tax returns, can't collect Social Security survivor benefits, can't use the Family and Medical Leave Act to care for their partners, and can't sponsor their partners into the country under immigration laws, just to name a few of the many rights that federal law confers. Even legally *married* same-sex couples can't do any of those things either, but that's because of DOMA. As we explain later in this chapter in the "Tackling the Defense of Marriage Act (DOMA)" section. Even if DOMA disappears, civil union partners still won't be able to do any of the things under federal law that married folks can.

The other designations are even worse

A *domestic partnership* isn't one status, but several different ones that (unfortunately) go under one name. Sometimes they're civil unions by another name, conferring all the rights and benefits of marriage. Some domestic partnership laws, such as in California, Oregon, and Nevada, attempt to create a legal equivalent to marriage. Sometimes they confer a smaller set of rights (as in Wisconsin). And the term is even more confusing because it also refers to local ordinances that confer a more limited set of rights. Check with your local government to see if your city or county offers domestic partnership benefits.

They differ from civil unions, though, in the procedures used to enter them. Even though entering into a civil union requires all the formalities of marriage, typically a person can simply register a domestic partnership — neither a license nor a solemnization is required.

Many domestic partnership laws and *all* laws going under any other name aren't nearly as comprehensive, such as the following:

- ✔ **Designated beneficiary:** This term is used only in Colorado. The status is like a limited domestic partnership status of a certain type: it allows same-sex couples an inexpensive way of creating estate-planning documents and of designating each other as the contact person in case of medical emergencies.

- ✔ **Reciprocal beneficiary:** This is yet another term for a law granting a few of the benefits of marriage. This status has been recognized in Hawaii since 1997, and it allows same-sex couples such rights as inheritance, property ownership under a status (*tenancy by the entirety*) usually reserved for married couples, and the right to sue for the wrongful death of their partner.

  Even though Hawaii now recognizes civil unions, a same-sex couple not wanting to take that step but still desiring some legal protections may want to enter into a reciprocal beneficiary agreement.

The first thing to understand is that most of these limited domestic partnership laws are really *ordinances,* local laws that apply only within a limited geographic region, such as a city. Usually at least one partner must live within that city for the couple to be eligible to register as a domestic partnership. Sometimes a couple can register if one of them *works* for the city, even if neither of them lives there.

These local domestic partnerships don't do anything near enough to protect you as a couple. After all, how many rights are available under local laws in the first place? But they're not useless and for some couples are definitely worth looking into.

Although every local domestic partnership law is different, they often allow the following:

- ✔ City employees can enroll their domestic partners in healthcare or other benefit plans.

- ✔ City employees can take sick leave for their same-sex partners.

- ✔ Registered domestic partners can avoid local real estate transfer taxes when buying or selling property between them.

Note that most of the benefits go to local government employees; these ordinances generally do little to help the couple in dealing with other third parties. For example, you generally can't use them to demand health benefits from your *private* employer for your same-sex partner.

If you live in a domestic partnership community that's located within a domestic partnership state, you may not be able to enroll in both registries. Before enrolling for a second time, check with your local or state domestic partnership registrar to see if you're required to de-register from one before enrolling in another. Furthermore, make sure you're enrolled in the registry that offers the most benefits.

Considering whether marriage is right for you

Just because your state gives you the right to marry, enter into a civil union, or register as domestic partners doesn't mean you *should*. This statement may sound obvious but you can easily get caught up in the civil rights/equality aspect of marriage, perhaps even to the extent of striding briskly down an aisle when your relationship isn't ready.

In general, couples shouldn't marry without very clear understandings and expectations between the partners. Ask yourselves these questions to see if you're ready to take a big step:

- ✔ Will you have joint finances, or keep them separate?

- ✔ Do you agree on whether you want to raise kids? If so, will you try to adopt, or will you go the surrogacy or sperm donation route?

- ✔ What are your behavioral expectations for each other? You should have a frank discussion about marital fidelity and whether monogamy will be strictly required. (By the way, opposite-sex couples would benefit from this discussion, too.)

You don't necessarily have to agree on all these issues, but you should certainly discuss them, even (perhaps especially) if the conversations are difficult. Be sure you have a realistic sense of whether marriage and civil unions can work in the long run because they're hard to get out of (domestic partnerships, often less so).

And these questions aren't meant to be an exclusive list. Think hard about what needs to be on your list: What's important to *you, as an individual and as a couple*? Here are some pros of entering into legal unions:

- ✔ You and your partner receive many rights and benefits that aren't available to unmarried couples.

- ✔ You may be able to avoid some of the exhaustive and expensive legal documentation that same-sex couples otherwise need to protect themselves. Just don't assume that the default rules that marriage creates are the ones you want.

✔ Perhaps most importantly, you express your love and enduring commitment to each other, to family and friends, and to the broader community, just as straight couples have been able to do since, well, forever. You can still express your love even without the legal recognition of marriage, but for some people it's not quite the same.

On the flip side, here are some cons to entering a legal union:

✔ Marriage doesn't confer only rights; it also imposes obligations, especially if your relationship ends. Do you want your partner to receive a substantial share of your assets and possibly even support payments if the marriage doesn't work?

✔ Marriage can affect the legal obligations between partners relating to the children of either one of them. Do you want that?

✔ Same-sex marriages and civil unions can be even harder to get out of than opposite-sex marriages. Consider this con, especially if you live in a state that doesn't recognize your union, and you would have to leave that state to tie the knot. We discuss this knotty problem in greater detail in Chapter 10.

Tackling the Defense of Marriage Act (DOMA)

The progress on marriage equality needs one very large and ugly asterisk, and it's called the Defense of Marriage Act (DOMA). Enacted by the US Congress in 1996, DOMA throws a smothering blanket over state laws granting marriage rights to same-sex couples. Here's what it means, in summary: Even if you're married in your state, your marriage doesn't count under federal law.

What are the real-world consequences? DOMA means that legally wed gay and lesbian service members can't get into housing that their opposite-sex counterparts are eligible to use. DOMA means that same-sex couples that want to file joint *state* tax returns have to work through their federal taxes *twice* — once as single taxpayers (the feds view them as single) and then a second time, as a *dummy* joint filing for the state joint filing to work from. DOMA means that legally married federal employees can't put their spouses on their health insurance plans. You get the idea.

In this section, we walk through the law and its effects on your union.

Deciphering the law (it's nothing good)

To better understand how DOMA affects you and your partner, you need a quick overview of the law. DOMA has two central provisions:

- ✔ **Section 2 tells the states that they need not respect same-sex marriages from other states.** Section 2 doesn't do much that the states can't already do. You may think differently after reading the full faith and credit clause to the US Constitution (Article IV, section 1). That provision states that each state is obligated to honor "the public acts, records, and judicial proceedings of every other state." But the clause has been read to afford less "honor" to laws than to judgments, and states have sometimes invoked a "strong public policy" exception to get around the clause. So states can effectively ignore the "full faith and credit" clause when they want to.

  At most, then, Section 2 of DOMA underlines the states' right to disrespect same-sex marriages celebrated in other states. Of course, one might ask why Congress is getting into this issue at all, but that question is better asked of the next section.

- ✔ **Section 3 defines marriage as the union of a man and a woman under federal law.** This section, which overrides state marriage laws only where same-sex marriages are involved, is almost unprecedented. It gets the federal government into the business of deciding who is married and who isn't, an issue that's usually left up to the states. And it involves the government only to the extent of making sure that same-sex marriages don't count under federal law.

The bottom line is that even if you and your partner are legally married in Massachusetts, Iowa, or any of the other states that recognizes same-sex marriages, *you aren't married under federal law.* The result, of course, is that you're not eligible for any of the hundreds of federal benefits that go along with marriage.

What happens when you're in a civil union, domestic partnership, or some other recognized relationship? DOMA doesn't apply in those cases, but you still aren't eligible for federal benefits. There's no such thing as a federal civil union. The federal laws that refer to marriage make no mention of civil unions or domestic partnerships. These novel legal entities exist at the state (or local) levels only, so it would take a new federal law recognizing civil unions for a same-sex couple to be able to take advantage of all the federal benefits, such as joint tax filings, Social Security partner benefits, the spousal privilege under immigration law, and so many more. For now, these benefits are only available to married couples — straight only, please — and not to those in any other kind of union.

Assessing the effect on your marriage

DOMA has created a bewildering situation. After all, what does it mean to be married for some purposes, but not for others? Here's an example of a couple, Jill and Michelle, whose home state allows them to marry.

Jill and Michelle are married in New York. After they marry, Jill bears a son, Max, conceived with an anonymous sperm donor. Jill, an Iraqi war vet, is a successful lawyer with the US Department of Justice, earning almost $200,000 per year. Michelle remains at home and has primary childcare responsibility for Max.

Based on these facts, the couple would be able to file a joint state tax return but not a joint federal return. Because filing a joint return is most beneficial in cases with one low (or non-) wage earner and one high wage earner, their inability to file a joint federal return could cost them thousands of dollars compared to a married opposite sex couple.

And Jill would not be able to obtain health insurance coverage for Michelle, either. Because Jill is a federal employee, she is not married in that capacity. She could, however, obtain benefits for Max.

By the way, if Jill worked for a private employer, she still might not be able to include Michelle as a spouse for health benefits purposes. If the employer is self-insured, then a complex federal law known by the acronym ERISA (the Employee Retirement Income Security Act) would apply, and the federal definition of marriage could kick in. (Many employers in this situation, though, choose to extend health benefits to same-sex partners anyway.)

Finally, even were Michelle covered, the amount of money the employer would pay for her coverage would be considered income, and

taxed against Jill under the provisions of the Internal Revenue Code. An opposite-sex couple wouldn't have to pay for these benefits because both spouses fall under a rule that exempts the value of health benefits from the calculation of income.

Now add this fact:

Jill and Michelle move out of the state and into Pennsylvania, which has no marriage equality law and also has a statute that prohibits same-sex marriages. Soon thereafter, Jill is killed in a tragic water skiing accident caused by the negligence of Fred, who was driving another boat. She is buried in a veterans' cemetery in New York State. Jill's parents come forward to sue Fred under Pennsylvania's wrongful death law, lay claim to Jill's estate, and claim custody of Max.

What rights does Michelle have here?

Start with the fact that the state of Pennsylvania probably won't recognize the couple's relationship as a marriage. Because of both Section 2 of DOMA and the state's own law expressing its own strong public policy against same-sex marriages, a court would likely rule as follows:

✔ Michelle probably would lose a suit against Fred for causing Jill's death. Wrongful death laws in most states, including Pennsylvania, define a limited class of people who are eligible to sue. The list includes parents and spouses, but because the move from New York to Pennsylvania rendered the marriage inoperative, Jill's parents could sue to collect whatever money they might have been expected to receive from Jill during the rest of their lives. Michelle, though she almost certainly lost more than Jill's parents, would get nothing.

(continued)

(continued)

✔ If Jill didn't have a will, Michelle might have no claim under the *law of intestacy,* which protects married couples. In that case, the parents would once again be the winners. If Jill did have a will naming Michelle as a beneficiary, Michelle would be able to recover to the extent specified in that will.

✔ Although it's unlikely, Michelle might even lose custody of Max. Because she didn't adopt him — she should have, because New York would have permitted it — the court might, in the course of disregarding the marriage, consider Max not to be the legal child of Michelle. In that case, the court would look with fresh eyes at who would be the best legal guardian for Max. Although that analysis would seem to strongly favor Michelle, there's no guarantee.

Doesn't sound great, does it? And for good measure, when Michelle eventually dies she will not be eligible to be buried in the veterans' cemetery next to Jill. Even though the cemetery is in New York, federal law controls veteran issues, and the two women aren't married under federal law.

Remember: Even if you're in a state that recognizes same-sex relationships, you're nowhere near as well protected as your opposite-sex counterparts. Federal law doesn't recognize your relationship. Most other states don't, either, and DOMA reminds them that they don't have to.

Taking on DOMA: The ongoing challenges

DOMA is really bad news for your marriage, but the good news is that help might be on the way. What are the options to getting rid of DOMA? This section focuses on some of the ongoing challenges to defeat DOMA.

Repealing the law

Congress could always repeal the law with The Respect for Marriage Act (RMA). Repeal efforts are gathering momentum as we write this, and a repeal bill has many co-sponsors in the Senate and in the House of Representatives. However because of the makeup of the Senate and House, the chances of a repeal getting through both houses of Congress in the short term and then being signed into law aren't great. Consult the nearby sidebar for more information on the RMA.

Challenging the law on constitutional grounds

A more promising development is a batch of lawsuits challenging DOMA on constitutional grounds. These suits question only Section 3 of the law — the section limiting marriage to the union of a man and a woman under federal law, and the section doing the most damage.

The suits claim that Section 3 of DOMA deprives gay and lesbian couples of equal protection under the law by treating their marriages differently than straight unions. Most of the plaintiffs are residents of states like Massachusetts, who are challenging their inability to access federal benefits. But Massachusetts itself is also a plaintiff. The state claims that the federal government is interfering with its right to define marriage as it sees fit by imposing an unconstitutional condition on its participation in federal-state partnerships. The most sympathetic example involves veterans' cemeteries located in the state. In order to qualify as a veterans' cemetery, federal rules mandate who can be buried there; these rules follow DOMA by allowing opposite-sex spouses, but not same-sex spouses, to be buried next to vets.

The Obama administration, which has decided that it can't defend DOMA because of its unequal (and unconstitutional) treatment of gays and lesbians, supports these suits. That's good news for DOMA opponents, but the majority in the US House of Representatives controls lawyers who are representing what it sees as the government's interests.

The suits have been successful in the lower federal courts, and in one federal court of appeals. Expect the Supreme Court to weigh in within the next couple of years.

We expect these suits to succeed, in part because the challenge is so limited to only Section 3. In a line of cases, the Supreme Court has repeatedly stated its view that the states have the right to decide who's married. DOMA interferes with that prerogative, and the Court probably won't like that.

For now, DOMA is the law — and it complicates your life.

Repealing DOMA with RMA

As long as DOMA is law, the legal situation confronting same-sex couples is likely to remain confounding, confusing, and frustrating. But a move is afoot in Congress to repeal the law and to clarify and expand the interstate rights of legally married same-sex couples. This measure is called The Respect for Marriage Act (RMA). RMA would repeal DOMA. But that's not all.

RMA would also grant federal recognition to any marriage validly entered into in any state. The law would therefore allow a gay or lesbian couple residing in a state that doesn't recognize their marriage to marry in another state and immediately gain federal recognition of their marriage, forever, and no matter where they choose to live.

Although RMA would be a huge step forward, it wouldn't bring full marriage equality, because it wouldn't compel *states* to grant or recognize same-sex relationships. But because most of the benefits of marriage are federal, RMA would get gay and lesbian couples most of the way home. After a couple was married in any state — or even in another *country* that recognizes same-sex unions — that couple would be federally married, period.

"Mini" DOMAs: The states get into the marriage "protection" racket

DOMA already exists. The public policy exception stating that states don't have to recognize same-sex marriages celebrated in other states also exists.

If those weren't enough, many states have passed an additional law that seeks to further protect their citizens from the menace of out-of-state marriages by same-sex couples. These "mini DOMA" laws can be broken down in a couple of different ways.

Where in state law are they found? And why does it matter?

How states mandate these mini DOMAs is important. States basically have two options when enacting mini DOMAs:

✔ **Some states have statutes that define and limit marriage to the union of "one man and one woman."** Statutes are easier to eliminate. The legislature passes them, and the legislature can repeal them. This has already happened in some states, like Washington.

Courts can also declare statutes to be in violation of their own state's constitution, which has happened in a number of states, including Massachusetts, Connecticut, and Iowa.

✔ **Some of these "one man, one woman" provisions have been written into state constitutions.** Where these laws are placed into state constitutions, the climb to repeal is much steeper. California is a good example: After a decision by the state supreme court declaring unconstitutional a law that banned same-sex marriages, the voters passed Proposition 8. That measure amended the state constitution to prevent same-sex couples from marrying in the future. Constitutions trump statutes. (The litigation challenging Prop 8 that you've probably heard about argues that this constitutional provision violates the *federal* constitution, and the US Constitution trumps everything else.)

How broad are these laws?

Whether these anti-equality laws appear in statutes or constitutions, you need to understand exactly what they do, and don't, prohibit.

✔ The first wave of these laws prohibited only same-sex marriages. They typically used language like this: "Only a marriage between a man and a woman is valid or recognized in this state." The effect is to keep same-sex couples from marrying within the state and to establish (or reinforce) the state's "strong public policy" against same-sex marriages.

✔ A second, more recent wave adds civil unions and any other legal entity that is the substantial equivalent of marriage to the list of nonrecognized same-sex unions. These laws began to come into existence after states began to create these marriage equivalents.

These broader laws have sometimes had consequences that were probably unintended by the state legislature.

One noteworthy example comes from Michigan, where a constitutional provision stated: "the union of one man and one woman in marriage shall be the only agreement recognized as a marriage or similar union for any purpose." Michigan Constitution, Art I, § 25. In 2008, the Michigan Supreme Court interpreted this law to prohibit public employers (such as state universities) from providing benefits to the registered domestic partners of employees. To the court, granting such benefits was recognizing a domestic partnership as a "similar union" to marriage for "some purpose."

There have even been some suggestions that some of the more broadly worded laws could upset private contractual agreements between same-sex partners, but so far that hasn't happened — and it isn't likely to. You should create the documents discussed throughout this book, because those documents will likely be respected — even where state law isn't on your side!

Examining Same-Sex Marriages: What Happens Across State Lines?

Because of the crazy patchwork of state marriage laws, trying to figure out exactly what happens when you and your partner cross state lines can be a challenging task, to say the least.

For example, say you and your partner live in Topeka, Kansas, which has a constitutional amendment barring the recognition of same-sex marriages, and you decide to drive the four hours to Des Moines, Iowa, to get married. Iowa will let you do this, by the way. Like most states, Iowa doesn't have a residency requirement, so people from anywhere in the country can drive or fly in, marry, and return to their state of residence. Then what happens?

These sections explain what you can expect. Hang on for a dizzying ride on the legal tilt-a-whirl!

Answering the question: "Did my wedding ring just disappear?"

Venturing to Iowa — or any other state that performs same-sex marriages — may hardly be worthwhile for you and your partner if you're returning home to a state that doesn't recognize your union. Many states have *marriage evasion laws*. These laws apply to state residents, and state that they may not travel to another state for the purpose of entering into a marriage that would be void in the state of residence. If they do, the marriage will be declared void in the home state — just as if the marriage had been entered into there.

So if you live in Kansas, your wedding ring will *probably* disappear as soon as you leave Iowa. In a sense, it didn't exist anyway because your marriage was never of any legal effect. (If you and your partner decide to move to Iowa later, though, voila! You're married again!) And if you live in a state that recognizes your marriage, you didn't need to leave in the first place.

You need to be aware of a few important qualifications to the general rule that your marriage will evaporate as soon as you cross back over into a non-recognition state.

- ✔ If your state recognizes some other kind of same-sex relationship, such as a civil union or domestic partnership, then your state may recognize your out-of-state marriage in the same form of recognized union in your home state. Just don't count on it. Make sure you check before you marry out of state, if you're in a civil union or domestic partnership state.

- ✔ You may live in a state that has no specific law either way on marriage. In that case, your state might recognize your same-sex marriage performed in another state. Until recently, New York was such a state, although now residents have gained full marriage equality. Maryland was to the same effect, but a marriage equality law is scheduled to go into effect there in January 2013 (unless the voters repeal it in the November 2012 election). So that leaves only one state, New Mexico, that has no official policy one way or the other. In 2011, the state attorney general issued an opinion stating the view that a same-sex marriage celebrated in another state would be recognized in the Land of Enchantment (New Mexico's nickname: didn't you know?).

- ✔ So if you live in New Mexico, going to another state to marry might be worth a try. But no court has ruled on the attorney general's opinion, which isn't binding. You and your partner might be the pioneers bringing the test case. (Let us know how it turns out.)

Even if your marriage has no legal effect in your home state, it may be useful for other purposes. You or your partner may be able to use it as proof to an employer of your domestic partnership and therefore qualify for benefits on that basis. Or if your employer doesn't yet provide benefits to domestic partners, you may be able to use it to emphasize that you're in a real and committed relationship, and that basic fairness demands equal compensation to all employees — and benefits are a significant part of compensation.

Maybe you and your partner just want to get married in a state that recognizes your union as equal to that of your fellow citizens, even though you know that it isn't legal in your home state. You can of course have a commitment ceremony in your equality-challenged home state, but for some people the legal piece of the puzzle is significant, whether or not it carries back across the state's border.

Many attorneys would advise a same-sex couple whose marriage won't be recognized in their home state not to leave the state to get married somewhere else, because it can be difficult to *end* a marriage or similar union if your home state doesn't recognize it — harder than getting married in the first place! See Chapter 10 for a fuller discussion.

Rubbing the Crystal Ball: What the Future of Marriage Equality Holds

The law that applies to same-sex unions is an unruly mess. States are all over the place, starting at full marriage equality and then moving down through civil unions and domestic partnerships before finally hitting bottom with broad laws that ban any kind of relationship recognition. Add to that the overlay of interstate issues and the presence of DOMA, and you have a situation likely to confound a law student taking a final exam. Those individuals not in possession of a law degree are likely to be even more confused.

We think it's highly likely that one day in the not-too-distant future the situation will be resolved in favor of full marriage equality, everywhere in the United States. We reach that conclusion for a few reasons:

- ✔ As a practical matter, the current situation isn't sustainable. Courts have already had to deal with complex interstate recognition issues, and the situation is only going to get even more complicated as more and more same-sex couples enter into various kinds of recognized unions and then take their legal show on the road. State legislatures are going to come under increasing pressure to fix this problem.

- ✔ The movement is solidly in the pro-equality direction. The number of states fortifying their same-sex union bans continues to drop, and some states, such as Nevada and Washington, have even maneuvered around or outright repealed these bans. At some point the story will be about how discriminatory laws in a minority of states are denying equality to same-sex couples without a good reason.

- ✔ The younger a voter is, the likelier he or she is to support full marriage equality. And after people are in favor of equality, they don't often change their minds. So as younger people continue to push up through the age brackets, before long such substantial majorities will be in favor of same-sex marriage recognition that equality will simply become inevitable.

How long will all this take? Our crystal balls aren't *that* good. Unless something dramatic happens within a few years, achieving full equality in every state might drag on for another generation, or even two. Some states are still pretty far away from seeing marriage equality as a necessary part of full citizenship, and even the fall of DOMA wouldn't get us all the way home. Federal recognition of state marriages wouldn't compel the states to do anything, unless something dramatic happens.

How California could affect marriage equality

California has had an extensive battle since 2008. An ongoing federal court case contends that Proposition 8, which was a ballot initiative that passed and disallowed same-sex marriages, violates the US Constitution. (Refer to the nearby sidebar, on the history of marriage equality in California since 2008.) This case has now been appealed to the Supreme Court. So the result for marriage equality could be dramatic and decisive — or not. Here are the possibilities, in escalating order of drama:

- ✔ The Supreme Court could decline to hear the case. The Court has plenty of discretion as to which cases it will hear. It may decide to allow the issue of same-sex marriage to percolate through state legislatures and local courts for a few more years before weighing in. In that case, the final decision by the Ninth Circuit Court of Appeals, finding the law unconstitutional, would stick.

- ✔ The Court could decide that same-sex couples don't have any constitutional right to marry. In that case, Prop 8 stands, but nothing else to the drive toward marriage equality changes. The states can go on banning or recognizing same-sex relationships, state courts can continue interpreting their own constitutions (which can confer broader rights than the US Constitution), and DOMA will remain in effect.

- ✔ The Court could decide that Prop 8 is unconstitutional but not rule more broadly that all states must recognize same-sex marriages. The "animus rationale" used by the Ninth Circuit court invites the Supreme Court to decide that Prop 8 was passed because the voters wouldn't take away the name marry (but leave full domestic partnership rights in place) unless they just didn't like gay and lesbian people. If the case is decided in that relatively narrow way, then other bans on same-sex marriages aren't automatically unconstitutional. But they would come under a legal microscope!

- ✔ The Court could end the whole marriage equality debate once and for all by holding that same-sex couples have a constitutional right to marry on the same terms as opposite-sex couples. Such a decision would effectively sweep all state same-sex marriage bans off the board and effectively repeal DOMA at the same time. (We said this was the most dramatic!)

Recapping the marriage equality in California

Through a set of incremental steps, California had gotten all the way to a comprehensive domestic partnership bill by the late 2000s. But that wasn't enough for several same-sex couples who brought suit in state court contending that they were entitled to full marriage equality, including the name "marriage."

In 2008, the California Supreme Court agreed. The court held that same-sex couples were entitled to not just the rights and benefits of marriage but also to the term "marriage." Same-sex marriages therefore began in the late summer of 2008.

Equality opponents responded with Proposition 8, a ballot initiative that sought to amend the state constitution by defining marriage as the union of a man and a woman. In November 2008, the measure passed with 52 percent of the vote. Same-sex marriages were no longer allowed in California, and the law thus reverted to the domestic partnership compromise previously in effect.

Prop 8 opponents then *returned* to the California Supreme Court and claimed that the measure wasn't a valid change to the state's constitution. They lost, and the amendment stuck, but those couples married during the few months when same-sex marriages were allowed were still married. (The court found that the law didn't apply retroactively.)

That might have been the end of at least this particular legal story. But a plot twist came in the form of super-lawyers David Boies and Ted Olson. The two had faced off in the well-known case of *Bush v. Gore* but now joined forces to bring a federal lawsuit on behalf of couples challenging Prop 8 under the US Constitution, which, of course, trumps the California state constitution. The suit claims that same-sex couples have a fundamental right to marry, and that, by denying them that right, Prop 8 is a violation of the constitutional guarantee of equal protection under the law.

After a long trial, the plaintiffs were successful in the federal district court. Prop 8 proponents then appealed to the Ninth Circuit, the federal court that hears appeals from federal cases from California and a few nearby states.

Earlier this year, the plaintiffs succeeded in that court, too. A three-judge panel ruled that Proposition 8 was passed because of *animus*, a legal term for prejudice against gays and lesbians. Under Supreme Court precedent that the Ninth Circuit found applicable to this case, laws based on animus deny equality in the most basic way.

After that defeat, the defenders of Prop 8 asked for a review by a larger panel of the Ninth Circuit. (This is called *en banc* review.) But the Ninth Circuit declined that request, and Prop 8's supporters have now asked the US Supreme Court to take the case.

What other legislation could impact marriage equality?

As long as we're crystal ball–gazing, we may as well discuss and speculate about how other legislation could affect the marriage equality debate. In general, any advance in equality for LGBT people is likely to advance the cause of marriage equality. Likewise, any setbacks in the march to LGBT civil and social rights could temporarily derail marriage equality, too. But the greater momentum rests with the pro-equality side.

The repeal of the military's Don't Ask, Don't Tell policy, for example (see Chapter 18 on life in the military after the repeal of this law), has already created marriage equality issues. Married opposite-sex couples are eligible for housing together, but same-sex couples (whether legally married or not) are not. Given that straight and gay couples work side-by-side in the military, this kind of very visible inequality is likely to advance the case for repealing DOMA.

On the state level, laws establishing civil unions and domestic partnerships create momentum toward full marriage equality. After the state has gone far enough to provide same-sex couples with all the rights and benefits of marriage, continuing to withhold the name *marriage* seems, in a way, even more discriminatory and needlessly confusing. So in several states, civil unions or domestic partnerships have given way to full marriage equality.

In addition, advances in the rights of same-sex couples to adopt children, such as joint and second-parent adoptions (refer to Chapter 7), also advance the cause of marriage equality. If a state allows same-sex couples to adopt kids on the same basis as straight couples, withholding the marriage that would further cement the family's legal status makes little sense.

But the march toward marriage equality won't come only from changes in legislation. It will also come from the lives of real lesbian and gay couples, raising children, caring for aging parents, being good citizens and dedicated members of their local communities, and piecing together their legal protection as best they can in a system that often regards them as strangers. People who know LGBT personally are likelier to support equality; they observe these real-life situations firsthand and understand the basic humanity before them.

Until equality is reality, though, same-sex couples need to continue cobbling their legal protection into a workable result. For now, this book can help you do that cobbling together.

Chapter 3

Eyeing the Challenges that Same-Sex Couples and Their Children Face

In This Chapter

▶ Sorting out the legal rules that apply to families headed by same-sex parents

▶ Dealing with the school environment

▶ Understanding and responding to discrimination against you and your family

*I*n most states, gay and lesbian couples can adopt children — either jointly or one at a time. But because of laws like the Defense of Marriage Act (DOMA) and state law additions to DOMA, same-sex partners can be legal strangers to each other.

What is the result? The kids get two moms or two dads, but in the eyes of the law, their parents are unmarried, a result that many of the opponents of marriage equality would otherwise deplore.

The fact that your children's parents aren't legally related is a problem in obvious and not-so-obvious ways, and we explore some of the ramifications in a few different contexts:

✔ Family benefits

✔ The treatment of your kids (and you) in the public and private school environments

✔ The legal and social difficulties your family may face in the broader society

This chapter opens the lens a bit more to look at how the law looks at families headed up by same-sex couples. In short, the situation is even messier as soon as kids come into the picture. You can face some of these obstacles with knowledge of the law, an unholy level of patience, and . . . a good sense of humor. But LGBT families face unique challenges.

Knowing When a Family Is and Isn't a Family

For same-sex couples, the word "family" has two different meanings, and the gap between those two goes a long way toward identifying the problem that we discuss in the following sections:

- ✔ The first use of "family" refers to the facts of your life — you, your partner, and your children are a family in every way that matters to you. If you're lucky, you're also a family to lots of other people: other family members (including your pets), neighbors, friends, and even complete strangers who understand what families are.

- ✔ The second use of "family" refers to the law, which doesn't recognize your family — at least not completely and consistently.

The following sections examine how state laws can affect same-sex families and what that nonrecognition means to you and your family.

Identifying problems same-sex families face: When the law gets in the way

Legal parent status is often the biggest problem. Your children may have only one legal parent (you or your partner), or they have two legal parents, but one of them is a third party — neither you nor your partner.

Some states don't allow unmarried couples to adopt kids jointly. Because same-sex couples are always unmarried in these states, they can't adopt as a couple. The law is changing quickly, and in some places courts allow same-sex couples to adopt even where state statutes don't specifically allow them to do so. So whether one of you is the biological parent or not, in some states your child will have one legal parent, not two. We explore adoption in more detail in Chapter 7.

These laws in some states are a bit absurd, allowing a couple to adopt children together but then denying their parents the right to legally marry (or at least enter into a civil union). It's also the situation, in every state when it comes to federal rights: no marriage, because of DOMA.

The consequences of this nonrecognition of one partner as the legal parent of their children are significant. Here are just a few of them:

✔ If the children are injured and taken to the hospital, the nonlegal parent will have no legal right to visit them, much less make decisions relating to their care. (Recent federal regulations now allow people to designate their visitors, but they don't apply to young children.)

✔ The nonlegal parent can't make medical decisions relating to the child.

✔ Both the nonlegal parent and child may be prevented from suing someone who caused harm to their relationship. (Chapter 16 discusses these types of lawsuits.)

✔ If the nonlegal parent dies, the child can't receive federal survivorship benefits from Social Security.

If you're considering adopting children, look for an agency that deals with gay and lesbian parents. Their case workers should know the ins and outs of the law, and they can advise you on the best course of action.

In some states, both members of a gay and lesbian couple can be legal parents; they can either adopt jointly, or if one is the biological parent, the other will be permitted to do a second-parent adoption. A number of states, such as Pennsylvania, for example, recognize both partners as the parents of their children, but they don't afford any recognition to these same parents *as a couple*.

This legally absurd situation can cause financial hardship to a same-sex family with minor children. All the state benefits that go along with marriage are denied to couples that can't legally marry, and the federal benefits are denied to all same-sex couples — even if they can marry or civilly unite in their state. The following sections take a closer look at the financial effects at the state and local level and then at the federal level.

Financial effects under state and local law

The inability to access state and local benefits obviously can wreak financial havoc on the family. Compared to legally recognized, opposite-sex couples, same-sex families have less money to work with.

There are really too many to explore in detail, but consider a few of the most significant financial effects:

✔ When one partner dies, the estate of that partner will be subject to the estate tax. (Married couples don't face this problem because the laws in every state create an exemption in favor of the survivor.)

✔ State income taxes must be filed separately.

✔ Compensation under various state programs (such as funds available to the victims of violent crimes and their "families") may be denied to an unmarried partner.

✔ If you want to add your partner to the deed to your home, you often have to pay a local transfer tax; married couples enjoy an exemption.

✔ Less directly, but no less painfully, some employers still tie health and other benefits to legal marriage. In addition, a nonbiological parent may not be able to add the child that she or he can't adopt onto an employer's policy, either.

You can avoid at least a few of these problems through the creation of a living revocable trust. We discuss these vehicles, which are extremely valuable for same-sex couples, in Chapter 13.

Financial (and other) effects under federal law

If anything, the situation is even worse under federal law, which isn't surprising because Uncle Sam provides most of the benefits doled out to married couples. Here are a few of the most pernicious effects of DOMA on your family. This list of the many legal disabilities visited on same-sex couples is nowhere near complete, even if they're validly married under state law:

✔ Just as with state law, estate and income tax laws treat your partner as a nonentity: no estate tax exemption, and no right to file a joint income tax return. The income tax rule can be hugely expensive in homes where one partner earns a high salary and the other stays home to raise the kids.

✔ If one partner dies, the other won't be entitled to Social Security death benefits — and neither will a child whose relationship to the deceased parent isn't legally recognized.

✔ The family can also be devastated under immigration law. Although citizens can sponsor their spouses for permanent resident status, federal laws deny that right to same-sex couples (see Chapter 18 for details).

✔ Military families are given special consideration when it comes to housing and the care of children. The law doesn't require the same for families headed by same-sex couples.

The point should be clear (and sad) enough by now. The nonrecognition of the marriage of same-sex parents heading up a family is serious and can even be destructive, forcing survivors from their homes, breaking up families with one noncitizen, and more.

Realizing what nonrecognition of your union means to your family

As anyone in a gay or lesbian partnership, especially but not exclusively one with kids, can attest, the whole or partial nonstatus of your family has other negative implications, too. For some, they may be worse than the legal issues.

First, some good news: Most studies have shown that children raised by same-gender parents do just as well as those raised by opposite-sex couples. That still doesn't mean that the kids don't suffer from the fact that their parents' relationship isn't legally recognized. Just as gay and lesbian kids suffer from discrimination and mistreatment, the children of same-sex parents also often experience social marginalization. Other children and even other parents who disapprove of same-sex relationships and parenting often ridicule or harass them.

Would marriage equality change how some people treat LBGT parents and their kids? Given how normalizing marriage is to most people, saying that it would help is probably safe. Although not every heterosexual adult or child would change their behavior and thoughts the day after a state enacts a marriage equality law, over time the legal recognition would lead to greater social acceptance.

In the meantime, you and your partner aren't helpless. Working on your own relationship can help your kids, too. Studies of kids raised by lesbian parents suggest that the better the relationship, the better equipped the kids are to handle the societal scorn they sometimes face. Where the parents have greater relationship satisfaction, a healthy division of paid and unpaid labor, and regular contact with other relatives, the kids do pretty well.

Recognizing the Challenges LGBT Families Encounter in Schools

Whether legally married, civilly united, or totally unrecognized by the law, gay and lesbian parents and their children face challenges in school that require care, attention, patience, and a good knowledge of your legal rights. These sections discuss important issues that same-sex couples need to consider when they have children in schools.

Figuring out the right school: Is a private school an option?

When you have children, you must consider whether to send your kids to private or public school. If private school is an option for you, be sure to research whether the school welcomes diverse families. Some schools are making an affirmative effort to attract families headed by LGBT families. They'll reach out to you, make themselves available, and host open houses where gay and lesbian parents speak in glowing terms about the experience their family has had in the school.

At the other end, some private schools speak volumes by their silence or may send signals by touting the school's inculcation of traditional values in the students they serve. You obviously want to avoid those schools.

Of course, most schools fall somewhere on the spectrum between these two extremes. Make sure you ask school administrators hard questions:

- ✔ **Are there (or have there been) LGBT-headed families here?** If so, would you seek their permission to be contacted?

- ✔ **What do you teach the students here about LGBT issues, and especially about LGBT families?** Many will likely say that they teach broadly about "diversity." Plumb more deeply.

- ✔ **How do you handle teachers and students who give the sons and daughters of LGBT parents a hard time?** Here you want the administrator to say that their teachers understand and appreciate all kinds of diversity, and if they don't, the school administration will decisively deal with them. They should also speak to the initiatives they've put in place about how to teach students respect, and how to deal with any teasing or bullying that does occur. (We discuss bullying in more detail in the "Bullying (and what to do about it)" section later in this chapter.)

You're looking for an environment that strikes you as welcoming and an administration that takes your questions and concerns seriously. In order to know, you have to be willing to ask the hard questions.

The worst thing you can do is fail to bring these issues to light and hope that things will work out. We have heard plenty of stories of schools expelling or retracting admissions offers for students after they find out that their parents are of the same gender. Many states don't have any legal remedy for this kind of discrimination by a *private* organization. And in any case, you don't want a legal remedy — what you want is a school where you never need to think about litigation in the first place!

Sending your child to a public school

For most LGBT families, though, private school isn't an option. For whatever reason (cost, location, and so on), they send their children to a public school. Knowing how to navigate issues that are likely to arise is important. These sections help you.

If cost is the only reason you're dismissing the private school option, consider that many private schools provide scholarships and need-based financial aid to families that can't afford the often-steep tuition. It's worth looking into.

Whether your child is entering kindergarten, or your family has just moved to a new school district, your first assignment begins well before your child even enrolls. Be proactive and

- ✔ **Find out what the district has to say about diversity.** Figure out whether an official statement or policy applies to LGBT-headed families.

- ✔ **Investigate whether local or state antidiscrimination laws apply to protect you and your children from intentional acts that negatively affect their education.** Although you hope never to need them, such laws can be an important reminder to school employees that your family deserves equal treatment.

- ✔ **Look into the experiences of other gay and lesbian parents.** If a large LGBT population lives in the area, perhaps you can contact a Family Pride group. If not, you may have trouble uncovering anything.

If you decide a public school is the best option for your child, make sure you read the following sections so your child doesn't face any discrimination because you're LGBT.

Dealing with school administrators and teachers

Before you make the final decision on whether a public school is right for you, you'll want to meet with the school principal to discuss your family. You'll want to make sure the principal has an open door so you and your partner can schedule an appointment whenever you have a concern.

This appointment with the school principal will speak volumes about the kind of experience you're likely to have as a parent who insists on and advocates for fair and respectful treatment of your family. Ask the same questions that you'd ask of a private school principal (which we discuss earlier in this chapter).

Be upfront and clear about your family. Your own style and comfort level will dictate how you go about discussing your family, but one very useful move is for *both* of you to meet with the principal together, if possible. (Even if you're an LGBT parent raising kids on your own, though, you should be open about your situation right away.)

After you know who your child's teacher is, meet with him or her. The focus will be on your child's education, of course — and part of that discussion should be about the learning environment. Gauge the teacher's comfort level with your family situation. At this point, you may or may not want to probe into how particular problems may be addressed in the classroom. But you should at least discuss the need for communication on issues that are of particular concern for your family.

If you discover — or even suspect — that the teacher has a problem with LGBT families, you have another decision to make. You may want to ask the principal to schedule a meeting that includes all parties (principal, teacher, and parent(s)) to resolve any issues. But if you're really uncomfortable, you may want to request another teacher. Make sure to document your reasons and make your case as clearly as you can.

Being involved in your child's education

People who personally know LGBT families are much more likely to accept them. As a result, make sure you get involved. Many public schools welcome parental involvement, so do what you can — go on field trips, participate in a parental support organization (such as Parent Teacher Association, an after-school group, and so on), and volunteer for events.

By so doing, you're more visible and you normalize your family for those who may have little experience with gay and lesbian families. Let other parents and teachers see you and your partner at events together and with your kids.

Even if you're busy working long hours, you can do volunteer e-mailing, fundraising, and so forth in the evenings. Build some good will while helping out. But really do try to get to some events. Your kids will appreciate it (at least until they reach a certain age).

Your involvement won't ensure that your kids won't have some negative experiences in school, just because their parents happen to be gay or lesbian. The more proactive you are, the better the chances you can avoid major problems.

You also want to make sure your kids are comfortable telling you what's going on. You need to have discussions with them about the possibility that some kids (or even adults) won't treat them respectfully. Start young, and speak in terms they can understand and that support (rather than scare) them. You want them to come to you with any problems they're having, and they'll be likelier to do that if you've had that talk.

If your child does encounter some harassment or problems because he or she has same-sex parents, you want to weigh how much you want to fight against the toll that this kind of stress might be having on your child. You can respond following these steps:

1. **Talk to the teacher.**

   In some cases, the teacher can bring in the parents of kids who are causing problems. If the problem is the teacher, though, then you should go to the principal.

2. **If the teacher can't handle the problem, meet with the principal.**

   Often the principal can mediate between you (and your family) and a teacher, if the teacher is the source of the problem. But if the principal really doesn't understand the problem's severity — or worse, doesn't want to understand — then go to Step 3.

3. **Report the problem to district personnel (such as the school superintendent) or to a local civil rights commission (if the commission has jurisdiction over LGBT issues).**

   Sometimes an LGBT community or advocacy group can help.

4. **You may have to consider requesting a transfer to another school.**

   Often transferring schools is the best solution, but sometimes the overall climate is so toxic that you may even need to think about moving. In some cities, the atmosphere is improving, but there's still a long way to go.

In extreme cases, such as when your child is being bullied, aggressive countermeasures are required (check out the next section for advice on how to handle a bully).

Bullying (and what to do about it)

Your children may encounter bullying because of their gay and lesbian parents. When other students' conduct toward your kids escalates beyond teasing into *bullying* (repeated, aggressive behavior designed to intimidate), you need to act right away! Don't ignore teasing! If it's directed against your kid in more than a playful way, it can preview or even constitute bullying. Even if your child hasn't been seriously harmed yet, the emotional damage has already started. And bullying can quickly escalate into acts that cause serious injury.

You can deal with the bullying by following the same steps we outline in the previous section, although now your response should be more urgent. What else can you do? You can also

- ✔ **Investigate anti-bullying programs in the school and the district.** See what is required by state law, and make sure the school has implemented the law. Even if the law isn't helpful, many schools have programs designed to combat bullying. But some don't, and you may not have the option of waiting to see if you can help build the program from the ground up.

- ✔ **If you feel your child's safety is at risk, notify local law enforcement authorities.** Many bullying activities are also criminal, and even if the bully is too young to be prosecuted, authorities can also put pressure on parents or school officials who are allowing it to continue.

- ✔ **In extreme cases, consider a lawsuit.** Sometimes, even the specter of litigation will grab the attention of school personnel in a way that you hadn't been able to accomplish before. See the nearby sidebar for more information.

Litigation is *not* where you want to be in these cases. By the time you're there, terrible things — often, extreme violence — have already happened, but knowing that lawsuits are at least a possibility is useful. You may need to mention litigation when you're confronting an unsympathetic school administration. Remember that they don't want to be on the receiving end of a lawsuit, for both financial and public relations reasons.

Identifying Challenges in the Broader Society

Your family is likely to encounter continued challenges to your legitimacy in many places. Many gay couples can recount a story of visiting a restaurant with their two children and being asked if it's "mothers' night off." (Answer: "Every night is mom's night off! These are our children." Lesbian couples, change the parental role for your story!)

Although this kind of encounter likely won't bother you much (as long as the server is okay with being gently corrected), think about preparing your kids for the plain fact that not everyone is going to be familiar with families like yours. Remind them that they should be respectful, and as they get older, ready to educate people about their family. Of course, most of the information people need is conveyed by the simple act of seeing your family together.

Yet some encounters are not so benign. The following sections give you some more insight on what you can do during different situations.

Combating legal discrimination

More than likely your family will encounter some discrimination in many phases of your life. You don't have any control over other people's actions, but you can control how you respond to this discrimination. Here we offer a few observations about what you can do, as a practical matter, even where there is no legal remedy. Chapter 4 discusses antidiscrimination law.

For example, what if your employer extends health benefits to married couples, but not to your (legally unmarried) family? No law may prohibit that distinction, especially if your employer is a private company.

For complicated reasons, certain private employers don't even have to provide health or other benefits of employment to same-sex married couples, even if they provide them to opposite-sex married couples. (Some employer plans are covered by federal law, in which case DOMA applies.) But that doesn't mean they can't provide benefits to your family — and they should do it. Just because this discrimination may not be illegal doesn't mean you have to put up with it.

Again, your job is to educate — and to persuade. Often, it's just a matter of being persistent. Bore them to death with facts. Here's how:

- ✓ **Gather information on the value of the benefits that your family is being denied.** You can point out how the practical result is that you're undercompensated relative to legally married families.

- ✓ **Find out and present information on the increasing number of corporations that are providing benefits to same-sex couples.** Some companies won't want to get too far ahead of the curve, so showing them that it's now common to provide such benefits can allay that concern. You can also use these facts to make the argument that gay-friendly policies will make your employer an attractive choice for talented employees — like you.

- ✓ **Reassure your employer that extending benefits to its gay and lesbian employees' partners isn't expensive.** Doing so isn't, and you can find the data to prove it.

- ✓ **Identify advocates from among your fellow employees — and not just the LGBT ones.** Of course, having a few of the higher-ups in your corner wouldn't hurt.

- ✓ **Team up with straight folks who aren't married but need benefits for their partners, too.** This strategy is sometimes a good one, because the employer can see that the "marriage only" rule for benefits excludes not just same-sex couples but also other couples in committed, long-term relationships.

The CD contains links to, and information about, LGBT advocacy groups. Some of them offer useful information on how to go about getting employment benefits.

You're also going to run into all kinds of other issues. Maybe your health club won't allow unmarried partners and their kids to join as a family. Sometimes these hurtful actions are illegal, and sometimes they aren't. Perhaps the best thing you can do is to become an activist — on whatever level works for you. Flip to Chapter 19 for how you can become an activist.

Handling family, friends, neighbors, and strangers

Society is just getting accustomed to LGBT faces. Only recently did LGBT people start coming out in large numbers. Dealing with same-sex families is an even more recent development for many people. They can say and do hurtful things.

Taking the school district to court

Framing a lawsuit against school officials or the district itself is a bit too technical for this book, but if you're considering filing a lawsuit against your child's school district, make sure you contact a lawyer or an advocacy group that is familiar with (and preferably has experience with) these issues. A few of the different legal theories that may apply are

✔ Intentional torts, such as battery, assault, and the intentional infliction of emotional distress. (These lawsuits are usually brought against the bully, but under compelling circumstances school officials who enabled the conduct may also be found liable.)

✔ Constitutional claims (such as the failure to provide due process or equal protection under the law) for deprivations of your child's rights.

✔ If your child is LGBT, you may also have recourse under Title IX of the Civil Rights Act if the bullying is because of perceived nonconformity with behavior "expected" of his or her gender (the Obama administration has taken a very aggressive position on this, and the Justice Department has even moved to intervene on behalf of bullied students).

✔ In some states, nondiscrimination laws may apply.

Yet the very proliferation of LGBT families, especially in certain parts of the country, has started to change the perception. After all, being involved in a committed couple, and, even more so, raising children is understood by everyone to be a huge responsibility. It's also a connecting one.

Your extended family, your neighbors, and even strangers see their kids getting along with yours. They start to view you as a parent with the same concerns for your kids as they have for theirs. And they're reminded of how the connective tissue of humanity is truer than whatever preconceived notions about "the gays" they might have had.

That doesn't mean that there aren't rough waters to navigate. Even friends can say things that wound — sometimes consciously, but more often, not. And no one kind of response will fit every situation. Sometimes you need to be direct. Sometimes pointed humor is the best riposte. Sometimes you just need to let it go. And sometimes, unfortunately, you need to cut your losses and move on — there are plenty of friends you haven't met.

Chapter 4

Facing Discrimination and Seeking Help

*W*hether you're single or partnered, or gay, lesbian, bisexual, or trans-gendered, chances are very good that you've experienced discrimination in some form or other.

Sometimes the law doesn't recognize the discrimination, but the discrimination infuriates or wounds you anyway — like when your kid's friend isn't allowed to play with your child just because her parents are lesbians, or, worse, when your own family members reject you and your gay partner.

In other cases, the discrimination may be masked by something else, so that you don't even know it's happened. Are you sure that you didn't get that job just because someone else had a better résumé? Or that the waitress is just "accidentally" taking forever to get to your family's table? Sometimes, people's motives aren't easy to identify, even to themselves.

In some situations, you can clearly determine what's happening, and also that there is — or *should be* — a law protecting you against actions that discriminate against you just because you're a member of the LGBT community. Sometimes a law does exist, and sometimes it doesn't. And even when a law exists, filing a lawsuit isn't always your best or only option.

In this chapter, we lay out what discrimination is, including the different categories of classes that the law protects, discuss some of the most important legal categories of discrimination, and explore ways of dealing with it.

Discrimination can shatter your life and ripple through your family. You need to know how to deal with it — how the law protects (or doesn't protect) you, how to know when you've been treated unfairly, and what your options are.

Much of the material in this chapter pertains to discrimination that you experience as an individual, not necessarily as a member of a couple, but separating the two is often difficult. If your application for housing is denied because you're a gay man, your family is obviously affected. Less obviously, if you're not hired, not promoted, or fired because you're a lesbian, your family is also affected — both by the loss of income and by the emotional toll that discrimination takes on everyone around the victim.

How the Law Views Discrimination against People in the LGBT Community

Here's a statement that could startle you: *In general, the law allows discrimination.* This sentence emphasizes the value society places on individuals' right to associate with whomever they want to, which generally means that employers, social clubs, and even landlords can refuse to hire, associate with, or rent to people that they plain don't like. If the decision maker doesn't like your personality, your red hair, or your interest in tennis, he or she can refuse to hire you, turn you away from the club, or rent to someone else.

They can't base their refusal on discrimination against individuals in legally protected categories. Although the following list varies a bit from one state to another, and between federal and state law, in general the protected categories include

- ✔ Race
- ✔ Sex (sometimes referred to as "gender")
- ✔ Pregnancy
- ✔ Disability
- ✔ Religion
- ✔ National origin
- ✔ Age
- ✔ Marital status

You probably noticed that "sexual orientation" or "gender identity" isn't on this list. We exclude it because discriminating on the basis of sexual orientation and gender identity is perfectly permissible in many parts of the country for employers, landlords, and ice cream shops to refuse to hire, rent to, or serve anyone who's gay, lesbian, bisexual, or transgendered. In some states, sexual orientation is a protected class, but gender identity is not, meaning that transgendered folks — who often are the most in need of legal protection against discrimination — have no legal recourse.

The patchwork is actually even more complicated than state by state. Even within a single state, certain cities or counties may offer antidiscrimination protection and others don't. And the *extent* and coverage of the protection offered can also vary. In these ways, legal treatment of sexual orientation and gender identity discrimination differs from how the law sees other kinds of discrimination.

That's because federal law doesn't do much to protect you and your partner. If you're discriminated against by the government itself (either federal or state), you might be able to claim that your constitutional rights to equal protection and due process of law were violated, but these cases are hard to win. So for the most part, you have to rely on legal protection other than the US Constitution. And here your problems begin.

Although battles have been waged in Congress for years, no federal statute specifically protects the LGBT community in the workplace, which is the source of much of the most stressful (and costly) discrimination. No federal law guarantees you access to public accommodations (which we discuss in the next section), and there's limited protection in the area of housing.

The situation at the federal level is currently better than we just indicated because the Obama administration has interpreted some federal laws to protect LGBT folks, even where the laws don't list sexual orientation as a protected category. Unfortunately nothing guarantees that these LGBT-friendly interpretations will remain in place, because a subsequent administration can simply overturn them. That's why legislation is needed.

The information on antidiscrimination law that we discuss throughout this chapter is general, so don't rely on the information as a source of current legal rules. Federal regulations change constantly. State laws expand, and sometimes contract, protection. Municipalities vote in protections in housing and accommodations. If you feel you've been discriminated against in a way that has you considering legal action, do some preliminary research on the current state of the law, and then, if appropriate, contact an attorney.

Mapping Discrimination by Category

You, your partner, and your family may experience discrimination in many different ways. Some of them, like snubbing by your family of origin or by complete strangers in a social setting, can't be dealt with legally; they require a set of adaptive behaviors, including education, humor, and a thick skin. But typical antidiscrimination laws do cover several areas. The following sections discuss four main areas of discrimination typically covered by state laws. Remember that laws vary state to state.

Employment

One area where discrimination can occur is in the workplace. Employment discrimination can take place in a number of ways:

- ✔ **Discrimination in hiring:** You may not get the job you're the best qualified for, just because you're LGBT, or in a same-sex relationship.

- ✔ **Failure to promote:** If you come out after starting at a job, you may find that your qualifications for a promotion are trumped by your sexual orientation — and be denied the step up that you deserve.

- ✔ **Getting fired:** Your boss may fire you after discovering that you're LGBT.

- ✔ **Hostile workplace environment:** You haven't been fired, but life on the job is miserable, just because you're LGBT.

A federal law protecting the LGBT community against workplace discrimination is vitally needed, but it's been elusive. For more than a decade, equality-minded members of Congress have been pushing the Employment Nondiscrimination Act (ENDA), which would simply add sexual orientation (and probably gender identity) to the list of groups protected against workplace discrimination. ENDA is a major goal of the mainstream LGBT rights movement. Many LGBT advocates had reason to hope that the law would finally pass during the Obama administration (the president supports it), but it hasn't come to a vote in Congress. Because no federal law prohibits employment discrimination, what are your options?

- ✔ **You may have a federal claim under Title VII.** This part of the Civil Rights Act protects against discrimination in the workplace based on sex. Under current interpretation of the law, this statute can be especially helpful to transgendered employees but can sometimes also be used by gay and lesbian workers. (See the nearby sidebar for details.)

- ✔ **You may be fortunate to live in a state that covers sexual orientation, making it a prohibited ground for discrimination.** The state law may even cover gender identity, although fewer states do so. If you're in such a state, you may have recourse under state law. (Just don't assume that because you're in a state that seems to cover employment, you have a possible claim. State laws are a crazy quilt, with different types of employers exempt for different reasons — size and religious purpose, to name two.) In some cases, where relocation is a good option for you, you may even consider state law in choosing your employer.

- ✔ **You may choose to work for an employer who has its own antidiscrimination policy that protects you.** Many employers today have their own written antidiscrimination policies. Job listings may even say that the employer is seeking candidates to increase diversity in the workplace and list sexual orientation (or even gender identity) as one category of diversity. Even though these policies aren't law, they're important none-theless. They signal that the employer is at least on record as welcoming you. And the policy may also suggest that the employer has a sympa-thetic Human Resources Department.

"Sex stereotyping": Using federal law to combat workplace discrimination

Even though federal law doesn't name LGBT workers as protected from workplace discrimi-nation, you and your partner may have recourse under Title VII of the Civil Rights Act, which is the section that deals with employment.

That's because one of the protected categories under Title VII is "sex." In a series of important decisions going back to the Supreme Court's 1989 ruling in *Price Waterhouse v. Hopkins,* courts have held that "gender stereotyping" is impermissible sex discrimination and therefore covered by Title VII. This interpretation of the law may help you or your partner in two ways:

✔ **If you or your partner is transgendered:** In April of 2012, the Equal Employment Opportunity Commission (EEOC) ruled that Title VII covers workplace discrimination against the transgendered: "[I]ntentional discrimination against a transgender indi-vidual because that person is transgender is, by definition, discrimination 'based on . . . sex,' and such discrimination therefore violates Title VII." The EEOC is charged with enforcing Title VII, and it has author-ity to investigate and sue employers found to have discriminated, so its interpretation is entitled to great weight. But it's not law in the same way that an Act of Congress is law, so a court could disagree, or the EEOC (perhaps in another presidential adminis-tration) could overrule itself. But for now, at least, transgendered people in workplaces covered by Title VII (generally those with

at least 15 employees) have coverage they didn't have less than a year ago.

✔ **If you or your partner is gay, lesbian, or bisexual:** The use of Title VII is more complicated. Unlike transgender status, discrimination on the basis of sexual ori-entation isn't obviously discrimination on the basis of sex. Depending on the alleged discriminatory conduct, it may be dis-crimination based on stereotypical views of appropriate behavior for men and for women. The key here is often how the com-plaint is worded.

For example, in the 2009 case *Prowel v. Wise Business Forms,* a federal appellate court sided with an employee who alleged workplace harassment. The man's fellow workers had tormented the guy for not being "manly enough" (including, bizarrely, for pushing the buttons on his machine "with pizzazz" and "filing" his nails rather than "ripping them off with a utility knife"). The lower court had thrown out the case, saying that the employee was trying to get around the fact that the law didn't cover sexual orientation by trying to reframe his complaint as arising under sex or gender stereotyping. The appellate court dis-agreed; if he could establish mistreatment based on impermissible stereotyping, he had a claim, whether or not he also hap-pened to be gay.

Before you take a job (if you have the luxury of choice), do some research about potential employers. Even in a state that has antidiscrimination protection that covers you, make sure you're in an environment where you don't need to go to court to vindicate your rights. Choosing a publicly gay-friendly employer doesn't insure that you won't experience discrimination, but it does improve your odds. Look for an in-house mechanism that deals with discrimination if it does occur.

Housing

Housing is another area where discrimination can occur because of sexual orientation and gender identity. The Obama administration has improved the legal situation for LGBT folks. In a ruling that went into effect in March, 2012, the Department of Housing and Urban Development (HUD) issued a rule interpreting the Fair Housing Act (FHA) to prohibit discrimination on the basis of sexual orientation and gender identity in housing. The new rule means that you can't be asked about your sexual orientation or gender identity, nor denied housing on those bases. Furthermore, you can't be denied financing, just because you're a member of the LGBT community. (Chapter 5 has more detail on this rule and on housing discrimination more generally.)

As with the improved federal situation with employment, though, an important caveat applies: A subsequent administration can undo this rule, because it's not required by the express terms of the statute. That's why there are moves afoot in Congress to provide housing protection to the LGBT community. It's even possible, although probably not likely, that a court could strike down this new HUD rule. The basis for doing so would be that the law, as passed by Congress, sets out certain categories of those protected against housing discrimination, and that sexual orientation and gender identity aren't included in that list.

Another source of housing protection may be at the state or local level. Check out your local laws to see whether they may cover your situation. Look to answer these questions:

- ✔ Does the law cover discrimination by lenders or only by those who own or rent the property?

- ✔ Is there an exemption for certain properties, such as those occupied by the owner, or those smaller than a certain number of units?

- ✔ Are there religious exemptions for owners or landlords who object to same-sex couples (or often to any unmarried couples)? It's not clear that such laws would still be upheld by courts, but make sure you check in any case; such an exemption could factor into your decision.

Public accommodations

Of all the areas of antidiscrimination law, the law ensuring equal access to public accommodations is the most complex and ill-understood. And unlike the federal laws relating to employment and housing, which at least offer *some* protection against *some* discrimination against *some* of the LGBT community *some* of the time, the federal statute dealing with discrimination in public accommodations law doesn't. It covers only race, color, religion, and national origin. Not sex. Not disability. And certainly not sexual orientation or gender identity or expression.

On the other hand, the law isn't that comprehensive in the first place. Enacted in 1964 as part of the civil rights movement, it covers only hotels, restaurants, and places of "entertainment" (including theaters, concert venues, and sports arenas). That's it.

So how do you know if you (and your partner) are protected from discrimination based on public accommodation? The following sections can help clarify.

Turning to state or local laws

If you (and your partner) are going to gain protection against discrimination in connection with public accommodations, you have to base your case on state or local law. And that's when all legal craziness breaks loose. Here are the biggest questions that arise in the public accommodations context:

- How does the law define *public accommodation*?
- How have courts in a particular state interpreted the language of the law, where its application to a particular situation isn't clear?
- Does the law cover discrimination based on sexual orientation? Gender identity or expression?

Although the term "public accommodation" may suggest that protection is limited to government-run operations, in fact, state statutes are typically much broader and cover privately owned businesses that offer to the public not just what you might think of as "accommodations" — perhaps facilities — but also good and services.

Statutes don't necessarily cover every business that such a broad term suggests they might. Often exceptions exist for "distinctly private" businesses or entities with a religious mission — thereby leading to headaches for courts (and state civil rights commissions) charged with drawing the line between public and private. This confusion isn't necessarily anyone's "fault" — defining every situation in advance is difficult.

Looking at legal precedents to see where you stand

Some cases are easy. For example, if someone refuses to serve your family in a restaurant, or the employee of a large hotel chain withholds the key to your hotel room upon seeing the two of you together, then the only question may be whether the law's protection includes sexual orientation. These places are held open to the general public — in other words, they are public accommodations, even though privately owned.

But some cases aren't so clear. Two well-known cases illustrate the potential power and scope of public accommodations laws for gay and lesbian couples:

✔ In a New Jersey case, a lesbian couple brought a successful claim against a church-affiliated group in Ocean Grove, after their request to rent the church's oceanside pavilion for their civil union ceremony was denied. The church group had accepted a public subsidy for the facility and had agreed in writing to make it available to the public.

✔ When a photographer in New Mexico politely declined to photograph a lesbian commitment ceremony, the couple successfully claimed that the refusal violated the state's public accommodation law. The photographer didn't bother to claim that other commitments took precedence, but instead admitted that it didn't do same-sex ceremonies. The state civil rights commission and two state courts have sided with the couple over the photographer's religious objection.

A couple of lessons emerge from suits like these two:

✔ These suits have often been mischaracterized as a reason not to allow same-sex marriages. Those individuals with strong religious or moral objections to these unions are being forced to take actions against their beliefs. However, these cases arose in states without marriage equality (New Jersey has civil unions, and New Mexico has no same-sex relationship recognition at all). These cases show the power of the public accommodations law and send this message: If you're engaging in commerce, you have to be open to all.

✔ Although the harms suffered in public accommodations cases won't, on average, be as great as those incurred because of the denial of a job or a place to live, pursuing these claims can still be valuable because of the following possible benefits:

• State civil rights commissions often investigate these claims, and their findings of discrimination have weight with courts if the cases are appealed. And because the commissions are charged with enforcing the civil rights laws, they'll often do much of the work.

- Even though your hard damages are often less than other forms of discrimination, sometimes they're real enough (you have to pay extra, and spend extra time, to find replacement services). And don't discount your emotional distress.

- These cases serve an important educational function, reminding the public that discrimination against you, your partner, and your family isn't okay, and is illegal! You're entitled to the same services as everyone else.

Education

Title IX of the Civil Rights Act says that any educational institution that receives federal funds can't discriminate on the basis of sex. Although many people consider Title IX as the vehicle that's improved athletic opportunities for girls and women, in fact it applies to all aspects of education.

Although Title IX wouldn't seem to do much for the LGBT community, in fact the Obama administration has taken the aggressive position that gender stereotyping is a form of sex discrimination — just as in the employment context, where the case law is more clearly in support of this position. So the law has been used to combat the bullying of LGBT kids, on the (sound) theory that this kind of mistreatment is a kind of gender stereotyping.

Some states also have laws protecting against discrimination in education that may be of assistance to you, but not many of them. Still, you want to check if you feel that a school has discriminated against you, your partner, or your kids. Often you can informally resolve these issues within the system, but obviously sometimes they can't be resolved. (Chapter 3 covers some of these issues.)

Taking action if the law doesn't cover sexual orientation or gender identity

The law has huge holes when it comes to protecting sexual minorities, despite broad readings of existing federal laws and ever-expanding state and local protections. You may find yourself in a situation where the discrimination is clear and has been costly, but the context in which it occurred just isn't an area where the law (local, state, or federal) protects you. If you're really determined to seek legal recourse, the good news is that you may have other options.

You're not just a gay, lesbian, bisexual, or transgendered person. You have multiple, overlapping identities: you're a woman, or an older American, or disabled, or African-American, or Asian, or (fill in the blank). You get the idea. An interesting debate revolves around whether the law should protect in the categorical way that it does, rather than just prohibit discrimination on any basis that doesn't have to do with job competence. For now, though, you have to be in a protected category, and *be able to show that the discrimination you've experienced is because of your membership in that category.*

As a member of the LGBT community, you may (reasonably) think that your employer or the landlord who's offering implausible reasons for refusing to rent to you are doing so because of your sexual orientation or gender identity. The situation may be more complicated though. The discrimination may be rooted in a stew of prejudices that are related. In other words, the discriminator may be a homophobe — and a sexist, a racist, and an ageist. If you suspect that one of these other identities is at play, you have the ability to file a complaint (or to go through internal channels, like the human resources office at work).

We don't mean to encourage bringing claims that aren't based on some reasonable basis. Your lawyer (if the case gets that far) can only do his or her job if you tell the truth about what happened.

One other thing to consider is a claim based on marital discrimination status, if your state law recognizes that protected category. These claims have sometimes been made in connection with a few issues, like:

- ✔ Whether an employer's refusal to grant benefits to the partners of same-sex couples is discrimination based on marital status
- ✔ Whether denial of family housing to same-sex couples is discriminatory on that basis

---

A note on HIV status as a disability

In 1998, the Supreme Court decided *Bragdon v. Abbott.* The case involved the question whether a woman was disabled, for the purposes of federal legal protection, when she had HIV but was asymptomatic. The Court held that, because HIV interfered with a major life function (reproduction), it constituted a disability even though the plaintiff could generally go about her daily activities.

The plaintiff in *Bragdon v. Abbott* had alleged discrimination against her dentist, and many HIV+ people can recount stories of discrimination by medical professionals, real estate agents, and restaurant owners. Although these problems are probably less frequent than they were a decade ago, disability based on HIV status (alone) is an actionable ground of discrimination. But because at least some people continue to discriminate against those with HIV, you may want to consider how much you want to disclose your status in the first place.

The bad news: Courts are inconsistent — and even confused — on this issue. Considering the marital discrimination route is worthy in some states, especially if you have no protection for your relationship otherwise. The good news: Some favorable precedents exist.

For those who are HIV+, you may also be able to bring a federal claim (and, often, a state claim) on the theory that HIV constitutes a disability. (Check out the nearby sidebar.)

Fighting Back: Identifying and Dealing with Discrimination

If you're a member of the LGBT community, you've probably already faced some form of discrimination in your life. If you haven't, consider yourself fortunate. The sad truth: Many people are discriminated in some form at one time or more in their lives. Some cases are more obvious than others. In the employment context, you may have an employer who says openly homophobic things (thereby contributing to a hostile work environment), or you may discover a document that worries about the effect of hiring gays on business. A prospective landlord may quote you and your partner a rental rate that you know is twice as high as what's being charged for the identical apartment across the hall. Or — as in one well-known, real-life case — a bakery may reject your attempt to order a Pride cake.

Many times discrimination is papered over by some other explanation: Even though you were the most qualified, you weren't promoted because fellow employee X has better "people skills." Your LGBT swim team was kicked out of its facility not because two team members exchanged an innocent kiss on the deck, but because the school needs to make more lap swim hours available to its students. And so on. Sometimes you'll be absolutely convinced you were discriminated against, and sometimes you'll be left wondering.

So how can you deal with discrimination that you or your partner encounters? Consider the following options.

If you don't want to pursue a court case, you have other avenues that may be more productive. Unless the consequences are severe (either financially or emotionally), consider doing nothing. Yes, nothing. More than likely, you've probably done nothing plenty of times. Going through life as a LGBT person or as one-half of a same-sex couple without experiencing multiple acts of discrimination is nearly impossible. Sometimes turning away is the best response. Other times the situation may call for pointed humor (if you can manage it), and other times a serious but respectful confrontation is the way to go.

Trying the informal route

If you do want to do *something*, you can consider informal means of dealing with the problem. For example, a baker wouldn't create a Pride cake. Or what about another baker who refuses to do a same-sex wedding cake? These examples may be trivial, but you can use them to highlight your options. What are they? Consider the following:

✔ **You can go to another business.** You can move on down the road to another bakery. Sometimes, that's all you feel like doing. You don't have to fight every battle. To some people, this response seems unsatisfying, and it leaves the bakery free to continue discriminating.

✔ **You can engage the person in a conversation.** In this case, talk to the baker about why he or she is refusing your business. Doing so may or may not be productive. If the reasons are based on deep-seated religious beliefs, discussion may not get you far.

✔ **You can tell others.** Here, you can publicize the bakery's discrimination in any ways that are available to you by speaking to other members of the LGBT community, blogging (if that's your thing), and even writing to the local newspaper or contacting television stations to tell your story.

✔ **You can check with the local or state government.** If your town, city, or state protects discrimination against LGBT people in public accommodations, you can contact the relevant civil rights commission, if one exists. (Even if not, more than likely some governmental entity is set up to receive reports of discrimination.) Often, a simple word from an agent of such an agency, especially if backed up with the threat of a fine, if available, can be enough to change policy. You may even get a nice apology out of the deal, and the value of "I'm sorry" shouldn't be underestimated.

✔ **You can contact an LGBT legal advocacy or political group for help.** You may want to consult with a local LGBT human rights group. If the discrimination is more serious (and especially if the implications seem broader), you may even want to contact a national LGBT human rights group.

If the group considers the case an important piece of litigation, it may pursue legal action on your behalf. At minimum, the involvement of such an organization can sometimes kick-start a dialogue that ends up changing the discriminator's views, or at least their actions, going forward. Some national groups that may be interested in helping, or referring you to other sources of help, include the following:

- **Human Rights Campaign (HRC):** This advocacy group (www.hrc.org) doesn't do litigation but can publicize the situation and educate the public about what's happened.

- **Lambda Legal:** This organization (www.lambdalegal.org) chooses high-impact cases for litigation.

- **National Gay and Lesbian Task Force:** This advocacy group (www. thetaskforce.org) works at all levels, from the ground up, to build public support for LGBT equality.

✔ **You can consider filing a lawsuit.** If a lawsuit is a possibility, you *may* consider going that route. If you decide to pursue a legal case, make sure you know what you're pursuing. Because people are getting savvier about avoiding overt discrimination (for both legal and cultural reasons), proving discrimination may be difficult. A good lawyer can help you put together a case from circumstantial (or, sometimes, from statistical) evidence, if that's the route you choose to take. Sometimes just the threat of a lawsuit will make a business, especially a small business, back down. But ask if a lawsuit is really worth it.

Going the formal route

Sometimes discrimination is too hurtful or damaging to try the informal route. If the discrimination is more serious than a bakery refusing you service, you need to consider a more formal response.

For example, say your boss sees a picture of you and your partner on your desk and then demotes you the next day, despite your excellent record. Even if you're highly employable, you can't deal with this demotion by just picking up your stuff and walking down the street to another place of business. To state the obvious: It's not like choosing a bakery.

Even if no law protects you, someone from human resources may be able to help, which is especially true if the employer has a nondiscrimination policy in place that applies to its LGB (and maybe even T) employees. The HR people will often investigate this kind of action, and the end result may even be that it's your boss — not you — who's walking down the street in search of other employment.

Your employer probably will take a series of steps, beginning with informal discussion and proceeding all the way through to a formal grievance and discipline procedure that you may be able to avail yourself of when discrimination strikes.

Even if a lawsuit is a possibility in these cases, often your contract — or good common sense — requires you to move through in-house steps before going the litigation route. If so, consider yourself lucky: Although litigation seems like a good idea, and may in some cases end up being your best or only remedy, regard it as a last resort. Lawsuits have a tendency to destroy everyone.

Part II
Everyday Law and Your Family

The 5th Wave
By Rich Tennant

"I'm entering all the bank's requirements for a mortgage, and we either need to buy a computer with more memory, or start looking for a smaller house."

In this part . . .

*T*he legal and social landscape that confronts you
affects your everyday life. Every significant decision
you make — whether to move in together, to combine
assets, to bring children into your family, and to plan for
the illness or death of one of you — is shadowed by the
law's different (and often unequal) treatment of your
family.

This part walks through these topics and provides sound
advice on how to make these decisions given these legal
hurdles you must clear. We emphasize the details in each
case and also provide information on two subjects many
would rather avoid: taxes and breaking up!

Chapter 5

Home Sweet Home: Living Together

In This Chapter

▶ Figuring out whether you and your partner are ready to move in together

▶ Deciding whether to rent or buy a home

▶ Knowing what you need to do to rent together

▶ Buying a home: What it entails

▶ Making a living-together agreement

*T*he decision to move in with your partner may be one of the most significant milestones of your relationship, especially for LGBT partners who can't legally marry. In terms of commitment and emotional and financial investment, moving in together may be as important as a wedding or starting a family. It may seem like a dream come true!

Of course your dream can turn into a nightmare before you know it. If you're expecting your new living-together life with your partner to unfold blissfully like a romantic comedy, you may be shocked to discover that moving in together can inevitably change your relationship. Whether it changes for the better or worse is entirely up to you and your partner.

So if you're going to make the big leap into living together, make sure you do it right. We can't promise that you'll live happily ever after, but if you read this chapter and follow the tips and suggestions we describe, more likely than not your experience will be less like a nightmare and closer to that dream you are imagining.

No matter if you've been dating for one month or a few years, at some point, couples reach a crossroads in their relationship where they must decide whether or not to:

✔ Make a long-term commitment

✔ Maintain the status quo

✔ Go their separate ways

When a couple elects to make a greater commitment to one another, they often choose to get engaged, get married, or move in together. Of course the capacity to take part in these options is largely dependent on a couple's sexual orientation and/or where they live. Straight couples — and gay and lesbian partners living in a marriage equality state — can marry if and when they choose. But, because of federal and state laws denying marriage rights to LGBT partners, legal marriage is off the table for gay and lesbian couples living in nonmarriage equality states.

Besides marriage, you can strengthen your relationship in a variety of ways. For example, where available, you may want to register as domestic partners or enter into a civil union. If you live in an area where these options don't exist, the next best thing may be to draw up legal documents, such as a will, living revocable trust, and/or advance directives to give each other inheritance rights, hospital visitation rights, and medical decision-making authority. We discuss these documents in more detail throughout the book.

Even when legal marriage rights are a viable option for couples who are ready to commit, more and more of them are choosing to live together outside of marriage before rushing to the altar.

In this chapter we discuss the pros and cons of living together and give you a few tips to help you recognize and avoid pitfalls that might needlessly damage or destroy your relationship as you transition from dating to cohabitating.

Determining Whether It's Time to Move in Together

Regardless of how long you've known your partner, at some point you may want to play house for a while to see if you'd make good roommates. After all, you don't really know a person until you've lived with him or her, right?

When you live with your partner, you can see how the person of your dreams handles the responsibility of paying the rent and utilities and doing household chores. You can also discover new things about each other and see another side of your partner that you otherwise never would.

Moving in together may be a boon to your relationship. After all, you can divvy up the cost of rent, food, utilities, and other expenses. You can have lots of unscheduled, impromptu intimate time together, and you can wake up each morning with your sweetheart lying in bed beside you.

Perhaps you'll be blissfully happy for the rest of your days or maybe you'll discover your partner has annoying habits that are just too much to bear. However it turns out, living together is a good way to see whether you can adjust to one another's quirks before making your relationship legal (or as legal as you can).

Keep in mind you and your partner will be sharing more than just an address — you'll be sharing your lives. So, if you're ready to take a chance on moving in together, you need to make sure you're going about it the right way. That's where the following sections can help you.

Being honest about your feelings, needs, and expectations

Having a preliminary discussion about whether you're both really ready to move in together is probably a good idea. This conversation is useful to have because if you can't get beyond this threshold issue, the question of whether you're ready to live together answers itself.

On the other hand, if you both agree that you're indeed ready to live together, make sure you discuss the following things before you start packing:

- ✔ **Money:** The discussion about money is difficult, but essential. Will you split the bills 50-50 or will you divvy them up a different way because of income disparity? The share each partner is responsible for contributing should depend on the total amount of rent, utilities, and other expenses as well as on each partner's income. Check out Chapter 6 about joining your assets together.

- ✔ **Cleanliness and clutter:** Although these things may seem insignificant now, if your partner is a neat freak and you love to kick off your shoes and let it all hang out, you could be in for some fireworks — and not the good kind.

- ✔ **Household chores:** Talk about who will cook and/or do the dishes, do the laundry, empty the trash, and so on.

- ✔ **Politics and religion:** Some couples find they can't tolerate living with someone who has vastly divergent views on these sensitive issues. Better to know now where your partner stands — and whether you can deal with his or her viewpoint — before you find yourself in a screaming match after voting for a candidate that your partner opposed.

- ✔ **Music, movies, and TV shows:** This discussion may seem petty and insignificant. Even though you may think you know, ask before you share a living space to avoid potential heated arguments later. If your tastes are compatible, that's great. If not, you'll need to negotiate TV viewing, movie rentals and what music (if any!) you want piped into your living space in the evenings and on weekends.

✓ **Furniture and décor:** You may think having this discussion is silly before you move it, but you need to answer questions, such as whose furniture will grace each room and what color will you paint the walls. In heterosexual relationships the woman stereotypically is in charge of decorating (although not always), and the man just doesn't care. But LGBT couples don't fit into stereotypical gender roles, and anger or hurt feelings may result when you tell your partner you think his or her favorite lamp is ugly.

✓ **Pets:** If both partners have pets, you ought to make sure your Rottweiler won't eat your partner's African Grey parrot the minute you leave them alone in the house. People are sensitive about their pets and tend to take their side in a fight. If your pets can't live under the same roof, you and your partner may not either. If only one of you has a pet, the petless partner needs to let the other know if he or she has allergies or issues with pet dander all over the house.

✓ **Daily routines or habits:** Chat about what you want to maintain after you move in with your partner. If the activity is quiet, like meditation, yoga, or reading, your partner probably won't object. However, if you play a musical instrument, especially something noisy like drums, you probably need to work out a schedule where you can enjoy your hobby without driving your partner crazy.

✓ **Your families, friends, holidays, and traditions:** Talk about all issues. Will your families come to your home to visit? Will they stay for dinner or sleep over for a couple of nights? Do you like to cook a meal for friends? Do you enjoy having your pals over for drinks or to play cards? How will you deal with major holidays? Will you adopt your partner's holiday traditions or will the two of you create your own, new customs? These areas can cause a lot of friction and stress if you don't discuss and know what to expect.

There is no right way to have this discussion. If you find you're unable to agree on important issues, you may want to postpone living together. If simply talking about your expectations results in an emotional meltdown, you probably need to reconsider your decision.

If you feel remotely uncertain about giving up your own place to move in with your partner, you may want to consider having a trial run while maintaining your own separate residence. You and your partner can take turns staying at each other's place for a month or so. Give yourself enough time to get to know each other and see what your beloved is like when not on his or her best behavior.

Just because you decide to move in with your partner doesn't mean you must also relinquish your independence. Maintain the friendships and activities that you currently enjoy. If you do, you'll feel more content, and your happiness will nourish your relationship with your partner.

Considering the pros and cons

Love is often blind. When you first fall in love, you either don't see or just don't care to see the imperfections your sweetheart occasionally reveals. However, one surefire way to knock your rose-colored glasses off your face is to spend every day together so you can get a good look at those warts. Of course as with all things, living together has its advantages and its disadvantages.

Potential benefits of living together include

- Getting to know all sides of your partner's personality, such as routines, habits, and temperament
- Having sex whenever the mood strikes without having to arrange a date and time
- Enjoying a deeper commitment with your partner
- Taking care of one another when one of you is sick
- Sharing responsibilities, household expenses, and chores
- Feeling like you're part of a team
- Having a companion to share good times and bad

Possible negative consequences of moving in together are

- Having different ideas about money, such as how and when to save or spend it and what it gets spent on
- Discovering that one of you is organized and fastidious and the other is a messy slob
- Finding out you simply can't tolerate each other's friends, family, religious beliefs, and/or habits and customs
- Realizing you can't live with your partner after you've sublet or sold your previous home and are strapped with the responsibility for your share of rent or mortgage payments

For couples who live in nonmarriage equality states, if you want to share a life with your partner, living together outside of marriage is your only real alternative. For those fortunate few who live where legal marriage (or some equivalent, like the civil union) is an option, you get to decide which course is best for you.

Moving in with your significant other is a big step that may change your relationship forever, for better or for worse. Thus, prior to loading up the moving van, make sure you and your partner have weighed all the pros and cons of living together before making any rash decisions.

Figuring Out What You Will Call Home

After you decide to move in with your partner, the next step is to consider what residence you will call home. You probably have a few choices, such as the following:

- ✔ **A home you choose to buy or rent together as a couple:** Some couples, though, choose to buy or rent a new home — on the view that they want to make a life together where neither of them has any territorial issues.

- ✔ **You or your partner's home that you own, rent, or sublet:** If you choose to move into a home that one of you owns or rents, you have to decide which home. Making this decision usually depends on a wide variety of factors, including the relative size of the home, number of bedrooms and baths, where the home is located, and so on.

If you own or lease the home you and your partner will live in together, here are some matters to consider:

- ✔ The percentage of rent and/or utilities your partner will pay, if any. For instance, if one of you earns less, is a student, or is unemployed, you may want to divide the rent and utilities according to each partner's ability to pay. (Refer to the section "Choosing to have unequal ownership" for more information on what to do when incomes are unequal.)

- ✔ Whether you should add your partner's name to the deed, and, if so, whether you will own equal shares or some other percentage depending on your partner's investment of cash and/or sweat equity. Before adding your partner's name to the deed of a home you've invested in, you should carefully think it through. After the deed is recorded, your partner will own whatever percentage of interest you decide to give to him or her. If you've been with your partner for a reasonable period of time and he or she is invested in the property by helping with the mortgage, upkeep, and/or physical labor, you probably owe it to your partner to give him or her a stake in the investment. (See the section "Having ownership stake with sweat equity" for a broader discussion on the issue of sweat equity.)

- ✔ If one or both of you are renters, you need to carefully read through your *lease agreement* (a contract between the landlord and tenant that lays out a tenant's rights to live in a rented property and a landlord's rights to enter the property or terminate the lease) to determine whether you can terminate the lease or invite your partner to move in with you. A *tenant* is a person who owns or rents a home, apartment, or other real property by deed, under a lease or by paying rent. (Refer to the section "Renting a Home" for more information.)

Be prepared for your landlord to demand more rent or an increase in the amount of your security deposit when you ask if your partner can move in with you. Check your lease to make sure you're able to add a roommate without paying more rent. If you live in a state or community with a rent control ordinance, your landlord may not have the right to raise your rent at all or only as much as allowed under the ordinance.

Whichever home you choose to live in, the bottom line is this: deciding to move in with your partner requires much thought, a lot of communication, and careful planning.

Deciding Whether to Rent or Buy

Determining whether to rent or buy depends on many factors that are subject to your individual circumstances. Figuring out whether you want to rent or buy includes more than just comparing your monthly rent payment with a monthly mortgage payment.

If you plan to stay in your home for more than seven years, buying may be a better strategy. On the other hand, renting a home may be wiser if you live in an area where monthly rental payments are lower than average (and are expected to remain so) or if you intend to move in a couple of years.

Buying a home is an investment — under normal economic circumstances — that should increase in value the longer you own your home. In normal economic times, due to some big up-front closing costs and higher monthly payments, it can take five to seven years before buying becomes a better deal than renting. Keep in mind that as you pay your mortgage you're also building *equity* (an owner's financial interest in a home or other real property; calculated by subtracting the amount owed on the mortgage from the value of the property) in your home.

On the other hand, a common argument against renting is that it's a waste of money. This can be true, especially because the recent mortgage crisis has resulted in a dramatic drop in real estate prices. Unless you live in a super-expensive housing market like New York, San Francisco, or Seattle, buying is now better than renting in almost all large US metro areas, with cities like Detroit, Phoenix, and Rochester, New York, being among the best cities to buy an affordable home.

To help you calculate whether renting or buying is better for you, we suggest you use one of the many free, rent-versus-buy calculators and other tools that are easily found by searching the Internet.

Breaking up co-ownership of a house is often more difficult than it is to get a divorce; it's longer, more expensive, and more difficult. Enter the situation with your eyes wide open and don't buy a house with someone you don't know very well. (Refer to Chapter 10 for issues you may have to face when breaking up and owning a house together.)

Renting a Home

Although home ownership is said to be The American Dream, as of this writing, more and more Americans are opting to rent rather than buy, even though home foreclosures and a decrease in the value of real estate have created a *buyers' market* (economic conditions that make it more favorable to purchase a home).

If you and your partner are just starting out in your relationship, renting may be less risky than purchasing a home. Leases end more cleanly and definitively than ownership does. For instance, when you buy a home with someone you don't know very well, you could end up in a messier-than-a-divorce scenario with no automatic legal remedies to ensure an equitable distribution of jointly owned property.

So if you're considering renting, the following sections have lots of helpful information for you, including what the advantages are to renting and other issues you need to know.

Naming the pros of renting

Besides the risk of a messy break-up and a bad economy, plenty of other good reasons exist to lease a home or apartment. For example, the money you pay in rent may allow you to enjoy services and amenities that you otherwise couldn't afford if you were buying your own home. Often, rental properties come with desirable features, such as

✔ A balcony overlooking the ocean or a view of the mountains

✔ A swimming pool, tennis courts, workout room, sauna, and/or hot tub

✔ Some or all utilities included in the monthly rental fee

✔ Little or no maintenance, such as mowing, weeding, painting, shoveling snow, and so on (although you may have to pay a maintenance fee, which can increase your monthly tab)

✔ No responsibility for structural maintenances, such as fixing or replacing a roof, unclogging septic pipes, and making other repairs, which are the landlord's responsibility

In addition to these advantages of renting, moving is a lot easier when you don't own your home. Even if you're still obligated under your lease agreement to pay rent, you can easily sublet for an amount equal to or slightly less than your monthly rental obligation or break your lease and pay the outstanding balance, and be out of your home in a matter of weeks rather than the months or years it might take to sell your property.

Dealing with potential housing discrimination issues

Until January of 2012, the federal Fair Housing Act (FHA) provided zero protection to same-sex couples who were discriminated against by landlords of privately owned property and public housing units. The good news is under a new Equal Access to Housing rule issued by US Department of Housing and Urban Development (HUD), landlords of HUD-funded housing, or housing whose financing HUD insures, are now prohibited from asking about your sexual orientation or gender identity or denying you housing based on your response.

The bad news: Because this rule was enacted under the Obama administration, a future US President can easily rescind this policy.

The Equal Access to Housing rule only applies to rental property that is affiliated in some way with HUD — in other words public or low-income housing. The rule doesn't affect a discrimination of LGBT couples by landlords and owners of privately owned rental property that isn't covered by HUD program.

If you're lucky enough to live in a city or county that has enacted an antidiscrimination ordinance that includes sexual orientation, you may have a legal claim against a discriminatory landlord whether or not the property is affiliated with HUD.

If you feel that a landlord or property manager of property covered by HUD has discriminated against you on account of your sexual orientation, you should contact HUD's Office of Fair Housing and Equal Opportunity for help at (800) 669-9777, or the state or local office that deals with housing discrimination claims.

Keep in mind that even if you do live where there are protections against housing discrimination, any landlord who wants to deny your application to rent can use a plethora of other reasons, such as bad credit, bad references, and so on, to mask his or her real motives. In that case proving the discrimination is based on your sexual orientation may be difficult.

When LGBT couples who rent have no legal protections for LGBT couples, the results can be ugly — higher rents, a higher incidence of harassment and bullying, and worse.

Knowing your rights as a tenant

If you're renting with your partner, your rights differ depending on whose name is on the lease agreement. As is almost always the case, legally married couples have more rights than unmarried partners, even when they sign a lease as co-tenants (also called *joint tenants,* a *co-tenant* is someone who signs a lease agreement with one or more other individuals).

Whether or not you live in a state or community that doesn't recognize the legality of your relationship, if both you and your partner sign the lease as co-tenants:

✔ Both partners have equal rights to live in the rental unit.

✔ You're both equally responsible for paying rent and other expenses spelled out in the lease.

✔ You're equally liable for failing to abide by the terms of the lease agreement.

If your relationship isn't legally recognized and your name isn't on the lease, you aren't legally responsible to the landlord for rent or other expenses pertaining to the agreement. If you break up and your partner abandons the home, you may be able to sign a new lease or negotiate a transfer of the current lease into your name. Keep in mind there is no guarantee the landlord will agree to let you do so. On the other hand, if your name isn't on the lease but your partner's name is, if you break up and move out, your partner will continue to be responsible for paying rent and the other expenses spelled out in the lease.

If only one partner signs a lease, you need to make sure the agreement clearly states your ability to let the other partner move into the unit with you. Even when the lease specifically allows for a roommate, if you live in an area that provides little or no legal protections for LGBT people, we suggest you get your landlord's permission to avoid future problems or even an eviction. Your landlord may or may not legally be able to stop you, so be proactive and avoid the problem in the first place.

If you live in a marriage equality state or a state or municipality with legal rights for LGBT partners, only one partner may be required to sign the lease, and the entire family will also have the right to live there with you. In other words, most lease agreements allow you to live in your rented home along with your legal spouse or partner and other members of your family.

If you're the legally recognized partner of a tenant and you didn't sign the lease agreement and your partner moves out or dies, you may be able to stay in the rental unit and

✔ Continue to pay the rent

✔ Communicate with the landlord regarding necessary repairs, complaints, and other issues

✔ Make repairs or improvements to the property that aren't in violation of the lease terms

You will probably need written permission from the tenant (your partner who signed the lease) before you can prematurely terminate the lease.

Not only will you have responsibilities to your landlord, as a co-tenant with your partner you also have certain obligations to each other as roommates. What those obligations are depends on the needs, wants, and expectations of both partners. A good way to make sure you're on the same page and that you understand one another's expectations is to write a *co-tenant agreement* that details and describes your responsibilities to each other as co-tenants, including how you will split the rent and what you will do in case of a break-up.

You can review a sample co-tenant agreement (Form 5-1) on the accompanying CD.

Buying a Home: What to Do

Making a decision to purchase a home together may be one of the clearest indications of a couple's commitment to their relationship. A home is often the most expensive single purchase you'll ever make. After you make the decision to buy a home, you need to look at other important considerations, such as the following sections discuss.

Choosing a competent LGBT-friendly real estate agent

Finding a gay or gay-friendly real estate agent who knows what he or she is doing is as easy as doing an online search for that exact phrase. A gay or LGBT ally as your real estate agent not only can help you find a home, but he or she can also steer you to neighborhoods where your relationship will be accepted.

Just because your agent is gay, lesbian, or LGBT friendly doesn't mean he or she is capable, skilled, or experienced at selling real estate. Make sure your agent is good at his or her job before signing a contract. The best way to find someone competent is to ask someone who frequents or works at a local bookstore, bar, community center, organic restaurant, food co-op, coffee shop, and so on. If an agent's name comes up more than a few times, you can bet that person is qualified to help you find a house. You can also check your local paper or gay/lesbian-friendly magazine for real estate listings that focus on promoting LGBT real estate agents.

Luckily and more often than not, when it comes to selling a house, even straight real estate agents are more concerned about making money than they are about discriminating against a willing and qualified buyer. Your real estate agent should also be able to hook you up with a LGBT-friendly bank or mortgage company.

As with renting, few laws prevent a real estate agent from discriminating against an LGBT couple who is shopping for a home. For couples living in non-marriage equality states, only properties with some ties to HUD have antidiscrimination policies that include protections for gay and lesbian partners. And even those protections remain intact only if the next US president chooses to not to rescind the Equal Access to Housing Rule enacted by the Obama administration or unless Congress passes a law extending antidiscrimination protections in housing to the LGBT community.

Although no federal law exists against housing discrimination on the basis of sexual orientation or gender identity, at least 21 states and several major US cities have enacted such laws.

Some state and local zoning laws don't allow unrelated people to live together in a single family dwelling. Fortunately, these laws are rarely enforced, but they could be! Ask your real estate agent if the area in which you're looking to buy is zoned only for people who are legally related.

Deciding on how you'll own your home

Property law (laws that govern ownership of real estate and personal property) in most states was originally written to protect the rights of legally related individuals, especially married couples. Because LGBT partners aren't legally recognized by a majority of states, you must take extra caution when purchasing something as valuable as a home.

When an unmarried couple moves in together, each partner's income and assets aren't automatically seen as owned jointly by both of them. In the event that one partner invests most if not all the cash into the home, the couple needs to decide together how they'll handle this unequal investment. For instance, the couple may want to:

- ✔ Own the home 50-50, even though one of them is contributing more to the down payment and/or mortgage

- ✔ Own an interest in the home that is commensurate with each partner's relative investment

- ✔ Own the home with only one partner's name on the deed and/or mortgage

The following sections explain these ownership options you have.

Eyeing your options for buying property together

In about half the states in the United States, when legally married spouses buy a home, unless they specifically say in writing that they want to own it another way, both spouses automatically own the whole property as *tenants by the entirety* (both spouse own a 100 percent interest in the home). The word *tenant* refers to owners as well as renters of property they possess, occupy, or lease.

The primary advantage of owning your home as tenants by the entirety is that, when your spouse dies, the house is and always has been 100 percent yours. No one can take all or part of the house from you — even if your deceased spouse had to use government benefits to pay for long-term or nursing home care. The state may place a lien on the property, but the state can't force a sale to collect their money until after your death.

On the contrary, unmarried partners, whether LGBT or straight, need to decide how they want to own property together. Because tenancy by the entirety isn't an option for unmarried partners, you have just two other possibilities available, which we describe in the following sections.

Joint tenancy with right of survivorship (JTWROS)

With *joint tenancy with right of survivorship (JTWROS),* you and your partner each own an interest in the property. When one partner dies, his or her interest automatically passes to the surviving partner, and therefore it doesn't pass to the deceased partner's family. JTWROS is different than tenancy by the entirety in a couple of ways:

- ✔ Each tenant only owns a 50 percent share of the property and tenants by the entirety both own a 100 percent interest. When partners have a deed naming them as JTWROS, both of them own a legal one-half interest in the property, even if one partner didn't pay a dime toward the down payment or mortgage. Thus, when the house is sold, the profits of the sale will be divided 50-50 between the partners.

✔ With JTWROS, one partner can sell his or her interest in the property without getting permission from the other tenant. Tenants by the entirety aren't able to sell without both parties agreeing to the sale.

Owning property as JTWROS is easy to do. If you're buying a home together, at the closing, make sure you tell the real estate agent and the title company to add the magic words "rights of survivorship" to your deed. If you already own a home together, check your deed to make sure those words appear after your names. If they don't, you should sign a *quit claim deed,* (a legal document transferring real property from one person to another and then recorded in a county's public land and/or records office) to transfer your property from yourselves as tenants in common (refer to the next section for more information on tenants in common) to yourselves as JTWROS. If you're adding your partner's name to the deed as a JTWROS, use the same quit claim deed to transfer ownership from yourself as an individual to yourself and your partner as JTWROS.

Although you can file a quit claim deed without an exchange of money, the person whose name is being added to the deed may have some tax implications. For instance, if the value of the equity in the property exceeds $13,000 (the current IRS cap for unreported gifts), then the difference may have to be reported as a gift on the added partner's federal and possibly state income tax return. You may want to check with an accountant for more information on the specifics of your plan to quit claim your property to your partner. In addition to a potential gift tax, if a lien was placed on the property before the quit claim, then both partners are liable for settling the lien when the property is sold.

We include a sample quit claim deed on the CD for both JTWROS and tenancy in common. Form 5-2 is Sample Quit Claim Deed creating a Joint Tenancy with Rights of Survivorship (JTWROS), and Form 5-3 is Sample Quit Claim Deed creating a Tenancy in Common.

Unless you own your property as tenants by the entirety or as JTWROS, you absolutely need to draw up a will in order to have a say in who gets your share of the property when you die. Without a will, by law your share of the property will pass to your legal relatives and not to your partner.

If you chose a competent LGBT-friendly real estate agent, he or she should have contacts with other qualified professionals who regularly work with LGBT clients, including the attorney who will draw up your deed. In that case, the attorney should know to add the magic words: "with rights of survivorship" so that a deceased partner's interest in the property will automatically pass to the surviving partner and not to the dead partner's relatives.

Tenancy in common

With *tenancy in common,* you and your partner each own an interest in the property (either equal or some other way). When one partner dies, his or her interest doesn't automatically pass to the surviving partner but rather to someone the deceased partner names in his or her will or to the deceased partners' next-of-kin.

When you own property as tenants in common, you can give each other unequal shares in the property. For instance, if you invested 70 percent of the down payment, closing costs, and mortgage payments and your partner provided the other 30 percent; you should state these percentages of ownership on the face of the deed. In most states, even if you own property 50-50, unless you use the magic words "with rights of survivorship," your deed will automatically create a tenancy in common.

Unlike a JTWROS, a tenancy in common is subject to probate because your share of the property doesn't pass automatically to the surviving partner upon your death. Instead, your share will transfer to whomever you name as the beneficiary in your will. And, if you don't have a will, your share of the property will pass to your next-of-kin according to your state's law.

About a third of US states offer transfer-on-death (TOD) or beneficiary deeds as a means to pass property to a partner or other loved one outside of a trust (and still avoid probate). For those leery of transferring ownership of a home to a partner, a TOD deed offers a safer alternative because the homeowner isn't relinquishing sole ownership rights or the right to 100 percent of the proceeds from a potential future sale. In fact, a TOD deed doesn't take effect until the homeowner dies.

If one partner has children from a previous relationship, a tenancy in common may make sense, especially if you want your children to inherit your share of the house.

Make sure your deed is worded correctly. (Check with your real estate agent or an attorney.) Otherwise, if your partner dies before you, you could find yourself co-owning your home with your deceased partner's hostile family members.

Choosing to have unequal ownership

If one partner makes a larger financial contribution to the down payment or mortgage — or if one partner has a substantially higher income than the other — you may want the percentage of ownership to reflect that difference. If you decide to go this route, check out these next few sections to see if they're applicable to you and your partner.

Having ownership stake with sweat equity

Sharing a home with your partner may be more important than the percentage of ownership each of you has in the property. Plus, the partner with less money may be able to contribute *sweat equity* (an ownership interest created as a direct result of hard work by a partner with less or no money to invest) in the form of remodeling or making improvements on the property. To be fair to the partner who invests his or her labor, you need to make written provisions to protect his or her investment. You can accomplish this in a number of ways, including:

- ✔ By creating a deed with both partners as co-owners with their relative percentage of ownership calculated according to the value of the sweat equity to be invested

- ✔ By having the partner who invested cash (and is the sole owner) draw up a will or trust that names the partner who will contribute sweat equity as beneficiary of the house

- ✔ By making a separate written agreement describing how the sweat equity will be calculated and the degree of ownership that will accrue as the work is completed

Every state in the country has a version of the *statute of frauds* (a law that requires an agreement giving ownership rights for real property has to be in writing). Therefore, if you're a partner in a relationship that isn't legally recognized in the state where you live, and if your name isn't on the deed to the property that you've invested sweat equity into, you have no legal ownership rights to that property, period.

You can, however, sign a written sweat equity agreement with your partner that clearly sets out the expectations and duties of both partners. For example, you can determine the value of a specific task by asking for an estimate on a specific project, and after the work is completed, you will have earned in sweat equity the value of that job.

Drafting a sweat equity agreement between partners as co-owners of property is essential, but it can also be challenging. Quantifying investments of cash is easy, but accurately calculating the value of labor for different work projects related to remodeling, repairing, or improving property can be difficult.

Even if your partner shook your hand and said he or she intends for you to be a co-owner of the property, the law won't recognize that agreement unless it's in writing. You can't rely on your partner's spoken agreement or a handshake.

Besides complying with the statute of frauds, another reason to put your agreement in writing is the simple fact that people have selective memories. Especially if you and your partner break up, you can have misunderstandings or hold hard feelings. What would happen if you've completed most or all of the work only to find yourself in a break-up with no place to live? Without a written agreement, how can you prove you're entitled to some degree of compensation?

Your sweat equity agreement should be signed and notarized and, where allowable, recorded in your county's office of lands records along with the deed. Please see the sample sweat equity agreement (Form 5-4) on the CD.

If you're unable to come to an agreement about how your sweat equity will be earned and ownership in the property allocated, it's probably a sign of trouble ahead. On the other hand, if you're okay contributing labor without owning an interest in the property, feel free to proceed without a written agreement.

Moving into one partner's home

One partner may own a home prior to the relationship and have his or her partner move into that home. Unless the home has another co-owner (an ex-partner or someone else) on the deed, the owner of the home may want to protect his or her partner by:

- ✔ Drafting a will or trust naming the partner as beneficiary to inherit the house.

- ✔ Giving the partner a *life estate* in the property (a type of ownership that only lasts for the lifetime of the partner; after the partner dies, the property will pass to a different beneficiary).

If the relationship is stable and you've been together for five or more years, you may want to add your partner's name to your deed as a JTWROS or as a tenant in common.

Examining tax and exemption issues relative to unmarried co-owners

Unlike legally married spouses, unmarried LGBT and straight couples can't file joint federal income tax returns. Thanks to the federal Defense of Marriage Act (DOMA), even gay and lesbian partners who are legally married in their home state can't file a joint federal tax return. (If your state recognizes your marriage or your civil union, you can file joint *state* tax returns.)

Not being able to file a federal return can be good or bad news, depending on how your income falls in with the *marriage tax penalty* (when combined incomes push married couples into a higher tax bracket). The bad news is that LGBT partners can't claim each other as dependents on your tax return, but the good news is that even if you live together and benefit from your combined incomes, you can't be taxed at a higher rate because the government doesn't see you as a family unit.

Because unmarried straight and LGBT partners can't file joint federal tax returns, if you own a house together, you need to figure out how you're going to handle mortgage interest and property tax deductions. For instance, you can

✔ Split the deductions 50-50, which can be problematic if one of you makes significantly more than the other because the deductions will create more tax savings for the person with the higher tax rate

✔ Let the partner with the higher income claim the entire deduction and compensate the other partner in some other way

Legally married heterosexual spouses can give each other an interest in separately owned property, tax-free. However, if an unmarried LGBT or straight partner adds his or her partner's name to the deed of a house they already own, they have to consider federal (not state) gift tax implications. All but two states (Connecticut and Tennessee) repealed their state gift tax. As of this writing, the Tennessee legislature passed a bill repealing that state's gift tax and it is awaiting the governor's signature.

In 2012, transfers of an interest in property valued up to $13,000 aren't subject to the federal gift tax. However, if the value of the gift (or interest in the property transferred) exceeds $13,000, the partner giving the property interest (the donor) will be taxed. The IRS calculates the gift tax by taking the value of the gift (what the partner's share of the property is worth) and subtracting any available exclusions, exemptions, and/or deductions. As of this writing, the maximum gift tax rate is 35 percent.

The IRS rule only applies to *lifetime gifts* (gifts made while you're alive). If your partner inherits your home through your will after your death, it's subject to federal estate taxes, but only if the value of the property inherited is worth more than $5 million.

Unlike an estate tax (which if owed is paid out of the estate and is based on the value of the entire estate), an *inheritance* tax occurs after a beneficiary has received his or her share of the estate. In other words, it's a tax on the amount received and the beneficiary pays it. Inheritance taxes are levied by most but not all states. States that do have an inheritance tax assess different exemption rates, depending on the beneficiary's relationship to the deceased. If you're worried about leaving a large inheritance to your partner because he or she may be required to pay an inheritance tax, check with a local accountant or attorney to see whether you can do anything to lower or eliminate inheritance taxes.

Keep accurate records showing each partner's contribution to the mortgage payments and taxes as financial proof that both partners contributed to the jointly owned property. Otherwise the IRS may determine the deceased partner was the home's sole owner, which would place the entire property tax burden on the surviving partner.

If you really loved me, you'd put my name on the deed!

If you own a home with only your name on the deed and then ask your partner to live in the home with you, at some point you'll need to think about making your partner a co-owner of your property. Before you put your partner's name on the deed, you may want to consider the pros and cons to doing so.

Reasons you may want to add your partner's name to the deed are as follows:

✔ Your partner has substantially added to the value of your home by contributing money or sweat equity.

✔ Your partner has been living in your home for many years and your relationship is stable.

✔ You and your partner have children, and you want your partner to raise the kids in the home if you die before they grow up.

Reasons to avoid putting your partners name on the deed to your home are as follows:

✔ Your partner has bad credit or is generally bad with money.

✔ Your partner has a bad habit like gambling, alcoholism, or a drug addiction.

✔ Your partner has a disability that may result in the need for government benefits now or in the future. When a person receives financial benefits from the government, often it will result in a *lien* (a financial liability on the property to secure the debt owed to the government) being placed on the property. When the property is sold (or the person receiving the government benefit dies), the government may enforce the lien. As a result, the government may force the property's sale or require the joint owner to repay an amount equal to the lien. (Refer to Chapter 9 for a more in-depth discussion on protecting property with an irrevocable trust.)

✔ Your partner only recently moved in with you or you've lived together for five years or less.

✔ You own the property with someone else or it's your family's ancestral home.

✔ Your partner threatens to leave you if you don't submit to his or her demands to be made a co-owner of your home.

Before adding anyone's name to your deed, check with your mortgage company to see whether doing so will trigger a "due on transfer" provision in your mortgage agreement, resulting in the need to refinance your home!

If you own your property as JTWROS, at the death of one partner, the property isn't subject to probate because it automatically passes to the surviving partner. Keep in mind, though, that property owned as JTWROS may be subject to federal estate or gift taxes. The property's entire value you and your partner own jointly will be included in the gross taxable estate of the first partner to die. As long as you keep careful records showing you contributed all or part of the expenses on the property, the amount you've contributed will be excluded from your deceased partner's taxable estate.

Financing your home

Because no federal laws protect an LGBT couple from discrimination by a private mortgage lender (one who isn't using HUD for financing), getting a home loan with your same-sex partner can be difficult when you live in a non-marriage equality state. And even when a lender isn't inclined to discriminate against a couple for being gay or lesbian, any unmarried couple is expected to jump through more hoops than would a married couple simply because the law sees married spouses as a family unit and unmarried partners as two separate and unrelated individuals.

Because banks located in a particular state tend to follow local laws and customs, when a married couple applies for a mortgage to buy a home, only one spouse is generally required to qualify for the loan. When a state sees an unmarried couple as unrelated, more often than not, a bank does too.

Lenders can require that each partner must meet income requirements for the mortgage. In other words, the lender may not allow the partners to submit their combined income for consideration. Therefore, LGBT partners are usually required to submit two separate applications. And if a partner has problems with his or her credit rating — unless one partner can carry the burden alone — chances are the application for a mortgage loan will be denied.

Before you schedule an appointment with a real estate agent to look at property, make sure you first figure out how much money you can afford to pay for your home. Although one rule says you can afford a house if it costs less than or equal to three times your *gross* (total amount before any deductions) yearly income, a more accurate measure is to figure out what you and your partner can actually afford. To calculate this, follow these simple steps:

1. **Sit down with your partner and add up your combined incomes, savings, and cash.**

2. **Deduct from that total what you're currently paying for nonhousing related expenses.**

3. **Subtract the amount you expect to pay for monthly mortgage payments on your new home, plus any taxes, insurance, maintenance, and any expenses relating to remodeling or expanding the home.**

What remains after this calculation is probably closer to the amount you can actually afford to pay for a home.

You can do an online search for a free mortgage calculator to find out how much of a mortgage you and your partner can qualify for.

If you decide to take out a joint mortgage, both partners will be required to fill out a credit application, which shouldn't be a problem unless one of you has credit problems, especially if you haven't been honest about it with your partner.

If either one of you has bad credit (as of this writing a credit score of 730 is considered a minimum requirement to qualify for a mortgage), the combined score for both of you will be lower. If either you or your partner has a credit problem, before applying for a mortgage, take the necessary steps to correct any errors and try to improve your credit score. You can get a free credit report online at one of the major credit bureaus, like Equifax, Experian, or TransUnion. (You may want to check out *Credit Management Kit For Dummies* by Stephen R. Bucci [John Wiley & Sons, Inc.].)

Before You Actually Buy a Home: Going Over an Important Check List

Before you purchase a home, you can make sure your experience proceeds smoothly and successfully. This section includes a check list with tips and suggestions. We cover some of these tips in greater depth in this chapter, but for your convenience, we list all important pointers here. After you complete each tip, check it off your list.

- ❑ **Plan ahead.** Start getting all your financial ducks in a row at least one year prior to the date you plan to purchase your home. Preplanning enables you to correct any problems you may have with your credit and gives you time to find the home of your dreams.

- ❑ **Communicate with your partner.** Set aside enough time to talk to your partner so that you can both lay out every detail of your individual needs, desires, and expectations before making such a huge financial and emotional investment. If you can't talk about and settle your differences before buying a house, you really ought to reconsider taking such a big step together.

- ❑ **Create a budget.** Find a free, online budget calculator to help keep track of your wages and spending for one year. You may be surprised to find out what you spend your money on. By shining a light on your bad spending habits, you can begin to get control over your budget.

❑ **Do a one-year mortgage try-out.** After you figure out what mortgage payment you'll be making (refer to the "Financing your home" section for help), try setting that amount aside each month for one year. Doing so can be a good way to test your ability to afford making your mortgage payments. At the same time you're building a nest egg to help with the down payment, closing costs, and moving expenses.

❑ **Save for a rainy day.** Even if you don't save as much as you would be spending on your mortgage, consider saving as much as possible to cover the cost of unexpected maintenance and repair issues that can arise after you move into your home.

❑ **Get referrals for a competent real estate agent.** You need a good, hard-working, LGBT or LGBT-friendly real estate agent who is savvy and can help you find a home and connect you with other professionals who understand the challenges faced by unmarried LGBT couples who are looking to buy a home. (Check out the earlier section, "Choosing a competent LGBT-friendly real estate agent" for more information.)

❑ **Find out all you can about mortgages.** Even if numbers aren't your thing, recent events in the mortgage and housing market should pique your interest in the subject at least to the point that you don't become one of those unwitting buyers who didn't read the small print or understand the terms. If you aren't sure what you are getting into, don't get into it! Before you sign anything, take a copy of the mortgage contract to an attorney, financial planner, accountant, or banker who will, for a small fee, review it with or for you and explain in plain English what your obligations will be over the duration of the mortgage.

❑ **Get prequalified for a mortgage.** Before you start house-hunting, apply for and (hopefully) qualify for a mortgage payment you can afford. Getting prequalified enables your real estate agent to find and show only the houses that are within your price range and that meet with your other needs and expectations.

❑ **Focus on location.** You can't spend too much time investigating the neighborhood around the property you're interested in buying. If you find a beautiful and affordable home that's located in a community filled with intolerant, hostile, or unfriendly neighbors, your dream home may soon become a nightmare.

❑ **Negotiate the price.** You'll be surprised to discover how often a seller is willing to accept an offer well below the listing price, especially if you're house-hunting in a buyers' market.

❑ **Decide how you want to own the property.** Do you want to own as JTWROS so that your partner will automatically own the home if you die first? Would you prefer owning as tenants in common so that you can give your share of the property to someone other than your partner when you die? Or perhaps only one of you will legally own the property, with just one partner's name on the deed and mortgage.

❑ **Find a home loan counseling center.** Ask your real estate agent or mortgage broker whether a home loan counseling center is near you. If they're unable to answer, do an online search. Home loan counseling centers provide classes on fixing your credit rating, finding the right home, what to look for in a real estate agent and mortgage lender, and how to budget for a down payment, closing costs, and so on.

❑ **Get good homeowner's insurance.** Make sure your homeowner's insurance policy will insure your partner's property, especially if his or her name isn't on the deed or mortgage as a joint owner. If you're unable to find an insurance policy to cover your partner's belongings, he or she will need to purchase renter's insurance.

Drawing Up a Living-Together Agreement

Legal marriage is essentially a contract that provides specific rights and protections, including the equitable division of property and spousal support during a legal separation and after a divorce. So, if you and your partner live in a marriage equality state and want all the legal protections that are available to legal spouses, perhaps you'll want to get married. On the other hand, if you live where legal marriage isn't an option — or if you just don't want to get married — you need to create a *living-together agreement* (also called a *cohabitation* or *partnership agreement*), or run the risk that you and your partner may be treated as legal strangers in the event of a future break-up.

While legal marriage is a civil contract that is automatically conferred the moment you say "I do," a living-together agreement (LTA) is a private contract between you and your partner, which establishes some but not all of the rights and obligations that married people obtain by custom and by state law. Chapter 10 discusses LTAs and how to set up one.

Why having a living-together agreement is important in the law's eyes

A majority of states are non–community property states, which means if a legally recognized couple (married or its equivalent) breaks up and they can't agree on how to divide their money and property, a judge may do it for them using the *equitable division of property doctrine* (the system by which a court utilizes a fair and just method to divide jointly owned property in a divorce/dissolution proceeding). Unfortunately, equitable doesn't necessarily mean equal.

When a legally recognized couple lives in a community property state and one partner buys something or deposits money in a jointly held account, generally the other partner automatically owns a one-half interest in it. On the other hand, in a non–community property state, the other partner doesn't have rights to the property until the couple dissolves the legal relationship or the first partner dies.

Courts in non–community property states generally take the following factors into consideration when determining how they will divvy up jointly owned assets:

- ✔ Whether one partner contributed more substantially to child rearing, preparing meals, shopping, cooking, cleaning, and laundry

- ✔ Whether one partner sacrificed opportunities to advance his or her education and/or employment in order to contribute to the relationship

Assets and property that are required to be divided equitably are those that were acquired after a couple gets married, enters into a civil union, or registers as domestic partners. Generally, property owned before the legal relationship — as well as personal gifts and family inheritances — belongs solely to the individual partner and isn't subject to equitable division of property.

If a court gets involved in a dispute over the division of property, it must first figure out what property is jointly owned and its fair market value. A professional appraiser may be called in to do an inventory of your property and then figure out what it's worth. After the court has this information, it will consider other factors (like those previously listed) and then divide the jointly owned property between the partners.

If your relationship isn't legally recognized, the doctrine of equitable division of property doesn't apply to you. The law sees you and your partner as unrelated roommates at best — or strangers at worst. That means your rights to any property you own with your partner will come down to who has possession of it when the time comes to break up.

Chapter 6

A Quick Lowdown on Joining Assets

You've finally found the light of your life, you've moved in together, and now you have to figure out how you're going to deal with paying the rent, buying food, and so on. If you're just starting, perhaps you're still basking in the excitement of your new living-together adventure. If so, you probably can't imagine that the day may come when an ice-cold bucket of money problems could snuff out your little flame of love.

More often than not, couples don't bother to work on mundane financial details before combining their money and other assets, which can result in too many relationships ending over fights about money.

But don't fret! You can take steps now to avoid many of the typical mistakes couples make about money. You have to be willing to take the time to map out a plan for how the two of you will manage your shared financial responsibilities.

The both of you will be far better off if you can agree — before you step foot over the threshold of your new digs — on how you'll split the rent or mortgage and whether and how you'll divvy up the cost of food, utilities, and other shared expenses. Most importantly, after you've agreed on a plan, you have to stick to it!

Every couple is unique, so no one blueprint can work for everyone. In this chapter, we provide material that you can customize to your personal needs. You can use this information to map out a plan that'll prove successful for years to come. If both partners take the necessary time to get to know and feel comfortable with one another's individual needs and desires — especially when it comes to money — your relationship should endure even as the fantasy fades and reality sets in.

Considering Money Issues for Partners Living Together

Problems with money can trigger huge arguments between partners who want to live together — whether legally married or not. Unless one partner has an expensive addiction (such as a compulsive spender or gambling problem), you should be able to work through your differences by making an effort to really understand one another's underlying beliefs and fears surrounding the issue of money.

In fact, before you and your partner take the risk of comingling your finances and moving in together, we suggest that you keep them separate, at least until you've had the opportunity to get to know and trust each other's fiscal judgment.

If you live in a marriage equality state (or a state with an equivalent law, like civil unions) and you get married, unless you have a written agreement that says otherwise, everything you earn and acquire from your wedding day forward may be subject to the doctrine of *equitable division of property* (the fair and just division of jointly owned property in a divorce/dissolution proceeding) if you split up. However, as long as you remain unmarried — either by choice or by law — you need to make ongoing decisions about whether or not to merge your finances or keep them separate. As you weigh your options, consider the following facts:

- ✔ The law doesn't confer automatic legal protections to unmarried partners, so if you're not married or in a civil union and you break up, you have no guarantee you'll be able to recover all, or any, of the assets you personally contributed.

- ✔ If your partner runs up a shared credit card or fails to make payments on a joint loan, you'll be responsible to the creditor for 100 percent of what is owed.

- ✔ If you deposit most, if not all, of the money into a joint bank account, your partner can waltz right in and lawfully remove every last penny.

Because unmarried partners are economically vulnerable when finances are combined, no matter how much you love your partner and think he or she can do no wrong, you need to proceed with caution before plunging headlong into these potentially shark-filled waters.

You can take steps to make it more likely than not that you and your partner can safely navigate these waters. If you make a realistic budget together, you may not have smooth sailing all the time, but doing so should make the sharks fewer and further apart. In the next couple of sections we give you practical advice that can help you and your partner achieve a successful financial relationship.

Having an honest discussion about debts and assets

Before you and your partner move in together, make sure you sit down and have that hard but absolutely essential conversation about money. During this conversation, be honest about your individual income and expenses and don't hold anything back. Don't try to make yourself seem better off than you actually are financially by hiding the size of your student loan or the amount of your monthly car payment. The truth will inevitably come out, and a purposeful deception, or even an inadvertent omission, may cause permanent damage to your credibility and your relationship.

This conversation is your opportunity to lay the groundwork for how you and your partner will ultimately handle your separate and joint finances. That's why working out your differences beforehand is imperative. Let your partner know if you feel any trepidation about comingling your money and make it clear to your partner what you want to maintain control over and what you are willing to share.

Are you not sure how to approach having this discussion about money or are you afraid of scaring off your partner? Here we offer some specific suggestions to help make these conversations easier for you and your partner, including what to discuss, how to do it, and what to do if you get stuck.

Making the money conversation productive

When you and your partner are ready to have the important money discussion, the best time is before you open your mailbox or on-line account to find an overdraft notice. Choose a day that's convenient and reserve at least an hour of time when you expect no interruptions to occur. Make sure the meeting space is quiet, comfortable, and private; in other words, turn off the TV, put away your phones, and turn off the computer.

If you're not sure how to get the conversation rolling, take the initiative by sharing your own feelings about a financial matter that concerns you. You may begin by telling a story from your childhood about how money issues affected your family and the ways in which that experience colors your current views about money. If you don't want to start with a story to ease into the discussion, just start the conversation by directly saying "We need to talk about money so there are no misunderstandings."

Believe it or not, if you figure out how to communicate with your partner, you can have an open and honest conversation about almost any subject. To help you realize healthier communication, try using these steps in your conversation to get you started:

1. **Echo your partner's words.**

   In other words, listen to what your partner has to say and then repeat back without judgment and in your own words what you heard your partner say. If you heard wrong, give your partner the opportunity to repeat and clarify, and you can again attempt to echo back what you heard.

2. **Validate what you've heard.**

   Just hearing your partner's words isn't enough; you also need to validate what he or she is feeling. Validating isn't about what you believe is right or wrong; it's about letting your partner know he or she is entitled to those feelings.

3. **Strive to understand what your partner says.**

   After your partner expresses his or her feelings and you've correctly repeated them and you validate those feelings, put yourself in your partner's shoes. Doing so allows you to see things through his or her eyes and express honestly that you can see the point he or she is trying to make.

4. **After you work through this process, switch places with your partner.**

   Your partner should also echo, confirm, and be understanding with you.

If you really want to have a healthy and fulfilling money talk, you have to try to avoid the normal patterns couples often get into. Stay clear of these bad habits that many people exhibit when discussing a difficult topic, such as money. Most people

- Don't really listen. They're just waiting until their turn to speak.
- Are more concerned about being right than about understanding their partner's point of view.
- Feel attacked and respond defensively to what their partner is saying.
- Tend to give a long and loud speech when it's their turn to talk.

Try to remember to pull yourself back from unhealthy communicating if you find yourself drifting away from our suggestions in this section. If you want to discover more about how to resolve money issues with your partner, visit www.dummies.com/how-to/content/how-to-resolve-marital-money-differences.html.

Knowing what to do when your discussions fall apart

If you find you're unable to have a civil discussion or the negatives of joining assets outweigh the positives, you don't have to break up. You may just want to choose one of the following options:

- ✔ **Keep everything separate.** No matter what you buy or rent, don't do anything jointly. You may still be able to share a living space and some expenses but with only one partner's name on the lease and utility bills. You still need to decide how you both can contribute to mutual expenses, such as rent, food, utilities, and so on, but at least you'll always be in control of your own financial affairs. If you choose this path to keep everything separate, the partner whose name is on the lease and other bills should make sure he or she can afford to pay for everything without the assistance of the other partner, in case that becomes necessary.

- ✔ **Get help from a third party.** If your problems arise solely as a result of a disagreement about how to manage your money, a financial counselor may be able to help you work through those differences. On the other hand, if one or both partners have deep-seated fears or unrealistic expectations about money, you may need to seek the help of a couple's counselor.

In the end, coming to an understanding about every single financial matter may be just too difficult. In that case you may want to focus on the bigger issues (like buying a home) and let go of the small stuff (for instance, whether to buy cheaper generic corn flakes or more expensive brand-named cereal).

Planning out a budget and setting financial goals

A good budgeting plan creates a solid foundation for a healthy fiscal life. Moreover, having your financial ducks in a row can lead you and your partner to greater stability in all areas of your relationship. A budget is a useful device to help you realize your long-term goals of buying your dream house, raising a child, going on a cruise, or whatever your goals may be.

These sections give you some hands-on advice that help you understand why a budget is important and how you and your partner can go about creating one that works for the both of you.

Recognizing why a budget is essential

Whether you live on a shoestring or have money to burn, knowing where your money is going each month and how you can do a better job of allocating your resources is important. Just because you use a budget to track your expenditures doesn't necessarily mean you can't go out to dinner or buy a new pair of shoes. A budget is simply a tool to help you control your financial bottom line.

A budget not only allows you to work out a system for paying your day-to-day bills, but it also gives you an opportunity to set goals for your future. For example, will your budget include long-range retirement planning or simply short-term activities, such as handling day-to-day expenditures?

When you start to discuss putting together your budget, keep these points in mind:

- **Make sure that both partners come to an agreement on what expenses to share and what to keep separate.** If one of you makes a higher salary than the other, you may want to split the expenses in a manner that reflects your unequal incomes. (Check out the "Merging Finances: Yes or No?" section later in this chapter to help you decide if you even want to comingle your money or keep it separate.)

- **Set aside something each month to achieve those long-term objectives.** Watching your nest egg grow can be a very exciting pastime.

- **Resist the temptation to fritter away your nest egg.** Having a bit of extra money around can be tempting. If you feel your determination to save is waning, ask your partner to remind you about the reason for the nest egg to begin with. It may help to put a photo of whatever you're saving for (European vacation, your dream house, a boat, or new car) on your fridge as an incentive to forgo that night on the town.

Even if you feel creating a budget is just a waste of time, you may be pleasantly surprised to discover how valuable a budget can be. In fact, a good budget can help you realize how much money you've been wasting because you weren't paying attention to where it was being spent. When you start budgeting, it can be like uncovering a treasure trove of cash that finally lets you afford to take that European vacation sooner than you expected or pay for renovations to your garage that you didn't think you could afford.

Coming up with a budget: The how-to

The hardest part of making a budget may be actually sitting down and doing the tedious work of collecting and organizing all your financial data, including your account balances, incomes, and expenses. After you have that information in front of you, you need to decide what type of budgeting system to use. Thanks to modern technology, several efficient and easy budget-making tools are available to make your job a tad easier:

- **Online budgeting software:** Usually free or very affordable, these programs allow you to input your financial information, and the program calculates your total income and expenditures. It also shows you where you can make changes that can enable you to track your bottom line. One of the biggest advantages of using an online budgeting service is convenience. Most come with apps for your smartphone and tablet so you can input data and access your information anytime and just about anywhere. The disadvantages are privacy and the potential for someone to hack into the service to retrieve your financial information.

- **Offline budgeting software:** You can purchase this software, either as a downloadable file from an online store or from a retailer that carries computers and computer-related tools. If you have a primary computer and don't rely on a smartphone or tablet, this option may be best. Most software of this kind has automatic updates, and it keeps track of your checking account balance as well as your incomes and expenditures.

- **Good old-fashioned paper:** If you're technologically illiterate or you just feel better having a hand-written budget plan, then a paper budget may be your thing. Because you can write a paper budget in a notebook, this system may be the best one to start with.

- **Envelope method:** If you and your partner don't want to go through all the trouble of creating a formal budget to pay expenses, you can use this method of budgeting. The *envelope budget* is the process of labeling envelopes with the name of the shared expense (rent, food, electric, and so on) and the total amount owed (you can also write the amount owed by each partner if you're not splitting expenses 50-50).

To be on the safe side, always pay your share of the bills electronically or with a check. Don't pay with cash, even in the rare cases where it's still possible to do so. Later, if a dispute over who paid what arises, you have proof of your own contribution.

Whatever budgeting system you use, make sure you stick to it! If you use a program you can access from your phone, laptop, or tablet, or if your paper budget is small enough to carry in your purse or pocket, you can and should enter expenses in real time as they happen.

Immediately calculating expenditures helps you keep track of how much you're spending, and on what. Keeping track can really help to keep a lid on unnecessary spending, which in turn can mean peace on the home front and more money to buy that big ticket item or take that fabulous trip.

Merging Finances: Yes or No?

One of the first decisions you and your partner need to make is whether or not to handle your finances separately or jointly as a couple. You may continue to have your own personal expenses, but you may also be sharing expenses for housing, food, utilities, and maintenance. If you decide to merge some or all of your finances, you both need to decide whether to do one of the following to pay for shared household expenses:

- ✔ Merge your finances into a joint account.
- ✔ Keep totally separate accounts.
- ✔ Open a joint account to pay shared expenses and a separate account for personal expenses.

We want to help you so you can figure out which choice is right for you both. These sections explain what to consider before making any decision and then point out different circumstances you and your partner may be in that can affect your final decision about merging your finances (or not).

Just because you've decided to share a living space with your partner doesn't mean you have to merge your finances. If you're happy with the status quo (each partner paying his or her own way), then you don't need to fix what isn't broken.

Don't forget that as unmarried, same-sex partners, your relationship lacks many of the legal safeguards that the law extends to married couples. Unless you live in a marriage equality (or its equivalent) state, you won't have any legal guidelines to aid in separating your jointly held assets. If your partner defaults on a joint loan or fails to make timely payments on jointly owned property, you'll be responsible for 100 percent of what is owed, even if you don't have the property in your possession.

Still, for many same-sex couples, merging assets is a natural extension of creating a life together. And traditionally, that's what married people do — for better, or worse. Merging assets creates a sense of togetherness because it allows you and your partner to share in each other's successes and to help one another through tough times.

Calculating your net worth of both partners before making a decision

Before your merge any assets, you first want to figure out the *net worth* (the total value of your assets minus the total amount you owe) of both partners. Your net worth is a snapshot of your current financial situation.

Calculating the net worth of you, your partner, and the two of you together can help you better understand how to merge assets, if at all. Doing so also comes in handy as you figure out whether it's fair to split expenses 50-50 or some other way because one of you has a substantially larger net worth. (Check out the next section if you and your partner find yourselves in this situation.)

When you figure your net worth as a couple, follow these steps:

1. **You should both separately add the values of all your personally owned belongings and property to find their individual net worth.**

    Don't take your salary into consideration, just what you each presently have. You both simply add the values for the following:

    - Your bank accounts (checking, savings, money market, and CDs)

    - Your homes (what you could sell it for)

    - Your cars, boats, RVs, and/or other vehicles

    - Your retirement and/or investment accounts

    - Your life insurance policies and/or annuities

    - Your collectables (antiques, jewelry, artwork, and the like)

    - Your furnishings, furniture, appliances, electronic, and entertainment equipment

2. **You both separately add your total *liabilities* (financial debts and obligations) that include the values of the following:**

    - Your balances of bank loans (car, mortgage, and so on)

    - Your student loans, if any

    - Your credit card debt

    - Your balances on any personal loans from family or friends

    - Any outstanding medical, dental, or other bills

    - Outstanding *liens* (a hold against real or personal property to ensure payment of a debt after that property is sold)

3. **If you've already accumulated assets and property with your partner, determine the value of your combined net worth.**

4. **Do the same with your individual and joint liabilities.**

   To do so,

   1. Add the amount you owe, what your partner owes, and what you owe together, if anything.

   2. Subtract your total liabilities from the total value of your assets and the result will be your net worth.

   3. Do the same for your partner and then for the two of you together.

   This final number is your net worth as a couple.

Unequal incomes: Bearing the greatest financial burden for paying expenses

When unmarried partners enter into a living-together arrangement and one of you earns or is worth more than the other, sharing expenses 50-50 may not only be unfair, it may be financially devastating for the less wealthy partner.

Unequal income and access to money can lead to feelings of frustration, anger, and resentment. If you and/or your partner feel anxious or uncomfortable about the inequality in your incomes and worth, the best thing to do is to sit down and calmly discuss your concerns. Keep in mind the money talk can be hard, so use the therapeutic communication techniques that we discuss in the "Having an honest discussion about debts and assets" section earlier in this chapter.

You have a couple of ways that you and your partner with unequal incomes and assets can divvy up shared expenses:

✔ **Split everything 50-50.** If you chose this option, you may want to try to live within the means of the poorer partner so as not to cause an undue financial burden, which can lead to anger, resentment, and eventually arguments over money.

✔ **Divide the bills in a manner that reflects each partner's relative income and net worth.** Choosing to split the bills according to each partner's ability to afford them is more likely to result in a more peaceful future for both partners.

   For instance, if Zelda Smith-Jones earns a $6,000 per month and Edith Smith-Jones brings home $4,000, each month, the couple doesn't necessarily have to split everything 60/40 to be more equitable to Edith. They could choose to live in a less expensive neighborhood or choose fewer cable channels to help make up the difference.

However, if Zelda makes $7,000 and Edith just $3,000, they have a more significant difference in their incomes and in their relative ability to pay for shared living expenses. Zelda could agree to split the expenses 70/30, which may make life easier on Edith and have the added benefit of creating an equality of sacrifice. However, if Zelda has personal expenditures (graduate school loan payments, child support payments, fees associated with her profession, and so on) that take a large chunk of her monthly salary, the couple should factor those expenditures into the decision on how to divide shared expenses.

The important thing is to do what is fair and what works for your relationship. As long as the partner earning more money is more interested in making the relationship work than on insisting on a 50-50 division that isn't feasible, the two of you should be able to work it out.

Comingling your money: The pros and cons

If you've had that difficult money talk, both partners probably have a pretty good idea about one another's priorities, goals, and expectations. Understanding your own and your partner's feelings about money can go a long way in helping you decide what to do with your finances. Many couples decide to comingle their money, which can have its own pros and cons.

If you decide to comingle your funds in some combination of shared and personal expenses, your options are as follows:

- ✔ Open a joint account with your partner where both of you will make deposits to cover only those expenses that are shared.

- ✔ Maintain a separate account in your own name to pay your personal expenses.

If you decide to comingle your funds and have a joint account, doing so has its advantages, including:

- ✔ Forcing both partners to have frequent discussions about finances and/ or expenses because you need to make sure the account has enough money to pay what is owed

- ✔ Creating a sense of common purpose as you work together to accomplish at least some of your immediate financial goals

- ✔ Causing both partners to be more cognizant of and accountable for spending money that's in the joint account

Comingling your funds in a joint account does have some dangers though, which are as follows:

✔ Your partner may bounce a check and decide not to deposit sufficient funds to cover it. If that happens, because you're a joint owner of the account, you're equally liable for any fees or legal actions resulting from the overdraft.

✔ Your partner has a legal right to spend some or all the money in the joint account on anything he or she wishes, and you have little or no legal recourse.

✔ Your personal credit rating as well as your credibility may be damaged because of your partner's irresponsible spending.

✔ You may encounter challenges in trying to keep track of who is writing what checks and/or using debit cards associated with the account, which can make record keeping problematic unless you work out a solution ahead of time.

✔ If you break up, proving what part of the balance in the account belongs to you may be difficult or impossible.

You can avoid some if not all of these potential pitfalls simply by using the word "and" and not "or" on the account. For instance, instead of "Zelda Smith-Jones *or* Edith Smith-Jones," use "Zelda Smith-Jones *and* Edith Smith-Jones." Using "and" instead of "or" means both partners' signatures are required on all checks. If you're concerned about your partner misusing funds in the joint account, you should also steer clear of debit cards.

What you decide to do about these and other challenges depends on your particular circumstances and the decisions you both make during and after the money talk we discuss earlier in this chapter.

Getting joint credit cards or keeping them separate

You also may want to discuss whether you want to have a joint credit card or if you want to keep those cards separate.

Having a joint credit card presents some of the same dangers as jointly owning a bank account that we discuss in the previous section. You're equally responsible for paying off any debt accumulated by your partner even if you didn't authorize or know about it. Even worse, any late payments or defaults by your partner will negatively impact your credit rating too.

If you're considering having a joint credit card, you can create a joint credit card in one of two ways:

✔ **By opening a new joint credit card account together:** If you go this route, both partners are required to complete separate credit card applications (depending on whether your home state recognizes the legality of your relationship). As holders of a joint credit card, both of you are equally responsible to pay all charges — even if your partner charged an item that you didn't know about or approve.

✔ **By adding your partner to your existing credit card as an authorized user:** To add your partner as an authorized user, just contact the customer service department by phone or online and ask what you need to do. After authorized, your partner will be issued a separate credit card in his or her name. Any charges or payments will be affiliated with your credit card account and only you will be legally liable for paying the balance. In other words, only your credit rating will be affected either positively or negatively.

Before you open a new card with your partner or add your partner to your current card, make sure you closely examine the fine print. Credit card agreements, terms, and regulations are written such that it's often impossible to know what you're actually getting into. For instance, you need to know:

✔ **Your annual percentage rate (APR):** *APR* is the interest rate on a credit card for the entire year. It is a finance charge expressed as an annual rate. For example, if your APR is 20.99 percent, for every $10.00 you charge, the credit card company will add almost $2.10 in interest!

✔ **The limit you can charge, if any:** Credit cards almost always come with a *credit limit* — the maximum amount you're allowed to charge on your credit card. Unless you sign up for an option to charge over your limit, your card will be declined for any purchase over that limit.

✔ **Whether cash advances have a different limit or APR:** The APR for cash advances is often higher than for credit card purchases. Cash advances often begin accruing interest at the time of the withdrawal, and they often have additional fees other than an APR. Bottom line: Make sure you understand your cash advance fees and rules before taking one.

✔ **Any fees for going over your limit:** If you charge more than your credit card limit, you may be hit with over-the-limit fees, a lower credit limit, and/or possibly other penalties, such as having your interest rates raised or even your account closed. Perhaps the worst outcome is the negative effect overcharging can have on your credit score because it makes you seem like a high-risk borrower.

✔ **Fees and penalties for making late payments:** More than likely, you'll be hit with a late fee ranging from $15 to $35; that fee continues to collect interest along with your remaining credit card balance. If you're more than 30 days late, the incident is added to your credit report, where it can live in infamy for the next seven years. If you're more than 60 days late, chances are your interest rate will go up to the *default rate* (the highest interest rate charged by a creditor). Being late can cause a decrease in your overall credit score, which affects your ability to borrow money for a home or car or get a new credit card.

✔ **Hidden fees:** Federal law prohibits credit card companies from hiding fees from consumers, but that doesn't mean that all credit card holders fully understand how fees accrue or what actions (or inactions) can trigger higher interest rates or additional fees. Read the fine print.

✔ **Annual fees:** Some credit card companies charge an annual fee ranging anywhere from $30 to over $100. Most who do charge the fee also offer to waive the fee for the first year as an incentive to sign up for a card. At the end of the first year, the charge is automatically added to your bill, and you can either pay it or cancel the card and (if you have a decent credit rating) sign up with a different credit card company. Because there's so much competition between credit card companies, call to get the annual fee dropped — at least for an additional year. Because credit card companies don't announce in advance when the fee will appear, keep a record of the date you first received your card so you can make the call for a waiver of the annual fee.

If you get a credit card together, make sure you keep accurate records of one another's credit card charges to make sure you're both within the limit. Mismanaging your credit card payments is a surefire way to destroy your credit rating:

✔ Thirty-five percent of your credit score is your payment history, so late payments can be significant.

✔ The second most important part of your credit score is the level of your credit card debt. Having high credit card balances (relative to your credit limit) decreases your credit score.

✔ Completely ignoring your credit cards bills is much worse than paying late. Each month you miss a credit card payment, you're one month closer to having a charge-off on the account.

Are you scared yet? The bottom line is this: Don't get a joint credit card just because you're in love. Nothing sours a romance faster than financial ruin.

If you have a joint credit card with your partner and then you break up, make sure you close your account. Don't risk waiting for your partner to take care of this important task. As long as he or she is able to make purchases on the card, you're liable to pay.

When you want to merge only some but not all financial accounts

Comingling your money doesn't have to be an all-or-nothing proposition. In fact, you can pool your financial resources in several less traumatic ways. For instance, you can keep your individual checking, savings, and credit card accounts and open a joint account strictly to pay for shared expenses, such as rent, food, and utilities.

If you decide that merging some but not all of your money is the best option for you and your partner, you still need to figure out what amount each partner will contribute to the joint account. In other words, you may want to do one of the following:

✔ **Deposit an equal amount regardless of your relative worth and income:** Contributing an equal amount to the joint account may help to ease certain money-related tensions in the relationship. Why? Because the partner with a lower income may not feel as though he or she is being subsidized by the wealthier partner and the higher income partner may not feel as though he or she is being penalized for being successful. A potential downside to this arrangement would be if the less wealthy partner has to struggle to make ends meet while the other partner has money to burn.

If you're thinking of contributing an equal amount to a joint account and one of you makes a lot less than the other, you may want to have a written agreement that provides a safety net to the poorer partner.

✔ **Deposit an amount proportional to your relative incomes:** A more equitable method of handling a joint account may be to deposit an amount proportional to your relative incomes (like in the nearby sidebar). The upside of choosing this more equitable option is that neither partner will feel pressured to live up or down to the other's earnings, and the relative income disparity between the partners may not have a negative effect on the rest of their relationship.

Any money deposited into a joint account belongs equally to both partners, and either one can withdraw some or all the money at any time. If you live in a state that doesn't provide legal recognition for your relationship and you break up, you have no automatic guarantees that you'll get back what you deposited. To protect yourself against a potential loss, you may want to maintain a small balance — just enough to cover your expenses for each month. Refer to the earlier section, "Comingling your money: The pros and cons" about some tips to protect yourself.

Comingling the proportional route

If one partner makes significantly more money than the other partner, you may want to have a discussion and decide to deposit an amount proportional to each person's income. Consider this example: Rudy Hill and Charlie Dunn have dated for six months before deciding to move in together. Rudy is a software developer who makes $5,900 a month. Charlie is an aspiring actor who is working as a barista at a hip coffee shop until he gets his big break. Charlie makes $2,500 a month, including tips.

Charlie and Rudy decide to open a joint account to pay for shared expenses, and both agree to contribute an equal amount per month, or $1,000 each. This works out great until Charlie's boss substantially cuts back on his hours because the local college students — the majority of the coffee shop's customers — leave over the summer months.

Now, when Charlie is required to deposit enough to cover half of the couple's shared expenses, he's forced to choose between paying his car payment or his credit card payment. One bill will be paid late, which will have a negative effect on Charlie's credit rating.

Because Charlie's money shortfall isn't a result of his bad behavior, and because it's a temporary condition that will resolve itself when the students return (or he gets a part in a play), Rudy could easily afford to pitch in a little more each month until Charlie's circumstances change. If Rudy refuses to help, Charlie may start to resent him, which could (and probably would) put a strain on their relationship.

Because Charlie's salary is equal to 30 percent of the household income and Rudy earns about 70 percent, they can make a budget that calculates the total amount of their shared monthly expenses, and then each of them will deposit into the joint account an amount that is based on their proportional incomes. In other words, Charlie will deposit $600 per month and Rudy will deposit $1,400 each month.

Merging your money doesn't have a right and wrong way. You just need to find a method that is equitable and fair and one that feels right to both of you. Even after you've decided on a solution, if it doesn't work out, you can always try something else.

Maintaining Separate Finances

After your money discussion, you may decide the best decision at this time is to keep your finances separate. Here we discuss the advantages and disadvantages of doing so.

As long as your relationship isn't legally recognized, simply living with your partner doesn't make you responsible for his or her debts. Furthermore, if you separately maintain your money, even if your partner defaults on a loan or declares bankruptcy, your assets won't be at risk.

Your financial security can completely disappear if you do one or more of the following:

- ✔ **You and your partner sign a contract or agreement to purchase something together.** You're both responsible for the entire purchase price.

- ✔ **You cosign a loan for or with your partner.** You are both liable for the entire loan amount, including interest.

- ✔ **You open a joint account or get a joint credit card.** You're both liable for the entire balance (see the earlier section, "Getting joint credit cards or keeping them separate" for more information).

- ✔ **You and your partner legalize your relationship by getting married, entering into a civil union, or registering as domestic partners.** Legal spouses and partners are considered one legal entity starting from the date of their marriage, civil union, or domestic partnership. Therefore, any debts acquired by either partner after that date are considered to belong equally to both partners. Unless the lender is willing to accept a written waiver that lets one of the partners off the hook, both are equally responsible for paying 100 percent of the debt.

If you don't do any of these previous actions and you simply live under the same roof with your partner, each of you is responsible for your own financial affairs.

One of the primary reasons partners say they want to keep their financial matters separate is to eliminate fights over money. When deciding whether or not to keep your money separate, ask yourself the following questions:

- ✔ **Will maintaining separate accounts make you less responsible for your own finances?** If you're worried about becoming a slacker, don't merge your money with your partner. Sometimes when people share financial accounts, they can easily fall into a pattern of letting their partner take the responsibility of balancing the checkbook, paying the bills, and so on. If you keep your money separate, you have the responsibility of paying your debts and keeping your accounts balanced.

- ✔ **Does the thought of comingling your money give you the willies?** If the mere thought of comingling your money makes you break out in a cold sweat, then don't do it. Often partners can't or won't check in with each other before making purchases from a joint account. When you're in charge of your own money, you always know what's going on. You don't need to worry about someone else spending money you don't have, and you can buy what you want or need without asking permission from your partner.

> ✔ **Are you and your partner in agreement about how you want to spend money and plan for the future?** If you and your partner disagree on what purchases to make or not to make — or on how much you should save for retirement or a rainy day — don't put your money in a joint account. Sometimes, couples have vastly different financial patterns and philosophies. Perhaps you're a penny pincher and your partner likes to buy linen with the highest thread count he or she can find. If this scenario describes you and your partner, keeping your money separate may be a relationship saver.

Even though the notion of keeping everything separate may provide you with a sense of relief, it may also make you feel more distant or less intimate. Separate accounts may not be for everyone, but if it works for you, then go for it.

If your relationship isn't legally recognized, you need to have a written living-together agreement (LTA) between you and your partner. An LTA spells out how to divvy up your property and allows you to prove you bought something by presenting a receipt or cancelled check. (Refer to Chapter 10 for more information about how to create an agreement.)

Chapter 7

Creating a Family:
Yours, Mine, and Ours

*A*mong the many difficult decisions that you and your partner will make, none is more difficult — or more important — than whether to bring a child into your family. This choice is hard for all couples (even the straight ones), but at least they're operating in a society with plenty of support for their decision to raise a family. Things are much, much more complicated for gay and lesbian couples, and sometimes even for single LGBT folks who want to adopt. The challenges are legal, practical, emotional, and social in ways that are unique to the LGBT community.

In this chapter, we explore the many dimensions of the challenges you face — in deciding whether to have kids in the first place, in taking the steps to make that happen, and then in dealing with how the law and society place infuriating obstacles in your path.

Because same-sex parents can't accidentally procreate the way opposite-sex ones can, the children you have together are *intentional*. Whether you choose to navigate the adoption process, or deal with sperm donors, egg donors, and gestational surrogates, you invest a great deal of time, thought, and (often) money into bringing a child into your home. In other words, your kids are *wanted*. Don't forget to keep that positive thought in mind as you deal with the often difficult challenges of creating a family.

Figuring Out Why You Want to Become a Parent

By the time you reach the point of deciding whether to bring children into your home, you should already have navigated a bunch of other decisions.

You've made a permanent commitment to each other. If you live in a state that affords recognition to your relationship, you've likely gotten married (or civilly united). Even if not, you may have had a formal commitment ceremony, signaling the seriousness of your commitment to your family and friends. Almost certainly you have moved in together. If you live in a state where your legal rights aren't protected, you may have taken steps to protect your rights through various agreements and documents that we describe throughout this book.

You now have decided to expand your family and bring children into your home, but you want to ask yourself a simple question first: *Why do you want children?*

This simple question isn't so simple to answer, but doing so is vital so you and your partner (or you alone if you're planning to do so by yourself) can think about this question before plunging ahead. Perhaps you want to adopt a kid (or more than one) in need of a home. Some couples want to adopt or foster-parent older children or children with special needs. Maybe you and/or your partner think being biologically connected to your kid is important, so you're thinking about sperm donation or surrogacy. But these questions only get you started, because the bigger issues involve your hopes and expectations for your family, not only *how* the family grows in the first pace.

 Be honest with yourself: Do you love being around kids? Are you the nurturing type? Are you a good mentor? And how much do you value your kid-free life, and how happy will you be after that's gone? Of course, many of these things are unknowable until you actually *have* the kids, and at some point you simply need to jump in. But these questions are serious and deserve serious thought. Be sure you both agree that you want kids — and talk about why you do.

Making Sure You Agree on Parenting Issues

After you decide that you want kids, you still need to make sure you and your partner are on the same page concerning your parenting styles. This isn't the time to be indirect or to hide your feelings from your partner for fear that you won't come across as sympathetic or sensitive.

Before you explore the different options of having a child, you need to make sure you share the same parenting philosophy with your partner. Ask yourselves some of these questions before, rather than after, having a child. Even if you're single and looking to have a child, answering these questions can help solidify your intentions and desires:

✔ Will one of you be the primary caregiver, while the other works? Or will you try for a more egalitarian approach?

✔ How strict a parent will you be? Do you and your partner agree on discipline?

✔ Are you religious? Is your partner religious? Do you follow the same religion? If you want your kids to be raised with religion, which one will you choose?

✔ What about schools? Depending on where you live, your income, and your views, public school may be the best option, or not. Do you want to consider private schools or even home schooling?

✔ Are you living in a place where you'll feel comfortable raising your kids? Is it safe? Is it friendly to LGBT families?

Of course, this discussion may seem *way* premature when you're first thinking about kids, and you don't need to make every decision right away. In fact, you *can't* figure some of this stuff out until the kids actually appear. Raising children turns things upside-down, and whatever you thought about your parenting philosophy may not survive the reality! But thinking about the big questions early and often is so important. Not being able to agree on these major life items may tell you something instructive about whether kids are really for you (at least as a member of this couple).

Considering Your Options to Bring a Child into Your Home

If you want to welcome a child into your home, you need to answer a big and most central question: How? For many gay and lesbian couples considering starting a family, this is the biggest question — one that calls up issues about what they value and about their deepest hopes and fears. This is also true, of course, for many opposite-sex couples, but often only faced where the couple isn't able to conceive "the old-fashioned way." (If you don't know what that is, you're reading the wrong *For Dummies* book.)

You have a few options for welcoming a child into your home. Understanding these options and what is involved with each decision is important to know what you're getting into. Some are quite costly, so read these sections to get a better grasp of your choices.

Adopting a child together

Perhaps the first option you and your partner thought of for bringing children into your home was adoption. Many children are in need of parents, and more and more LGBT couples and even single people are adopting kids and giving them the love and support they deserve and need. If you're considering adoption, these sections explain how you can go about doing so.

Going abroad or staying home

A gay or lesbian couple essentially has two ways to adopt a child: internationally or domestically.

For now, the international option is bleak for LGBT couples, even for those who can afford the time and considerable expense involved. Although several countries once allowed same-sex couples to adopt (often, as long as they were mum about their relationship), those international adoptions are much more difficult than they used to be. That option has been closed off, at least for now and in most places, in part because more and more countries are signing onto the Hague Adoption Convention, which requires more transparency.

Today, even agencies that strongly support gay and lesbian adoptions will often refuse to work with you in your "don't ask, don't tell" effort. And if your union is legally recognized, then you can't claim to be "single" in any case.

On the other hand, if you're single and if the country you're considering allows single people to adopt, this option may still be a good one for you. Generally, though, you'll have to keep your sexual orientation mum while the process unfolds, so decide whether you can deal with this situation.

International adoptions can sometimes be problematic for another reason, too: In some cases, the child(ren) you're seeking to adopt can have physical or emotional issues that aren't disclosed, and that you don't discover until you meet the child (if then).

The domestic angle of adoption presents more options for you. Many thousands of kids are waiting to be adopted in the United States, and in many states, you can create your family in this way.

Adoption by gays and lesbians is complicated in many states. Only Florida has a statute that expressly bars "homosexuals" from adopting, but an intermediate court has declared the unconstitutional, and its status is currently unclear. (Some gays and lesbians have lately been able to adopt kids there.) A few states, like Utah, bar "cohabitating," unmarried couples from adopting. (Arkansas's recent law to the same effect was struck down by that state's Supreme Court.) Questions exist about whether you and your partner can adopt jointly, or one after the other (called a *second parent* adoption). We explore these issues throughout this chapter, but you need to make sure you know what you're legally getting yourself into from the jump. Check your state laws, because the results can vary from one part of a state to another.

If you decide on a domestic adoption, you also want to consider the following questions before proceeding:

- ✔ Are you willing to consider adopting a special needs child? By some estimates, as many as half of all domestic adoptions are now of children who have learning, physical, or emotional problems.

- ✔ Would you consider adopting an older child? Many older kids are in need of adoption. Adopting an infant is more difficult.

- ✔ Would you be comfortable with an *open adoption,* in which the birth mother (or, less often, both birth parents) maintains some contact with the child after the adoption goes through?

- ✔ What about the delicate issue of race? Do you care whether the child is the same race as you? Having this type of conversation may be difficult, but doing so is important. Many factors, including whether you're in a biracial relationship, where you live, and what your own general views on transracial adoption are, may affect your decision. You also need to honestly check in with your own feelings.

For an adoption agency, denying a foster placement or adoption to any prospective parent or child on the basis of a person's race, color, or national origin is a violation of Title VI of the federal Civil Rights Act of 1964. In other words, you can consider race, but the agency can't.

Considering your adoption options

After you figure out a few more specifics about the type of child you're interested in adopting, you have to consider another set of issues in order to welcome your new family member into your home. If you want to adopt domestically, you basically have four avenues to pursue:

- ✔ **Private adoption:** Many couples go through a private adoption agency. If you're determined to adopt an infant, this option is especially good. The agency can provide information about you and your partner to women (and girls) who are planning on giving up their children for adoption, and the birth mother then can choose the parent(s) she prefers.

- ✔ **Independent adoption:** Sometimes, the couple and the birth mother agree on this option. As the name implies, the parties arrange the adoption without an agency's intervention. Most states allow them, but not all do, and in any case they're regulated carefully, so be sure to check on local law before plunging in. Hire to an attorney to address all necessary legal issues.

In some states, one attorney may not represent both parties (the one relinquishing the child and the adoptive parent). This prohibition should suggest extreme caution in "sharing" a lawyer with the birth parent, even if that's allowed in the state whose laws apply.

✔ **Public agency adoption:** This type of adoption generally involves kids who have become wards of the state. Often, these children have come through the foster care system. Parental rights may have been terminated, sometimes against birth parents' wishes. Infants and babies rarely become available in this way, because the law provides time for birth parents to turn around their lives. But if you're interested in adopting older kids — and, often, kids who have bounced around among foster homes, and perhaps with some time spent with the birth parents — this option may be the best for you. In many cases, the kids in the public dependency system are special needs children.

✔ **Open adoption:** Sometimes, you and your partner agree to allow the birth mother some kind of access to your child, ranging from annual photos all the way to occasional visits. You should seriously consider whether you want to do an open adoption. Is contact with the family of origin a good idea? And what if you decide that the relationship with the birth family is no longer a good idea? Even though the birth parents generally have no legal rights (except in a few states, where contracts for contact may be honored if in the child's best interest), breaking off contact can be painful for everyone, including the child. Be sure to discuss a potential open adoption thoroughly with the agency and understand your legal options if the openness isn't working for your family or for your child.

Adopting jointly? Can you and your partner do it?

Even after you've steered your adoption ship through the wavy seas and tried to figure out which adoption method is right for you, more complexity waits! Of course, if you're in a relationship, you and your partner want to adopt your child together — as the couple that you are. But can you do a *joint adoption?*

The good (and straightforward news): If you're in a legal marriage civil union, or domestic partnership, the answer is "yes" — you and your partner can adopt your kid jointly, just the same as any other married couple.

But for the majority of people in the United States who don't live in marriage-equality states, the answer isn't as clear. The rule in many states is, surprisingly, that *no rule* about joint adoptions exists! Many state laws don't spell out whether unmarried couples can adopt kids jointly. In nonequality states, you and your partner are (in this respect) like other unmarried cohabitants, except that some judges look at a same-sex couple differently than an opposite-sex, unmarried couple. The practical results of this lack of clarity vary:

✔ In some states, a judicial ruling or consistent practice is in your favor. Although the statute may not be clear, you'll have no problem jointly adopting a child.

✔ In other states, practice actually varies from one county to another, or even — absurdly — from one judge to another. In these cases, a good adoption agency can often steer you to the right place. But be aware that the law isn't clearly in your corner.

The CD contains a list of references (Appendix B) for the laws pertaining to adoptions by gays and lesbians, in couples or as single parents. Be sure to check to see how up-to-date these sources are before proceeding.

Even if you can't jointly adopt your child, the two of you may still be able to become the child's legal parents. In some cases, the parent who didn't adopt first may be able to become the child's legal parent through a second parent or a stepparent adoption. The law in this area is complex, but you should make it happen if at all possible. Otherwise, the law will see the second parent as a legal stranger to the child. The consequences to that parent and the child can be quite serious. Here are a few of the most dramatic:

✔ Getting the child on the parent's health insurance policy is difficult if not impossible.

✔ That parent has no authority to make decisions — medical decisions, enrollment in school, and so on — for the child.

✔ The child can't get benefits, such as Social Security death benefits, from that parent.

✔ If the adoptive parent dies or becomes incapacitated, the other parent has no legal status (although some courts may find this parent to be a *de facto parent* [a person who has acted as an important caregiver for some time to the child], and confer legal status anyway).

✔ If the two of you split up, the legal parent may be the only one with custody or visitation rights (again, some courts look at the actual relationship between the child and the nonadoptive parent and grant that parent the right to continue his or her relationship with the kid).

Adopting your partner's child as a second parent

If you live in a state that doesn't permit joint adoptions, another option may be to adopt your child *serially* — one of you becomes the legal parent first and then the other adopts the child as a second parent. This possibility arises in two very different situations:

✔ **Where one of you has been in a previous relationship (usually a marriage) in which both you and your former partner were the legal parents of a child.** This situation often arises in cases where one partner was in an opposite-sex relationship. The partner who isn't a legal parent needs to do a *stepparent adoption*, but the problem is that typically only married (or legally equivalent) couples have this option. In a stepparent adoption, the married partner who isn't the biological parent is permitted to adopt the other partner's biological child only if the *other* biological parent — the third party who isn't part of the couple — consents (or if that person's parental rights are terminated).

✔ **Where there's no third party (besides the biological parent who isn't part of the couple, and whom we can ignore for now) to complicate the adoption, but the state (or locality) where you live doesn't permit same-sex couples to adopt jointly.** But even in nonequality states, you may be able to do a *second-parent adoption*. The law in many states is unclear and can even vary from court to court and county to county. In places that have permitted second-parent adoptions, the process resembles that of petitioning for an individual adoption. The prospective parent files a petition to adopt his or her partner's child. The adoption court will then conduct a home study.

In states where there's no official recognition (or record) of the parents' relationship to each other, the couple may need to provide the court with evidence of it. Letters of support from family and friends who know the couple and the reality of their family's life together can be indispensable in some cases.

At the risk of sounding repetitive, contact a lawyer who is very familiar with LGBT adoptions if you're considering a second-parent adoption. Often confusing court decisions, inconsistent local practices, and other issues can complicate the procedure. An experienced lawyer can help you navigate this scary complexity.

Relying on science: Sperm, eggs, and surrogates

Many same-sex couples want to have some biological connection to the child. You may not care so much, but you may be concerned about the stress and uncertainty of adopting a child that has no connection to your biological family. If either of these reasons for finding an alternative to adoption applies to your family, you may want to consider creating a family through using a sperm donor or an egg donor/gestational surrogate.

Before we dive more deeply into these waves, a little terminology to help you understand what we mean:

- An *egg donor* is a woman who has agreed to sell one or more of her eggs to people who need an outsider's egg to create their family.

- A *sperm donor* is a man who has agreed to sell his sperm to people who require it in order to start their own family.

  Often, these donors are anonymous — as a legal matter, it is (or should be) impossible for anyone to find out their identities.

- A *surrogate* is a woman who carries the child.

- Often, the term *gestational surrogate* is used to emphasize that the egg donor and the surrogate are two different women.

Using a sperm donor

Lesbian couples often have it easier than gay couples when using a sperm donor to have a child. A woman simply finds a sperm bank, identifies a suitable anonymous donor, and then becomes inseminated with that donor's sperm. You know the rest (we hope). Here are a few additional details:

- Although the donor is anonymous, the sperm bank typically supplies information about the donor's age, race, height, weight, eye color, and other physical characteristics. Many sperm banks now offer much more information, including the donor's educational level, interests, and so on. You can follow the advice from that old song, and "shop around"!

- Women can perform self-insemination using a device, such as a syringe.

- For some women, medical assistance is necessary (or desired). In that case, you can provide the sperm to a healthcare professional who can perform the task.

- In some cases, neither of you can (or want) to carry the child yourself; in that case, you can employ the services of a surrogate. (Read the next section for more info.)

When couples plan to have more than one child, sometimes each mother agrees to carry one (or more) of the fetuses. And sometimes one partner donates an egg to the partner who plans to become pregnant, although doing so involves additional expense. This option may either be medically necessary or simply a way for the partners to share in the process.

Another option that some lesbians choose is asking a friend or in-law to donate some sperm. Although the attraction of this choice is obvious — you know the person's history, you want him to be involved in the child's life, and you want your kid to have his genes rather an a complete stranger's — we suggest you be wary of this decision. Although laws and court decisions in different states vary, listen to this general and *very loud* warning. Because the biological father's identity is known, courts may be tempted to invest him with the rights and obligations normally accorded to fathers. This tendency can be more pronounced in states that don't allow the nonbiological parent in a same-sex relationship to adopt the child, because in that case the donor may look to the court more like the other parent.

If you're set on using a close friend's sperm, you can try to get around these problems by making sure that you and the donor clearly understand the agreement and that the potential donor is someone you trust implicitly. Better yet: Draft an agreement with this known donor, making clear exactly what role, if any, he will have in the child's life. You may want to spell out that he will have no obligation to provide support, either. (Rights and responsibilities are often seen as two sides of the same coin; if you're clear that you're not expecting support from him, your argument that he has no legally enforceable rights is more sympathetic.) Of course, you need to consult an attorney to determine how the courts and legislatures in your state look at these known donors. *Don't omit this step!*

No matter how careful you are, though, we can't in good conscience tell you that there's *no* chance that this donor won't have a greater role in your child's life than you want. A court can refuse to enforce your contract with the donor. There's also just the possibility of unneeded hassle if your relationship with the guy goes sour. You don't have any chance with this hassle if you use an anonymous donor. Furthermore, anonymous sperm donations are lawful in every state (although not in some other countries). On the other hand, a court could possibly compel an involved donor to contribute to the child's support, because the child's best interest is always foremost.

Using an egg donor and a gestational surrogate

Gay men who want to make a biological contribution to their family have a more difficult and a much more expensive route to travel. They need an egg donor and a gestational surrogate. One or more eggs will be fertilized and then implanted into the gestational surrogate.

If you do decide to go this route, be sure to decide what kind of relationship (if any) you want your child to have with the gestational surrogate and discuss this with the surrogate.

Although some places employ services where one woman can do it all — be the biological mother and carry the fetus — almost all surrogacy arrangements these days divide those responsibilities. Doing so is smart because courts have held that the biological mother who carries the fetus to term has a superior claim to that of the biological father's spouse (and that's even likelier to be the case where the court is dealing with a same-sex couple, especially in a state without marriage equality or civil unions).

So to reduce any issues you may face, we suggest you obtain eggs from a donor. Hire a gestational surrogate. Keep these two roles separate.

Even if you do use a separate egg donor and a surrogate, the legal landscape is rocky. States are all over the board on this issue. Some states have specific statutes that address these issues, and others don't. The actual practices within states are sometimes even inconsistent with what the law seems to require. The problems aren't with egg donation but with surrogacy. Here is a quick thumbnail sketch of the different possible rules that explain why the landscape is so fuzzy:

- ✔ Surrogacy is illegal.

- ✔ Surrogacy isn't illegal, but contracts for surrogacy can't be enforced (so if a problem comes up, you have no legal remedy).

- ✔ Pre-birth parentage orders may not be granted, forcing the nonbiological parent (or even both of you!) to adopt the child after it's born (if second parent adoptions are even permitted in the state).

- ✔ No rule exists; the law is unclear.

Is the situation hopelessly confusing? Well, not hopelessly. A few agencies serve as middlemen between the couple and the surrogate. They're experts at navigating the often uncharted legal waters so that the child is able to come into your family without too much difficulty. If you choose to proceed without an agency, make sure to figure out all you can *and* to find a lawyer with some experience in these matters *in your location.*

One excellent reference source is *Surrogacy Across America,* an article by Diane S. Hinson and Maureen McBrien, a 2011 publication by Creative Family Connections. (The publication is available at `http://creativefamily` `connections.com/50state.html.`)

The CD contains a state-by-state guide to surrogacy laws (see Appendix B). They're complex, so you need an expert to guide you through the process.

Opening your home to foster children

The most recent data available showed that more than 400,000 children were in foster care. For some gay and lesbian couples, caring for one or more foster children is an appealing alternative (or addition) to adopting kids.

The foster care system was created for children — including all kids up to the age of 18 — who can't live in their first homes for a variety of reasons. They become *wards* of the state, which is a legal way of saying that the state takes on the responsibility of their care. Wherever possible, the state places these kids with families (although some states still have group homes).

As a foster parent, you have limited status. You're not the legal guardian, but you're responsible for the day-to-day care of the children in your custody. You receive a stipend to care for the children. Generally, the amount is sufficient for basic needs and a bit beyond, but not for extras, such as extracurricular activities, camp, and so on.

The idea of bringing kids into your home who desperately need a place to live sounds appealing, and it is, for some people. Here are some things to consider before making that decision:

- ✔ **Foster care is intended to be temporary.** The ultimate goal is either to reunite the kids with their birth family or for the children to be adopted.

- ✔ **You're expected to cooperate with the state (and any agencies it contracts with to provide supervision of foster care) in achieving that goal.** You still have to cooperate, even if you firmly believe (or even know) that the child would be better off remaining with you.

- ✔ **You may have to deal with the emotional distress of giving up the child.** Even foster parents who aren't interested in adopting often find the day when the foster child is removed from their care to be very difficult. And until you've been a parent, you have no idea how difficult it can be to surrender a child, even if that child is placed in a good home for adoption. (It's even worse if the child is heading to a place you know won't be good for him or her.)

- ✔ **Being the foster parent may give you a practical advantage if and when the child becomes available for adoption.** The federal Adoption and Safe Families Act (ASFA) is intended to move kids into permanent homes more quickly. If the birth parent(s) are unable to get their acts together within a relatively short time, the law presumes that the goal should change from reunification to adoption. If you're already the foster parent, you stand a better chance of being able to adopt the child (if legally permissible in your state) when the goal change happens.

- ✔ **You may specify that you only want to foster children where the goal is adoption.** You may ask: Why would I foster a child who should be adopted? But this happens because the court needs to approve a goal change and the birth parent's rights need to be terminated. So a significant period of time can occur between when the agency changes the goal to adoption and the child can actually be adopted. In fact, you have no guarantee that it will ever happen (although it usually does).

State and local agencies are typically underfunded, understaffed, and often overwhelmed. If you and your partner are good foster parents, the agency may try to persuade you to take foster children where the goal is still reunification. Even if the case workers really believe that the child will ultimately be placed for adoption, you're putting yourself at substantial emotional risk if you agree.

Raising Children Together

Congratulations! The two of you have just welcomed the newest member of your family. Given the many obstacles the law, and nonlegal, players have put before you, your journey probably hasn't been easy so far. But the journey has just begun and it's going to get harder, because now the two of you actually have to raise the kid (or kids!) together. Whatever issues you've considered, whatever plans you've made, and whatever contingencies you think you've anticipated are about to be thrown into the crucible of real life. Parenting won't be made easier by the fact that you are (after all) a same-sex couple, but we hope the following sections can help ease any parenting challenges you may face as an LBGT parent.

Giving support to your kids

In restaurants, at your kids' school, around your parents' friends, and . . . everywhere else, you can expect to be viewed and treated differently than opposite-sex parents. Complete strangers may ask "where you got" your kids. Some people will wonder aloud about how the kids will fare without an appropriate role model of the opposite sex from that of you and your partner. Fellow students doubtlessly may give them a hard time, in various ways.

You need to think about how your family is going to handle these challenges. To do so, we suggest the following:

- **Supply your child(ren) the tools to respond to the inevitable questions and comments.** These tools include accurate and complete information, instructions on patience and how (or how not) to respond, and a sense of humor. Talk to your kids about the plain fact that you're a family headed by two moms or two dads. You need to let them know — by telling them, but more importantly by *showing* them — that they can discuss any issues that arise. Remember that it can get tough for them at times, and that they may even sound resentful for being in a different kind of family. No matter what, don't get defensive! Acknowledge their feelings, even if doing so is, well, painful.

- **Consider getting involved in a supportive group.** Look for a local parents' organization that stages various activities for gay- and lesbian-headed families. These family activities include camping trips, holiday parties, sports events, and so on. Sometimes you can even find "break out" groups, such as a gay dads' organization that can host brunches for the kids to meet and play, and for the parents to discuss matters of interest for their particular subgroup.

✔ **Spend vacation time with other families like you.** If you're not in an area with a good LGBT families group (if your time and finances permit), you can choose an organized event, such as Family Pride Week in Provincetown, Massachusetts, or Gay Day Family in Orlando, Florida (with visits to Disney and other local attractions). Or you may just get together with other lesbian- or gay-headed families for a week that shows your kids (and your friends) that other families are like them. Again, showing is more powerful than telling.

Dealing with the "Mommy" and "Daddy" labels

What are you going to have your kid *call* you? Same-sex couples don't have an obvious nomenclature because the "mommy" and "daddy" labels are engineered to suit opposite-sex couples. Do you have them both call you by the default "mommy" or "daddy" name? You may want to consider several other options that are available.

Use your imagination and find something that fits. After all, one of the great things about being a same-sex couple is that you're likely to think more carefully about everything, including the name that works for your family.

Some gay dad families use "daddy" and "papa"; some use the more challenging "dad" and "daddy." Lesbian families seem to have no end to the creativity. "Mom" and "mommy" or "momma" or some variant work for some; others just choose to use the same name for both and let the kids decide on ways of differentiating the two parents as they get older. One well-known activist uses the terms "Short Mom" and "Tall Mom."

Whatever you decide, remember that your child will have to use these terms around others. In one case we know of, the mother who identified as more masculine (though still as a woman) was referred to as "Daddy." If reading that is startling to you, imagine how it comes across to the straight society. Is your commitment to a particular name strong enough to deal with — and have your child deal with — the fallout from a particularly provocative name? Maybe, but think about it.

Handling birth certificate issues

Birth certificates are important for many reasons because those individuals listed as parents on the birth certificate are presumed to be responsible for the child's support and are also presumed to be the decision-makers for the child. In other words, if you're listed on the birth certificate as a mother or a father, you're the child's legal parent. As a result, getting on the birth certificate is important, if you can, but doing so can be difficult.

Before going any further, we need to break down the two situations in which birth certificate issues can arise:

- ✔ In the case of adoption, a new birth certificate is issued when the adoption is made final. Thus, the adoptive parent, or parents, is listed on that new document. (Refer to the earlier section, "Considering your adoption options" for issues involving joint and second-parent adoptions.) The bottom line is that the birth certificate will reflect the legal status of the partners as parents of the children.

- ✔ In the case of surrogacy or sperm donation, the issue is whether the nonbiological parent can be added as a parent on the birth certificate.

If the two of you live in a marriage-equality state that has marriage equality, then the issue should be clear in the case of adoption. As long as you're legally united at the time of the adoption, you shouldn't have any impediment to your ability to jointly adopt a child with your partner.

If one of you already has a child when you marry, we suggest that the nonparent adopt the child. That's the only way to be certain that both of you will be full legal guardians of that child (assuming that's what you want).

The more difficult issue involves surrogacy and sperm donation. The biological parent, of course, will be on the birth certificate. What about the nonbiological parent? In the case of opposite-sex couples, this issue doesn't usually arise, because the law presumes that the husband of the woman who gave birth is the legal father — and his name is therefore on the birth certificate. But does that presumption apply to you and your partner?

In some states that have recognized the legally equality of same-sex couples, both of your names will be placed on the birth certificate when you bring a child into your family through surrogacy or sperm donation. But other states have resisted! In Iowa, a state with full marriage equality, state officials refused to put the name of the nonbiological mother on the birth certificate unless and until she first adopted the child that her spouse had given birth to. A lower court judge ruled that the state had misinterpreted the law, and that the nonbiological mom didn't have to adopt. The case is on appeal as of this writing.

The legal professionals who are helping you with your adoption and legal parenting issues should be well versed on this area of the law. Make sure to discuss your concerns about your legal status as a parent with them. Because county government often handles vital records (including birth certificates), your ability to get the nonbiological parent named on the birth certificate may not even be consistent within a given state. A lawyer well versed in the local law can navigate this situation with you.

Do whatever you can do to adopt the child that you and your partner want to raise together — even if you're in a state where marriage equality is legal, because other states may not recognize that equality.

In states without marriage equality, you may or may not be able to get the nonbiological parent's name on the birth certificate. The answer depends on whether you can both be adoptive parents. So what happens if that's not possible? If only one of you can be on the birth certificate or can adopt, how will you protect your rights as parents? The next section explains what to do.

Create a co-parenting agreement to protect both parents and children

Even if you can't both be the legal, adoptive parents of your children, you and your partner can enter into a *co-parenting agreement* (a contract between two partners — one being a legal parent and the other having no legal parenting rights). The agreement ordinarily stipulates how the partners will co-parent the child while living together as a family and how to share parenting responsibilities, custody, support, and visitation if the partners break up.

Because the contract is between the parents and no one else, the co-parenting agreement should only contain the responsibilities and obligations agreed to by the co-parents. If the legal parent wishes to authorize the co-parent to interact with third parties (such as teachers, doctors, and so on), he or she will need to draw up additional legal documents, which we describe in the "Giving a nonlegal co-parent key decision-making rights" later in this chapter.

A good co-parenting agreement sets out both parents' responsibilities and expectations for the raising of the child. They should cover, in as much detail as possible, such huge issues as:

- ✔ Time committed to child care by each parent
- ✔ Financial responsibilities to the child
- ✔ Medical and other key decision-making rights
- ✔ How decisions will be made in case of disagreement
- ✔ How disputes will be resolved if you split up
- ✔ Visitation and support in the event of a breakup
- ✔ Intent to make the nonlegal parent the child's legal guardian (although you should supplement this intent by nominating the co-parent as guardian in a separate document and in the legal parent's last will)
- ✔ Intent to share custody of the child even after a breakup

At the outset, we need to point out that these arrangements may not be legally enforceable. Courts in many states won't enforce these agreements per se. That's because they're rightly quite concerned about the child's welfare and want to retain authority to do whatever's needed in that child's best interest. Yet co-parenting agreements nonetheless serve very important purposes, but they're still worth creating for the following reasons:

- ✔ You and your partner can focus on the big issues that are otherwise too easy to put off, or avoided altogether, unless there's a crisis.

- ✔ Even if the agreement isn't enforceable, it can serve as useful evidence of you and your partner's intent. This agreement can be extremely valuable in many contexts, but especially if you and your partner split up and the legal parent wants to fence the other parent out of custody or even prevent visitation.

- ✔ Recent custody and visitation cases have shown that the legal system may be starting to catch up to the reality of the cultural diversity of American families. In a recent Ohio Supreme Court case, a nonlegal parent lost her custody battle after the court held that a legal parent must show by written contract or by evidence of behavior that he or she clearly ceded all parental rights in favor of shared parental rights with a nonlegal parent.

  The couple in this case did have several legal documents drafted by an attorney and signed by both parties, which explicitly stated the legal parent wanted her partner to be her daughter's "co-parent in every way." However, the court determined that the language was insufficient proof that the legal parent intended to relinquish sole custody and decision-making rights.

Therefore when making a co-parenting agreement, make sure that you clearly state the legal parent's intention to "share custody" of the child with the co-parent even after the couple breaks up.

Messy breakups have often caused legal parents to invoke the law against their former partners, trying to get the court to find that their exes are legal strangers to the children. As the nonlegal parent, you want to prevent this. As the legal parent, you should welcome a co-parenting agreement as a way of protecting your child from your own future temptation to use the law in this way.

We include a sample parenting agreement (Form 7-1) on the CD.

Nominating a Guardian for Your Child

Nominating a guardian for your minor child is easy, and every responsible parent ought to take the time to do so. When LGBT partners decide to have a child, more often than not only one of them is the legal parent, at least until the couple can obtain a second-parent adoption. In the interim or if a second-parent adoption is unavailable, the legal parent should nominate his or her partner as guardian of their child.

If a lesbian couple is using a sperm donor, as soon as there is a viable pregnancy, the pregnant partner should nominate her partner as guardian. Doing so ensures that the nonlegal partner has access to the newborn baby in case she has complications during childbirth.

In addition to naming your partner as guardian, the legal parent should also nominate an alternate guardian in the same document in case your partner dies before you or is otherwise unavailable (for example, if both partners are involved in the same accident).

If a legal parent dies without nominating his or her partner as guardian, especially if the partner has no legal relationship to their child, the court will appoint someone, usually the child's next-of-kin. The problem is that this person may be someone who disapproves of your family or even someone your child doesn't know or love.

These sections explain why you need to appoint a guardian for your minor children and describe the different types of guardianships, how a court determines who would make an acceptable guardian, and the mechanism by which you can select a guardian (either your partner or someone else you trust) for your children.

Understanding why you need to nominate a guardian

You typically have two ways to nominate a guardian for your child:

- ✓ **Adding a clause in your last will and testament:** In case you die while your children are minors (under the age of 18), you should name a guardian in your will to raise them. You should also appoint an alternate guardian in case your first choice is unable to carry out this responsibility.

If you're planning to add a nomination of guardian clause to your last will, you should be aware that this type of nomination is only legally binding in a few states. Courts in a majority of states have the right to overturn a parent's will nomination if they believe it's in the best interest of the child to do so and if the child is old enough (generally older than age 14) to choose his or her own guardian.

✔ **Signing a stand-alone nomination of guardian form:** Accordingly, even if you do nominate a guardian in your will, we also suggest you sign a separate, stand-alone nomination of guardian form.

We include a sample Nomination of Guardian form on the CD (see Form 7-2). We also add a sample nomination of guardian clause to insert in your will on the CD.

Generally, there are two types of state guardianship laws:

✔ **Court-appointed guardianships:** In states with court-appointed guardianships, regardless of the parent's preference, a court is required to weigh certain factors and then make a final determination as to who will be appointed the child's guardian. Ordinarily, the court factors in the deceased parent's preference as they weigh the relationship of the guardian to the child, whether the nominated guardian has, among other things, the time and financial ability to take on the role of guardian. Some states also factor in the wishes of the minor child if he or she is older than 14 (12 in a minority of states).

✔ **Parent-appointed guardianships:** In parent-appointed guardianship states, the guardian chosen by the legal parent will automatically be appointed as long as he or she is fit, and it's in the child's best interest to be raised by that person.

When states are considering what is in the best interest of a minor child, they sometimes decide to divide the duties of guardian into two categories:

✔ **Guardian of the person**: A guardian over the person of a minor child stands in for the parent. In other words, he or she cares for and nurtures the child and makes sure the child has everything necessary to reach his or her fullest potential: food, shelter, medical care, education, and so on.

✔ **Guardian of the property:** A guardian of the property is responsible for managing, in the best way possible, the property and/or money left to a minor child.

Passing control of a minor child's property and financial assets to a property guardian doesn't mean that the guardian is the owner of those assets. Ownership of the property remains in the name of the minor child. The only responsibility held by the property guardian is to oversee and manage the assets you leave to your child. Because he or she will be managing money on behalf of a minor child, the property guardian is required by law to maintain accurate records for all accounts.

More often than not, the same person is appointed to fill both roles, but occasionally the court gives physical custody of the child to one guardian and appoints another to manage the child's financial matters. If you want your partner/co-parent to perform both duties, you need to specifically add that preference in the written nomination.

If you appoint one person as guardian over the person of your minor child and a different person as guardian over the property, make sure they understand what your priorities and wishes are for your child's upbringing. Even more important, make certain they're willing and able to work together to carry out your directions.

Choosing a guardian

If you're in a relationship and your partner is co-parenting your child, your first choice for guardian will probably be your partner. Even so, you need to consider naming an alternate guardian in case your partner predeceases you or is unavailable to act as guardian for some other reason.

Contemplating the possibility of someone else raising your child can be difficult. Sometimes you and the co-parent may have difficulty on naming a guardian or alternate guardian.

To facilitate the process of choosing a guardian, you and your partner (or you alone if you're a single parent) need to make a list of all the family members and friends that both parents want to nominate. After you compile a list of names, make another list of characteristics and issues to factor into your decision. Each parent can add his or her own concerns, but the following list can help get the ball rolling:

- ✔ **Relationship:** Does your child like or love the guardian (and vice versa)?

- ✔ **Age:** How old is the guardian? The younger the child, the more care he or she requires. Also, the guardian shouldn't be too young to handle the responsibility or too old to manage childcare.

- ✔ **The guardian's physical and emotional health:** Raising children is a lot of work, and a guardian needs to be up to the task.

- ✔ **Maturity:** Your child's guardian should be mature and stable enough to take on the role of raising a child.

- ✔ **Philosophy and religion:** The guardian's child-rearing philosophy and world view should be closely aligned to that of the parents, especially as it relates to raising children.

✔ **Other commitments:** Being raised in a family with other children may be a plus or minus. If the guardian has a job with long hours, he or she may not be a good choice. If the guardian lives with another adult (spouse or partner), you also need to factor in that person's philosophy and personality.

✔ **Enthusiasm:** The guardian should be genuinely willing to step in as guardian. Have a long discussion to make sure he or she really understands the parents' expectations.

When you compare the list of potential guardians to the list of factors affecting the decision, the roster of potential guardians will probably get shorter. After you make a decision about who to nominate, encourage the alternate guardian to spend some time getting to know the child. Doing so gives the guardian and child an opportunity to develop a bond that may make any future adjustment much easier.

Realizing a court has the final say over who will be appointed guardian

Even if you nominate your partner as guardian, unless he or she has legally adopted your child as a second parent, a court will ultimately decide if it's in the best interest of the child to be raised by your partner.

Determining what is in the best interests of a child depends upon many factors, including some which may reflect a particular judge's antigay bias, such as, but not limited to:

✔ The age and gender of the child.

✔ The love and emotional bond between your choice of guardian and your child.

✔ The physical and mental health of the guardian.

✔ The *lifestyle* and other social factors of the guardian. As you can imagine, this is a very subjective criteria. For some judges, "lifestyle" simply means the potential guardian's work and travel schedule and whether the guardian is a single person who enjoys the nightlife to the point that it would hinder his or her stability and so on. In a few cases, a judge may consider the guardian's "alternative lifestyle" or sexual orientation and deny guardianship on the basis of the judge's personal belief that an LGBT guardian would — as a matter of fact — be detrimental to the child's well-being.

✔ The guardian's ability to provide food, shelter, clothing, and medical care.

✔ Whether the child is old enough to choose where he or she wants to live.

✔ Whether the child's current living arrangement is stable, safe, and desirable.

✔ Whether the guardian has a criminal record or history of child abuse.

Consider these factors and how they may be applied in states and jurisdictions where the determining court is biased against the LGBT community. As previously stated, some gay men and lesbian parents lose the right to raise their nonlegal children when their partner becomes incapacitated or dies, simply because he or she is gay or lesbian.

In most instances, a court gives your partner (especially if he or she is also the child's other legal parent) and your legal family members a preference in determining who will be guardian.

You must state in your will or nomination of guardian form that you want your partner to be the first choice of guardian. The court then seriously considers your suggestion while determining what is in the child's best interest. If you do name your partner as your child's guardian, check out the next section.

Often the most effective way to avoid losing custody of your child is to make every effort to have your partner adopt your child as a second parent as soon as possible. Refer to the previous section, "Adopting a child together," for an in-depth discussion of adopting a child.

Giving a nonlegal co-parent key decision-making rights

Because a nomination of guardian ordinarily doesn't take effect until the legal parent becomes incapacitated or dies, in order to extend immediate authority to a co-parent, the legal parent needs to sign a document giving the co-parent the authority to make important decisions for and about the child.

Commonly referred to as *Authorization to Consent to the Medical Treatment of a Minor Child,* this document can be drafted to suit each family's particular needs and circumstances. A thorough authorization includes

✔ Authorization for the co-parent to consent to emergency and nonemergency medical and dental treatment, including surgery

✔ The right of the co-parent to visit the child in a medical facility, even when the policy is limited to *family only.*

✔ The right of the co-parent to access copies of the child's medical and school records

- ✔ Permission for the co-parent to deal with the child's teachers and other school officials, including the right to consent to the child's participation in extracurricular and in-school activities, to transport the child to and from school, to sign report cards, to provide an explanation or notice of the child's absence or tardiness, and so on

- ✔ A directive that the co-parent be listed as an emergency contact

- ✔ Authorization for co-parent to travel with the child across state lines

You can find a sample Authorization to Consent to the Medical Treatment of a Minor Child form (Form 7-3) on the CD.

Financially Protecting Your Minor Child

Nominating your partner and an alternate to be guardian to your child is important, but it's not enough. You also need to make sure you leave enough money so that your child has an opportunity to live to his or her fullest potential.

If one parent dies, the surviving parent will continue to raise the child. However, if both parents die before the child grows up, the guardian will take over the parent's role.

Parents can do a few others things to ensure adequate financial resources are available to raise their child if neither of them is alive. The most important is to set up a child's trust — either as a stand-alone document or in a last will and testament.

A trust for children is the same as a trust for adults. When creating the trust, the parents will appoint a trustee — either the guardian or someone else — to oversee the finances they put into the trust for their child. In addition to other terms, the trust should include

- ✔ Provisions that the funds are only to be used for the benefit of the child and that the initial investment (principal) will stay in an interest-bearing trust account. Any income or interest earned on the principal will be used to pay for the child's health, education, maintenance, and support, with discretionary payments made for other activities such as vacations, pool passes, music, or dance lessons, camp, and so on.

- ✔ Parents may also want to consider the possibility that the alternate guardian may need financial support. For instance, if the guardian is required to cut back on his or her work hours, change jobs, or relocate to the child's community. In that case, the parents should consider letting the trustee of the trust subsidize the guardian's income.

- ✔ After the child reaches adulthood, whatever remains of the principal can be distributed in one-lump sum or paid out in installments over time.

If the parents are concerned that the guardian would (or might) mismanage the trust funds or use them for his or her own benefit, then they should make sure the guardian and trustee isn't the same person.

To fund the trust, the parents can open an account in the name of the trust (ask your bank, accountant, lawyer, or financial planner for help in doing this) and then make deposits into that account over time. Furthermore, parents can purchase life insurance policies naming the trust as the beneficiary so that when one or both parents die, the insurance proceeds automatically are deposited into the child's trust to be managed by the trustee.

The primary purpose in creating a trust for your child is to provide for his or her support and education if you and your partner die before your child becomes an adult. This kind of trust can be tricky to set up, so you may want to consult with an experienced estate planning attorney.

Chapter 8

Wading through Tax Issues for Unmarried Partners

. . . .

In This Chapter

▶ Understanding how the federal government views your relationship from a tax viewpoint

▶ Recognizing how same-sex marriage affects the way you file federal tax returns

▶ Figuring out how to claim your child and partner as your dependents

▶ Seeing how DOMA causes higher taxes for LGBT couples

▶ Distinguishing the different filing requirements for state tax returns

. . . .

*T*he very idea of filing tax returns can make April 15 a day of dread for millions of American wage earners. Not only are tax forms and their instructions ever-changing, confusing, and sometimes even contradictory, lots of folks also have a fundamental fear of all things related to the Internal Revenue Service (IRS).

As intimidating as tax day is to the average American, the day is worse for LGBT couples whose marriages, civil unions, and domestic partnerships are legal according to their state's law but — thanks to the federal Defense of Marriage Act (DOMA) — not recognized by federal law.

DOMA defines marriage as a union between one man and one woman and denies federal legal recognition of same-sex couples even when they're legally married, in a civil union, or are registered as domestic partners in their home state. (Refer to Chapter 2 for more details about DOMA.)

Because state law and DOMA create a patchwork of rights and benefits for LGBT families, tax penalties and benefits of all sorts may or may not be imposed on or available to you and your partner depending on where you live. This confusion creates a filing nightmare for couples trying to figure out what state and federal tax regulations do or don't apply depending on their particular legal status.

In this chapter we describe the different ways US federal and state tax policies affect LGBT families whether or not they're in a legally recognized relationship. We also discuss the impact of DOMA on how same-sex couples pay taxes — how it functions to deprive LGBT families of many federal and state benefits that are available to their straight counterparts.

Although this chapter is divided into several sections dealing with separate areas of tax law, there is no absolute boundary that clearly delineates between tax policies. Therefore, you may see some overlapping discussion, especially in regards to DOMA, as we try to help you sort it all out.

Recognizing What Legally Married Couples Get from a Tax Standpoint

A family's legal status triggers access to many tax benefits and obligations. When the federal income tax law was first conceived in 1913, it contained a $1,000 deduction for married couples. And ever since, tax law has continued to incorporate incentives and tax credits to benefit married couples and families.

For instance, as long as they meet certain income eligibility and other qualifications, legally married spouses and their families may do the following:

- File joint federal tax returns and merge their incomes even if one partner had little or no income
- Give one another tax free gifts and inheritances
- Receive an Earned Income Credit (EIC) for low-income workers
- Get a Child and Dependent Care Credit to recoup a portion of child care–related expenses
- Obtain an Adoption Credit to help offset the costs of adopting a child
- Qualify for a Child Tax Credit to provide tax relief to families raising children
- Receive higher education–related tax credits to help defray the cost of college tuition
- Receive a tax exemption for employer-provided health insurance and pension plans for the taxpayer, his or her legal spouse, their children, and other qualified dependents

Each year the federal tax code grows bigger. Finding an exact number of pages included in the Internal Revenue Code is nearly impossible, but lots of folks have tried. For sure the code includes thousands of pages, prompting much angst in some Americans, even to the point of inspiring a Taxed Enough Already (TEA) Party movement that claims to be against the creation of new taxes and in favor of simplifying or eliminating the tax code altogether. As Benjamin Franklin said, "In this world nothing is certain but death and taxes." If only he really knew the type of tax code today, he'd probably roll over in his grave.

Because the federal government doesn't recognize LGBT marriages, thanks to DOMA, you and your partner aren't given these rights. (Refer to the later section, "Seeing DOMA's Effects" for more information.)

Answering to Uncle Sam: Federal Income Taxes

Because the Internal Revenue Service (IRS) is a federal agency, it follows federal law (DOMA), not state law, when recognizing same-sex marriages or their legal equivalents (civil unions and domestic partnership registrations). But state tax agencies in marriage equality states do recognize same-sex couples as married for tax purposes.

Consequently, same-sex couples who are legally married, in a civil union, or in a registered domestic partnership must treat federal and state tax returns differently.

The following sections point out how LGBT couples must file their federal tax returns separately, how you can file if you have dependent children, and how you potentially can claim your partner as your dependent. We also discuss the marriage penalty, an often-discussed topic that unmarried couples, both gay and heterosexual, encounter when filing federal taxes.

Considering your filing options

For the purpose of this section, we divide this discussion about federal income tax into three separate categories depending on your legal status and state of residence:

✔ **LGBT partners who live in states with LGBT marriage or equivalent rights and who have opted not to enter into a legal union.**

✔ **LGBT partners who live in a non-marriage equality or equivalent state, whether or not the couple got married elsewhere.**

If your circumstances match one of these two options, the federal government deems you as unmarried for federal tax purposes. Because you're in fact not married or your state doesn't recognize your marriage, you must file your federal income tax return as a single person or as head of household (HOH). (We discuss how to file as HOH in the next section.)

✔ **LGBT partners who live in a marriage equality (or its equivalent) state who are married or otherwise legally united.** If your circumstances mirror this category, your tax filing is more complicated. Why? Because the IRS follows the federal DOMA and thus, even if you're legally married, you and your partner *can't* file your federal income tax returns as married couple.

Instead, if you and your partner are in this category, do the following:

- You must file federal income tax returns as single individuals (or as head of household if you have dependents).

- In some states, you must file state income tax returns as married filing jointly or married filing separately, depending on which option results in a higher tax refund or lower tax penalty. In states offering less than marriage (civil unions or domestic partner registration), a couple may not even have the option of filing a state return using a married filing status.

When a heterosexual married couple fills out their federal income tax return, they must then transfer the figures generated on the form to their state income tax return. Conversely, in the bizarre world that is LGBT legal rights, because federal and state tax codes sometimes see the status of LGBT partners differently, gay and lesbian partners in this category may need to generate *four* separate tax returns:

✔ **Each partner must file an individual federal income tax return as single individuals or as HOH — that's two separate forms.** Because the federal government doesn't recognize same-sex marriage, married gay and lesbian couples are required to file separate returns as single individuals. Of course, when you're legally married you *aren't* factually a single person; thus the federal government is forcing you to lie on a tax form that also requires you to sign beneath a paragraph that warns you that the information you provide on the form is "to the best of your knowledge" true. Doesn't that put LGBT couples in quite a pickle? (Refer to the nearby sidebar about how some couples are refusing to lie.)

Because you're being forced to lie about your marital status on your federal tax return, some tax experts advise you to add a note after your signature that you are actually married but were forced to file as a single person because of DOMA. Of course you can't do this if you file your forms electronically!

✔ **Using their combined income, deductions, and so forth, both partners should generate a mock federal income tax return showing figures that reflect a married filing jointly status — that's three forms so far.** You may create a *mock* (simply a regular old federal income tax return that is filled out but never submitted to the IRS) federal income tax return. What's the reason for the mock return? In order to come up with the figures necessary to complete a joint *state* tax return, you first need to calculate what your federal tax return would have been if you were legally able to file it.

✔ **With the figures generated from the mock federal form, depending on their state's law, the couple may or may not be required to file a state tax return as married filing jointly — and that is a total of four forms!** The purpose of the mock form is to generate the accurate figures for a married filing jointly status to input into a state tax.

Professional tax preparers say that because of the additional paperwork, time, and detail required to complete them, the fee for preparing tax returns for LGBT partners can be more than double what it costs to prepare returns for a married opposite-sex couple.

Some LGBT couples are refusing to lie

As of this writing, the IRS compels LGBT married couples to lie about their marital status on their federal income tax return forms. But as more and more states allow same-sex marriages, there is increasing tension between the law and the lie. This tension has resulted in a new political movement that is challenging the IRS's refusal to grant legally recognized LGBT partners the right to file federal income tax returns jointly as a married couple.

Although no one knows for sure exactly how many same-sex couples are refusing to lie and thus filing jointly as married couples, a website called Refuse to Lie (www.refusetolie. org) gives couples advice from those who've taken the risk.

Currently the LGBT community is split about whether or not breaking the law in an effort to make a point is okay. After all, if you get caught knowingly using the wrong filing status on your tax return, you may be assessed a penalty, plus interest.

For now, the IRS doesn't ask taxpayers to signify whether or not they are male or female, and they don't require proof on marriage. However, knowingly using the wrong filing status can get you into hot water, and we don't recommend it. Especially because more and more LGBT couples file jointly as married spouses, the movement may be getting the unwelcome attention of IRS auditors.

Until DOMA is overturned or the IRS changes its policy, if you knowingly file the incorrect tax return and the IRS discovers your deception, it will reject your filing and require you and your partner to refile using the proper returns. Because it can take more than a year for the IRS to reject your return, if you owe taxes, you're liable for any interest plus penalties in addition to the original tax bill.

Discovering more about the head of household filing status

If you or your partner have a child, one of you may be able to claim the child as a dependent on your federal tax return even though you're not legally married by filing as head of household (HOH). Taxpayers who claim the HOH filing status often benefit from a higher standard deduction and lower tax rates than single taxpayers, so it's worth looking into it.

If you have one or more children who meet the following four criteria, you can file as head of household (HOH) and claim a child as a dependent, which usually allows you to pay less tax than if you simply filed as a single person.

- ✔ The child must be your biological, adopted, step, or foster child. The dependent child could also be your younger sibling, your grandchild, or one (or more) of their children, for example your niece or great-grandchild.

- ✔ The child must have lived with you for more than six months over the course of the tax year.

- ✔ The child must be under the age of 19 at the end of the year, or if the child was a full-time student for at least five months out of the tax year, he or she must be under the age of 24. If the dependent person is totally and permanently disabled — regardless of age — he or she meets the dependent criteria.

- ✔ The child must have depended on you for at least half of his or her support during the tax year.

If a couple has two children, each partner may be able to claim one child as a dependent and file as HOH on their individual federal income tax returns.

Both partners can't claim the same child to qualify as HOH in the same tax year. If you have just one dependent child, you can take turns listing the child as your dependent in alternate years. Nothing gets the attention of the IRS auditing division more than two individuals claiming the same dependent in the same year.

Determining whether you can claim your partner as your dependent

Even if you don't have a dependent child, you may be able to file your federal income tax return as head of household (HOH) by claiming your unemployed or stay-at-home partner as your dependent. To do this legally, your partner (or another unrelated adult dependent) must meet all four of the following criteria:

✔ Have earned less than $3,700 in gross, taxable income or unemployment benefits (this figure is for tax year 2011 and it changes from year to year)

✔ Have received more than half of his or her support from you (things like food, shelter, clothing, education, medical care, and just about any other expense imaginable) for the entire tax year

✔ Be a citizen of the United States, a resident alien, or a citizen of Canada or Mexico

✔ Not be claimed as a dependent by another taxpayer in the same tax year

In addition to these four criteria, under IRS regulations, you can claim any adult as your dependent as long as your cohabitation doesn't violate federal or state law. Because the Supreme Court held antisodomy laws to be unconstitutional, unless any other legitimate laws make it unlawful for you to live with your partner, you've probably got nothing to worry about. More than likely, if a state has a law against you living with a person you claim as your dependent and somehow the IRS gets wind of it, the worst thing that'll happen is the IRS will deny your deduction.

If you're thinking of filing as HOH, make sure you've met the qualifications for claiming a dependent before submitting your forms. For more information about how to qualify for HOH, please check with your tax adviser.

Tackling the marriage penalty

Whether gay or straight, unmarried partners do have some advantages when filing federal income taxes. For instance, in some cases LGBT partners pay less in federal income tax than heterosexual married spouses, while in most other instances they pay more.

In fact, LGBT couples lose out on many tax benefits that are only available to heterosexual married spouses. According to a 2004 Government Accounting Office (GAO) report, there are a total of 1,138 federal rights associated with marital status, including federal income taxes.

One of the few disadvantages of having the right to marry for federal tax purposes occurs when both spouses earn equally large incomes. When this happens, a married couple can end up owing more to Uncle Sam than they would if the law considered them single. This scenario is known as the *marriage penalty* because unmarried partners are able to keep their incomes separate and thus pay less income tax even though they both benefit financially from their combined resources.

The marriage penalty exists because the United States has a progressive tax rate, meaning the more you earn the higher your tax bracket. For example, if you earn $75,000 a year and your partner earns $75,000, as long as you aren't married, you'll both be assessed a 15 percent tax on the first $35,350 and 25 percent tax on the rest. Both of you would have a tax bill of $14,780. After you get legally married, your combined income is $150,000, which puts you in the 28 percent tax bracket meaning you would owe Uncle Sam $29,779 or $219 more than if you filed as two single taxpayers.

If being married means you pay more taxes, why are gay men and lesbians fighting so hard for equal marriage rights? First of all, marriage equality is more than just a tax issue. Even considering just the tax considerations, being married is sometimes more advantageous, because being married and filing jointly doesn't always result in a penalty. Sometimes married partners get a *marriage bonus* instead.

Take for example a scenario where one spouse earns substantially more than the other. Say one spouse earns $175,000 and the other spouse earns much less at $35,000. Because they can file a joint tax return, their federal income tax bill is reduced. That's because more of the higher-earning partner's income gets taxed at lower rates and because married couples are entitled to bigger standard deductions than single taxpayers who are not heads of household.

Although federal income tax law doesn't let LGBT couples file joint returns, you can still make financial decisions that maximum your tax advantages. For example, if you own your home jointly with your partner and both of you are making mortgage payments (whether or not you pay an equal amount), either one of you may claim a mortgage interest deduction on your individual income tax returns (assuming you itemize your deductions).

Even if you don't own property together, you can give a tax-free gift of up to $13,000 annually (in tax year 2012) to your partner, to a child, other relative, friend, or charitable organization that can reduce your tax burden.

 Because the tax law changes so quickly and because the legal status of LGBT partners is ever-evolving, check with a local LGBT friendly tax planner or tax attorney who is familiar with LGBT-related tax issues and regulations in your particular state.

Seeing DOMA's Effects

As this book is being written, the federal DOMA remains the law of the land. Although the Obama administration believes DOMA to be unconstitutional, and his Justice Department recently asked the Supreme Court to determine the constitutionality of Section 3 of DOMA, it still affects you and your partner in many ways, including your wallet and how you file taxes. Section 3 of DOMA codifies the nonrecognition of same-sex marriage for all federal purposes (including the filing of joint tax returns). If the court agrees to hear the DOMA case, it's entirely possible that as early as 2013, the IRS will treat legally recognized same-sex couples the same as married heterosexual spouses and much of what is written here will be moot. (We will endeavor to keep you updated as the ever-changing laws affecting LGBT families at www. dummies.com/go/samesexlegalkit.)

Several DOMA lawsuits are working their way through the legal system. Although the administration will no longer *defend* the constitutionality of DOMA, the administration says it will continue to *enforce* DOMA until either Congress repeals it or the Supreme Court rules it unconstitutional.

Basically the administration *won't* argue the constitutionality of DOMA in a court of law but — if you file a lawsuit based on DOMA's effect on your individual rights — the administration *will* fight you in court as long as DOMA remains the law of the land. If you think that sounds like twisted logic, you're probably right.

A pending Supreme Court review would probably change DOMA's effect. Furthermore any changes in presidential administrations could change the way things are followed, with the worst-case scenario being a ban of same-sex marriages introduced as an amendment to the US Constitution.

For now, DOMA is in effect, and these sections examine the many damaging ways DOMA lays its ugly claws into federal taxes.

How DOMA affects the federal tax code

Because of DOMA, before the Supreme Court even rules on it, your LGBT family isn't recognized as a family in the eyes of the law. In 2004, the GAO issued a report identifying 198 federal taxation laws and policies that directly benefit heterosexual married couples but — on account of DOMA — are denied to married same-sex partners.

As long as DOMA is legitimate federal law, LGBT couples will suffer the following discrimination in the federal tax code:

✔ Legally married same-sex spouses are forced to choose whether to lie about their marital status on their federal income tax returns or risk having their jointly filed return rejected on the grounds that it was fraudulently filed. This puts couples at risk of being assessed a penalty plus interest on their original tax bill.

✔ Because married LGBT spouses can't file jointly, they're unable to add up the costs of their combined expenditures, such as uncompensated medical expenses, which may result in a loss of a federal tax deduction for those expenses.

✓ Comingled finances and expenses must be separated for the purposes of calculating individual taxes. This task is at best difficult and time-consuming, and at worst, impossible.

✓ If a married same-sex couple lives in a state that also allows them to file a joint state tax return, they need to re-mingle their income and expenses for the purpose of that state tax return. Check out the later section, "Considering State Taxes: A Mixed Bag" for more details.

✓ When married couples divorce, federal tax law lets them to equitably divide their marital property without being assessed gift and other taxes incurred when one person gives another person something of value. Conversely, when LGBT married partners split up, transfers of valuable property, such as a home, may be taxable.

✓ When one spouse is compelled to pay spousal support to the other in a divorce proceeding, those support payments can be deducted by the spouse who pays support. Not so for LGBT partners.

✓ When a heterosexual spouse dies, the surviving spouse can claim a marital deduction equal to the fair market value of the property transferred from the deceased spouse's estate to the surviving spouse. The deduction also postpones the requirement to pay federal estate taxes until after the death of the surviving spouse. Again, LGBT spouses don't qualify for this deduction.

As you can see, DOMA creates serious federal tax inequities for same-sex couples and their families. We hope that DOMA will soon be relegated to a footnote in American law like laws banning mixed-race marriages.

If DOMA gets overturned, married same-sex couples living in marriage equality states will probably be entitled to file federal income tax returns as married, filing jointly. Unfortunately, it remains unclear what will happen federally to those couples who have registered as domestic partners or entered into a civil union. Moreover, if a couple gets married in a marriage equality state and then returns home or moves to a state that bans same-sex marriages, will that couple have the right to file a joint federal tax return even if they are not able to file a joint state tax return? This and many other questions remain unanswerable today and possibly for many years to come.

Healthcare benefits are taxed and medical bills cost more

When a married heterosexual employee with employer-provided health insurance puts a spouse on his or her health insurance, the value of that health insurance benefit (for the employee as well as for his or her spouse) isn't considered income, so no tax is owed on the value of that benefit.

But because of DOMA, even same-sex partners who are legally married in their home state are seen as legal strangers in the eyes of the federal government, including the IRS. As a result, even if you're lucky enough to have employer-based health insurance that also covers your same-sex partner, you'll pay more in taxes because your employer and you are required to treat the fair market value of your partner's coverage as taxable income to you.

For instance, if the value of the health insurance coverage for your partner is $5,000 per year, that $5,000 is tacked on to your overall income, except to the extent that you contribute to that $5,000. Like your regular income, the value of your partner's health insurance benefit is then taxed as income, as well as being assessed a tax for FICA (the Federal Insurance Contributions Act that funds Social Security) and Medicare.

This additional tax burden has made it impossible for some LGBT employees to afford to add their partner to their health insurance plan. To address this inequity some larger, more progressive companies have offered to reimburse their LGBT employees to cover the additional taxes on a partner's healthcare benefit. (Of course, because that reimbursement is *itself* income, it is taxed, too! But at least you're then paying a much smaller amount.)

DOMA also creates disparity between heterosexual and LGBT spouses for healthcare expenses. For instance, under federal law, an employee is able to contribute pre-tax wages to a flexible spending account (FSA), which he or she can then use to pay healthcare expenses. When an employee's marriage is legally recognized, the feds let his or her spouse and other qualified dependents use the FSA as well, but because LGBT marriages are *not* recognized under DOMA, a same-sex spouse *may not* use the FSA to help pay his or her medical bills, unless that spouse is also a dependent.

Because a same-sex spouse of an employee with an FSA is still required to make co-payments and pay deductibles and uncovered health expenses using after-tax dollars, it's estimated that same-sex couples who take advantage of employer-based healthcare benefits are deemed to have *imputed income* (noncash compensation to an employees' taxable wages), and as a result they pay an average of $1,500 more per year than their straight counterparts.

Not only does this discriminatory policy hurt LGBT couples, but businesses that employ them incur extra burdens to payroll and additional administrative costs.

No deferral for inherited retirement account balance

If you and your partner aren't planning to rely solely on Social Security benefits in your golden years, one or both of you probably have Individual Retirement Accounts (IRAs) and possibly employer-based retirement accounts into which you contribute a bit each payday.

Assuming you've both named the other as a beneficiary on your retirement accounts, because DOMA doesn't recognize your marriage, when the first partner dies, the surviving partner will immediately have to start withdrawing annual *required minimum distributions* (RMDs), which is a set amount of money from the deceased partner's retirement account. That money is counted as income to the surviving partner and taxed accordingly.

Conversely, legally recognized surviving spouses can roll over a deceased spouse's retirement plan into his or her own IRA, and they're not required to start taking annual RMDs from the rollover IRA until after they turn 70½. Because RMDs are taxable, heterosexual spouses are allowed to collect more tax-deferral benefits than same-sex partners whose marriage isn't recognized by the feds.

Furthermore, because the Social Security Act is a federal law, a same-sex spouse isn't entitled to receive his or her partner's Social Security benefits either.

No tax-free employer benefits

Because of DOMA, gay and lesbian spouses can't take advantage of certain tax-free benefits from their partner's employer unless they qualify as a dependent of the employed partner. We discuss two of those benefits (tax-free health insurance benefits and payouts from FSAs) in the previous section, "Healthcare benefits are taxed and medical bills cost more."

Here are some of the remaining employer-based benefits that are regulated by federal law and therefore currently aren't available to LGBT spouses:

- **Family Medical Leave Act (FMLA):** FMLA allows employees to take a 12-week unpaid leave once a year to take care of a spouse or immediate family member with a "serious health condition." Thanks to DOMA, employers aren't required to offer medical leave to LGBT employees to care for their partners, even if the couple is legally married. But you can take time off to care for your child, and under an interpretation of the law by the Obama administration, even the one of you who isn't a legal or biological parent may also be entitled to leave.

✔ **Employee Retirement Income Security Act (ERISA):** ERISA sets minimum standards for private employer-maintained healthcare and pension plans. Among other things, ERISA determines whether a spouse of an employee has a right to use part of the pension in the event of the employee's death. Because the federal DOMA defines an employee's spouse as being someone of the opposite sex, it's unclear as to whether or not an employee's same-sex spouse is eligible to receive his or her deceased spouse's pension.

✔ **Consolidated Omnibus Budget Reconciliation Act (COBRA):** COBRA requires private employers with 20 or more employees to offer continued healthcare coverage for a defined period of time to employees and their spouses and children if the employee is fired, gets divorced, or dies. DOMA excludes married LGBT couples from automatic protection — leaving it up to employers to choose whether or not to continue coverage.

This list of benefits that are outright denied or at least not provided tax-free to gay and lesbian employees on account of DOMA is just a partial list. Although DOMA doesn't outright prohibit employers from offering benefits to LGBT employees, if the employer chooses not to do so, the employee has no legal recourse.

Considering State Taxes: A Mixed Bag

Even if you and your partner get married or civilly united, if you actually live in a state that doesn't recognize same-sex marriages or treat civil unions and domestic partnerships as marriage-like for tax purposes, you and your partner have to file as single people on both state and federal returns.

If your state *does* recognize the legality of your relationship — even though the feds don't acknowledge your legal union — you'll need to file your state tax returns as a married couple.

When filing a joint state tax return, you're generally asked to plug in the numbers from your federal tax return. But, because you don't file your federal return jointly as a married couple, you'll need to create a mock federal return to get the correct numbers for your state forms. This step is not only time-consuming but also expensive, especially if you use a professional to do your taxes.

The situation gets even "better" for LGBT couples living in community property states. A *community property state* is a state in which property acquired after marriage is considered as belonging to both spouses equally unless it was inherited or given to one spouse as a gift.

Recently the IRS said it would recognize community property owned by a same-sex couple, even though it doesn't recognize the relationship that created the community property in the first place. Generous, no?

So, if you live in a community property state and you're married or in a comparable relationship, because the income you and your partner earned during the year is also considered community property, you need to combine your incomes for state tax purposes and then divide it to file separate federal tax returns.

These new IRS rules have created quite a headache for tax preparers who complain that LGBT couples who divided their income and withholdings risk having their returns rejected by IRS computer programs because the numbers on the returns are inconsistent with those on their W-2s.

Worse, same-sex couples need to provide supplementary forms to their regular tax return explaining the steps they took to divide their property. Because of all of this extra and unusual paperwork, LGBT couples must send their returns by snail mail, which results in a much slower processing of their returns, perhaps six or more months.

Chapter 9

Living Together in Sickness and in Health

*O*ne of the worst indignities LGBT partners sometimes deal with is being treated unfairly and disrespectfully when a partner or child is seriously ill or injured. In addition to the fear and anxiety a partner or parent is already feeling, they face further insults when being made to stay away from their loved one's bedside and kept in the dark as to their partner or child's condition.

Unfortunately, despite social, political, and legal gains, some healthcare providers or hostile family members — in the most critical time of need — continue to treat LGBT Americans as though they're undeserving of kindness, empathy, and understanding.

Even partners who've been sharing resources and responsibilities for decades are sometimes denied the right to make medical and financial decisions and visit an ill or injured loved one in the hospital. Virtually every gay and lesbian person knows someone or has a friend of a friend who has suffered the heartache of being treated as a stranger to his or her partner.

Sometimes the decision to deny rights to same-sex partners is made on account of a stated policy, but every now and then someone, such as a nurse or bank teller, will decide to enforce a "rule" that may or may not be valid policy.

Fortunately for the LGBT community, in 1990, the US Supreme Court ruled that you have a constitutional right to direct your own healthcare, and, if you put your instructions in writing, those wishes must be followed.

The good news is that you can avoid anxiety and create financial and medical decision-making authority — as well as hospital visitation rights — fairly easily by making *advance directives* (financial power of attorney, living will, and medical power of attorney). This chapter explains what you can do to protect yourself and your loved ones before you find yourself in this situation. This chapter addresses other health-related issues you and your partner may face in your senior years, including Medicaid and nursing home care.

Advance Directives: Taking Action before an Illness or Injury

The term "advance directive" may sound self-explanatory. It simply means writing down your directions for financial and healthcare decision making in advance before something happens to you.

In this book we use *advance directives* to describe a set of legal documents that let you put your wishes in writing about who you want to make medical and financial decision for you and what medical treatment (if any) you want performed in case you're unable to speak for yourself. As we discuss advance directives throughout this chapter, we also explain about other supporting documents that enhance the power and authority you and your partner can give to each other.

Several kinds of advance directives exist that you can make, but for the purpose of this book we focus on the basic documents necessary to give LGBT couples specific rights, power, and authority over financial and medical matters. You want to sign these documents:

✔ A living will

✔ A medical power of attorney

✔ A durable power of attorney (DPOA)

Creating advance directives, especially for an LGBT couple, is imperative before it's too late. After your treating physician and another doctor who performs an examination determines competency, you're mentally incapable of making your own financial and healthcare decisions, that's it. You can't create advance directives if you aren't competent to do so. Therefore, if either you or your partner has a chronic health condition or a terminal illness, read this chapter and make your advance directives right away.

You can find sample advance directives (Form 9-1) on the accompanying CD. You can also find free, state specific legal documents online by searching the phrase "free gay and lesbian advance directives" or words to that effect.

In the following sections, we introduce you to the most effective means of using advance directives (in the forms of a living will and a medical power of attorney) to ensure your wishes for medical treatment are followed when you can't speak for yourself:

Making decisions about end-of-life treatment with a living will

All 50 states allow a competent adult to create a *living will* (a legal document that lets you make known your wishes regarding your medical treatment when you can't speak for yourself) to control decisions about his or her own health care. As long as you're mentally competent, you can revoke your living will and, if you desire, make a new one.

Gays and lesbians especially need to have a living will because it does the following:

✔ It informs your healthcare providers and your family about your instructions for your medical treatment in the event you aren't able to speak for yourself.

Generally, the treatment options in a living will are dependent on whether you have been diagnosed with a terminal illness, are in a persistent vegetative state (permanently and irreversibly unconscious) or are experiencing such a severe and worsening physical or mental deterioration that your quality of life is effectively nonexistent and you'll never again have the ability to make your own decisions.

If you're in the end stages of your life and don't want your life or suffering prolonged, a living will lets you choose whether or not you want doctors to provide or withhold the following treatments:

- Life-sustaining treatments (treatments that may not cure you, but will keep you alive)

- Treatment and care to make you comfortable and to relieve pain

- The care necessary to provide for your personal hygiene (bathing, combing your hair, and so on)

- Experimental drugs, therapy, or treatment that may or may not be effective in prolonging your life

- Cardiopulmonary resuscitation (CPR)

- Mechanical ventilation (ventilator or breathing machine)

- Blood transfusions

- Maximum pain relief, even if it hastens your death

- Artificial nutrition and hydration (food and water administered intravenously or via a feeding tube)

✔ It increases your partner's credibility when he or she makes medical decisions that may conflict with the wishes of your family members but that agrees with what you've stated on your living will.

✔ It lets you leave instructions about your own healthcare for a variety of potential medical problems and allows you to choose whether you do or don't want specific medical treatments and procedures performed.

A living will only handles these critical decisions if you aren't able to communicate your wishes. It doesn't take away your right to request life support, pain medication, artificial nutrition, or hydration if you're able to speak for yourself. Furthermore, if there is even a slight chance that you'll recover, your living will *doesn't* authorize your doctor or healthcare proxy to pull the plug on you.

Some living wills are stand-alone documents while others include healthcare powers of attorney and/or organ donation forms. We describe these and other advance directives in the next few sections. We include generic living will samples on the CD (see Form 9-2).

Each state has its own requirements for what to include in a living will, and those requirements can change from year to year. The sample living will on the CD exists only as a guide for how to fill out the various options that are on most living wills. Most living will forms also have blank spaces where you can add directions that may not otherwise be listed on the document. To get an up-to-date living will for your state, either visit an attorney or use one of the many online resources where you can obtain a free living will. Just type the phrase "free gay and lesbian living will" into a search engine for several sources.

Don't confuse a living will with a living trust or a last will and testament, which are legal documents for distributing your property after your death. We explain a last will in Chapter 12 and living trusts in Chapter 13.

Understanding how mental competency is established

Mental incompetence has both a medical and a legal meaning. For a last will and testament to be valid, the person making the will must be of sound mind. According to the law, you are of sound mind if you know who you are, where you are, and what you are doing.

For advance directives, no singular mechanism is in place to determine when your mental incompetence will trigger a reliance on the instructions set forth in your living will, powers of attorney, and other documents.

Obviously, while you're unconscious, you are at least temporarily unable to make your own decisions. In that case, your living will and other advance directives will be followed until you regain consciousness and your mental competence can be assessed.

If your condition appears permanent, your treating physician will establish incompetency after careful examination, diagnostic testing, and consultations with one or more specialists. If your physician's diagnosis is challenged, a court may need to make a legal finding of mental incapacity by reviewing medical records and hearing testimony from your healthcare proxy, family members, and/or medical experts.

Naming someone to oversee your health care using a medical power of attorney

A medical power of attorney, also called a *durable power of attorney for healthcare, a designation of healthcare surrogate,* or an *appointment of healthcare proxy,* depending on your state, allows you to name your partner or someone else you trust to make your medical decisions if you're unable to make them yourself. Some states merge a living will and medical power of attorney into one document, generally called an *advance healthcare directive.*

Just like a living will, a medical power of attorney has a unique format in each state. In order to make sure your document accurately reflects your state's requirements, you need to check with a local attorney or search online for free, state specific medical powers of attorney with language designed specifically for the LGBT community.

The accompanying CD has a sample medical power of attorney (see Form 9-3). The CD includes a table that lists the title of each state's medical advance directives and whether they're separate documents or are combined into one (see Form 9-4).

Selecting a healthcare proxy

Choosing someone to be in charge of your healthcare decisions is by far one of the most challenging jobs you'll ever ask anyone to do for you. If you're in a long-term, committed relationship, chances are you will want to appoint your partner to make your healthcare decisions. In this book we refer to your healthcare agent as your *proxy*. If you're single with children older than 18, perhaps you want one or more of them to act on your behalf.

If you're unable to communicate your wishes by speaking, writing, or gesturing, your healthcare proxy will step in to

- ✔ Interact and coordinate with your physicians
- ✔ Make decisions about your healthcare, therapy, medications, and treatment

 Appoint an alternate proxy in case your first choice is unavailable. Doing so guarantees you always have an advocate who can make sure your wishes are carried out — especially because you're most vulnerable when you're unable to communicate your wishes.

 If you're naming your spouse, partner, or child as your proxy, you likely already trust this person, and he or she probably knows your wishes. But if you're appointing someone who doesn't know you as well, you should at least choose someone you trust and who you believe understands and respects your feelings and wishes regarding what medical treatment you would want in various circumstances.

 Some states restrict who can serve as your proxy. For example, your healthcare providers are often prohibited to serve as your proxy because their judgment may be biased due to their self-interest.

The person you choose to be your healthcare proxy should also be self-confident and assertive enough to advocate for your rights, especially when your family members disagree with the decisions he or she is making on your behalf.

 You want to name only one person as proxy to avoid confusing your doctors with conflicting healthcare instructions. You can request that your proxy consult with others before making a final healthcare decision, but giving decision-making authority to more than one proxy at a time is unwise.

Granting authority to your proxy

In your medical power of attorney you have the option to give your proxy very broad authority over your medical decision making or you can limit that authority by specifying what areas of your healthcare your proxy does or doesn't have authority over.

Perhaps the most important feature of the relationship you should have with your healthcare proxy — regardless of their connection to you — is your belief in that person's willingness to instruct your physician to give or withhold medical treatments or procedures even when those instructions go against your proxy's own beliefs.

And every now and then a situation may arise that your healthcare directives don't directly address. For example, if your doctor proposes a treatment that isn't specified in your medical power of attorney, your proxy will be required to infer from all your other instruction what he or she thinks you would choose to do.

Any decision your proxy makes will be based upon his or her understanding of your wishes, the treatments recommended by your doctor, and the instructions written in your medical power of attorney and/or living will. So, before you fill in your medical power of attorney, sit down with your proxy and alternate proxy and tell them exactly what you need them to know.

If you and your partner break up, whether or not you enter into a new relationship, you may want to prepare a new medical power of attorney that reflects the change in your circumstances. No law requires you to name your spouse or legally recognized domestic partner as your proxy, but if you decide to name someone else to make your healthcare decisions, be sure you create that document after the date of your marriage or partnership. Otherwise, your legal marriage, civil union, or domestic partnership registration may automatically revoke your original medical power of attorney.

Tell your family members, especially those you anticipate will try to upset your partner, that you've made this document and that you appointed your partner or someone else. Just knowing you gave authority to someone else may be all that is needed to stop them from trying to usurp that authority.

In addition to granting authority to make medical decisions, you also want to give your partner hospital visitation rights. You can accomplish this by creating a stand-alone hospital visitation document or by adding a clause in your medical power of attorney.

We include a sample stand-alone hospital visitation document and an example of a hospital visitation clause to be added to a medical power of attorney on the accompanying CD (refer to Forms 9-5 and 9-6).

Comprehending medical privacy laws

According to the law in most states, if you're appointed as your partner's proxy to make healthcare decisions, you also have the right to access his or her medical records so that you can give *informed consent* (where a doctor fully informs you about medical treatments, tests, and possible side effects) before agreeing to a particular treatment or test.

Unfortunately, having a valid medical power of attorney granting you authority to act on behalf of your same-sex partner doesn't guarantee that some healthcare providers won't ignore that document.

Therefore, even if your medical power of attorney should be all that is necessary for you to access your partner's medical records, some medical institutions still require you to sign a Health Insurance Portability and Accountability Act (HIPAA) form.

Congress enacted HIPAA mainly for these reasons:

- ✔ To enable new employees to obtain health insurance coverage sooner
- ✔ To allow you to maintain your health insurance coverage between jobs
- ✔ To create national standards for securing electronically stored and transmitted healthcare information
- ✔ To keep your healthcare information and your medical records private

Given the potential for medical personnel and/or family members to disregard your authority — in addition to ensuring your access to necessary healthcare information — a HIPAA authorization form provides further proof of your partner's desires and intentions.

Many medical facilities have their own HIPAA form that is unique to their specific compliance efforts. If you have the opportunity to sign a pre-approved form prior to or at admission, you should do so.

However, if you're taken to a hospital in an emergency situation, you may not have time to sign a hospital approved form. Therefore, we provide a sample HIPAA form that complies with the federal statute (45 C.F.R. §164.508) on the CD (see Form 9-7) that should be acceptable to any medical facility.

Keep the original of your HIPAA form — along with your other medical advance directives — in a convenient, easily accessible location so that your proxy will be able to get them in case of an emergency.

Designating an agent to oversee your financial matters: Your DPOA

A durable power of attorney (DPOA) gives you the right to appoint an *agent*, also called an *attorney-in-fact* (someone you trust to pay your bills, write checks on your account, buy and sell property, make investments, and other financial decisions) while you're mentally incompetent — whether or not you will recover.

If you have a fully funded living revocable trust (refer to Chapters 13 and 14 where we discuss them in more depth), the authority granted under your DPOA will be limited to assets that are *not* in your trust. If you've appointed the same person as the successor trustee of your trust and agent under your DPOA, then this gives that person broad powers and control over all your assets.

These sections investigate the different powers in which you can give control to your agent and explain important pointers for you to remember as you select your agent if you decide to set up a DPOA.

Determining what power to give your agent

You can decide whether you want this power to become effective when you sign the document or if you would rather have it take effect when you become incapacitated. Your DPOA ceases to be effective upon your death. A power of attorney is *durable* because the authority it grants continues even after you become mentally incompetent.

You have the option of granting your agent broad power over your finances or you can limit his or her authority to just a few financial matters. Generally, a DPOA includes a list of powers with a space for your initials beside each one. When you initialize a power, you effectively authorize your agent to act as though he or she is you. Refer to the accompanying CD for a sample DPOA (refer to Form 9-8).

The list of optional powers may include the authority to:

✔ Pay your bills

✔ Handle your financial accounts, such as pay fees, make deposits and withdrawals, and so on

✔ Manage and maintain your real property, pay for upkeep, make mortgage payments, lease or sell your property, and pay your property taxes

✔ File and pay your personal taxes

✔ Invest your money in stocks, bonds, mutual funds, and so on

✔ Oversee your business's operation

✔ Fund your trust

✔ Hire professionals (lawyers, physicians, appraisers, accountants, and so on) as needed

You can and should modify your DPOA to fit your particular circumstances. For example, if you choose to give your agent the power to manage your real property, you may want to specify that the power granted doesn't allow your agent to sell your home while you're incapacitated.

A DPOA is a powerful legal document and thus you should carefully consider whether to create one. Never give so much power and authority over your finances to anyone you don't trust — even if that person is your partner.

Signing a DPOA authorizes your agent to act on your behalf. No one relying on the authority granted in this document will be held responsible for your agent's negligence, honest mistakes, or intentional wrongdoing.

State laws require an agent to be careful with your money and property. In other words, he or she isn't allowed to purposefully squander or steal your assets. As long as the agent acts prudently (wisely and with caution), even if your agent loses your money, he or she will not be liable for those losses.

Picking an agent

If you decide to create a DPOA, consider naming the person you named as your healthcare proxy as your agent to oversee your finances. (Refer to the earlier section, "Selecting a healthcare proxy" for more information.) Picking the same person should reduce the possibility of a power struggle between two people who would otherwise need to work very closely to make sure your medical and financial needs are met.

Most people choose their partner, close family member, or friend as their agent, and thus, when such losses occur, it may cause irreparable harm to the relationship.

If you are concerned about your agent having too much power over your assets — even if you do have faith he or she won't act inappropriately — you can direct in your DPOA that your agent provide a monthly or quarterly accounting of every transaction to another person you name.

Some states restrict who can serve as your agent. For example, an attorney or someone working for a financial institution may be prohibited to serve as your agent because his or her judgment may be biased due to self-interest.

If you decide to name an alternate agent in case your first choice is unable or unwilling to act on your behalf, use the same criteria you used in making your first choice.

Talk to the person you want to name as your agent under your DPOA. Of course, get this person's permission and tell him or her what you expect done. And don't forget to tell your family members — especially those you antici-pate will try to upset your partner — that you've created this document.

Signing the proper documents to protect you and your loved ones

Even though you don't like to think about issues of serious injury, sickness, and death, they're a fact of life. Preparing for what is inevitable makes sense so you're ready for whatever life presents you. State and federal laws already recognize every adult person has the right of self-determination in making healthcare and financial decisions — as long as that person is competent. You just need to make sure you sign the proper documents.

Each state has its own requirements as to what constitutes a valid living will, medical, and financial power of attorney. Some state legislatures provide a sample form right in the statute while others spell out specifically what language is required to make the document valid.

Several legitimate sources are available where you can get advance directives that are valid in your state:

- ✔ **From a local attorney:** Prices range anywhere from $50 to $500, just for these three documents.

- ✔ **From your local medical facility:** They're usually free of charge.

- ✔ **From Rainbow Law:** It has been providing free state specific advance directives for the LGBT community since 1999.

Perhaps you believe neither you nor your partner will ever experience sudden illness or injury that causes you to temporarily or permanently lose *mental capacity* (the ability to understand your current circumstances and the consequences of any decisions you make). That may be so, but even if you manage to live to be 100 years old, deteriorating changes associated with aging can, over time, affect your decision-making ability.

Because the inability to make rational and reasonable decisions for yourself is a foreseeable reality, make sure you take the time to plan ahead in order to spare your loved ones — especially your same-sex partner (who may be simultaneously dealing with hostile family members and medical personnel) — any additional and unnecessary stress.

Tell members of your immediate family (parents, siblings, aunts, uncles, and so on) that you created advance directives appointing your partner as your decision maker. Just by taking this one, perhaps difficult step, you may be sparing your partner a massive struggle with your family later on.

After you've signed your documents:

- ✔ **Create a small card to keep in your wallet or purse that names your partner as your agent and proxy.** Make sure his or her work, home, and/or cell numbers are also listed. If possible, laminate the card to keep it legible. Doing this may get your partner past that first hurdle of having been notified before anyone else with authority to act immediately established.

- ✔ **Make several copies of your medical advance directives.** Give one set to your treating physician and another to your proxy and alternate proxy.

- ✔ **Keep copies of your medical power of attorney and your living will in the glove box of all your vehicles and in the overnight bag you take whenever you travel.** Make sure these documents are ready to travel with you wherever you go. When you keep copies in your glove compartment and overnight bag, you're always ready for an unforeseen emergency.

- ✔ **Keep the original documents in a safe, convenient, easy-to-access location.** That way your agent or proxy can get to them no matter if an emergency occurs over a holiday or in the middle of the night.

- ✔ **Give copies of your financial DPOA to every financial institution where you have an account.** Do the same with insurance agents and so on, depending on the powers you initial on your DPOA.

If you belong to a church, synagogue, temple, or other religious organization, you may want to give a copy of your advance directives to your clergyperson. Then, if someone tries to thwart your wishes on account of a religious objection, your partner will have an excellent advocate to counter any argument made on religious grounds.

Knowing Your Rights as Your Partner's Decision Maker with Visitation Rights

LBGT people have to deal with unfair actions, laws, and policies all the time. These inequities are far worse when they happen during times of crisis, which is why having advance directives is important to protect the rights of your family of choice when you aren't able to stand up for them.

Unfortunately, just because you and your partner sign advance directives doesn't mean healthcare providers or family members won't challenge your rights and authority to act under them. Therefore you need to understand what rights you do have, and when those rights are violated, what you can do about it.

A real-world story leads to LGBT visitation rights

President Barack Obama was inspired to enact the new rule after hearing the story of Janice Langbehn, a lesbian, whose partner, Lisa Pond, died alone in a Miami hospital while she and their three adopted children — despite having advance medical directives authorizing health-care decision making and hospital visitation — were forced to sit for hours in a waiting room. Langbehn said a hospital social worker told her she was "in an antigay city and state" and thus she would not be allowed to see her partner.

In the memo issued with the new regulation, President Obama wrote: "In these hours of need and moments of pain and anxiety, all of us would hope to have a hand to hold, a shoulder on which to lean — a loved one to be there for us, as we would be there for them."

These sections reveal new rules recently enacted by the Obama administration that should help to put a stop to challenges by healthcare providers. In the event those rules are rescinded by the next president or if medical personnel ignore them, we also provide steps you can to take to assert the rights and authority granted to you by your partner.

The authority to make medical and financial decisions derives from the powers granted in your advance directives, and those rights should be honored regardless of the sex or sexual orientation of the person you appoint to make those decisions.

Enacting new rules for Medicaid and LGBT couples

Until recently, same-sex couples didn't have any guarantees that they would be allowed to visit their partner in the hospital — even with written authorization from the patient directing that a partner be given primary rights to hospital visitation. All that changed in January 2011 when President Barack Obama announced new federal Health and Human Services (HHS) hospital visitation regulations that extend to same-sex couples the same visitation rights as heterosexual couples.

Under the new regulations, LGBT patients being treated at hospitals and other medical facilities that accept Medicare and Medicaid now have the right to say who can visit and who can make medical decisions on their own behalf. Although this regulation is a positive step forward for LGBT rights, remember that the next president could just as easily reverse the hospital visitation rule.

In Chapter 19, we discuss ways that you can get involved in the LGBT equality movement. Marriage equality isn't just an interesting debate that gets heated up every four years in a presidential election season. As long as the law treats gay and lesbian families as non-families and LGBT people as undeserving of legal equality, the consequences to families will continue to be grave.

Dealing with biased healthcare providers

Opponents of equal marriage rights often say that same-sex couples can just sign a few legal papers and, like magic, their problems will disappear. Sadly, the reality is that valid legal documents don't always guarantee smooth sailing when a loved one is critically ill or injured.

Theoretically, with the new rules enacted by Obama requiring healthcare facilities receiving Medicaid and Medicare payments to honor the visitation and decision-making rights of LGBT couples, problems with narrow-minded medical personnel should be few and far between. Unfortunately, a few individuals will fail to follow the rules. When confronting a difficult healthcare provider, we suggest you do the following to be able to visit your partner:

1. **Remain calm and try to speak respectfully to whomever is caring for your seriously ill or injured partner.**

2. **Provide a copy of your partner's advance directives granting you hospital visitation and healthcare decision-making rights.**

3. **If that doesn't work, print a copy of the HHS rule and give it to the doctor, charge nurse, nursing supervisor, social worker, or someone working in the administrator's office.**

   You may want to contact the local media (TV, radio, and newspapers) to tell the story. Hospitals are businesses and don't like negative publicity.

4. **If you still can't get results you want, contact your local US representative or senator to report a violation of the HHS rule.**

   You may consider hiring an attorney as well to intervene.

We include a copy of the new Health and Human Services (HHS) hospital visitation rule, CMS-2010-0207-1232 for your convenience on the accompanying CD (see Form 9-9).

Sharing a last name with your partner and kids has its advantages

You may want to consider changing your last name so you and your partner share the same last name. Although you may have some costs associated with a name change, you may find a couple advantages of having the same name:

- ✔ Getting over the family-only policy may be easier so you can step in and immediately have the ability to make decisions for and offer comfort to your loved ones in their time of need.

- ✔ Your partner and children may be accepted as your immediate family by your blood relatives, friends, your children's teachers, doctors, neighbors, and your community — even where marriage and civil unions aren't available.

In other words, having the same name is often all that is required to establish a familial relationship with someone, which is the primary reason gay men and lesbians give for wanting to change their name.

Many LGBT partners have opted to change their last names. Some choose a hyphenated hybrid of both partners' last names, others choose to adopt their partner's last name, and a few choose to create and share a new name that didn't belong to either of them.

If you live in a state that recognizes same-sex marriage and you and your partner get married, you should be able to change your name simply by virtue of that marriage. People who don't live in a state that recognizes same-sex marriage needs to petition their local court for a legal name change.

Anyone can change their name, as long as he or she isn't doing so for fraudulent reasons. For example, you can't change your name simply to avoid paying a creditor or to elude a punishment or penalty for committing a crime. The cost of changing your name varies from state to state and can range from $100 to $500 or more, depending on whether or not you hire an attorney or do it yourself.

Some counties allow you to do a *pro se* (do-it-yourself) name change and offer free or inexpensive forms as well as detailed instructions on their website for proceeding. To find your county's website or phone number, type your county's name and the phrase "county clerk" into a search engine. If your county has no website, call the clerk's office and ask if it has forms available. When you perform the online search, even if your county doesn't have a website, the clerk's phone number should be listed in the results.

Several online document preparation services provide forms and instructions necessary to do your own name change. Again, the best way to find one of these sites is to perform an online search using the phrase "gay name change" or something to that effect.

Besides the cost of the initial filing of the petition, you also have the cost of a background check, fees for publishing one or more public notices in the newspaper, and money for postage for certified mailings and fees associated with notarial services. In truth, determining the exact cost of a name change is difficult because it depends on the circumstances of your particular case and your state or local filing requirements. You may have additional costs related to making necessary changes to your driver's license, Social Security card, and passport. You should also get a new birth certificate to reflect your new name.

Every time you change your name, you create a new alias and leave a trail of documents with different names along the way. That is why you should make sure your legal documents identify you not only by the name you now have, but also list your previous name in parentheses the first time your name is listed. For example, if you were born with the name Zelda Smith, and later change your name to Zelda Smith-Jones, the first time your name is stated on the document, it should read "Zelda Smith-Jones (also known as Zelda Smith)." Instead of "also known as" you can shorten it to "aka."

Coping with hostile family members

When your partner is taken to a hospital or other medical facility, more than likely you will be dealing with all sorts of emotions, including fear, anxiety, and helplessness. The last thing you want is drama with family members who don't respect you and your partner's wishes.

In the event that your partner was in an accident or had a medical emergency, you may not be notified until after your partner's family members have arrived and established themselves as being in charge. If you were with your partner or had notice of the emergency, you may be the person who registers your partner and will therefore have a chance to give copies of the advance directives before anyone else arrives. Whichever situation you find yourself in, chances are good that a disgruntled family member at any time can decide to disregard your authority over and rights to your partner.

Having legal documents in your hand is hardly comforting if your partner's family decides to interfere with your authority by giving orders to doctors that go against your partner's written directives. And you can certainly feel intimidated, sitting vulnerably in your partner's hospital room with a horde of disrespectful family members insulting you or just staring you down.

Although you may have advance directives, medical staff sometimes can ignore you even if they're sympathetic to your plight because pushy and aggressive family members bully them.

If you encounter your partner's hostile family, the most important thing is to remain calm and be patient, even in the face of possible insults and name-calling. Remember, you're here for your partner, not his or her family and not for yourself.

If you're forced to be in the same room with your partner's hostile family:

- ✔ **Try to avoid speaking to them.** If you must, keep the conversations neutral. Avoid discussing anything other than what needs to be said about your partner's healthcare.

- ✔ **Don't get lured into debating issues, like religion, politics, or other topics that tend to create conflict.** If one of them tries to engage you in a discussion that will probably become an argument, change the subject or leave the room.

- ✔ **Accept them for who they are.** Try to imagine how they're feeling. They also love your partner and must be just as worried as you are.

- ✔ **Try to be polite but realize you don't need to put up with their abusive behavior.** You can be assertive and set boundaries when one or more of them treats you in an unacceptable way.

- ✔ **Make sure you have your own support system.** If possible, ask your friends to take turns sitting with you while you're at your partner's bedside or in a waiting room with his or her family. Choose people who won't try to confront or antagonize the family.

- ✔ **Know when it's time to distance yourself from the unhealthy atmosphere.** If your partner's family can't be in the same room with you without saying or doing something rude, you may need to remove yourself from their presence. Ask the doctor or floor nurse to arrange a visitation schedule so you and the family can take turns sitting by your partner's bedside.

No matter the outcome, you and your partner's family will eventually part ways. In the meantime, you may need to remind yourself that it's only a matter of time before you get your life back, so take a deep breath and breathe. Chapter 20 has ten tips that can help if you encounter unsympathetic relatives.

Uncovering Problems with LGBT Seniors and Nursing Home Care

A greater and greater number of Americans are reaching old age (thanks to the baby boom after World War II). This increase includes those people who identify as LGBT. The number of gay men and lesbians in need of nursing home care is also rising as are concerns that traditional nursing home policies and staff may not be ready or willing to deal with the influx of LGBT elders.

Nursing homes and long-term care facilities tend to be staffed primarily by nurse's aides under the supervision of a nurse. Prior to the passage of the Nursing Home Reform Act (NHRA) in 1987, nursing homes were fraught with abuse and neglect by untrained and under-supervised staff.

The NHRA established specific rights of which all nursing homes receiving Medicaid and Medicare must bestow upon their residents. These rights include the right to privacy, the right to be free from abuse and neglect, and the right to be treated with dignity and respect.

Nursing homes that are in compliance have vastly improved the living conditions for most residents. Unfortunately, recent investigations by undercover journalists have revealed a different sort of abuse: discriminatory actions, and neglect and psychological and physical abuse of LGBT residents by uninformed, bigoted, and ill-trained nurse's aides and other auxiliary staff.

After many news stories were published revealing abuses to LGBT seniors in nursing homes, a new study was conducted by the Department of Housing and Urban Development (HUD) and LGBT advocacy organizations. These studies not only expose LGBT specific abuse, they also point out the need to update the NHRA to require additional education and training around the issue of LGBT rights. We hope these updates will result in a healthier and more accepting environment for LGBT residents of nursing homes.

Enforcing the rights of LGBT nursing home residents

Horror stories of NHRA violations describe how gay and lesbian residents of nursing homes are neglected, abused, and kept apart from their loved ones and other residents because of their sexual orientation.

Nursing home care for the "hidden population"

Because older gay men and lesbians have lived their lives in a society that's been hostile toward them, they may be more likely than heterosexual seniors to end-up living in a nursing home for these reasons:

✔ They may be estranged from their immediate family and thus don't have the luxury of moving in with supportive relatives when they're no longer able to live alone.

✔ Thanks to DOMA, same-sex partners are ineligible for certain tax and other benefits (automatically available to heterosexual married spouses) that provide more options for dependent care living. For example, the pensions of LGBT couples are taxed at the maximum withholding rate, and, unlike federally recognized legal spouses, gay and lesbian partners (whether married or not) aren't eligible for Family and Medical Leave Act (FMLA) benefits.

✔ According to a recent study by the Center for American Progress, because LGBT seniors are often reluctant to expose themselves to uninformed or antigay healthcare professionals, many delay seeking even routine medical treatment which can result in a "premature" admission to a nursing home facility.

If you're being abused in a nursing home, tell your partner, friend, or family member the next time they visit. If you don't get visitors, tell someone who is visiting another resident. If you have access to a phone, call adult protective services (look online for the number) to file a complaint. If all else fails, call a nursing home abuse lawyer. Generally, they are easy to find in the Yellow Pages under attorneys.

If you're visiting a loved one in a nursing home and notice bruises, unresponsiveness, poor hygiene, or other physical or emotional signs of abuse, don't ignore it! Instead, stay calm and do the following:

✔ **Ask your loved one (or another resident) what happened.** If he or she is reluctant to answer, make sure he or she isn't acting out of fear of retribution, loyalty to a staff member, or because they do not want to upset you.

✔ **If you have a camera, take photos.** Pictures speak louder than words, especially because wounds and bruises can heal quickly. A photograph provides a permanent record of the abuse that won't fade over time.

✔ **Ask to speak to the charge nurse or supervising nurse.** Have that person examine the resident and explain the cause of the injury or suspected abuse.

✔ **While the nurse is examining and explaining what happened, take notes or use your cell phone to record what he or she is telling you.** When you create a record of the explanation, you can challenge any future changes to the story. Because he or she will see that you're taking notes or making a recording, the nurse may also be less likely to embellish the explanation.

✔ **If you aren't satisfied that the nurse is addressing your concerns, by law, you have a right to discuss the issue with the facility manager.** Nursing homes are legally obligated to post the names and contact information of all staff members, including supervisors and facility managers.

✔ **If you don't already have a one, get a copy of the facility's written policy regarding injury, abuse, and neglect.** Nursing home facilities are required by law to maintain written policies and procedures regarding grievance procedures and other matters of concern to residents and families.

✔ **If you believe your loved one's life is in danger, call 911 immediately.** In case of a life-threatening emergency, you don't have time to go through a formal grievance process. You need to take immediate steps to remove your loved one from the facility. The best way to do so is to call 911 and let the authorities determine the best way to proceed.

Although you will be experiencing many emotions, try to speak to the aide, staff, and manager calmly and professionally — and give them time to explain what happened. We hope they have a reasonable explanation.

If the explanation is unsatisfactory or if you notice your loved one's condition isn't improving or getting worse, contact adult protective services and file a complaint against the facility. You can find adult protective services in the social services section of your phone book's Yellow Pages, on the website of the National Council on Aging, or by calling 800-677-1116. You should also consult with a nursing home abuse lawyer to discuss the situation and find out what legal steps, if any, you should take.

Choosing a facility that supports you and/or your relationship

If you have all the financial resources you need, you probably have a wide range of opportunities when deciding where to reside after you retire. On the contrary, disadvantaged LGBT folks with limited funds have very few options and may be forced to live in a nursing home or other facility that isn't gay friendly. Finding a nursing home where you feel welcome and respected and part of a community is important.

Studies show LGBT elders are likely to face discrimination by ignorant or unfriendly nursing home staff and fellow residents. We hope the NHRA will soon be updated to include new guidelines for LGBT residents, so every gay and lesbian living in a residential facility receiving Medicaid and Medicare will be treated with respect and dignity.

Frances's story: Nursing home nightmare

Frances, an out lesbian and New York City nursing home resident, was kept tied to her bed with restraints for so long that she suffered severe bed sores all over her body. The staff abused Frances because she was a lesbian, and they didn't want her interacting with the other residents. When Frances refused to stay in her room, the staff physically restrained her, and then ignored her pleas for help. Frances died of sepsis, resulting from untreated sores and ulcers, and her daughter sued the facility.

In 2009, the Third Circuit court held in favor of Frances's daughter and found that LGBT nursing home residents have the right to bring a private right of action against Medicaid-funded nursing homes for violating the NHRA.

This and other cases like it, along with proposed new LGBT-centered rules for NHRA, mean LGBT residents of nursing homes and other long-term care facilities can and should seek legal redress for abuse and neglect to themselves and their family members.

If you're a single gay man or lesbian, you'll simply decide for yourself where you want to live, and you don't necessarily need to worry about trying to interact with a partner while in a nursing home facility. However, if you're in a relationship, you probably want to move into a retirement facility with your partner where one or both of you can get increasing levels of care as needed.

Unfortunately, some facilities don't permit same-sex couples to live together as a couple (although they may let you live together if you claim to be siblings — something biracial couples can't get away with), and even when they do, some seniors report being shunned or worse by staff and/or other residents.

If you want to move to an LGBT friendly facility, you may need to move to one of these states that, as of this writing, have one or more LGBT retirement facilities: Arizona, California, Delaware, Florida, North Carolina, Massachusetts, Minnesota, New Mexico, Ohio, Oregon, and Texas. To locate an LGBT-friendly retirement facility, visit the national resource center for LGBT aging at http://www.lgbtagingcenter.org/resources/area.cfm.

Paying for long-term care: Get your financial ducks in a row

Nursing home care is expensive, and many times people end up paying thousands of dollars for this care when they need it. As a result, oftentimes they end up selling all their possession to pay for the care. Before you sell everything you own to move into a nursing home, you ought to consider a few things.

Differentiating between an assisted living facility and a nursing home

Residing in an assisted living facility is a bit like living in a college dorm. Residents have their own apartment in a facility that also provides planned activities and one or more communal meals each day. Some facilities also provide housekeeping, laundry, and transportation services as well as exercise and wellness programs. An assisted living environment can help seniors by providing opportunities for socializing with other residents and by assisting with activities that may be difficult or impossible to do alone, such as bathing, dressing, and remembering to take medication.

Nursing home residents live in an environment that is more like a hospital than an apartment.

Generally, residents are under the care of a licensed nursing staff (if in a skilled nursing facility) or of certified nursing assistants (if in an intermediate-care facility). Nursing homes are reserved for seniors and others with serious medical conditions, for example, if they're bed-ridden, have dementia, or are recovering from surgery or a serious illness.

Many of the new LGBT-centered retirement facilities offer the ability to transition, depending on your level of need, from independent living to assisted living, and then, if needed, to a nursing home — all located on the same property.

The best way to protect yourself and your partner is to buy life insurance policies and invest in personal retirement accounts. On these accounts and policies, make sure you name your partner as beneficiary. In Chapter 15, we explain how to go about setting up a retirement account and getting an insurance policy that will help to cover these expenses in your old age.

You can help pay for nursing home care using the following devices:

- ✔ **Life insurance policies:** One of the best ways to protect yourself and your partner is to buy a life insurance policy that names your partner as the beneficiary. Obviously, a life insurance policy doesn't pay out funds until the insured person dies. But if you and your partner own a life insurance policy on each other, when the first partner dies, the surviving partner can use those funds to pay for his or her own or the deceased partner's nursing home expenses.

- ✔ **Personal retirement accounts:** If you have an IRA, 401(k), or other retirement account, you'll be better able to afford the cost of a nursing home. If you name your partner the beneficiary of your account, assuming there's anything left in the account after you die, your partner will inherit the remaining funds to either pay off your expenses or his or her own.

- ✔ **Your private health insurance:** If you have it, you may not have access to nursing home benefits for yourself and your partner unless the policy specifically provides for domestic partners.

If you do have this coverage, you may need to provide your insurance company with a written statement that you and your partner are in a domestic partnership. You may also be required to officially register as domestic partners in your county or state. See Chapter 15 for more info on registering as domestic partners.

Because of DOMA, under Social Security law, you and your partner won't have access to survivor benefits or spousal retirement benefits. As a result, you need to consider the potential loss of income if the higher earning partner passes away first because the partner with a lower (or no) income may not have enough of their own Social Security or other retirement benefits to have a decent standard of living.

Federal pension and income tax law are geared toward heterosexual married spouses, therefore senior gay and lesbian couples should understand their retirement income and benefits will likely end upon their death, leaving little or nothing for their same-sex partner or non-legal family.

Understanding how a Medicaid lien works

When legally married spouses own a home together, each spouse owns a 100 percent interest in the home. The only way a married individual can own less than a 100 percent share of the home is if the couple agrees in writing that each spouse will own the home a different way. In other words, unless the couple makes other arrangements, both spouses automatically own the entire interest in any real estate they buy after they get married. This kind of ownership, called *tenants by the entirety*, is only available to legally married spouses.

For LGBT (and unmarried heterosexual) couples, the federal government views them as unmarried, so when they own a house, even if they are equal co-owners, each partner only owns 50 percent interest in the property. When one partner needs to go on Medicaid to pay for his or her nursing home and long-term care, this policy can have severe ramifications.

For example, if you become so incapacitated that your partner can no longer sufficiently care for you, you may need nursing home care for a period of months, years, or perhaps for the rest of your life.

Medicaid is the most common way to pay for nursing home care. When you apply for Medicaid, the government counts your assets to see if you qualify. Even though the Medicaid rules exempt your home from counting as an asset, after you receive Medicaid, the government may put a lien on your home to guarantee that the government is reimbursed for your nursing home costs.

If you have assets (money in the bank, stocks, bonds, and so on) in your own name, you'll be required to pay your own nursing home costs until you've spent nearly all your money (referred to as *spend-down*). After you have spent down, Medicaid kicks in to continue paying for your nursing home care.

Depending on the level of care you receive, nursing home fees can run between $9,000 to $15,000 per month. With the average nursing home stay being two and a half years, the total amount for nursing home care can end up costing between $270,000 to $450,000! If Medicaid paid for your entire stay, the amount of the Medicaid lien could easily exceed the value of the equity you have in your home. If you're legally married and you have a Medicaid lien on your home, the lien won't be enforced until after your death and the death of your spouse.

However, if you aren't married or if your marriage isn't recognized by your state's law, as soon as the partner who incurred the Medicaid lien dies, the state will step in and give your partner the option of paying off the lien. If your partner is unable to do so, the state may force a sale of the home and keep the proceeds from the deceased partner's share, up to the amount of the lien. Often this action leads to your partner, who may be elderly or otherwise incapacitated, to lose the home and possibly be forced into poverty.

Protecting your home and other assets from a Medicaid lien: Irrevocable trusts

If you and/or your partner are concerned about the future possibility that one or both of you will be forced to enter a nursing home or other long-term care facility, as soon as possible separate your jointly owned accounts and create other means of protecting those assets well in advance of the Medicaid *look back period* (the time preceding the person's application for Medicaid during which asset transfers will be scrutinized, normally five years).

The best way to protect your assets, especially your home, from a Medicaid lien is by creating an irrevocable trust into which you title your property and transfer bank accounts (see Chapter 14 for how to transfer property and assets into your trust).

After you have transferred your assets into the trust, the person for whom the trust is created (known as the trust's beneficiary) must not have direct access to trust funds so as to avoid a Medicaid lien. However, the beneficiary can continue to live in the home and have access to some funds as long as they don't exceed the maximum amount allowable to retain Medicaid eligibility.

You can set up an irrevocable trust, naming yourself as the trustee of the trust and your partner as the beneficiary or vice versa (refer to Chapter 13 for more information on trusts). According to the trust documents, the trustee can pay the beneficiary's expenses as well as the upkeep, maintenance, mortgage, and taxes on the house. Other benefits of an irrevocable trust include avoiding probate (flip to Chapter 12), providing protection from creditors of your children, allowing for distributions to minor beneficiaries in intervals, and so on.

We include a sample irrevocable trust to protect your home from a Medicaid lien on the CD (refer to Form 9-10).

Don't confuse an irrevocable trust with a living revocable trust. A living trust can protect your assets from probate, but it won't protect from nursing home costs.

Introducing the Affordable Care Act and Its Impact on LGBT Folks

In March 2010, President Obama signed the new healthcare reform law known as the Patient Protection and Affordable Care Act (PPACA, ACA, or Obamacare). The law is perhaps best known for requiring the much-maligned and misunderstood *individual mandate* (if you aren't covered by an employer or government healthcare plan, you're required to purchase coverage or pay a fine unless you're exempted by virtue of your religious beliefs or because the cost would be too great a financial burden).

Other well-known features of the ACA are that it prevents private health insurers from denying coverage on the basis of a pre-existing condition and it extends coverage of children under a parent's plan until they reach age 26.

Fortunately, the ACA will positively affect the LGBT community in several ways:

- ✔ LGBT partners will have access to coverage through their domestic partner's or their own employer.

- ✔ The Supreme Court recently ruled that the ACA, including the individual mandate, is constitutional and therefore the healthcare law will proceed as planned — with one exception: Medicaid. Originally, the Act called on all 50 states to expand Medicaid coverage to low-income residents by 2014, regardless of their age or disability. However, the court ruled that states can refuse to expand their Medicaid programs if they want to, and the federal government can't penalize them by taking away their overall

Medicaid funding. This means the expansion of Medicaid isn't a guaranteed outcome, which may substantially limit the scope of coverage for LGBT adults who live in states that refuse to participate in the Medicaid expansion program.

✔ Many gay and lesbian Americans who were without coverage due to a pre-existing condition now have the right to health insurance coverage for that condition. This is especially important for those living with HIV and AIDS who've had difficulty obtaining private health insurance.

✔ Beginning in 2014, *insurance exchanges* (where individuals and businesses can shop for insurance coverage through private insurers who supposedly will compete for clients) will begin to lower the cost of insurance premiums, and people with middle-class incomes will get tax credits to help offset the cost of those premiums.

✔ Rules prohibit insurance companies from canceling your policy because you made a mistake when filling out your paperwork.

✔ ACA ends lifetime dollar limits on crucial benefits, and it puts a ceiling on annual caps (caps won't be allowed after January 1, 2014). This permits coverage for the treatment of chronic diseases for as long as is necessary.

✔ It requires health insurers to cover preventive care without charging deductibles, co-payments, or co-insurance.

✔ The ACA will fund community-based preventative programs that address drug and alcohol abuse, obesity prevention, HIV-related care, nutrition, and exercise programs.

✔ The ACA also will address health disparities faced by LGBT individuals.

✔ It will also focus on training the medical field to be more sensitive to the special needs of the LGBT population and their families by hiring and training a more diverse and culturally competent healthcare workforce.

✔ It also increases funding for research and data collection methods regarding LGBT health disparities to better equip policymakers.

For more information about the Patient Protection and Affordable Care Act and how it affects you, visit `http://www.healthcare.gov/law/index.html`.

Chapter 10

Breaking Up Is Hard to Do

- -

In This Chapter

▶ Understanding the various forms of legal LGBT relationships

▶ Legally ending a relationship

▶ Remembering the Golden Rule

▶ Trying not to hurt the kids

- -

*B*efore we can begin our discussion of divorce, we first need to get a feel for the various legal rights LGBT couples are able to cobble together for themselves depending on their home state, home town, or where they work. Because the legal environment for LGBT relationship rights is so confusing, when a couple wants to break up or divorce, they may be unsure exactly what to do or what the process entails. This chapter explains what an LGBT couple can do to protect themselves, their children, and their property when they do divorce or break up.

Figuring Out How to Legally End an LGBT Relationship

As long as marriage has existed in the United States, the desire to get a divorce has too. In fact, the Supreme Court not only considers marriage a basic civil right, but the Court has also suggested that the Constitution protects the right to get divorced as well.

Just like anyone else, the more gay and lesbian partners enter into legally sanctioned relationships, the more they need access to divorce protections. Ever since LGBT couples rushed to the altar to take advantage of their brand-new legal rights (some without considering the consequences), there's been an almost frantic search for a legal escape hatch.

Although all 50 states recognize heterosexual marriage and divorce, a majority of states don't acknowledge same-sex marriage or civil unions — or their dissolution. With so many states now conferring differing degrees of LGBT legal rights (refer to Chapter 2 for a discussion of marriage and the other forms of LGBT recognized by states and municipalities), it becomes practically impossible for a state that doesn't have those legal categories to legally dissolve same-sex unions. This creates a myriad of complications for couples who don't live in the state in which they formed their legal status.

So, once you are legally bound to your same-sex partner by way of a domestic partnership, civil union, or legal marriage, if you do not live in a state that recognizes that relationship you may have trouble getting out of it. The following sections explain why dissolving a relationship isn't as easy as you may think. We also walk you through how to divorce or end your legal relationship.

Understanding why dissolving a legal LGBT relationship is unclear

Thanks to the Full Faith and Credit Clause of the United States Constitution, all 50 states must recognize the laws of the other 49 states, including marriage and divorce.

The federal Defense of Marriage Act (DOMA) defines marriage as a union of a man and a woman for federal purposes. But DOMA also expressly gives states the right to *refuse to recognize* a same-sex marriage performed in another state. If you think DOMA appears to violate the Full Faith and Credit Clause, you're not alone!

Because every state recognizes the legitimacy of heterosexual marriages performed in other states, an opposite-sex married couple can get divorced anywhere, and every state gives that divorce full faith and credit. Thus, the parties need only get past the following legal hurdles to be able to file for divorce. As long as one or both spouses meet these requirements, their divorce is likely to be granted:

- ✔ One or both spouses must meet the state's residency requirements, if applicable. A few states have no residency requirement for divorce, but most require one or both spouses to be a legal resident for six months or more.

- ✔ The spouse filing for divorce must have a legal basis for doing so. Today, however, all states recognize *no-fault divorce,* enabling the parties to dissolve their union if they're incompatible. In some states, though, spouses must be legally or actually separated for a specific period of time before the divorce will be granted.

Whether you're married, in a civil union, or in domestic partnership — even if you only had a commitment ceremony that wasn't legally recognized — in your own hearts, you and your partner almost certainly consider yourselves to be a family even though the law may disagree.

Because it involves the ripping apart of emotional, familial, financial, and legal ties, no matter if you're gay or straight, breaking up is never easy. But ending a legally recognized same-sex relationship may be much more difficult.

Ending a domestic partnership

Before you can proceed with ending a domestic partnership, you need to know what type you have. Basically three types of legally recognized domestic partnerships exist. The following sections identify these three types and explain how to end them.

Private domestic partnership

A couple voluntarily enters into a private domestic partnership when it draws up and signs a variety of legal documents that usually include a living-together or partnership agreement, wills, trusts, advance directives, and so on.

Because state and/or local legal obligations don't generally attach to a private domestic partnership, when an LGBT couple in this status wants to end their relationship, they follow whatever terms they agreed to in writing (for example, giving a 30-day written notice, waiting out a two-week cooling-off period, equitably dividing property, and so on) and then simply move out. However, if the couple signed a partnership or living-together agreement (we discuss this type of agreement later in this chapter) and one of them breaches or violates the terms of the agreement, a court may be asked to settle any disputes that arise from that breach or violation. Also, if the couple has children and both are deemed legal parents, they may be required to enter into a child custody, support, and visitation agreement that may or may not involve the intervention of a court.

Although doing so isn't legally required, both partners should *revoke* (cancel) or *amend* (change) their legal documents to reflect the change in their relationship status.

Employer-based domestic partnership

An employee enrolls a domestic partner as an eligible dependent for benefits offered by his or her employer under an employer-based domestic partnership. To end an employer-based domestic partnership, the employee should notify the benefits administrator of the change in his or her status and then follow the required procedures to remove the partner from the employee benefits. There is no waiting period before both partners are legally free to begin any other type of relationship with a new partner.

If you fail to notify your employer that your domestic partnership has ended, you may be liable to reimburse the employer for any benefits paid on behalf of your ex-partner.

Public domestic partnership

With this type, a couple registers their relationship with a state, county, or municipality that recognizes their legal status. The process for ending a *public domestic partnership* varies depending on the specific law. In some states and communities, ending a domestic partnership is as simple as filing a specific form notifying the state or local official that the relationship has terminated. In other jurisdictions, domestic partners must dissolve their relationship by filing for divorce — just as you would if you were legally married!

A state-by-state list of domestic partnership statutes (Form 10-1) is on the CD.

In order for a state or municipality to have the *jurisdiction* (legal authority) to dissolve a domestic partnership, one or both partners may be required to reside in that state or community for a specific period of time. Some states have no residency requirements for ending a domestic partnership, while other states require at least one partner to live in the state for six months prior to filing for dissolution.

Because legal rights attach to this type of domestic partnership, during dissolution proceedings, a court may divide the couple's assets and award child visitation, custody, and/or support. In most cases, domestic partners in this type of relationship may not get married or enter into a civil union or domestic partnership with someone else until their current partnership is legally terminated.

Dissolving a marriage or civil union in a legal equality state

As the law currently stands, most states that allow equal marriage and civil unions also extend those rights to out-of-state couples, even when their home state doesn't recognize their union. As a result, no matter where you live, you can travel to one of these states, get hitched, and then return to your home state to live happily ever after — or not.

If you decide you want to end your relationship — provided that you live in a marriage-equality or civil union state, or a state that recognizes your right to get a divorce — you simply follow the same procedures as a divorcing heterosexual couple.

Before we discuss *how* to get a divorce, you need to make sure you can get past a few initial legal hurdles:

- ✔ You must meet your state's residency requirements.
- ✔ You must have legitimate grounds (reasons) for wanting a divorce.

If you meet these requirements, next you have to

- ✔ File all of the required forms and financial statements with the court and then abide by any judicial orders that follow
- ✔ Give proper notice to your soon-to-be ex
- ✔ Wait for your final divorce decree

Because a civil union and marriage attaches legal obligations to both partners, neither person may enter into a civil union, marriage, or public domestic partnership with another person until the divorce is final.

Hundreds of counties across the United States now have free or inexpensive, online do-it-yourself divorce forms with instructions that you can download, fill out, and file yourself, without an attorney's help. To find out if your county offers this service, either check out its website or call the county clerk's office. You can find the number in the government section of your local phone book.

Don't try to do your own divorce if you and/or your partner are disputing the division of property or custody, visitation and support of children, or if you have a very large and complicated estate.

Getting a divorce in a state that bans same-sex unions and divorces

All divorces require the intervention of a court of law where a judge issues a final *divorce decree* (a court order declaring the legal end of a marriage or civil union). If you want a divorce in a state that bans same-sex unions and divorces, it depends on where you were married. The following sections discuss this question and possible solutions to help you obtain your divorce.

Where you were married is relevant

The state where you were married determines how you can divorce or legally end your relationship.

If you live in a state that bans same-sex unions and you were married or received a civil union or domestic partnership in another state (that does legally recognize those unions), you more than likely can't get divorced in your home state because your state law doesn't recognize the legality of your relationship in the first place. States that ban LGBT relationships argue that allowing gay and lesbian couples to divorce would inadvertently open the door to equal marriage rights.

Courts in states that have a *mini DOMA* (a state version of the federal Defense of Marriage Act prohibiting marriage of same-sex partners) almost certainly deny your divorce petition. Opponents of marriage equality in mini DOMA states feel divorce could be the first step down a slippery slope to full marriage rights for gay and lesbian partners.

Furthermore, you may not be able to get divorced in the state that granted your status because that state doesn't have *jurisdiction* (power and/or authority to apply the law) to grant divorces to nonresidents. This catch-22 situation gives a whole new meaning to the term 'wedlock'!

But even states like Rhode Island — a very progressive state that allows civil unions (a marriage-like status with all the same rights and benefits of marriage) — refuses to grant divorces to residents that were married in another state because "state law only contemplates divorce between a husband and wife." And that's true even though the governor has stated that Rhode Island will recognize same-sex marriages from other states.

Only one state, Georgia, has a mini DOMA that mentions the word "divorce." The federal and other state DOMA's only restrict access to LGBT *marriage* and are silent on the issue of divorce. Because those state DOMA's don't explicitly deny the right to same-sex divorce, why can't their courts grant a divorce decree to LGBT spouses married in another state?

If you live in a DOMA state and are trapped in a marriage you no longer want, why not file for divorce and see what happens? If the court denies your petition, you can appeal to a higher court on the grounds that your state's DOMA doesn't apply to divorce. Laws are always evolving, but they only do so when someone has the courage to challenge them. Thus, although ending a civil union, domestic partnership, or same-sex marriage may be technically *difficult* when your state doesn't recognize your relationship, it may not be *impossible*.

Creating a legal-limbo for same-sex couples

As long as states refuse to grant divorces to LGBT couples, gay men and lesbians who were married or entered into a civil union in a legal equality state will continue to be mired in a legal limbo. This uneasy state of affairs raises many questions:

What if a bisexual man marries his same-sex partner in Massachusetts and when visiting his parents in Florida, he meets a woman, falls in love, and marries her? Is he guilty of bigamy if Florida doesn't recognize his Massachusetts marriage? If he and his wife travel by train across the country on their honeymoon, will he be married to his partner or his wife as they travel through Iowa, which is a marriage-equality state?

Legal conundrums exist even for couples who *are* able to get a divorce. Many same-sex couples who marry have lived with their partner for many years before officially tying the knot. In that time they may have accumulated property together. Because their legal marriage happened long after they first set up house together, their marital property that is subject to equitable division would only entail that which they obtained after they wed. Will courts take into consideration property acquired prior to the legal marriage because that legal status was unavailable?

As more and more couples get married and move to states across the country, current inconsistencies in the law will eventually move the cause of same-sex marriage forward.

Most states have statues defining divorce as "the termination of the marital relationship between a husband and wife." This definition implicitly creates two requirements:

- ✔ That the couple be married.
- ✔ That the couple be of the opposite sex.

Because the LGBT couple is legally married in states where marriage equality (or its equivalent) is allowed, even if the home state doesn't recognize the marriage, the couple is still married and the first requirement is met. The divorce statute doesn't specify that the marriage needs to be *valid* in the divorcing state, thus courts don't need to read a validity requirement into their divorce statute. In the alternative, same-sex couples can ask the court to recognize their marriage for the limited purpose of granting them a divorce.

If the court refuses to grant a divorce under its own divorce statutes, why not ask if the state would agree to apply the laws of the state that granted the marriage in the first place? In contract disputes between businesses and across state lines, courts are often asked to apply the law from another state if there are "significant contacts" in the state with the more desirable statute (in this case marriage and divorce equality).

Establishing equitable relief

If the court refuses to apply its own divorce statutes or the statutes of the state that issued the marriage certificate, a divorcing couple could always ask the court for equitable relief. All trial courts have the power to grant *equitable relief* (a judgment based what is fair and necessary for a particular case) when a legal remedy doesn't exist.

To establish a need for equitable relief, one or both partners will need to show the following:

- ✔ **No other suitable legal remedy is available.** As soon as the couple is denied their right to divorce in their home state and the state that granted their legal status, the first requirement is met.

- ✔ **Without a divorce, the couple will suffer real harm.** Showing the harm a couple will suffer if they can't get a divorce is fairly easy. As long as they're married somewhere, they may perceive themselves to be unable to remarry and, if they do marry someone else, they'll be caught in a legal limbo where they will be married or not as they travel across state lines.

- ✔ **No equitable defenses would prohibit the court from granting a divorce.** To provide an equitable relief remedy, a judge doesn't need to determine the validity of the marriage per se; he or she merely needs to acknowledge that the partners require a judicial remedy that is otherwise legally unavailable.

- ✔ **The court has the discretion to grant the divorce based on equitable jurisdiction.** Although a couple may find equitable relief is better than nothing, it is not a divorce decree and therefore other states may not accept it as a valid termination of the marriage. If possible, ask the court to add language to the judgment declaring the marriage "dissolved," and from this point on the partners are to be considered "single individuals."

Using one or more of the preceding arguments for getting a divorce in non-equality states hopefully can result in the ability of a married same-sex couple to obtain a legal end to their marriage no matter where they were married and where they live now.

Planning for a Breakup While You're Still a Couple

When couples are at the beginning of their relationship the last thing on their minds is the possibility that someday they might break up. Unfortunately, stuff happens and so it's always better to be prepared for a rainy day, even if it never comes.

When legal rights attach to a relationship status, such as marriage, civil unions, and even some domestic partnerships, the law provides some automatic legal protections, ranging from equitable division of property to financial support for a partner who sacrificed their own financial gain on behalf of the relationship, and so on.

LGBT couples — regardless of where they live — have to face the fact that the legal landscape is ever-changing and that rights they have now may be expanded or contracted, depending on what political party gets elected and whether opponents of LGBT rights can successfully get anti-equality initiatives placed on statewide ballots. Thus, regardless of whether couples do or don't live in a state or community that recognizes same-sex relationships, committed partners should always create their own rights, protections, and obligations vis-à-vis one another.

One way to do so is by drawing up a variety of legal documents, such as *wills* and *trusts* (documents that let partners, among other things, leave property to each other), *advance directives* (that let partners appoint one another to make medical and financial decisions) and most importantly, a *living-together* or *partnership agreement* (a contract which sets out the terms of how partners will share property, money and expenses while living together and how they'll divide it in a breakup). (We discuss wills, trusts, and so on in Part III.)

If you can't get married (or simply choose not to marry), while you and your partner are still in love, we suggest you put into writing a living-together agreement (LTA) about how you will share living space, money, and property while you're living together and how you will divide it all up if you break up.

So is an LTA something you and your partner want to sign? Read the following sections to find out why it's so important and what you need to discuss with each other before signing one.

Realizing why an LTA is essential

Whether or not you and your partner enter into a legal union, there are plenty of reasons to draw-up an LTA. When you do, you should make sure your LTA covers most if not all of the following:

- How you will divvy up jointly owned personal property and financial assets in case of a break up.

- Whether one partner will be financially obligated to support the other partner while they're living together and/or after the relationship ends. This situation may occur if one partner has substantially more wealth, a partner quits his or her job to take care of the home and/or children, or one of you is disabled and unable to make a living wage.

- How you'll handle paying bills, expenses, and debts while you live together.

✔ What you'll do with the house you own together if you break up. For example, will you sell it to a third party and divide the proceeds or will one of you buy the other out?

✔ Although an LTA may not be legally binding, having one may help to define support, custody, or visitation rights for minor children. A court isn't obligated to follow what you've agreed to, but a court may find it useful to see that once upon a time both partners wanted the other to be a parent to your children. Having an LTA address parental rights and obligations can be especially important when one partner isn't a legal parent because the agreement helps to establish the existence of a parent-child relationship as a matter of fact if not a matter of law.

Knowing what to talk about when setting up an LTA

If we have one message in this section and this chapter, it's the importance of talking to each other honestly about your needs, wants, and expectations before living together. One of the advantages of sitting down to make an outline of your LTA is that it gives you the opportunity to have this essential conversation.

Only you and your partner really know what you want and expect from one another; therefore, your LTA is unique to your circumstances. You still need to include some basic matters in your discussion. The most important and essential topic of conversation (and probably the most difficult) is how you will deal with money. (We consider it so important that we devote all of Chapter 6 to this topic. We suggest you read all of Chapter 6 to discuss some of the following money matters in greater detail.)

Here's a checklist of things to discuss to help you get started on your LTA:

✔ **Merging bank accounts:** Some partners keep separate personal accounts and open a joint account for household expenses. If you decide to merge all of your money into one joint account — especially if you want to avoid conflicts over money or overdraft fees — we suggest you set limits on what you can spend beyond bills and expenses. You may want to put each other's names on your separate accounts for easier access in an emergency.

✔ **Keeping your money separate:** If you have good credit and want to keep it that way, you may want to keep you bank accounts separate. Having your own account can also go a long way in preventing arguments about money.

✔ **Deciding who will be in charge of paying the bills:** Whether or not you have a joint account, you want to keep detailed records of what bills were paid and what remain outstanding. If possible, take turns paying the bills — one of you pays for six months and then the duty shifts to the other partner for the next six months. Controlling how the money is spent can be powerful. Make sure you don't let it go to your head.

✔ **Designing a budget:** Make a list of your individual and combined monthly income and expenses. A budget helps to constrain unnecessary spending, and it lets you see how you can better allocate your resources. Use a search engine to find a good online budget tool. Most of them are free. For help on making a budget, you may want to check out the latest edition of *Personal Finance For Dummies* by Eric Tyson (John Wiley & Sons, Inc.).

✔ **Obtaining a credit report and sharing it with your partner:** Doing this task may be the hardest of all, particularly if you have a low credit score. If you're planning on having only one partner's name on the lease or mortgage, knowing one another's credit rating can help you determine which of you will assume that responsibility. Having a discussion about your relative credit ratings is just another way to get into the money conversation pit. Dealing with financial matters upfront and before they get too far along is easier.

✔ **Focusing on personal debt:** Reveal your outstanding credit card debt, auto, school, and/or other loans that you currently owe and pay for. The amount you make each month may not matter if all or most of it goes toward paying off your debts. It's only fair that both partners are fully aware of the other's ability to help out with expenses. Otherwise, one partner may end up picking up the slack for the cash-strapped partner.

✔ **Making break-up plans:** You may think it strange to start off your relationship by making plans for a possible future breakup. Breaking up may be hard to do, but doing so is even harder when you have property to divide. Even in the glow of your living together love-fest, you need to think about and plan for a time when you may be arguing over who gets the big screen TV and custody of the dog.

✔ **Dividing property:** If you're buying or already own a home together, and one of you has contributed more money than the other, add to the LTA that — in the event of a breakup — the partner making the larger investment will be reimbursed at the ratio of equity he or she put in to the home.

✔ **Laying out buy-out provisions:** In case one partner wants to keep the house after a breakup, decide whether that partner will pay the other partner an amount equal to half of the equity earned or half the equity minus any real estate agent's commission, brokerage fees, closing costs, and/or taxes that would have to be paid if the house is sold on the market.

✔ **Resolving disputes:** LTAs often contain mediation and arbitration clauses so that you can avoid a costly legal battle. *Mediation* is the process whereby you and your partner meet with an unbiased mediator to work out a mutually satisfactory compromise that is put into writing and signed by all three of you. An *arbitration* process is somewhat different in that you choose an arbitrator, your partner chooses another, and those two choose a third arbitrator. The partners then give their side of the story to the panel of three arbitrators who will render a decision in writing. If you agree in advance to abide by the arbitration clause in your LTA, unless the process was flawed, the arbitrators' decision is binding and a court won't hear your claim.

Because state law varies widely in the way property is divided when legally recognized and nonlegally recognized partners break up, your LTA should be drafted to clearly protect the rights of both partners so that neither of you incurs any unintended liabilities.

Drafting the LTA

Creating an LTA is a bit like setting up a business. You're simply making a plan for running your everyday lives and for divvying up your stuff in case it doesn't work out. And, figuring out all of these details in the warm glow of love is a lot easier than it will be with the bitter feelings that often accompany a breakup.

Depending on the complexity of your situation, you can either draw up your own LTA using the sample we provide in this book or you can pay an attorney to make one for you. The sample LTA assumes both partners want to share expenses equally as well as jointly own any property purchased after the agreement is signed. Otherwise, all income belongs solely to the partner who earned it as does any property given to a partner as a gift during the relationship or obtained prior to the onset of the relationship.

A sample LTA (Form 10-2) is on the CD. The attached LTA has three exhibits:

✔ Exhibits A and B are where each partner lists his or her individually owned property.

✔ Exhibit C is where the partners list jointly owned property. Only the property on exhibit C is subject to division in case of a breakup.

If your situation is more complicated, you may want to ask an attorney to review your do-it-yourself LTA or make one for you. Because an LTA is a contract, both partners should sign it before two witnesses and a notary.

No one can accurately predict the success or failure of a relationship. Entering an LTA with your eyes open is smart. In other words, hope for the best but plan for the worst.

Nonetheless, working hard on your relationship, including making it clear what you want and expect out of your living-together experience, is probably the best predictor of success. Do the work before you begin living under the same roof with your partner.

Some states that don't allow legal recognition of same-sex relationships do provide certain legal remedies for dividing up property owned jointly by non-legal partners. Because these remedies aren't automatically granted to same-sex partners based on their relationship status, a partner wanting to take advantage of them needs to file suit in the appropriate court. Remedies for dividing joint assets between unmarried partners are

- ✔ **Partition actions:** Either partner can file a partition action asking a court to divide jointly owned property between the partners, according to the percentage of interest owned (for instance, 50-50, 70-30, or some other way). The two kinds of partition are

  - • **Partition in kind:** Partition in kind usually involves the division of money or personal property where a judge orders the property to be equitably divided between the partners according to each partner's interest.

  - • **Partition by sale:** Partition by sale is usually reserved for more valuable property that is difficult or impossible to physically divide (such as RVs, boats, real estate, and so on). In a partition by sale, the court appoints a disinterested third party to have the property appraised and then sell it. After the property is sold, the proceeds are distributed between the partners, again according to the interest each of them owns.

  A partition action can be very expensive, including court costs, appraiser and seller fees, and more than likely, attorney fees.

- ✔ **Unjust enrichment:** When partners purchase property together and later break up, if one of those partners refuses to share the jointly acquired property or doesn't compensate his or her ex for the value of the property, the partner keeping the property is *unjustly enriched.* Fortunately for the partner without the property, the eyes of the law deem this status as unfair and may order the partner who keeps the property to pay restitution. The partner without the property can file a civil suit on the grounds of unjust enrichment, with the court awarding damages if the case is judged in favor of the partner without the property.

Lawsuits are expensive and can be stressful. It's almost always preferable for partners to enter into a living-together agreement (LTA) before or after moving in together rather than litigate property disputes in court.

Protecting Kids in a Breakup

When a same-sex couple has children, their responsibility for treating one another with respect during and after a breakup is even greater than it otherwise would be because the law often doesn't recognize the legal relationship between LGBT parents and their children.

 Whatever the situation, one thing is clear: When a breakup happens, children get hurt. And when a child loses both parents simply because no one took the time to create legal protections, it can be devastating.

Although partners in same-sex relationships naturally can't produce children, millions of gay men and lesbians are choosing to become parents. See Chapter 7 for an in-depth discussion on becoming parents and how best to raise a child with your partner.

 No matter how the parent-child relationship is established and regardless of whether or not the law confers legal rights and responsibilities on it, to the children, having the love and support of both parents is vital to their happiness and well-being.

Unfortunately, children often find themselves in an emotional tug-of-war with one or both parents fighting over custody, support, visitation, and worse, trying to win a child's affection and loyalty by pitting the child against the other parent. And, of course, the vast majority of same-sex partners with children do not have any legally recognized relationship with their partner or children at all.

If you and your partner have children and you later break up, do your best to make sure you don't become so angry and resentful that you use your child as a weapon against your ex!

Part III
Planning Ahead to Protect Your Loved Ones

The 5th Wave   By Rich Tennant

"It's a legal document authorizing you to carry out a Do Not Resuscitate order on my behalf, although heaven knows, you have a hard time cancelling a magazine subscription."

In this part . . .

Gay and lesbian couples have plenty of reason to be concerned about what will happen to whoever's left behind when one partner dies. The law isn't friendly, and stories of surviving partners being frozen out of their money, their homes, and even their children can be recited by too many members of the LGBT community.

This part shows you how to avoid all those potential nightmares. We discuss the importance of making sure your documents are up-to-date and clear. We provide lots of practical information about drafting wills and trusts and making sure your trusts are funded. We also discuss how to access health and retirement benefits, and how the law looks at the death or injury of your partner when caused by a third party's negligence. These topics look much less complicated after you pore over these chapters.

Chapter 11

LGBT Estate Planning: Laying the Groundwork

In This Chapter

▶ Explaining why LGBT couples need to create legal protections

▶ Understanding the basics of estate planning

▶ Making an inventory and getting organized

▶ Putting your plan into action

*U*nless your relationship is legally recognized, you and your partner are strangers to one another in the eyes of the law. Period. You may think the love and responsibilities you share with your partner are exactly the same as your heterosexual family and friends, but unfortunately, that isn't the case — the law sees it another way.

So what does legally recognized mean? As we explain in more detail in Chapter 2, a marriage sanctioned by the law bestows concrete legal and tax benefits upon married couples. The moment they say "I do" heterosexual spouses are eligible for more than 1,100 state and federal benefits, rights, protections, and responsibilities that are denied to same-sex couples who can't wed. And, thanks to the Federal Defense of Marriage Act (DOMA), even married same-sex couples who are able to access state benefits are denied valuable federal rights and protections. Moreover, the problem for same-sex couples extends beyond legal nonrecognition. Medical and corporate institutions, religious organizations, and even relatives, friends, and neighbors don't always see committed gay and lesbian partners and their kids as a real nuclear family.

So what can LGBT life partners do to protect each other from the harsh realities of legal, institutional, and familial discrimination in the event of legal separation, mental or physical incapacity, or death? For now, you must create your own legal rights and protections using wills, advance directives, contracts, and more. In a strange way, committed gay and lesbian couples are lucky in at least this way: Because the law often doesn't recognize same-sex relationships, the need for planning should be more obvious to them. But everyone — married or not! — needs an *estate plan*.

Comparing a financial plan with an estate plan: What's the difference?

The term *estate planning* is sometimes used in conjunction with or as a substitute for *financial planning* because financial planners frequently incorporate estate planning documents when creating a financial plan for their clients. But the terms refer to two different things.

A *financial plan* is the process of planning for your financial future by saving and making investments to accumulate wealth, provide security for your retirement, or pay for a dependent's college education.

An *estate plan* allows you to arrange, in advance, for the systematic and organized transfer of assets to beneficiaries following your death and for the continuity of asset management during an illness or injury. Most estate plans involve creating and signing specific legal documents that clearly spell out your wishes for how your property will be managed and to whom it will be distributed. A properly designed plan also lets you appoint someone you trust to make sure your instructions are carried out.

Although an estate plan can be part of a comprehensive financial plan, for the purpose of this book we limit our discussion to estate planning, focusing on creating written, legal documents to protect and empower LGBT families.

Because your relationship isn't legally recognized, we're here to help you do what is necessary to protect your rights, your relationship, and your property. This chapter explains the importance of having specific legal documents in place and makes clear what protections are essential for and available to unmarried partners. We also delve more deeply into the topic of estate planning to define what an estate is and help you understand how to recognize and assess the value of your estate. Having an estate plan in place before an unfortunate event occurs is paramount. Therefore we also provide directions on how to follow through with your estate plan so that it achieves your goals. An estate plan should not only provide after-death protection, but it also anticipates the possible need for long-term care in case of illness or injury. In this chapter, we explain the ins and outs of pre-planning for long-term care in order to protect your assets.

Figuring Out What an Estate Is

People hear the word "estate" and picture a wealthy tycoon, living in a mansion and driving a Lexus. In fact, an *estate* is simply all the stuff you own: your house, bank accounts, IRA, retirement accounts, stocks and bonds, car, personal property — even the toaster oven you received when you came out as a gay man or lesbian!

Here's another way to look at what an estate is: When you're alive, if you decide to get rid of some of your stuff, you can sell it on eBay or at a yard sale. After you die, your *executor* (the person you appoint in your will to administer or settle your estate after your death) may sell some of your stuff at an *estate sale.* Check out the classified ads in your local paper and more than likely you'll find yard sales and estate sales listed together in that section.

Whether you're legally married or not, providing for your loved ones is your greatest responsibility. If you want your partner to *inherit your estate* (receive your property) after your death and make medical and financial decisions for you when you're ill, you need to put your wishes into a legal writing — in other words, you need to make an estate plan, which we explain in this next section.

Defining an Estate Plan

An *estate plan* is simply a detailed and organized set of instructions — your instructions — which clearly describe how you want your assets to be managed while you're still living and after you die. More importantly, your estate plan should clearly state your wishes and identify whom you want to control and inherit your property after you are gone. That's really all there is to it.

The following sections introduce two fundamental estate planning documents and describe the basic structure of a good estate plan.

Identifying the document choices you have for your estate plan

Generally speaking, an estate plan comprises several legal documents, depending on your particular circumstances. Two main types of estate plans are available based on the following:

- ✔ **A last will and testament:** A will is a *testamentary document* (for example, it doesn't take effect or become valid until the death of the person making the will) that specifies how you want your estate settled and your property distributed after your death. (Refer to Chapter 12 for more information.)

- ✔ **A living revocable trust:** A *trust* is a legal agreement that takes effect as soon as it's signed and that clearly spells out how your assets will be managed, your estate settled, and your property distributed both during your life and after your death. (Check out Chapter 13 for more on trusts.)

What's in a name? Defining and simplifying all those scary legal titles

Throughout this chapter we use the terms *manager* and *decision maker* to describe those people you appoint in your documents to oversee your estate or assets and make medical and financial decisions for you. Individual states use different terminology for these positions. For example, the term *manager* refers to the person you appoint to *administer* (to supervise or be in charge of) your will. Some states refer to this person as *executor;* other states use the term *personal representative* or an *administrator.* Whatever term is used, the duties and powers of your manager are virtually the same. Likewise, the phrase *decision maker* refers to the person you appoint to make medical and financial decisions for you when you aren't able to make those decisions for yourself. Depending on your state's law, a decision maker may be called your *agent, personal representative,* or *attorney-in-fact.*

Each type has its own unique pros and cons, which we cover in Chapters 12 and 13. No matter which type of estate plan you decide to use, the important thing to remember is that *you should not put off creating legal rights and protections until it's too late.*

If you become ill or injured or you die before preparing estate planning documents, your partner and/or family of choice may not have the right to live in the home you shared together. Your loved ones may not receive your other property and assets. Your legal relatives — even those who you haven't spoken to in years — may have superior legal rights over your partner. It's your responsibility to put your wishes in writing before it's too late.

As long as you're of *sound mind* (not mentally incapacitated), you can cancel (the legal term is *revoke*) or change (*amend,* another bit of legalese) the documents in your estate plan. An amendment to a will is generally referred to as a *codicil.* You may want to revoke or amend your will and/or trust if:

- You break up with your partner.
- You move to a different state.
- You buy or sell your home.
- You have or adopt a child.
- Someone you named in your document dies.

Unless you want your ex to *administer* (have control over) and inherit your estate, you need to revoke or amend your will and/or trust after a breakup. You probably don't want your ex to be the *beneficiary* (the person who will receive assets and property under your will, trust, insurance policy, and so on) of your estate either.

Because each state has different laws governing wills and estates, you may need to revoke a will and create another will that is valid in your new home state. Because a trust is a contract, you only need to amend the trust to reflect your change of residence.

If you move to another town or city in the same state, you should amend your will and trust with your new address. You may also want to amend your trust or will to include a new beneficiary (for example, if you have or adopt a child) or to remove a beneficiary if someone you've named dies.

Making an estate plan: The how-to

After you decide to create estate planning documents, your biggest challenge is actually doing the work required to make your plan effective. Although doing so may be a bit time consuming, the pain and suffering you will spare yourself and your loved ones later is well worth the effort. Here is what you need to do to create an effective estate plan:

1. **Sit down and make an inventory or list of your valuable assets.**

   If you have a partner, you both need to take the time to do this. To make it easier on you, we've included a sample inventory as well as a blank asset and property inventory form on the CD. Doing so can help you organize your property and divide it according to specific categories.

   Valuable assets include but aren't limited to *real property* (house or land), motor vehicles (such as cars, RVs, and boats), cash, bank and financial accounts, art, jewelry, books, CD or DVD collections, antiques, tools, electronic equipment, specific items of personal property having sentimental value (family heirlooms), and so on. In other words, all the stuff that *isn't* real property is personal property, and everything should be listed.

2. **Decide who will be responsible to make medical and financial decisions for you and who will manage and distribute your assets and property after you die.**

   Use full, legal names and make sure you have updated contact information, including cell phone numbers and e-mail addresses.

   Include on your manager and decision maker list:

   - The name(s) of your *manager,* the person who will administer your estate and settle your affairs

   - The name(s) of your medical and financial decision maker

   - If your children are minors, the names of guardians to care for them

   - The name(s) of manager for property distributed to underage beneficiaries

In case one or more of the people on your list isn't able to act for any reason, you should name an alternate to take their place. Naming an alternate is important because you never know whether your first choice will be willing or able to act on your behalf. And, more importantly, if you don't choose an alternate and your first choice is unavailable, the court will appoint someone for you — and that someone may be the last person you would want to make decisions for you and manage your affairs. We know of or have heard of too many sad examples of grieving partners being shoved aside by homophobic or unsympathetic relatives of the deceased. You don't want to join this club!

3. Decide who will inherit your estate after you are gone.

After all, the whole point of creating an estate plan is to make sure your loved ones are cared for, right?

Using your asset inventory as a guide, decide how you want to divvy up your property. For many people, this assignment will be easy because you plan to give everything to your partner or to your kids. For others, your estate plan may be a bit more complicated. For example, you want to give most of your assets to your partner and/or children, but you also want to give something to other people and/or organizations.

4. Create your beneficiary list.

Your *beneficiary list* is exactly what it sounds like — it's a list of all the people and organizations you want to benefit from or inherit your money and property after you die. On the beneficiary list, make sure you provide, in order of *priority* (who do you want to be first in line to inherit, and, if that person isn't living, who do you want to inherit the deceased person's share):

> The name of your first choice of beneficiary (usually a partner)
>
> The names and birthdates of your children
>
> The names of others to whom you want to leave your property
>
> The names of organizations, groups, or causes you want to benefit
>
> Information about your pets, including names, descriptions, and caretakers

Use full, legal names and updated addresses and phone numbers. Be sure to describe the relationship you have with your beneficiary on this list and in your legal document (for example, your partner, child, sister, mother, friend, and so forth.) Although making these lists may seem like a chore, it really helps to gather and organize this information, in advance, to give you the opportunity to reflect on your choices and to ensure you don't unintentionally leave out some person or some organization you care about.

Don't forget to list alternates — that is, who should get your property if your first choice doesn't survive you.

Included on the CD is an estate planning worksheet with tips and suggestions to help you create your list.

5. Discuss your plan with those you want to empower and authorize.

After you determine who your managers and decision makers will be, ask their permission to name them as such on your legal documents. Make sure you tell them exactly what is expected of them and that they're willing and able to act on your behalf. Even more importantly, ask yourself if you feel the people you've listed are mature enough, trustworthy, and qualified to perform the required tasks and duties.

You also want to tell your parents or siblings that you have created legal documents and that you've appointed your life partner as your executor, as your agent to make your medical and financial decisions, and as the beneficiary of your estate. If you are reluctant to come out to your family, at least give them the basic facts about your decision without revealing your motives. Consider this: If you don't tell them yourself, your partner may be put in the awkward position of having to deal with their shock and anger while at the same time trying to juggle the duties of executor or healthcare surrogate.

The last thing you would wish on your partner is to have disgruntled family members fighting over his or her decision making powers and/or inheritance rights at this very stressful time — especially because you won't be around to able to defend your wishes.

Even if you don't tell your family you've signed legal documents that gives your partner the right to make decisions for you and inherit your property, those documents are still valid.

6. Go over your list with your partner.

Make sure you explain all your decisions so he or she isn't caught by surprise later on. Even better, sit down and make your list with your partner at your side.

7. Talk to those people you are naming as your decision makers.

Acting as executor of your will or trustee of your trust is a huge responsibility. You don't want to burden them with a duty they don't understand or wish to perform.

8. Give copies of your documents to someone you trust.

This person can be a family member or close friend, perhaps a clergy member, who may be able to intervene calmly on your partner's behalf. Sharing the documents can greatly ease the burdens of your partner and family who will be trying to care for you in your illness, or grieving over your death.

Who will take care of your kids if something unlikely happens?

Prospective adoptive parents have to seriously consider who would — or could — take care of their soon-to-be children if they become incapacitated or die. But this question is worth serious consideration by *all* parents of minor children, and perhaps especially by gay and lesbian parents whose death might be more likely to set off a squabble among relatives about who, if anyone, can or should take the kids in.

Stick to these steps to help you determine who will be your children's guardian:

1. **You and your partner need to think about which of the possible candidates would be best for raising *your* children.**

   Among the many factors you may consider are geography, parenting style, political philosophy (no homophobes need be considered!), the personalities of all involved (some kids and adults are better matches than others), and resources. Making this decision may be more difficult than either expect, so keep that in mind if you find yourself becoming more assertive or agitated than usual.

2. **After you settle on a potential home and parent(s) for your children, think about the conversation you want to have with those you've chosen.**

   Explain why you're asking them to take on this responsibility and listen attentively to their concerns and questions. If they seem ready to take on the burden, insist that they sleep on it and (if they're a couple) talk it over before committing. If they say no or seem reluctant, accept their decision and move on — without judgment, if possible.

Some LGBT partners worry that a disgruntled family member may try to interfere with the rights of their life partner. Fortunately, some states permit a competent adult to designate another person as their "family," or legal "next of kin." These written designations provide additional protections for couples whose family is not accepting of their lifestyle.

In addition to designating a partner as your next-of-kin, LGBT couples may want to consider petitioning the probate court for a legal name change so that both partners share a common surname. This option may be of particular importance to a couple if they have children or are planning to become parents.

Designing an Estate Plan to Suit Your Circumstances

Whatever your situation, your estate plan is the foundation upon which you will build security and peace of mind for your loved ones. Every relationship and way of life is unique, and your estate plan should reflect your particular circumstances. Partners in a committed relationship may choose to live together or apart. More and more LGBT couples are opting to have children. Older couples and those couples with special needs must create rights and protections where the law falls short.

Laws affecting LGBT legal rights vary from state to state, and the task of protecting rights and benefits can seem daunting, but with the help of this chapter and this kit, you can get a handle on what you need to do to protect your family and loved ones.

The following sections outline the basic structure of the typical estate plan and provide essential information about other techniques and tactics you may want to use to design your estate plan. We help you whether or not you decide to do it yourself or use an attorney. We also offer instructions for making your estate plan effective and official as well as directing what you should do with your documents after they are signed.

Identifying the parts of an estate plan

Depending on your personal situation — your marital status, where you live, what you own, your net worth, and so on — your estate plan will be very simple or quite complex. At a minimum, every person should have the following:

- ✔ **A will:** A *will* is a legal document that doesn't take effect until you die. A will enables you to appoint a person to settle your estate and name a person or organization who will receive your money and property after your death. (See Chapter 12 for more info about wills.)

- ✔ **A living will:** A *living will* lets you say, in advance of illness or injury, what medical treatment, if any, you want administered when and if you become ill or are injured with no hope of recovery or survival. (Chapter 9 provides more explanation about living wills.)

- ✔ **A medical power of attorney:** This legal document allows you to appoint someone you trust to make medical decisions for you when you're not able to make them yourself. (Check out Chapter 9 for more information.)

As you accumulate more assets and your situation becomes more complicated, you may need some additional estate planning tools. Also, special circumstances such as a legal marriage, breakup or divorce, remarriage, moving to a different state, having or adopting a child, a partner or child with special needs, and so on require legal documents specifically tailored to meet your new circumstances.

Additional estate planning tools may include:

- ✔ **Durable power of attorney:** Also known as a *DPOA,* this legal document lets you authorize someone you trust to manage your money, property, and business for you when you aren't able to do these things yourself. (See Chapter 9 for more in-depth information on DPOAs.)

- ✔ **Living revocable trust:** Also called a *grantor trust,* this document is a legal contract or agreement that, among other things, lets you appoint someone to hold title to your real estate and other valuable assets. (Check out Chapter 13 for the lowdown on these trusts.)

- ✔ **Irrevocable Medicaid trust:** A special type of trust that lets you protect your assets – especially the equity in your home – in case you ever need nursing home care or Medicaid benefits. (Chapter 13 has more details.)

- ✔ **A minor child's trust:** This trust lets you arrange for property and assets for a minor child or children to be managed by someone you trust until the child reaches a certain age. (Refer to Chapter 13 for insight into this kind of trust.)

- ✔ **A special needs trust:** This specialized trust takes care of a physically or mentally disabled child or adult without affecting his or hers eligibility for government benefits like Supplemental Security Income (SSI), Medicaid, food stamps, and so on. (Head to Chapter 13 for more details.)

Some of the more advanced estate planning documents in the preceding list are outside the scope of this legal kit. For example, if you need a special needs trust for a disabled loved one, have a large and complex estate, or have some other unique situation, hiring an attorney may be your best option.

Planning for the inevitable may not be the most enjoyable thing you have ever done. However, with effective estate planning, you can transfer the greatest amount possible in the least amount of time to the people you love. Every estate plan should do the following:

- ✔ **Assure continuity of control over assets:** Especially when the person you appoint to manage your assets is your partner, he or she should continue to have the right to access and control property and financial accounts as though you were alive and well.

- ✔ **Maximize access to assets:** Your estate plan should guarantee there is no delay in your partner's right to access money and property while a judge decides whether or not your documents are valid and legitimate.

✔ **Increase the preservation of capital:** Your assets should be able to increase in value while you're *incapacitated* (unable to manage your own affairs) or while your estate is being settled.

✔ **Maximize privacy:** No one but you should be able to appoint someone to manage and inherit your assets.

✔ **Assure adequate management of assets:** Your documents should clearly identify your assets, who will manage them, and where they are located.

✔ **Minimize time to settle estate:** Your documents should avoid *probate* (a court proceeding where the validity of a will is determined by a judge) because it can be very time consuming.

✔ **Minimize cost of estate settlement:** In addition to being time consuming, the probate process can also be costly because it involves attorney's fees and court costs.

✔ **Efficiently transfer estate to desired beneficiaries:** When your estate plan avoids probate, your beneficiaries receive their share of your estate more quickly.

Do-it-yourself or hire an attorney?

Your decision to hire an attorney or create your estate plan on your own is an individual decision and should be based on whether or not you:

✔ Have a complex personal, financial, and/or business life

✔ Have an estate which is valued at more than $5 million (see the nearby sidebar for more information)

✔ Have a messy personal life (in the midst of a breakup, child custody battle, and so on)

✔ Are uncomfortable creating your own estate planning documents

Beware the federal estate tax rollercoaster

Estates that exceed a certain value must pay federal estate tax, and the amount of that value changes from year to year. In 2011 that value was $5 million dollars and in 2012 it will increase to $12 million. More than likely, if you're like most Americans, your entire estate will pass to your beneficiaries free from any federal estate tax. *Note:* The higher exemption value is set to expire at midnight on December 31, 2012. That means, on January 1, 2013, the federal estate tax exemption will revert back to the $1 million dollar value — unless Congress extends the estate tax exemption before it expires.

Regardless of whether you draw up your own estate planning documents or ask an attorney to do it for you, as long as your relationship isn't legally recognized, you *must* put your wishes in writing to protect your rights and the rights of your loved ones.

If you want to use an attorney but would prefer someone who is gay or gay-friendly, contact your local LGBT organization, community center, or bar association and ask for a referral.

Before deciding whether to hire an attorney, you may want to:

- ✔ Read through this book to educate yourself about the fundamentals of estate planning
- ✔ Complete the estate planning worksheet on the CD
- ✔ Try creating some of the simpler documents
- ✔ Check your gut and trust your instincts

After you complete these steps, if you're sure you understand the basics of estate planning, and are confident of your ability to do-it-yourself, you're probably ready to give it a try.

If money is an issue and you cannot afford to hire an attorney to draw up your estate plan, consider creating your own and then find an attorney who — for a small fee — is willing to look over your documents and offer advice and suggestions that you can apply on your own.

Making your estate plan official

After you create your estate planning documents, you still need to take care of a few other items to ensure your documents are legally valid.

1. **You must sign your documents according to your state's law.**

   With exception of a few states, a person must be at least 18 years of age to sign a valid will, trust, or contract. In order to make a legal document stand up to a challenge, it should also be signed by two witnesses and a notary.

   Included on the CD is an Appendix with signing requirements in all 50 states.

2. **When you are ready to sign your documents, do so at a place where you regularly conduct business, such as your bank, real estate agent, insurance agent, and so on.**

   Generally, these places have a notary on staff, and a couple of employees can act as your witnesses. Signed copies of your documents are considered your originals. Make sure to sign in blue ink to help you distinguish photocopies from originals.

Having your lesbian and/or gay friends witness and notarize your documents generally isn't a good idea in case someone should challenge whether you were of sound mind or under undue influence at the time you signed. Will challenges alleging undue influence have occasionally been successful when a disgruntled family member suggests the deceased was surrounded by LGBT witnesses and a notary who then used coercive tactics to compel the deceased to name his or her LGBT partner as executor and/or beneficiary of the will.

What to do with your documents after they're signed

After you sign the documents, make at least one photocopy of each original (signed) document and then do the following:

- ✔ Give copies of your living will and medical power of attorney to your doctors to keep in your file.
- ✔ Put a copy of your living will and medical power of attorney in the glove compartment of your car.
- ✔ Give copies to the person you appointed to make medical decisions for you.
- ✔ Take copies of your durable power of attorney to your financial institutions, and they will be less likely to challenge your partner's authority to act.

After your documents are properly signed and photocopies are made, you need to put them in a safe place. Keeping originals of your will and advance directives in a safe deposit box may be unwise. For example, if something happens to you when the bank is closed, your next-of-kin (not your partner) may be able step in and make decisions that are counter to your wishes.

Put the originals of your legal documents in a large freezer bag and place them in the freezer section of your refrigerator. Your freezer is an easily accessible, fire-resistant safe. Whatever you do, make sure you tell those you name to manage your assets and settle your estate where your documents are stored.

Thinking About Long-Term Care Insurance

Life insurance can be an excellent tool to provide financial security for a surviving partner and children and should be part of any solid estate plan. Due to the inability to take the marital deduction (discussed in more detail in Chapter 9), it may be appropriate for an LGBT couple to have cross-owned insurance; that is, each partner is the owner and beneficiary of a life insurance policy on the life of the other partner. When an insured life partner dies, the surviving partner (as owner and beneficiary) can use the proceeds for expenses incidental to settling the deceased partner's estate, to replace loss income, and so forth.

The proceeds from a cross-owned life insurance policy aren't taxed as part of a deceased's partner's estate because that partner didn't own the policy.

If a cross-owned life insurance policy isn't an option, an LGBT couple may want to obtain long-term care insurance. Not only are these policies becoming more comprehensive and affordable, the premiums also may be deductible for income tax purposes (with some limitations) as a health insurance expense.

Premiums for long-term care insurance plans are expensive, and the fine print on your policy may be hiding important information, such as when benefits start, what amount of the maximum daily payout, how long benefits will last, and what services are covered. Some policies have strict eligibility conditions for paying benefits; thus, if you don't meet these conditions, you may be incurring long-term care expenses but won't receive any benefits to cover them. Before buying a long-term care policy, make sure you understand what you're really getting and how much it will cost. Contact a trusted insurance agent for more information about making life and long-term care insurance part of your comprehensive estate plan.

An estate plan isn't about death and dying — it's about life and love

Naturally, no one wants to think about illness, death, and dying — especially when it involves your own lives and those of your loved ones. Because thinking about end-of-life matters can be difficult, too many gay men and lesbians put off getting their legal ducks in a row until it's too late.

Sadly, as a result of this disparity, when a life partner dies, the surviving partner often suffers more than bereavement. He or she may lose the home or items of personal property. He or she can be denied access to the partner's children, even if he or she helped raise them. And the surviving partner can be shut out of important rituals and decisions associated with saying goodbye: Will the body be buried or cremated? What shape will the funeral or memorial service take? Will an organ donation pledge be respected? An estate plan spells out all this information.

Chapter 12

Last Will and Testament: Your Primary Estate Planning Document

A *last will and testament* (commonly referred to simply as a *will*) is a *testamentary document* (a legal document that doesn't take effect until after the death of the person who signs it) that lets you appoint someone to manage and settle your estate, and also allows you to name the persons or entities who will inherit your property after your death.

Depending on the state where you live, the person you appoint in your will to manage your estate is called your *executor* or *personal representative*. The persons or organizations you name to inherit your property in your will are known as *beneficiaries*.

Because the majority of states still don't recognize gay and lesbian relationships (see Chapter 2 for a discussion on marriage equality), same-sex couples should, at a minimum, have a will to ensure that their property passes to their family of choice rather than to their legal relatives.

Making a will is relatively easy, and most states let you write your own. When you create a will, you can make sure your wishes for leaving property to your loved ones are carried out after you die.

In this chapter we share with you why a will is necessary, what to include in your will, how to figure out how and who to leave property, how to ensure your will is valid, and why you shouldn't solely rely on a will (which doesn't take effect until after you die to protect and benefit your family of choice). We also discuss probate and why you should stay clear of it.

Where's There's a Will, There's a Way

When you have a will, you have a way to direct the manner in which your *estate* (all the stuff you own when you die) will be managed and distributed after your death. However, having a will gives you so much more.

All adults should have a plan in place for what they want to happen after they die. Unfortunately, because making a will forces a person to face the reality of death, estate planning tends to be the elephant sitting in the room that a majority of folks are determined to ignore.

If you don't have a will, you're risking unwanted outcomes and potential problems for your partner and any children you and your partner are raising as co-parents, especially if you're not a legal parent to the children. After all, a will lets you specify not only which assets you want to give and to whom, but also who you want to manage your estate and your choice of guardian for your minor children.

Even though it's perfectly natural to feel uncomfortable about making a will, doing so might make a big difference to your family of choice. And making a will really isn't that difficult. After you get past the emotional roadblocks, all it takes is a little knowledge and effort.

The following sections describe the reasons you absolutely need to have a will and why — if you and your partner are gay, lesbian and/or unmarried — you should use a will in conjunction with a trust and other documents to better protect and care for your loved ones and what happens if you don't have a will.

Understanding why you need a will

Putting your wishes in a legal writing is the most important thing you can do to protect your partner and/or family. A properly written and signed will can give you an incredible feeling of relief knowing your loved ones will be properly provided for after you're gone. Without a will (and a trust, as we explain in Chapter 14), same-sex partners have no legal rights to make decisions for one another, raise each other's children, or inherit one another's property.

When you draw up a will, you can put down on paper your wishes and decisions about vitally important matters. Make a will sooner than later; the motives for having a will include but aren't limited to the following:

> ✔ **A will presents a way for you to provide for your family of choice in a relatively simple and effective manner and at very little cost.** Caring for your family is your greatest responsibility.

✔ **A will allows you to leave special instructions for a loved one with special needs.** You want to make sure assets are distributed in such a way as not to qualify this person from government benefits.

✔ **A will reduces and possibly eliminates bitter and angry feelings between your family of choice and your biological family.** You can specifically spell out your choice of beneficiary of your property, manager of your estate (executor), guardian of your children, and alternate beneficiaries in case your first choice dies before you.

✔ **A will offers a way for you to name your partner as guardian of your children so their lives won't be even more devastated by the loss of both parents.**

If you and your partner have children and you're their only legal parent (by birth or by adoption), then, when you die, unless you've appointed your partner as guardian of your children in your will, they'll be considered orphans even though your partner has been a *de facto parent* (a stepparent or other person with equal or nearly equal parenting responsibilities of one or more children but without legal parenting rights) to them their entire lives. (Refer to the nearby sidebar for more information about de facto and the courts.)

To avoid the trauma of having your children ripped out of the arms of their surviving mom or dad, you need to do whatever is legally possible to create legal parenting rights for both partners.

In some states. even if you do nominate your partner as your child's guardian in your will, the courts aren't required to approve this nomination, and no guarantee prevents your relatives from trying to challenge the nomination. These challenges can lead to expensive and time-consuming litigation and are likely to cause emotional harm to your children and your partner.

If you don't have a partner, a will allows you to name a guardian to raise your children and choose someone to oversee your minor children's inheritance. (Refer to Chapter 7 for in-depth information on appointing a guardian.)

Don't put off making a will until it is too late. No one can predict when or if they'll experience a sudden illness or death, leaving no opportunity to sign a will.

Dying without a will: You're intestate

Recent polls show that between 60 and 70 percent of adults don't have a will. Chances are that the percentage is higher among the LGBT community because so many haven't come out to their families and/or to employers. They may not feel safe talking to a local attorney or putting into writing their wishes to empower and benefit their same-sex partner. Many who don't have a will, whether they're gay or straight, just don't want to think about their own mortality.

Whatever your reason for avoidance, you need to consider what'll happen to your loved ones and your property if you depart this life without having a will in place.

If you live in a state that has no legal protections for same-sex relationships and if you die *intestate* (without a will), your living loved ones can expect this to happen:

- ✔ Instead of you deciding who will be in charge of settling your estate and inheriting your assets, a judge will make that decision for you.

- ✔ When deciding who gets what, the judge will use your state's law of intestate succession (a law drafted by the state legislature that directs what happens to a deceased person's property when they die without a valid will) as a guide.

- ✔ Because the law of intestate succession always gives inheritance rights to legally recognized family members, your partner won't be considered a legitimate heir to your property.

- ✔ If you're raising a child who isn't your legal relative, that child won't have any legal right to inherit your property.

- ✔ If the judge determines you have no qualifying living relatives, the state itself — not your partner — is next in line to take your property.

Every state has its own intestate succession law and, although they differ slightly, they all give property and assets to your nearest legal relatives in a very specific order that goes something like this:

- ✔ If your state does recognize LGBT relationships and you and your partner marry or enter into a civil union, he or she will be first in line as your surviving spouse or domestic partner.

- ✔ If you have no spouse or partner (or if your relationship isn't legally recognized) and you have children, your kids will be first in line to inherit.

- ✔ If you have no spouse or children, your parents will get your property.

- ✔ If you have no spouse, children, or parents, your siblings are next, then your grandparents, aunts and uncles, next your nieces and nephews, your cousins, and so on down the line.

If your state doesn't protect the rights of unmarried partners, your partner won't be included on the list of legitimate heirs. The only way to ensure your same-sex partner has any right to control and inherit your property is by drafting and signing a valid will.

Protecting children's interests:
De facto co-parents and the courts

Courts understand that ongoing contact with both parents — even when the partner's break up — is always in the best interest of the children. In the absence of a legally recognized parent-child relationship between gay and lesbian parents and their children, nonlegal LGBT parents are sometimes denied custody of their children after the death of the legal parent.

Occasionally (unless the child has another legal parent that isn't the surviving partner), courts will decide that the nonlegal co-parent is the de facto parent of a deceased partner's children. A *de facto parent* is someone who has a parental relationship and is a regular caretaker of the child or children. Relevant factors a court uses

to determine whether or not someone is a de facto parent include

✔ If an established psychological bond exists between the nonlegal parent and child

✔ How much time the nonlegal parent has spent in the role of parent to the child

✔ Whether the nonlegal parent knows details about the child's medical history, school, religious activities, and so on that other parties don't know

As LGBT families are becoming more visible, courts are starting to integrate gay and lesbian parents and children into existing family law protections.

 If you live in one of the majority of states that offer no legal protections for same-sex relationships and you die without a will that names your partner as your executor and beneficiary, the state will treat your partner as a legal stranger to you. Your partner will have no right to manage your estate or inherit your property after you die.

Knowing What to Include in Your Will

You and your partner may have considered creating a will. If you're single, you may have thought drafting a will was something you wanted to do. Well, we're here to tell you: Do it. In this section we help you figure out what your will should and shouldn't say and how and to whom you should leave your property.

 After you decide to create a will, doing so only takes an hour or so of your time. The act of creating your will helps get rid of the uncertainty that's at the root of your nagging feeling. Even more important, having a will in place can spare your loved ones heartache, stress, time, and money.

Depending on the complexity of your lifestyle and the value of your assets, you may want to make a do-it-yourself will, use an online legal document preparation service, or hire an attorney or other legal expert to make a will for you.

You may want to use a preparation service, attorney, or legal expert to make your will if:

- ✔ The complexity of your relationships and size of your estate makes it problematic to use a simplified and generalized will format. For instance, if you have a strained relationship with family members who may challenge your will or if your assets are so valuable you think someone will try to undermine your wishes that everything goes to your family of choice.

- ✔ If you have a special situation that requires special planning, for instance, you're concerned that your choice of guardian will be challenged or you have a child or partner who is incapacitated or has special needs.

- ✔ If you own real estate in different states, your will should reflect the laws in each of those states.

If you feel you don't need the help of a preparation service, attorney, or expert and that you can make your own will with the help of this legal kit, you should make sure your will gets reviewed by an expert familiar with the estate planning laws in your state.

Before sitting down to make your will, fill out the property and asset inventory forms included on the CD (see Form 12-1).

The following sections are a guide to help you create your will. We discuss what your executor will do, how to choose an executor, and how to figure out how to compensate your executor.

Understanding what an executor is

One of the most important matters you have to deal with in your will is the appointment of the person who will settle your estate after your death. Depending on the state where you live, the person you choose is referred to as your *executor* or *personal representative*. Whichever title your state uses, the duties are identical.

Most of the duties your executor needs to perform don't require special expertise. Your executor can accomplish them without the help of an attorney or an accountant.

Generally, an executor of a will must

- ✔ Request certified copies of the death certificate
- ✔ Find and notify next-of-kin and beneficiaries named in the will
- ✔ Make an inventory and appraisal of personal property and financial accounts.
- ✔ Cancel credit and debit cards
- ✔ Collect snail and electronic mail and cancel any accounts or subscriptions, including online ones
- ✔ Notify government agencies (such as the IRS and Social Security Administration) of the death
- ✔ Collect proceeds from life insurance policies, employee death benefits, Social Security and/or veteran's benefits, union benefits, and so on

After the executor performs these preliminary duties, he or she needs to file the appropriate papers (including a death certificate and the will) with the probate court in the county where the deceased person lived. As soon as the probate judge issues an order giving the executor the authority to act, the executor must perform other duties, including:

- ✔ Organizing an estate sale of property that is not to be distributed to one or more beneficiaries named in the will
- ✔ Paying outstanding debts and taxes from the proceeds gathered from policies, accounts, and the sale of property
- ✔ Distributing remaining property and other assets to beneficiaries named in the will
- ✔ Filing income tax returns for the deceased and estate tax returns as required

 You can make the settling or administering an estate throughout the probate process easier if you refer to your executor throughout your will as an *independent executor*. Using this title should result in a simplified probate process that lets your executor act without a judge overseeing every little detail.

 In order to make certain your executor is able to act independently, add a sentence to your will directing that you want your will probated as simply and quickly as possible, and you want it probated free of court supervision. Some states may require your executor to file a petition requesting an independent administration. Check with your local probate court to determine whether your state requires a petition.

Choosing your executor

Your executor has a lot of important decisions to make, so you want to make sure you select someone who can successfully carry out the duties. Deciding who should be executor of your will is one of the most important determinations you'll ever make. Your choice of executor should not only be trustworthy and sensible but also organized and detail-oriented.

These sections look closer at who you should select and what happens if you don't select anyone.

Making the right selection

Whoever you choose, keep in mind that your executor is responsible for managing your assets, keeping accurate records, and interacting with financial and legal professionals. The person you choose doesn't have to be a superhero or a Rhodes Scholar, but the job does require persistence, intelligence, and commitment. The most important attribute when choosing your executor is a willingness to do the job. Ask permission and be sure to discuss in detail the duties that we outline in the previous section.

Your options for choosing an executor include the following:

- **Your partner:** For most people, the obvious choice for executor is a spouse or life partner because you probably trust this person more than anyone else to follow your wishes. If your spouse or partner is unwilling or unable — due to a disability or an aversion for performing one or more of the duties of executor — you need to choose someone else to settle your estate.

- **Friend or family member:** When your spouse or partner is unable to act as your executor, perhaps your next, best option would be to ask a close friend or relative who knows your wishes and is willing to do what is necessary to carry them out.

If your best choice for executor is a family member or close friend who lives in a different state, then for practical reasons you may want to consider appointing your second choice. Every state allows an out-of-state executor, but the executor may have more of a difficult time performing the routine duties necessary to settle your estate, particularly when he or she has to travel a long distance to do so.

- **Co-executors:** You many want to appoint two or more people, perhaps a couple (spouses or partners), siblings, or any two people you know who tend to work well together, to act as co-executors. The only way using co-executors can work is if everyone sees eye-to-eye on most if not all of the issues and if they're the type of individuals who can share responsibilities and duties well.

In many cases, having co-executors is probably a bad idea. When co-executors can't or won't work together, the time it takes to settle your estate may slow to a crawl.

✔ **Professional executor:** Although choosing someone you know and trust is better to serve as your executor, when you don't have that option, you may want to consider appointing a professional individual or organization (financial institution, lawyer, accountant, and so on) to administer your estate. Going with a professional is especially true if you have a large and complicated estate or if you have a beneficiary with special needs.

A professional executor will probably charge a fairly high fee for their services and, before you make your will, you need to make sure the professional wants to be appointed as your executor.

Knowing what happens if you don't appoint an executor

In the event you're unable or unwilling to choose an executor for your will, your will is still valid, but the court will appoint someone to be the *administrator* (someone to manage or administer your estate). Unfortunately, that person may not be someone you or your beneficiaries know or trust.

If you don't appoint someone as executor in your will, many states allow for the person who stands to inherit more than half of your property to serve as your administrator. When no such obvious person exists, the court may or may not choose someone based on their relationship to you and in the following order:

✔ If you live in a state with legal recognition of same-sex partners, the court will probably appoint your spouse or domestic partner.

✔ Your legal children if you have any. If not, then the court turns to your grandchildren. If you don't have any, then the court turns to your great-grandchildren as long as they're adults.

✔ Your parents, if they're alive. If they aren't, the court turns to your siblings, specifically, a brother or sister who lives in or nearest to your state of residence.

✔ Your grandparents, if they're alive. If they aren't, then the court turns to your aunts, uncles, and first cousins.

✔ Your legal stepchildren — in other words, the children of your legally recognized spouse or partner — if you have any. If none, then the court turns to your next nearest legal relative; in other words, according to the way your state's law views the term "nearest relative."

Keep in mind that a probate court has a lot of discretion about who it can choose as administrator. The court tends to choose an administrator who lives in the same state as the deceased person, if there is anyone. Otherwise the court may choose someone who lives closest to the deceased. In the states that have adopted a set of laws called the Uniform Probate Code, judges can disqualify anyone they find "unsuitable" — in other words, if evidence suggests that someone is dishonest, is mentally incapacitated, or has a drug and/or alcohol abuse problem, the court won't appoint that person.

If your partner and/or kids aren't legally related to you according to your state's law, they're not on the list! Thus, if the court can locate no living legal relatives, and you didn't appoint someone else as executor in your will, the court will appoint someone — possibly one of your creditors — to settle your estate!

For this reason, if you're able to choose an executor, make sure you appoint an alternate person to act as your executor just in case your first choice dies or becomes incapacitated prior to your death. Make sure you use the same criteria in choosing an alternate as you did in choosing your first executor.

Establishing how your executor will get paid

As you contemplate who it is you want to appoint as your executor, consider the issue of executor *compensation* (payment). Every state allows for an executor to be paid for administering a will. Depending on your state's law, the fee paid to your executor may be a percentage of the value of your entire estate (assuming the bigger it is, the more work will be required), or it may be what the law refers to as a reasonable fee (a fair and proper payment) for performing a particular duty or task.

If you appoint your partner or someone else who will inherit under your will, that person will probably perform the duties of executor at no cost.

When your executor isn't your partner or other beneficiary named in your will, we suggest you leave a sum of money to that person as compensation for the work they will need to do to settle your estate.

Deciding How to Leave Your Property

The primary objective of your will should be to empower and benefit your family of choice. Unlike heterosexual families, LGBT families are often seen as legal strangers in the eyes of the law. To counter this inequity, you need to carefully design the distribution of your assets depending on the complexity of your family structure.

For example, if you want everything you own to go to one or more persons, your distribution will be straightforward and fairly simple. If you have a plan to distribute property between individuals and organizations (like a charity) while also leaving specific items of property to others, you need to design a more complicated distribution plan.

Until LGBT Americans have equal civil rights in all 50 states, any distribution of property for LGBT couples, with or without children, will be more complex than for married, heterosexual families. Of course, everyone, regardless of their marital status or sexual orientation, needs to draw up a will to ensure that whatever property and assets you own go to people or beneficiaries you designate. Without a will, the court makes these decisions for you.

The criterion for leaving property applies equally to both a will and a living revocable trust (see Chapter 13 for how to establish a trust). Therefore, if you choose a trust as your primary document for leaving property to your loved ones, the following sections also apply to you.

In the following sections we discuss the best way to set up the distribution of property in your will, depending on the makeup of your family. Trying to categorize all the various familial models that exist in the LGBT community is nearly impossible. This is, in part, because historically gay men and lesbians have had to create their own families of choice after being rejected by biological family members. And, until recently, the law didn't define those relationships as familial.

Whether or not you live in a state that recognizes same-sex relationships, we identify four broad categories of family structures and then provide an all-purpose distribution plan for each category in the following sections. In the more comprehensive discussion that follows, we also consider other contingencies to guide you in expanding a distribution plan so that it better suits your individual circumstance.

Before leaving your property, think about your distribution as a pie chart. The slice of your estate that you give to a beneficiary is a certain percentage of the pie. So, no matter how many beneficiaries you name, when you add the total of all the individual slices, they should equal 100 percent. And remember, there is no one hard and fast rule. You know best what is fair relative to your relationship to your kids and your partner and their financial or other needs.

Whenever possible, if one of your beneficiaries or executors dies, make a *codicil* (a document that modifies or amends your will), an entirely new will.

Plan A: Leaving property to your partner and children

Distribution plan A involves a scenario where you're in a committed relationship with a partner (legally recognized or not), you and/or your partner have children, and you want to leave 100 percent of your property to your partner. This isn't a problem if:

- ✔ **You and your partner are both legal parents of your minor and/or adult children.** If your partner is a legal parent to your minor child or children, and you leave 100 percent to your partner, more than likely he or she will continue to support the children until they are grown. Then, when your partner passes, he or she will probably leave everything to the children — whether or not they are under the *age of majority* (under 18) — in his or her will.

- ✔ **You have adult, nondisabled children, and your partner isn't a legal co-parent to them.** If so, you can name your partner as your primary beneficiary and your children as your alternate beneficiaries to inherit after your partner or if your partner dies before you.

  If you die leaving everything to your partner, he or she has a right to leave that inheritance to anyone he or she chooses. So, if you want to be certain that your adult children will inherit something from your estate, you may want to give some, but not all, to your partner and the rest to your adult children.

- ✔ **You have a child who is incapacitated (whether or not an adult) and receiving government benefits (such as Social Security or Medicaid), or you have a minor child and your partner isn't the legal parent.** Make sure your distribution is written in such a way as to not disqualify your child from being eligible to receive those benefits. You want to add language that directs the trustee to use it to pay for the child's expenses and not to give it directly to your child. If this describes your situation, then you should seriously consider discussing your estate plan with an attorney who has experience in drafting wills that take care of disabled beneficiaries who are receiving government benefits.

  If one or more of your children is a minor or incapacitated in some way and your partner isn't the legal parent, you need to arrange for your child to inherit a portion of your estate that will enable your child's caretaker to raise your child in a manner that will enable your child to live to his or her fullest potential, which may mean taking out a life insurance policy on your life that names your child as the beneficiary. If you do leave property to your minor or disabled child, be sure to add language to your will that puts that property into a trust for the child until he or she is mature and responsible enough to manage a large sum of money. You can also appoint someone to manage this property for your child throughout their minority. Chapter 13 discusses this topic in greater depth.

Plan B: Leaving property to your partner if you have no children

Use distribution plan B if you're in a committed relationship with a life partner and you have no children. Assuming there is nobody in your life who is depending on you for financial assistance, you can leave 100 percent of your property to your partner with no worries about inadvertently harming someone who is vulnerable.

If you choose plan B, don't forget to name one or more alternate beneficiaries in case your partner dies before you.

Plan C: Leaving your property when you have children but no partner

Distribution plan C is a good plan to use if you have no partner but do have children or other dependents. Like plan B, you can leave 100 percent of your property to one person or you can divvy it up, leaving equal or unequal shares to a number of beneficiaries, depending on the closeness of their relationship to you or their relative need. You need to make sure when all the shares are totaled that they equal 100 percent.

As in plan A, if you have disabled or minor dependents, you should set up a trust in your will to hold the property you give to them and appoint someone to manage that property. Make sure you add language to your will to protect the eligibility of government benefits for the disabled dependent and consult with an attorney to prepare or at least look over your documents.

Plan D: Leaving your property if you have no partner and no children

If you're single and you don't have children or other dependents, you can use distribution plan D. In this scenario, no legal or social conventions dictate how you should divide your property. You can leave it all to one person, an organization or charity, or you can distribute it among various friends, family members, and organizations.

When you have multiple beneficiaries, you need to think about who will get a particular beneficiary's share if they die before you. For example, you can divide it between the surviving beneficiaries, give it to the children of the deceased beneficiary, or leave it some other way (to a different person altogether, a charity or an organization).

Be sure to name alternate beneficiaries to inherit your property if your first choice of beneficiary dies before you. If you don't, your state's law of intestate succession (refer to the earlier section, "Dying without a will: You're intestate" for more information) will kick in and your property will be distributed to your next-of-kin.

Making Sure Your Will Is Valid

The most important point of having a will is ensuring that it's *valid,* or legitimate. If your will is held to be invalid (not legitimate), some if not all of your wishes won't be followed and some if not all of your property may go to people or institutions you didn't name in your will. In other words, the law acts as though you died intestate — or without a will. For more information on what happens when you die without a will, see the previous section, "Dying without a will: You're intestate."

Therefore, before you even make your will, verify that you know what to do to make sure your will is legally valid. For example:

- ✔ **You must be 18 years of age or live in a state that allows exceptions to certain minors.** Some states permit an underage person to make a will if they are married, serving in the military, or legally *emancipated* (a judge issued order liberating a minor from the control of his or her parents or guardians).

- ✔ **You must be of *sound mind* (mentally competent).** In order to have the mental capacity to draw up a will, the law requires that you understand what a will is and what it does, and that you're aware of what property you own and who will inherit it.

If you meet the preceding criteria, you're capable of making a will. Nonetheless, in order for the will to stand up in court, additional requirements must be met. Although the details differ a bit from state to state, in general a valid will must contain the following:

- ✔ One or more specific provisions for giving away your property and/or naming someone to care for your minor children or pets.

- ✔ Your signature and the date the will was signed (refer to the later section "Examining the process for signing your will" for more information)

- ✔ The signature of two witnesses who aren't named in the will as your beneficiary or executor (check out the later section, "Choosing your witnesses: The how-to" for selecting your witnesses).

You must clearly state your intentions in the provisions you write. In other words, a person reading your will should have no difficulty understanding your wishes so that they can be carried out.

We place a sample will on the accompanying CD to help you determine what you need to include in your will (refer to Form 12-2).

If you decide to create a do-it-yourself will (via a kit or software), use a computer or word processor to ensure that your words are legible. Use high-quality paper and a laser printer to print your will. Documents printed on inkjet printers tend to fade over time and smear when they get wet. If you don't have a laser printer, save your will on a disk or zip drive and take it to an office supply store or print shop to have it professionally printed.

Except for your signature, the signatures of your witnesses, and the date, you should *never* use a pen or pencil to write or scratch out words or phrases on your typed will. A will that is both typed and handwritten may be held to be invalid because determining whether the typed or handwritten words actually reflect your wishes or whether someone else wrote on your typed will after you signed it is extremely difficult.

These sections discuss some important points you need to know and potential problems to avoid to ensure the validity of your will. If you're serious about making a will, you must read these next sections so you will better understand what you should and should not do.

Recognizing problems with handwritten and spoken wills

Some states allow for handwritten or holographic wills as long as the entire will is handwritten. Often, a handwritten will doesn't have to be witnessed in order to be considered valid. If someone were to challenge the validity of a holographic will, your executor will have a very difficult time if not impossible time proving the handwriting belongs to you, especially if the will isn't witnessed.

As for a spoken or oral will, in order for it to be legitimate, the law generally requires that a mortally wounded person or someone facing imminent death speak it. The dying person must be desperate to express his or her last wishes and have no other means to do so except by uttering them to a nearby person. A court generally doesn't recognize the validity of an oral will unless the person uttering the will dies unexpectedly, as in a war or in an accident.

Handwritten and oral wills can cause a ton of legal problems for your loved ones who would have difficulty trying to prove the handwriting is yours or that you verbally articulated a legitimate oral will on your deathbed. Thus, even if you do live in a state that allows for handwritten and/or oral wills, doing so can be extremely dangerous and foolish for you to attempt to use either of them to protect your same-sex partner.

The law assumes a person who wants his or her property to pass to someone other than legal heirs will take the time to put their wishes in writing. Therefore, because you're reading this book, you presumably have lots of time to write a proper will.

Choosing your witnesses: The how-to

After you die, your executor must present your will to your local probate court which then begins the process of validating your will. In other words, the court must determine whether or not the will is actually yours.

In order for a will to be held as valid (and perhaps survive a legal challenge by someone claiming your will was forged or that it's a counterfeit), two witnesses need to be present when you execute it (sign). Both witnesses must see you sign the will, and they must also see each other sign it. In order for the will to be valid — just like the person making the will — the laws in most states require your witness to be older than age 18 and of sound mind.

When choosing witnesses to sign your will, keep these important considerations in mind:

- ✔ **Make sure they aren't named in your will as a beneficiary, guardian, or executor.** A witness should never be someone who has a vested interest in your will. When a person is in line to inherit property or benefit in some other way, his or her credibility as an unbiased witness to the signing of your will is compromised. In order to make sure a witness is more likely to testify as to your state of mind when you sign your will, he or she shouldn't have a dog in the fight.

- ✔ **Ensure the witnesses don't have any undue influence over you.** If someone has excessive power that causes you to do something against your will over you, and it can be proved that you were pressured into signing a will you didn't wish to sign, your will may be considered invalid on account of that pressure.

- ✔ **Select someone who is heterosexual if you live in a state that doesn't legally recognize your relationship and that is hostile to LGBT rights.** Don't ask your gay and lesbian friends to witness or notarize your will.

If you do, a disgruntled relative may be able to convince a probate court that your gay and lesbian witnesses and notary coerced you into giving your Svengali-like partner everything you own.

✔ **Verify your witnesses will be around, if necessary, to testify to the authenticity of your signature after you die.** Whenever possible, try to pick witnesses who are healthy and younger than you are and don't ask someone to witness your will if you know he or she is planning to move away.

Because you can't predict the future and be certain your witnesses will be available when you die, consider creating a *self-proving affidavit* (a notarized document) that you and the two witnesses who watched you sign your will and heard you say that it's your last will and testament sign. A self-proving affidavit can potentially save your partner and other loved ones from having to endure a long and costly probate process by adding an extra layer of protection.

We include a sample self-proving affidavit on the accompanying CD (see Form 12-3).

A good way to have your will and other documents witnessed and notarized is to visit your bank, insurance, or real estate agent and use the notary they have on staff and other employees as your witnesses. Sometimes these types of business provide notary services free to their customers, and, even if they do charge a fee, they're professional people with whom you do business and who know you have the capacity to sign and that you aren't being pressured to sign against your will.

Examining the process for signing your will

To prepare for the signing of your will, you first need to coordinate the date and location with your witnesses and notary and then familiarize yourself with the legal requirements for signing a valid will. In general, those requirements are

✔ You, both witnesses, and the notary must be present in the same room at the same time to sign the will and watch each other sign it.

✔ Before executing your signature, say out loud that this is your last will and testament (doing so is important because some states require that you acknowledge that you're aware that you're signing your will).

> ✔ Place your initials on the bottom of each page on the lines provided, if any, and if not, initial the bottom right corner of each page. Adding your initials should prevent someone from actually removing and replacing one or more pages and also may prevent an accusation by a disgruntled relative that your partner removed and replaced pages in your will.
>
> ✔ You and the witnesses must sign the last page of your will in the presence of each other and while you're all watching. Make sure you sign your name as it's printed on the will.
>
> ✔ Have the witnesses print their names and addresses on the lines provided on the signature page of your will.

The contents of your will are nobody's business, and your witnesses are only there to witness your signature and not to read the names of your executor, your beneficiaries, or what property you are giving and to whom. In order to keep that information private, just place a sheet of paper over everything except where you and the witnesses will sign.

Making sure your executor knows where your will is located

After your will is signed, keep it in a location that your executor can easily access. Make sure you tell your executor where your will is stored. If you place it in a locked box or cabinet, either give your executor the combination to your safe, a copy of the key, or tell him or her where the key is hidden.

A good place to store your legal documents is the freezer section of your refrigerator — in a waterproof container of course. Not only is your fridge easy to get to, it's also fire-resistant. Better yet, we doubt that your executor would forget such an unusual storage space.

If an attorney makes your will, chances are he or she will also store a signed original in the law office. Some online services, such as Rainbow Law, offer secure, online storage of your signed documents. Rather than keeping a hard (paper) copy of your will, the service scans the signed will and stores it electronically, giving you a password to download your will as needed.

Creating multiple copies of your will

Before making a photocopy of your will, consider using a black and white photocopy machine because newer color copiers make it almost impossible to tell the difference between originals and copies.

You may want to print extra unsigned copies of your will to give to your partner, executor, or other loved ones so they know your intentions. If you decide to do this, make sure you add a watermark or write the word "duplicate" on each page.

Making two original wills to sign simultaneously may not be a wise choice. If you give one original to your executor or some other trusted person and then later forget you did so, it may cause a conflict if you later write a new will. Any time you make a new will, make sure it includes a sentence that revokes any previous will. Failing to do so can cause potential confusion about which reflects your most recent intentions.

Identifying Documents That Support Your Will

Although a last will and testament, standing alone, should empower and protect your partner and other loved ones, you may want to consider other documentation to enhance and support what you're trying to accomplish with your will.

You can create a variety of legal and nonlegal documents to accompany your will. For the purpose of this book we limit our discussion to the documents that are more likely to reinforce a will written by and for LGBT partners and families. We discuss four important documents in the ensuing sections.

Other documents supporting your will, which we more thoroughly discuss in Chapter 9, include a healthcare directive, living will, power of attorney for finances, and so on.

Preparing a separate writing to your will

A separate writing lets you give particular items of personal property to people you specifically name in a separate document entitled "a separate writing to your last will and testament."

For example, perhaps you're leaving almost all your property to your partner, but you have one or more family heirlooms that your parents or grandparents passed down to with the understanding they would remain in the family. Or, maybe you have a good friend who has repeatedly said he or she admires a work of art you have in your home.

In order to be deemed as valid, a separate writing must

- ✓ Be referenced by your will (or your living revocable trust)
- ✓ Be handwritten and signed by the person making the will
- ✓ Explicitly describe the items of property to be given and identify the recipients of the property with reasonable certainty

Although your will should reference a separate writing, it doesn't prescribe to any format. You can simply place the title "Separate writing to my last will and testament" at the top of the page and then list the property and the name of the person you want to have it.

You can make the separate writing before or after the will is signed, and you can add property and recipients to it or delete them as needed without updating or amending your will (or trust). You can also designate an alternate beneficiary for the property in case your first choice dies before you.

The separate writing isn't a formal legal document and thus doesn't need to be typed out or formatted in a specific way. It's just a sheet of paper (or more if your list is long) with the title "separate writing to my last will and testament" at the top of the page. Underneath the title, write a description of your personal property and the names of the people to whom you want to give that property. At the bottom of each page you should write your initials and add the date and your signature to the bottom of the last page.

You can find a sample separate writing on the accompanying CD (check out Form 12-4).

Making a disposition of remains

In Chapter 9 we discuss the need for LGBT couples to create *advance directives* (revocable living will and medical and financial powers of attorney) to give one another powers and authority in case of illness or injury. These documents cease to be valid as soon as you die. Therefore, even if your partner has been making medical decisions for you up to the moment of your death, as soon as you die, your partner's power to have any say over what happens to your body no longer exists.

And, even though you may have nominated your partner as executor in your will, because a judge must first approve of your partner's designation as executor, your family may swoop in and take control of your remains before your partner can get a court's order to stop them.

If this little detail bothers you, take heart! Most states have a law that permits you to create a disposition of remains to authorize your partner as your agent to take charge of your cremation or burial.

A *disposition of remains* form is a written communication of your wishes regarding what happens to your body after you die and who will be in charge of carrying out your wishes. Having a disposition of remains form is especially important if you want your body to be cremated because if you haven't put your wishes into writing anywhere else, a funeral director may require the consent of your legal relatives. If even one of them refuses to consent, the funeral home may decide not to cremate your remains.

Even when your state has no statute specifically dealing with the power to appoint someone to carry out the disposition of your remains, you should create one anyway. Just having such a document in hand may be all that is required to stop a disgruntled family member from adding insult to injury to your partner as he or she is in the process of grieving your death.

You can see a sample disposition of remains form on the accompanying CD (see Form 12-5).

Providing important information to your executor

In order to settle your estate after you die, your executor — even if he or she is your partner — must have access to certain information that can hasten the process. The best way to give most if not all of that important information to your executor is to create a separate document, commonly titled *information for executor,* that includes the following information:

- ✔ The name and contact information of all of the people, organizations, and institutions named in your will

- ✔ The names and contact information of your treating physician, accountant, insurance agent, financial planner, clergy member, and so on

- ✔ The name, address and phone number of your emergency contact person

- ✔ Your Social Security number

- ✔ The location of your safe deposit box or combination to your safe

- ✔ The location of your original legal and valuable papers (original will, trust, durable power of attorney (DPOA), bank and financial accounts, and so on)

> ✔ A list of places and people you gave copies of your DPOA, will, health-care directives, and other legal documents to
>
> ✔ Your wishes regarding a funeral or memorial service and how you want your body to be disposed of (burial, cremation, donated to science, and so on)

Communicating most of this information is better suited in a document separate from a will because the more personal information you share in your will, the more vulnerable it becomes to a legal challenge.

In addition to providing the preceding information on this document, depending on your particular circumstances, you may also want to add one or more of the following:

> ✔ An explanation as to why you want to leave property to certain people or institutions and why, if relevant, some beneficiaries are getting more than others — or why someone is getting nothing at all
>
> ✔ Directions for the care of your pets
>
> ✔ Instructions for dealing with your digital profiles — e-mail, social networking, websites, blogs, and so on, including user names and passwords

We include an example of this form on the CD (refer to Form 12-6).

You may want to add a handwritten note, write a separate letter, or record a video that tells the world that you consider your partner to be your spouse and, as such, you expect the courts and your legal family members to respect your feelings and commitment to your partner. Doing so is especially important if you and your partner got married in a state that recognized your legal union and then returned home or moved to a state that doesn't recognize your marriage. The letter or video announcing your feelings about your partner can clarify your intention to empower and benefit your partner, which can help to reduce efforts to challenge your will.

As you make your lists, write your letter, or record your video, be very careful not to say anything that in any way contradicts what you have stated in your will. Otherwise, you risk the possibility of creating confusion about your intentions, which may cause problems for your partner and result in all or part of your will being invalidated.

Why lawyers charge more for a living revocable trust than they do for a will

When an attorney drafts a legal document (unless she is fresh out of law school) she doesn't start each new document from scratch. In fact, most attorneys now rely on document assembly programs that merge your personal information into a form template. After the merging process is completed, the attorney reviews your document and modifies it as necessary.

As a consequence, these days it takes about as much time and effort to draw up a simple living revocable trust as it does to draft the average will. Nonetheless, even for a relatively straightforward and uncomplicated estate, a lawyer charges between $200 to $500 to draft a simple will and $2,000 to $5,000 to draw up a living revocable trust.

Nearly every will ever written by an attorney has the lawyer's name and contact information printed on the cover of the will or in the margin of each page. The lawyer does this knowing that after a person dies, there's a good chance the executor will contact the lawyer for help with the probate process. When this happens, the lawyer can expect to get paid a few thousand dollars in attorney fees. However, because a trust avoids probate, the lawyer services won't be needed later on.

In other words, the fee an attorney charges for making a trust often includes what she would have made for probating a will. She simply adds the probate fees upfront when drafting a trust.

Thinking about adding a living revocable trust to your estate plan

A will by itself may not be a sufficient estate plan for empowering and benefiting your same-sex partner and family of choice. Chapter 13 discusses the pros and cons of creating a *living revocable trust* (a legal document that lets you give property to your family of choice, avoids probate and — unlike a will — takes effect the minute you sign it) and how it may better protect the rights of LBGT families.

After reading Chapter 13, if you decide you would rather have a living revocable trust, you still need a will. However, when you have both a trust and a will, you must add a pour over provision to your will. A *pour over provision* is a paragraph in the will that allows and empowers your executor to take property that wasn't put into your trust prior to your death and retitle it in the name of your trust. This pour over provision ensures that your valuable property will pass to your beneficiaries through your trust and thus avoid probate, which we discuss in the next section.

You can peruse a sample pour over will on the accompanying CD (see Form 12-7).

Getting the Lowdown on the Probate Process

The probate process, in particular, for LGBT couples and families, often evokes one particular feeling. Dread. *Probate* is a legal procedure that starts shortly after a person dies — with or without a will. The job of the probate court is to find out whether or not a will is valid.

Doing what you can to avoid probate is your ultimate goal. These sections outline why you should stay clear of it and what happens if a will is challenged.

Understanding why you want to avoid probate

Before settling on a will as the document to pass property to your partner and family of choice, ask yourself why you would risk putting your partner through the dreaded probate process if you can avoid it. Fortunately you can keep your wishes private and pass property to your partner immediately after your death — without going through the probate court. The most effective method for avoiding probate is by drawing up a living revocable trust, in which we discuss in detail in Chapter 13.

The three main reasons LGBT couples should avoid probate are

- It opens the door to a will challenge, resulting in court costs and attorney's fees (if an attorney is hired to defend the will). A will doesn't take effect until you die and therefore, if someone steps forward to challenge it, you won't be around to defend your will. More than likely, if a challenge happens, your partner — or other executor — will be forced to fight the will challenger in court, resulting in having to pay an attorney to help plus any fees associated with filing documents or holding hearings with the court.

- It's a public process and the entire spectacle plays out in the community at large and becomes part of public record so anyone can stick his nose in your business and see what property you owned and who you left it to.

- If your will is challenged, assets will be frozen (perhaps for months or even years) until the court can determine whether or not the challenge is legitimate. When a will challenge occurs, a judge will put a hold on your partner's (or other executor's) right to distribute money to your beneficiaries, sell your house or other property, and so on, until the judge determines that your will is valid.

If you don't have a will or living revocable trust, the court will rely on state law when appointing an executor and distributing property. If you live in a state without legal recognition of LGBT partnerships, more likely than not your partner won't have any rights at all. To discover more about what happens when you die without a will, refer to the earlier section, "Dying without a will: You're intestate" for additional help.

Knowing what might happen when a will is challenged

If a will is to be probated, a probate court will appoint someone as executor of the will to oversee the decedent's assets and pay outstanding bills. More often than not the court will appoint the person who was nominated in the will unless the nominee is shown to be dishonest, lacking in character, or immoral, or has some other characteristic making him unfit to administer an estate.

The traits that may prompt a court to disqualify your partner as your executor may be in the eye of the beholder. So, if you're living in a state (especially in a rural area) where same-sex relationships are regarded as immoral or sinful, your partner may be disqualified by a biased probate judge. All a biased judge would need in order to disqualify your partner is for one of your more motivated and pushy relatives to accuse your partner of having undue influence over you.

Even if a judge isn't biased, she personally doesn't know you or your partner and therefore would be required to at least investigate claims made by your family member.

If the court ultimately decides not to disqualify your partner as executor (yet), the probate process can still be destructive because it's a public matter and the entire community will have access to the proceedings. That means everything that is in your will — all the property you own, the debts you owe, your partner's sexual orientation, and who you are giving your property to and who you are disinheriting — will be out in the open. This information can be especially damaging to school-aged children and to your partner if he or she isn't out to family or at work.

And even worse, if you own a house (or have bank accounts) in only your name, because your estate may be frozen during a will challenge, your partner may be barred from living in the home until the probate process has been completed.

It could be many months if not years before your partner (and possibly your children) would be able to reside in your home and have access to your bank accounts. In the end, if your will is held to be invalid, your family of choice may never have the right to inherit your property. Instead, your assets will be passed to your legal relatives according to your state's intestacy laws. In all but a handful of states your property goes to your family of origin and not your family of choice.

Chapter 13

The Living Revocable Trust: The Keystone to Your Estate Plan

. . . .

In This Chapter

▶ Defining and analyzing trusts

▶ Explaining how a trust works

▶ Knowing how to draw up a trust

▶ Understanding how to put a trust into action

. . . .

*U*nderstanding trusts and how they function isn't as complicated as you may think. If you know a little bit about *contracts* (a legal agreement where one party promises to do something or pay a sum of money in exchange for another party promising to do or give something in return) and *property rights* (the right to own and control real estate and personal property), then figuring out how trusts work is like a walk in the park.

Even if you don't have a firm grasp of contracts and property rights, getting a figuring out trusts shouldn't be too difficult. A *trust* is basically a legal contract that spells out exactly how you want your property (cash, investments, real estate, motor vehicles, and so on) to be managed when you become *incapacitated* (unable to manage your own affairs) and passed on to your *beneficiaries* (persons named in a will, trust, or insurance policy to receive money and/or property) after your death.

The idea of trusts began way back in medieval times when knights used them as a way to prevent the King of England from taking their land and property while they were off on crusades or slaying Huns. Like the Pilgrims, the law of trusts traveled to the New World on the Mayflower, and ever since wealthy families have used them to reduce estate taxes and pass property to their heirs (legal relatives with rights to inherit the estate of a deceased person) outside of a will. (Chapter 12 gives you more information on wills.)

In this chapter we explore what a trust is and explain why it's the most effective tool for protecting the rights of unmarried partners.

Defining a Revocable Living Trust and Its Characteristics

The word "trust" means faith and confidence in another. Hence, a *revocable living trust* creates a legal relationship where the trust's creator is counting on others to cooperate in carrying out certain duties and responsibilities. The law of trusts recognizes many types of trusts with a variety of functions and uses. This section focuses on revocable living trusts, also known as *grantor trusts* or *living trusts*.

Coincidentally — and unbeknownst to the brilliant minds who invented trust law — living trusts are simply a fabulous way to empower and protect LGBT families. Gay men and lesbians are better off using a living revocable trust together with a will because:

✔ A trust is a good way to avoid probate (Chapter 12 discusses the ins and outs of probate and Chapter 14 discusses putting property into a trust to keep it out of probate).

✔ A trust is less likely to be successfully challenged by disgruntled family members.

In most contracts, the parties making an agreement are two or more separate entities (people, businesses, or organizations). In a revocable living trust, the parties entering into an agreement are the *grantor* (the individual drawing up a trust) and the *trustee* (the person who manages the property held in the trust). As we explain throughout this chapter, the grantor and trustee in a living trust are the same person — *you!*

The following sections introduce three fundamental principles of a revocable living trust, including what it is, how it works, and who is involved.

A trust is living because it takes effect as soon as it is signed

A trust is *living* because it's created during your lifetime and takes effect as soon as you sign it. Shortly after signing a trust, you have to transfer your valuable property into the trust, using a concept called *funding* (the act of retitling your property from your own name to the name of the trust). Chapter 14 explains how to fund your trust. We include a sample trust (Form 13-1) on the CD.

After you have fully funded it, the trust immediately owns any property held in the trust, which can include bank accounts, real estate, motor vehicles, insurance policies, personal, and so on.

Because a trust takes effect immediately when signed, it's very difficult for someone to successfully challenge its validity. Of course anyone can try to challenge a trust, but because you interact with the trust throughout your life — by making deposits and withdrawals from bank accounts, buying and selling trust property, and so on —it's practically impossible for someone to convince a judge that you unknowingly or unwittingly named your life partner as the beneficiary of your property.

On the flipside, a will doesn't take effect until after your death and is therefore extremely vulnerable to a challenge by disgruntled relatives. Some unaccepting family members of a deceased gay or lesbian person have been known to accuse a same-sex partner of coercion and undue influence in a will challenge.

After you die, if a family member does decide to challenge your will, you won't be around to defend your partner's inheritance rights. Because a probate judge is required to investigate any reasonable accusation of undue influence or other wrongdoing, your partner may be forced to try to prove your intentions in a court of law. You can easily avoid this sad outcome by creating and properly funding your revocable living trust.

A trust is revocable because it can be cancelled or changed

As long as you're mentally competent (able to manage your own affairs), you can *amend* (change the terms) or *revoke* (end or cancel) a revocable trust. A trust is revocable because, as the name suggests, it can be cancelled in whole or in part as long as you're living and mentally competent. After the grantor dies, the trust becomes *irrevocable* (unchangeable).

Amending a revocable living trust

In order to amend a trust, a grantor simply draws up an *amendment* (a legal document that spells out the changes you want to make), signs it, and stores it with the original trust. An amendment doesn't cancel out your original trust; it simply changes some of the *terms* (the way the trust is worded) of the trust. If you ever decide to cancel or revoke your trust, you need to do so in writing.

You don't need to give copies of the amendment to anyone as long as the original trust clearly states that any future amendments will automatically be merged into the original trust.

Here are a few (but not all) of the occasions you may want to cancel or amend your trust:

- ✔ After moving to a different state
- ✔ After a breakup
- ✔ After the death of your partner or someone else named in your trust
- ✔ After having or adopting a child
- ✔ After changing your mind about giving money or property to someone
- ✔ After the death of the grantor

We include a sample trust amendment (Form 13-2) on the accompanying CD.

Revoking a trust

If you want to revoke a trust, tearing your trust into little pieces and throwing it in the trash isn't enough. If you've properly funded your trust, more than likely you've given copies to your bank, your insurance agency, the DMV, and other entities. In that case, you not only need to sign a revocation, you must give copies of the signed revocation to every person, business, agency, and so on where you have accounts or property you previously put into your trust.

Furthermore, if you've opened financial accounts in the name of your trust, you need to close them. If you've named your trust as beneficiary of your insurance or other policy, you need to name a new beneficiary. In fact, you must place any property that you retitled into the name of your trust back into your own or someone else's name after you revoke your trust. Chapter 14 provides more information on what to do before and after you revoke your trust.

The accompanying CD includes a trust revocation form (Form 13-3).

A trust is private and not part of the public record

Unlike a will (where after the death of the person, the will is filed with the probate court and made part of the public record), a revocable living trust is a private document. Rarely does anyone — not your homophobic family members, your ex-partner, or your nosy neighbor — ever have access to the information in your trust regarding your beneficiaries, your financial status, and how much and to whom you're leaving your property. Only in the very rare instance when a named trustee is unavailable or when one or more terms of the trust require interpretation by a court is a trust ever made part of the public record.

When you go to banks or other institutions to fund your trust, you don't need to produce your trust document. In fact, you can and should draw up and sign a separate document, called a trust certification (Form 13-4) to use when you want to open a financial account, change a beneficiary, retitle a car, or record a deed. This document is a condensed version of your living trust that includes only the information necessary to set up a trust account or to retitle property or assets into the trust. Otherwise, the certificate leaves out private information such as the value and identity of your property, the names of your beneficiaries, and what you are leaving them.

A trust avoids probate

Probate is a court proceeding where a judge determines the validity of a will and grants permission (via a court order) to the will's executor to transfer the deceased person's property to the beneficiaries named in the will. (Refer to Chapter 12 for more information on probate.)

The reason you, as an LGBT person, would want to avoid probate is simple: The probate process opens up a potential can of worms because it provides an opportunity for disgruntled relatives to challenge the validity of a will, thus undermining the wishes of the deceased person to leave property and other assets to a same-sex partner. Consequently, a properly funded revocable living trust is able to avoid probate entirely and therefore provide a faster and more efficient transfer of property to your family of choice after you die. (Chapter 14 discusses how to fund a trust.)

The probate process can be very stressful and time-consuming, taking months or years to complete. Because the judge personally doesn't know the parties to the will, any accusations the family members make, suggesting the deceased person was coerced into giving all of his or her property to a same-sex partner, will likely slow down the probate process even more. Thus the value of the partner's inheritance may be greatly diminished when he or she is forced to spend thousands of dollars on court costs and attorney's fees just to defend the will.

A trust can avoid all of this anguish and hassle because — through the act of funding — you actually transfer ownership of your property to your trust. Afterward, even though you continue to have complete control over that property as trustee of your trust, the law no longer recognizes you as owning that property. And because you're not the owner of the property, it doesn't get included in your will — and it won't be subject to probate.

Grasping Irrevocable Trusts (and How They Differ from Revocable Trusts)

When a grantor becomes incapacitated or dies (and no longer has the ability to change or cancel it), a revocable trust then becomes irrevocable. *Irrevocable trusts* are trusts that can't be changed. Many types of irrevocable trusts are designed to accomplish a variety of estate planning goals. Because we focus on helping the LGBT community members protect their relationships and rights with revocable trusts, in this book we offer only a brief analysis of irrevocable trusts.

Generally, irrevocable trusts are used for the following reasons:

✔ **Lowering the overall value of an estate to reduce estate taxes:** Some irrevocable trusts are drafted to protect the wealth of very rich families. They use these trusts to remove valuable property from a large estate so the property won't be taxed after their death.

✔ **Caring for a disabled loved one:** Planning for a child or other loved one with special needs may include the use of an irrevocable *special needs trust*, which can be established as a subtrust under your living revocable trust or will, or as an irrevocable stand-alone trust.

✔ **Protecting assets from creditors:** This type of trust (also known as a *Medicaid trust*) is often used in the event of a long-term care illness, such as cancer, multiple sclerosis, Alzheimer's, and so on. The ill beneficiary doesn't own the assets funded in an irrevocable trust; therefore, his or her creditors will probably be unable to reach them.

More and more gay men and lesbians are using irrevocable trusts to protect their property from a Medicaid lien in the event that one or both partners need long-term or nursing home care. The irrevocable trust is used for this purpose because federal and state law denies marriage rights to same-sex couples, and thus spousal protection from a Medicaid lien isn't available unless a home is placed into an irrevocable trust. See Chapter 9 for more on what Medicaid liens are and how to protect your assets against them.

Opting for an irrevocable trust is a big decision. The most significant difference between a revocable and an irrevocable trust is about the right to control the property in the trust. When a person signs a revocable trust, that person is both grantor and trustee. And as trustee, the grantor retains total control over the property placed into the trust.

By contrast, when a person signs and funds an irrevocable trust, she appoints someone else as trustee of that trust. As a result, the grantor who created the trust (more than likely the owner of the property that funded the trust) relinquishes ownership rights as well as control of the property. The right to control the property in an irrevocable trust is transferred to the trustee.

The grantor creates and funds the trust, but the grantor has no further control. The trustee has *legal ownership* of the trust, which means that she has the legal right to control the property. But that control is to be exercised on behalf of the beneficiary, who has the right to use and enjoy the property subject to the trustee's control. Not surprisingly, the beneficiary's interest is referred to as *beneficial ownership*.

None of the three — grantor, trustee, or beneficiary — has tax liability for the property held in the irrevocable trust. Instead, the trust has its own tax ID number.

Identifying How a Revocable Trust Works

You can use a revocable living trust to create rights, benefits, and obligations between you and your LGBT partner (or heterosexual unmarried partners), even as the law treats them as legal strangers to one another. In the following sections we use the art of storytelling to unravel the mysteries of a trust and reveal how they work to protect LGBT rights. In these sections we delve deeper into the workings of a trust including the players and the parts.

Identifying the cast of characters in a trust

A trust has a cast of characters who each play a role in the creating, managing, and receiving the trust. Having a solid understanding of these people and their roles in relation to each other and the property held in the trust can help you see the big picture.

Every living trust has the three important characters. The good news: All three of these individuals are often one and the same.

 ✔ **Grantor:** The most important character in a trust, the grantor is the person who makes the trust. Without this person, there would be no trust in the first place. In some *jurisdictions* (the state or other area over which a court's authority extends) the grantor is called the *trustor* or the *settlor*. We prefer the title grantor because the name itself describes the act of granting (or giving) something to someone, which is the primary role of the grantor.

A trust begins when a grantor *funds* or *retitles* property (changes the name of the owner) from the grantor's name to the name of the trust (generally, the name of a trust includes the grantor's name and the date the trust was signed). After the grantor has completed the task of creating and funding the trust, the trust has been activated. Although the grantor can continue to add property to and remove property from the trust, for the most part, the grantor's role is finished.

✔ **Trustee:** This person is who the grantor appoints to take over the care of the trust after it's signed and funded. The trustee has a duty to manage and grow the value of the trust property and to be prudent and wise when dealing with trust funds. The law calls this trust relationship a *fiduciary duty*.

Just as the grantor did before putting property into the trust, the trustee has the authority to do whatever is necessary to increase the value of trust assets. For example, a trustee has the right to lease property or invest money in order to generate income for the trust. If the trustee causes the trust to decrease in value — by intent or by neglect — the beneficiary has the right to sue the trustee who may then be removed as trustee and/or held liable for reimbursing the beneficiary for the value of the lost assets. Generally, a trustee remains in charge of the trust until the trust's funds are exhausted or when the trustee resigns, is removed, or dies. If a beneficiary wishes to sue his or her same-sex spouse or partner for breach of fiduciary duty, it's allowable; however, due to the nature of the relationship between the partners, it rarely happens.

✔ **Beneficiary (beneficiaries):** The *beneficiary* is the party to the trust who receives the benefit of the trust. With a revocable living trust, this person can also be the grantor and the trustee.

The reason the grantor made a trust in the first place was to benefit somebody. In a simple revocable living trust, the grantor is also the trustee and the beneficiary. This means the trustee manages the property to benefit him or herself as the beneficiary. And when the successor trustee takes over, if the grantor/beneficiary is still living, the trustee can't run off with the trust funds. Rather, the successor trustee must use the money to care for the grantor/beneficiary. After the grantor dies, the successor trustee distributes whatever remains in the trust to the grantor's alternate beneficiaries (one or more beneficiaries who will inherit under the trust if the first beneficiary dies before the grantor).

Recall that in a grantor/living trust, the trustee, grantor and beneficiary are the same person. However, if the grantor becomes incapacitated, his successor trustee takes over as trustee. When that happens, the grantor/beneficiary has two roles:

- To receive money and other assets from a trust

- To act as auditor of the trust to make sure the trustee is being responsible with the trust funds

> If the successor trustee is spending the funds inappropriately or improperly investing the funds, then the beneficiary is responsible for removing the trustee and replacing that trustee with another who will run the trust properly.

The ins and outs of a trust: Legal fiction

To fully grasp how a trust works, you need to know that the law of trusts uses something called a *legal fiction* (the law pretends something is what it clearly isn't in order to achieve a desired result). When a person signs a trust, the law pretends that person becomes two separate beings with different titles and responsibilities. Even more bizarre, the law no longer sees the signed trust as a piece of paper but rather as a container that can hold the grantor's property!

A good example of a legal fiction is a *corporation* (a business or a group of individuals authorized to behave as though they're a single entity). According to the law, after a business files articles of incorporation with a state, it becomes a legal person.

Although it's clear to everyone that a corporation most certainly is *not* a living, breathing soul, the law pretends it is a person in order to give the corporation certain rights that are otherwise reserved only for actual human citizens. For example, a corporation can enter into contracts, sue and be sued, and (more controversially) exercise free speech rights.

Eyeing the role of the successor trustee

A revocable living trust lets you appoint a *successor trustee* to take over the role of trustee when and if the original trustee — you — becomes ill or dies. When that happens, the successor trustee steps into your shoes and has automatic and immediate access to all the property you put into your trust without any waiting for the probate proceeding. Everything is private with no notice published in the newspaper or public hearing. You can read the later section, "Choosing a competent and trustworthy successor trustee" for some advice of picking a successor trustee for your trust.

Remember a trust is a legal fiction, and the grantor and trustee are both you. Thus you don't literally give yourself property you already own — it's just a legal sleight-of-hand. Also, the trustee or successor trustee of your trust isn't allowed to run off to Las Vegas with your money. Rather, the successor trustee must use the assets in your trust to take care of you — to maintain your property and pay your bills — just as you did before you created a trust.

Considering Key Issues When Drafting a Revocable Trust

Before drafting your trust, you need to be very careful to set out all of the specifics. Keep in mind that planning, drawing up, and funding a living revocable trust may take a bit more time than making a simple will.

To help you get ready to draft your trust, we include worksheets for making your lists, a sample inventory, and blank asset and property inventory forms (Forms 13-5 and 13-6) on the accompanying CD.

Estate planning involves thinking about hard stuff, including your own vulnerability and mortality. Make sure you take time to list all the people and organizations you want to name in your trust and to try and imagine as many "what ifs" as possible. (Refer to Chapter 11 for a complete discussion of estate planning.)

Here we help you understand the importance of choosing the right people to manage your property and to identify the best way to distribute your assets after you die.

Choosing a competent and trustworthy successor trustee

The successor trustee is someone you select to have the same rights and power over your property as you have now. The idea of giving someone complete power over all your assets may sound scary — even insane — so you want to choose someone competent and trustworthy. Whomever you choose, remember that a successor trustee has a fiduciary duty to the beneficiaries named in the trust, and that duty is both ethical and legal.

A majority of grantors choose a successor trustee with whom they're close and familiar. A trust is an effective way to pass property and rights to a same-sex or unmarried partner, especially when the partner is also the trust's successor trustee. If your partner can handle money and is honest and trustworthy, choosing your partner as your successor trustee may be the way to go.

In some cases, a spouse or partner — although wonderful in every other way — may just be a lousy money manager or may be incapacitated (severely ill or disabled) in some way. In that case you may want to go another route and choose a trusted friend, relative, or perhaps a professional person, such as an accountant or lawyer.

If you decide to choose someone else besides your partner, consider the following points:

- ✔ **Age of the person you want to appoint as your successor trustee:** You certainly don't want to choose someone who lacks the maturity and experience to manage your property, and you should be equally as wary of choosing someone who is much older than you are. More than likely, many years will pass before your successor trustee will step into your shoes. When that happens, you need this person to be able to perform the necessary duties and tasks.

- ✔ **The size or complexity of your estate:** If you have a large or complicated estate, you may want to use the services of a professional successor trustee, such as the trust department of a bank or other financial institution, an attorney, or an accountant. Professional trustees generally charge a monthly or annual fee based on a percentage of the assets they are managing. One disadvantage of using a professional trustee is the potential lack of sensitivity that may be required in making certain decisions.

Think long and hard about the ideal candidate to manage your trust and don't simply focus on the closeness of your relationship or his or her technical and financial competence. Perhaps the most important characteristic is whether your successor trustee will be motivated and enthusiastic about carrying out your wishes and instructions.

Perhaps you want to choose more than one person to act as trustee of your trust. If you decide to nominate two or more successor co-trustees, consider their personalities and try to imagine whether they will have difficulty making decisions together. If so, you may want to make their appointment *consecutive* (your second choice will only act if your first choice is unwilling or unable). Although tempting, nominating two people as successor trustee isn't very wise because it may complicate a process that would otherwise proceed smoothly.

Be sure to get permission from your prospective successor trustee before drawing up and signing your trust. The task of managing your trust and settling your estate involves some time and effort, and the successor trustee needs to accept the role in writing. As long as you're mentally competent, you can always amend your revocable living trust if you change your mind and decide to nominate someone else to be your successor trustee.

We include Sample Acceptance as Trustee (Form 13-7) and Resignation of Trustee forms (Form 13-8) on the accompanying CD.

Disinheriting relatives who might want to assert inheritance rights

Generally, the law of trusts permits you to name anyone you wish to be your beneficiary and lets you divvy up your property and assets in any manner you desire. It also lets you disinherit or omit someone (your parents, adult children, siblings, aunts and uncles, and so on) who would otherwise have a legal right to inherit your property.

The disinherit rule does have a few exceptions: in some states you may not be allowed to disinherit your legal spouse and/or minor children. Because the law in most states does protect a surviving legal spouse from being completely disinherited, it is imperative that the LGBT community prevail in our struggle for equal marriage rights!

If you live in a state that doesn't legally recognize your relationship, your trust should be drafted to not only to empower and protect your partner, but also to ensure that your biological family members are not able to circumvent the directives spelled out in your trust by asserting their rights as your legal heirs (those designated by law to be the rightful persons to inherit your property upon your death).

In order to successfully disinherit your legal relatives and thwart a potential challenge to your partner's right to inherit, you should:

- ✔ Add specific language to your trust that designates your partner as your primary beneficiary
- ✔ Incorporate precise disinheritance language that includes the legal names of your relatives and their relationship to you
- ✔ Include an additional *love and comfort clause*, which reiterates your intention to benefit your partner

We include an inheritance and disinheritance language as well as a sample love and comfort clause (Form 13-9) on the CD.

Using an in terrorem clause to prevent challenges to your trust

An *in terrorem clause* (also called a *no-contest provision*) is a clause in a trust (or will) that threatens to disinherit a beneficiary if that beneficiary challenges the terms of the trust or the amount of their inheritance in court. Adding such a clause and then notifying your beneficiaries that you've done so may be enough to prevent them from making a challenge in the first place.

We include a sample in terrorem clause (Form 13-9) on the CD.

Here is how it works: Say you live in a state that doesn't recognize LGBT rights, and you have a same-sex partner and two adult children from a previous relationship. Assuming you want to divide your property between your partner and your children, you devise a plan where your partner will inherit 60 percent and your children will equally share the remaining 40 percent between them. Suppose one or both of your children resent your partner and have indicated to you that they don't think it's fair that your partner will receive a greater share of your estate.

In order to maintain harmony and save your partner a lot of grief, you decide to include an in terrorem provision in your trust. More than likely, your children — who are each slated to receive a 20 percent share of your estate — would think twice about making a challenge, especially because doing so would mean they'd risk losing everything.

Including a no-contest or in terrorem clause may leave you with a false sense that they you've avoided a family crisis. However, the enforceability of these clauses in wills and trusts varies from state to state. In some states the clauses are unenforceable. In others they're enforceable unless the challenge is based on probable cause and/or good faith. Therefore, if you're truly concerned about a disgruntled family member making trouble for your partner, consider disinheriting him altogether. Any beneficiary named in your trust is entitled to an *accounting* (a record of financial accounts and transactions) from the trustee, which may be enough of an opening for them to wreak havoc.

Even if you disinherit a loved one in your trust, you can still benefit him by purchasing a life insurance policy on your life and naming that person as the beneficiary. When you do this, the proceeds of the policy will pass directly to that beneficiary outside of the trust. Problem solved.

Taking care of vulnerable beneficiaries: The special needs subtrust

If you have a beneficiary (your partner or someone else you care about) who is vulnerable, physically or otherwise, you may want to create a *special needs* subtrust in your revocable trust to take care of that beneficiary. A special needs trust can be drafted as stand-alone document or as a separate subtrust within your living trust. As a subtrust, your successor trustee funds the special needs trust upon your death.

You may need to include a special needs subtrust when a beneficiary

✔ Is a minor under the age of 18

✔ Is physically disabled or intellectually impaired

✔ Has a mental health condition

✔ Is addicted to drugs or alcohol

A special needs subtrust enables a minor child or an adult who is under a physical or mental disability to have an unlimited amount of assets held in the trust and managed by a trustee for the benefit of the under-age or vulnerable individual.

If a special needs subtrust is properly drawn up and funded, money and property held in the trust won't be counted as assets belonging to the beneficiary (or the trustee). Because neither the beneficiary nor the trustee owns the trust assets, the beneficiary retains his or her eligibility for government benefits (Supplemental Security Income [SSI], Medicaid, vocational rehabilitation, subsidized housing, and so on).

Unlike a revocable living trust, which uses the grantor's Social Security number, a special needs trust is its own *entity*, which means it requires an Employer Identification Number (EIN) as its tax ID number. An EIN is issued by the Internal Revenue Service (IRS) and is free of charge.

You will find the IRS forms for obtaining a federal tax identification number (FEIN) and copies of IRS forms SS-4 and 56 on the CD.

A special needs subtrust is irrevocable (it can never be cancelled and should only be amended when necessary) and ought to include provisions for the trust to end when the beneficiary attains a certain age, upon the death of the beneficiary, or when some other significant event occurs.

Depending on your comfort level and the complexity of your estate, you may need to hire an attorney to draft a special needs subtrust. However, with the right guidance, you may be able to create a special needs subtrust yourself, with the help of a document preparation service or by using legal document software.

If the trust is to be funded with funds owned by a beneficiary rather than your own money, complicated, state-specific rules may apply. In that case you really ought to get input from a lawyer experienced in drafting special needs trusts.

Knowing What Happens When a Grantor Becomes Incapacitated

When someone is *incapacitated,* he is generally unable to manage his own affairs due to an inability to communicate and/or effectively process information. A person may be incapacitated due to a mental or physical illness, advanced age, a head injury, stroke, learning disability, or a specific disease (including Alzheimer's).

Incapacity can be short or long term. For some people, after capacity is lost, it never returns, and others (due to congenital or other conditions that develop early in life) may have never had capacity in the first place. For most people, incapacity develops gradually, over the course of years and due to the aging process. Less often, incapacity results from an unexpected and acute illness or injury.

A person can have a *disability* (be in bad health, lack the ability to see or hear, or be unable to use one or more limbs) and not be incapacitated. In fact, incapacity only becomes an issue when a condition is so serious it prevents a person from doing what is necessary to provide for his own healthcare, food, shelter, clothing, and personal hygiene.

After you're incapacitated, it'll be too late for you to inform the successor trustee of the whereabouts of your documents, the specifics about where your assets and papers are located, and so forth. That's why meeting with your successor trustee as soon after you sign your documents as possible is important so you can fill him in on what it is he needs to know to take over the role as trustee.

Being prepared before it happens

As soon as a revocable living trust is signed and funded, the grantor should have a meeting with the successor trustee to go over the trust (and other legal documents) to become acquainted with the trust and its provisions. Before a grantor becomes incapacitated, the successor trustee needs to be ready and know the following:

- The location of the original trust
- The names of financial institutions and account numbers for assets held in the trust
- The location of insurance policies and other important papers
- The names and addresses of successor trustees and beneficiaries
- The names and contact info for doctors, funeral directors, and so on

If a grantor is uncomfortable sharing account and other financial information, he should write it down on a separate sheet of paper and store it in a location that the successor trustee knows and can easily access.

Proving the grantor's incapacity

Before the successor trustee can step into the shoes of the grantor, it must be determined that the grantor is unable to manage his or her own affairs. If that determination hasn't been made by the grantor's family, physician, or someone else, the successor trustee must take the necessary steps to prove the grantor's incapacity. In order to do so, the successor trustee needs to obtain sworn statements from two doctors — one of them being the grantor's treating physician — corroborating that the grantor isn't physically or mentally able to handle his or her financial affairs.

After it's determined that a grantor is no longer able to act as trustee, the successor trustee should notify the grantor's financial and other institutions (where trust accounts are held) that the grantor is incapacitated and the successor trustee is now in charge.

Financial institutions don't give access to customer accounts just because someone waltzes in and claims to have authority to act. Thus, a successor trustee must provide copies of the incapacity statements from the grantor's doctors as well as a certificate of trust (a shortened version of the trust document) to the grantor's financial institutions before they will permit access to the grantor's accounts.

We include a certificate of trust form (Form 13-4) on the accompanying CD.

As long as the trust was properly funded, the successor trustee should be able to step in as trustee and manage the grantor's financial affairs quickly and easily, without the need for a court order.

Understanding the successor trustee's role

Upon the incapacity or death of the grantor, the successor trustee has a responsibility to perform certain tasks according to the directives spelled out in the living trust.

A successor trustee has a duty to

- ✔ Follow the instructions in the trust document
- ✔ Keep trust accounts separate from their own finances
- ✔ Refrain from spending trust assets for his own benefit unless the beneficiary and successor trustee are one and the same

> ✔ Invest trust assets in a *prudent* (conservative) manner in order to increase the value of the trust estate
>
> ✔ Maintain accurate records, filing tax returns, and reporting to the beneficiaries as directed by the trust's terms
>
> ✔ Distribute the trust assets to the beneficiaries according to the terms of the trust

The following list walks you through the steps that detail the successor trustee's role after the grantor is shown to be incapacitated:

1. **The successor trustee locates the trust document.**

   Before doing anything else, if the grantor has children or pets, the successor trustee makes arrangements for their care. If the trust provides specific instructions, the successor trustee follows them.

2. **The successor trustee finds out if the grantor has assets other than financial accounts and then makes an inventory of what those assets are, what their value is, and where they are located.**

   If necessary, the successor trustee should put together a budget in order to figure out what cash is on hand, what bills need to be paid, and so on. Making a budget is a good way to get organized, and it can also help you stay on top of the day-to-day management of the grantor's financial affairs.

3. **The successor trustee gives copies of the grantor's healthcare documents to the grantor's treating physician and all other medical facilities whether or not the grantor has empowered the successor trustee to make the grantor's medical decisions.**

   These forms include the medical power of attorney, living will, and so on. If the grantor has appointed someone else to make healthcare decisions, the successor trustee should notify that person and, if appropriate, help him perform his duties as the grantor's healthcare surrogate.

4. **The successor trustee reads through the grantor's healthcare and long-term care insurance policies to ascertain the scope and limits of what will and won't be covered.**

   If the grantor has any assets held outside of the trust, the successor trustee may not be able to access them unless the grantor has also signed a Durable Power of Attorney for Finances (DPOA) that names the successor trustee as an agent or attorney-in-fact. Chapter 9 provides a thorough explanation of what a DPOA is and how it functions.

   The CD also contains a sample DPOA (Form 9-8).

   If the grantor's incapacity appears to be long-lasting, the successor trustee should consider applying for disability benefits on behalf of the grantor. Benefits that a grantor may qualify for are:

- Disability benefits through grantor's employer
- Social Security Disability Insurance (SSDI) or Supplemental Security Income (SSI)
- Private insurance
- Veteran's benefits and services

5. **The successor trustee begins to receive and deposit funds, pay the grantor's bills and, in general, use the grantor's assets to take care of the grantor and any dependents until the grantor either recovers or dies.**

   White transacting the grantor's business, the successor trustee needs to promptly file any insurance claims on behalf of the grantor; keep careful records of medical expenses, income received, and bills paid; and of course, make sure income taxes are filed and property taxes are paid on time. Throughout the grantor's incapacity, the successor trustee has a duty to provide the grantor and beneficiaries with a regular accounting.

If the grantor recovers from the incapacity, the successor trustee will resign as trustee in writing, and the grantor will resume the role of trustee. As long as the trust is properly drafted and funded, the transition from successor trustee back to the trustee should be smooth and simple and shouldn't require an order from a court.

You can find a sample trustee resignation letter and a detailed list of the duties of a successor trustee on the CD (Forms 13-8 and 13-10).

What Happens When a Grantor Dies

When the grantor dies, the successor trustee has all the same duties and responsibilities that we discuss in the previous section but with a few minor differences. These sections focus on what the successor trustee needs to do after the grantor dies.

Requesting death certificate copies

As soon as possible after the grantor's death, the successor trustee needs to obtain copies of the grantor's death certificate.

To request copies of the grantor's death certificate, the successor trustee is required to visit or write to the vital statistics office in the state and county where the grantor died. Whether writing or requesting the certificate in person, be sure to provide the following information:

✔ Grantor's full, legal name, gender, and date of birth

✔ Name of the city, county, and state where grantor died

✔ Date of grantor's death

✔ A copy of the living trust or the certification of trust indicating authority to obtain the grantor's death certificate

✔ Successor trustee's driver's license (or other form of government-issued identification)

Ten or twelve certified copies of the grantor's death certificate may be necessary to complete the task of settling the estate.

When requesting the death certificate in writing, a self-addressed, stamped envelope should be provided.

A sample letter requesting a death certificate is included on the CD (Form 13-11).

Performing other duties

While waiting for the death certificate, the successor trustee has a few other important duties to carry out. Those duties include

✔ **Carefully read through the trust and will.** The successor trustee should read over the section that spells out the trustee's powers and duties to make sure it's understandable. Find the names of the beneficiaries and make sure their contact information is up-to-date. Look at Schedules A and the Notice of Assignment of Property to get a rough idea of what assets have been funded into the trust. Review Schedule B and the separate writing attached to the grantor's will, if any. If there are items of personal property the grantor wishes to give to a beneficiary outside of the trust, the trustee should set that property aside and notify the appropriate beneficiary of the grantor's intention.

✔ **Secure the grantor's home and take an informal inventory of its contents.** The successor trustee needs to do so as soon as possible after the grantor's death. The successor trustee should make a written list of the valuable assets in the grantor's home — and, if possible, take photos — so as to document what's there. Among other reasons, doing so helps to establish proof of what the grantor owned so that later, if an item goes missing, the successor trustee will have evidence that it belongs to grantor's estate.

✔ **Locate financial account information.** These documents include bank accounts, investment accounts, stocks, bonds, life insurance policies, annuities, pension plans, or other assets that have designated beneficiaries.

✔ **Draft letters to send with copies of the death certificate and certification of trust to the appropriate financial institutions and insurance agencies.** The letters inform them of the grantor's death as well as request information about the balance remaining in the grantor's accounts and the value of the grantor's insurance policies.

Sample letters requesting a financial account and insurance policy information are included on the CD (Forms 13-12 and 13-13).

✔ **Obtain a federal tax identification number (FEIN) for the trust.** While a grantor is living, the trust is revocable (can be cancelled or changed), but after the grantor dies, the trust becomes irrevocable (can no longer be cancelled or changed). As a result, the trust needs to have its own tax ID number.

The successor trustee can easily obtain it by following the easy-to-locate links on the Internal Revenue Service (IRS) website at www.irs.gov. While on the IRS website, the successor trustee can submit IRS Form SS-4 and IRS Form 56 to arrange for trust-related tax correspondence to be delivered to the successor trustee's address.

We include detailed instructions for obtaining a federal tax identification number (FEIN) and copies of IRS forms SS-4 and 56 on the CD.

After the successor trustee has accomplished these preliminary duties, here are the next steps you follow (if you're the successor trustee):

1. **Inform the grantor's family that you've been appointed by the grantor to be in charge of the grantor's estate and final arrangements.**

   If the family is just finding out, or if they disapprove of the grantor's "lifestyle," you need to be prepared for a struggle. See Chapter 21 for tips on how to deal with disgruntled relatives.

2. **Determine whether the grantor has left instructions or made arrangements for cremation, burial, and/or a memorial service, and then take whatever measures are necessary to follow the grantor's wishes.**

   Depending on the law in your state, you may need to draw up a separate document authorizing your partner (or someone else you choose) to make arrangements for the burial or cremation of your body after your death. To err on the side of caution, you should state your wishes as to the disposition of remains in your will, trust, and on a separate disposition of remains document. Chapter 12 discusses this document in more detail.

We include a sample disposition of remains on the CD (Form 12-5).

3. **Collect the grantor's death benefits (Social Security, life insurance, and/or retirement plans) and put them in an interest-bearing account until the assets are distributed.**

4. **After the death certificates arrive, contact the financial institutions where trust funds are located.**

   Notify them that you're the trustee and provide to them a copy of the grantor's death certificate, your photo ID, and the certification of trust.

5. **Gather the grantor's valuable personal property and have the items appraised by a qualified appraiser.**

   Valuable personal property may include antiques, collections (stamps, coins, books, art, and so on), expensive tools, musical instruments, office and/or electronic equipment, designer clothes, décor, furniture, furnishings, motor vehicles, boats, and so on. Having the property appraised is important so the value of the property can be calculated and included in grantor's overall estate. If necessary, arrange for an estate sale to dispose of household goods and personal effects that aren't slated to be given to a beneficiary named in the grantor's trust.

6. **Keep careful records of bills and income as well as expenses incidental to settling the grantor's estate and file medical claims as soon as possible.**

   These bills can include medical and funeral expenses, appraisal, accounting, legal, and other fees.

7. **If necessary, hire an accountant to prepare final income and estate tax returns.**

   Depending on the size and complexity of the grantor's final return, you may feel you need the help of a professional; otherwise you can do it yourself or use the help of tax preparation software.

8. **Make a final accounting to give to the beneficiaries named in the grantor's trust.**

9. **If any assets or property need to be distributed to one or more beneficiaries, divvy it and transfer ownership according to the instructions in the trust.**

   If the grantor's trust has a special needs subtrust and the assets need to be diverted into that trust, you need to acquire a new tax identification number. You, as the successor trustee, have a duty to manage those assets according to the terms of that trust. In addition, you need to maintain accurate records and follow specific reporting guidelines.

Because the grantor created a revocable living trust rather than relying on a last will and testament, you don't need to wait for a probate judge to issue an order. You can immediately distribute the grantor's possessions to the beneficiaries named in the trust.

After all the grantor's assets have been distributed, the trust is dissolved and your role as successor trustee is done.

We include a detailed list of the duties of a successor trustee on the CD (Form 13-9).

Using a Joint Trust: Yes or No?

A *joint trust* is simply a revocable living trust with two grantors and two trustees. A joint trust generally is reserved for legally married couples who own most if not all of their property jointly. It makes sense for an opposite or same-sex married couple to create a joint trust because the law recognizes and supports their relationship to one another.

A joint trust between married (or legally recognized) partners is sometimes called an *A-B trust* because, when the first spouse dies, the joint trust is split into two trusts:

- ✔ Trust A contains the surviving partner's personal property as well as the jointly owned property.

- ✔ Trust B contains the deceased spouse's individually owned property, which can be immediately distributed to the beneficiaries according to the deceased spouse's wishes.

A joint trust may be advantageous for couples who have children from a previous relationship because, even if a surviving spouse/partner doesn't like the terms of trust B (or his or her stepchildren), it becomes irrevocable as soon as the first spouse dies, and the provisions can't be changed.

The terms of a joint trust generally allow for a surviving spouse to continue to use and enjoy all the property and assets held in the trust even after the first partner dies.

Owning property in a joint trust isn't the same as owning property outside of a trust as co-owners. Both partners who co-own property not held in a trust each have (usually) a 50-50 interest in that property. Most LGBT couples try to own property as joint owners with rights of survivorship (JOWROS) in order to create a basic legal right to inherit property from one another. If everything goes smoothly, JOWROS property should pass to a surviving partner immediately upon the death of the co-owner.

So is a joint trust right for you and your partner? The following sections explain when to use and when not to use a joint trust.

When to use a joint trust

When a couple has been together for five or more years (in other words, is in a stable, long-lasting relationship), gets legally married (or enters into a civil union or domestic partner registration), and lives in a community property state, creating a joint trust to hold jointly owned property probably makes sense.

Likewise, if a couple is very wealthy, a joint revocable trust may provide them with a federal estate tax shelter. The federal estate tax exemption (which conservatives like to call the *death tax*) has been increasing exponentially every year, and in 2012, an estate must be valued at more than $5.12 million dollars before it's subject to federal — and not necessarily state — estate taxes. Chapter 8 discusses estate taxes in more detail.

When to use separate trusts

Having a joint trust isn't always preferable, especially when partners own much of their property individually or when they've only been together for five years or less. Creating a joint trust in a state that denies them legal recognition may be risky, especially if the state has a constitutional amendment prohibiting couples from trying to create the "incidents of marriage."

To the extent that a couple plans to keep some but not all property separate, each partner should create a separate trust to hold such property. In that way, there can be no question as to each partner's intent regarding who owns what property and how it will be managed during the grantor's life and distributed after the grantor's death.

Even when a couple creates separate trusts, they may still want to draw up a joint trust to hold their community property. Because of the unusual nature of trust law, same-sex partners are limited only by their imagination as to how to protect one another's rights using one or more revocable living and/or irrevocable trusts.

Chapter 14

Funding: Transferring Assets into Your Trust

*W*hen you *fund* a trust, you simply transfer legal title of your property to your trust. How you fund your trust depends on the type of property you are signing over. In this chapter we spell out the types of assets that need to be transferred into a trust as well as the steps you must take in order to properly fund your living trust.

As soon as you fund your trust, you must also indicate what property has been transferred to your trust by listing it on a separate page attached to your trust on Schedule A. *Schedule A* (Form 14-1 on the CD) is one or more sheets of paper attached to the end of your trust. On this schedule, you list the real property, financial accounts, motor vehicles, and so on that you have put into the name of the trust. After you list everything, you must sign the Schedule A. We explain other aspects of Schedule A in this chapter.

Explaining Why Funding a Trust Is Key

A trust allows you to place your property into it so that after your death, your successor trustee distributes your property to your beneficiaries. Consider what would happen if you didn't fund your trust and put any of your assets into your trust. In that case, the trustee would have nothing to manage, and worse, after your death, all your beneficiaries would receive nothing. Imagine their surprise!

Executing a durable power of attorney

If your trust isn't properly funded prior to your incapacity or death, then very likely your estate may be subject to probate. However, in cases of emergency, you do have a possible exception. If you *execute* (sign) a Durable Power of Attorney (DPOA), you can authorize your partner — or someone else — to take care of funding your trust for you.

Note: You should only use a DPOA to fund a trust via a DPOA in extreme circumstances, such as when you're so seriously ill or injured and you're unable to carry out the function of funding your own trust. Transferring your own property into your trust is much easier and less hectic than using a DPOA. After all, people are less likely to

question your right to transfer assets you own into a trust you created. Unfortunately the same may not be true if while you're incapacitated, your partner attempts to transfer your property into a trust where he or she is both the successor trustee and beneficiary. Moreover, a DPOA is only good as long as you're alive. If you die before your trust is fully funded, your partner will no longer have authority under the DPOA to fund your trust. Whatever property remains outside of your trust will be subject to probate. Chapter 9 provides more information about creating a DPOA, and Chapter 13 deals with how a successor trustee may use a DPOA to access accounts not already transferred into a trust.

Not having a funded trust puts your partner — especially if you live in a state that doesn't recognize your relationship — back at square one, having to rely on the kindness and generosity of your legal family members or being forced to assert his or her rights in probate court. Chapter 12 has a detailed description of the probate process to better understand why you should avoid probate whenever possible. This scenario is what you want to avoid. That's why creating legal documents to protect the rights of your partner and/or family of choice is so important.

Don't postpone funding your trust until later or when you have time. Later often translates to never, and if you *never* fund your trust, then your assets will be subject to probate even though one of the primary reasons you created a trust in the first place was to avoid probate.

The following sections describe what you need to do to transfer property you own into your trust, thus funding your trust. The procedure for doing so varies, depending on whether or not the asset has a title, deed, or certificate of ownership.

Property with no proof of ownership

Transferring property that has no proof of ownership may be the easiest funding step you take. All that is required to put items of personal property with no documentation proving ownership into your trust is to draw up and sign a *Notice of Assignment of Property*.

Like Schedule A, the notice is essentially a blank sheet of paper with the title, Notice of Assignment of Property (Form 14-2 on the CD), at the top and your signature at the bottom. Between the title and signature you simply make a list of your *valuable* personal property. You can find a sample document on the accompanying CD. By *valuable,* we mean property someone would want to receive because it has monetary or sentimental value. (Check out the nearby sidebar for how to determine whether different items in your property are valuable.)

By and large, most of your property doesn't have documentation proving you're the owner. You list this type of property on the Notice of Assignment of Property. This type of property generally falls into the following categories:

✔ Furniture, furnishings, and appliances

✔ Pets (yep, they are property)

✔ Jewelry

✔ Antiques

✔ Art work, books, and collectables

✔ Clothing

✔ Computers and other office equipment

✔ TV, DVD player, stereo, and other electronic equipment

You don't need to list each and every item individually unless it is something unique or specific. Just make sure you have it all listed either as an individual item or by category. You can group different types of this property together on this list in the following types of ways:

✔ For the usual appliances (large and small), such as a refrigerator, stove, toaster oven, microwave, and so on, just write "all my large and small appliances."

✔ For your collection of tools like wrenches, hammers, screwdrivers, and so on, you can write "hand tools."

✔ For electric, gasoline, compressed-air, and battery-operated tools, write "power tools."

✔ For furniture, you can categorize by room, as in "living room furniture" or by type as in "antiques."

✔ For property that doesn't fit into an identifiable category, such as nick-knacks, ornaments, figurines, baubles, decorations, trinkets, tchotchkes, and other novelty items, you can lump them together as "miscellaneous items of personal property."

TIP

Determining whether an item of property is valuable

You only list valuable property on the Notice of Assignment of Property. How exactly do you decipher whether a piece of property has value? A good way to assess the sentimental value of your property is to ask those closest to you if they would like to have anything in your home after you're gone. If so, add those items to your list of valuable property.

Sometimes — as with an antique family heirloom — property may have both sentimental and monetary value. But even if an item of property doesn't have a monetary value, it may have sentimental value. For example, who but your loved ones would want that lop-sided lump of clay you made in your ninth grade arts and crafts class? Well, if someone does want your lump of clay, you'll either give it to him or her outright or make sure it gets included on the Notice of Assignment of Property.

After you list all your items of valuable personal property on the Notice of Assignment of

Property, the property that remains are those items that can be thrown out or given to charity. After all, unless you're a famous celebrity, no one is going to want locks of your hair or your used and out-of-style wardrobe!

Another way to gauge whether an item of personal property has monetary value is to don your imagination cap: Suppose you win a three-day, all-expense-paid trip to Disney World. What if the promoter of the drawing is a thief who designed the sweepstakes as a scam to lure you away for three consecutive days and nights so he could break into your home while you're off schmoozing with Mickey Mouse? Imagine yourself walking into your house after the thieves took every item of valuable property they believed they could resell. Whatever is left in your imaginary ransacked house doesn't need to be transferred into your trust.

Property with legal proof of ownership

Other kinds of property — generally property that has a higher monetary value — require documentation proving you are the owner. Funding your trust with this type of property takes a little more work on your part. Although transferring property you already own into your trust may seem like a hassle, doing so is well worth your time and energy if your goal is to protect your loved ones from losing inheritance and other rights after you are gone.

Each category of property gets funded in a unique manner. The types of property with proof of ownership fit into the following categories:

- ✔ Real property (your home and any other real estate)
- ✔ Financial (bank and investment) accounts
- ✔ Motor vehicles (cars, boats, RVs, ATVs, and so on)

> ✔ Business interests
>
> ✔ Stocks and bonds
>
> ✔ Life insurance, annuities, and retirement accounts

Check out the next section for the ins and outs for funding these types of property into your trust.

Ensuring Property with Proof of Ownership Gets Funded into Your Trust

More than likely, your most valuable assets are those that have documentation showing you as the owner. When added together, such property (real estate, financial accounts, life insurance, motor vehicles, and so on) may be worth tens of thousands of dollars. When one or more of these valuable assets are left out of your trust estate, they may be subject to probate and therefore may lose value or worse, not go to your partner or others you name in your trust.

These sections provide specific directions for funding various types of property with proof of ownership into your trust.

Putting in real property

Your home is often the most valuable asset you own. Making sure your home is funded into your trust could make all the difference to your partner (and possibly non-legally related children) who may otherwise find themselves homeless upon your death.

In order to transfer real estate (your home and any other real property you own) into your trust, you need to sign a grant or quit claim *deed* (a legal document that transfers ownership of real estate) granting ownership from you as an individual to yourself as trustee of your trust. Even if you own your property as a joint owner, you can use a grant deed to transfer your interest in the property into your trust.

When you transfer real property from yourself as an individual to yourself as trustee of your trust, the grant or deed includes your name and the date the trust was signed. (You can find sample grant and quit claim deeds on the accompanying CD. Form 14-3 is the sample grant deed, and Form 14-4 is the sample quit claim deed.) For example, if Zelda Smith-Jones created a trust and wanted to put her home into it, her deed transfer would look something like this:

Zelda Smith-Jones, an individual, to Zelda Smith-Jones, as Trustee of the Wilma B. Flintstone Living Trust, dated September 31, 2012

To make the grant or quit claim deed official, the process follows these steps:

1. **Sign your deed.**

   Use the exact same name as is on your current deed. If you've changed your name in the meantime, use your new name and add in parentheses "also known as" and then list your previous name. Doing so can help in any future title search when and if you ever sell your home. You probably need to have your signature either witnessed, notarized, or both. Check with your local land records office and ask for the proper deed signing requirements.

2. **Get any relevant information on any transfer tax from the county tax assessor, county recorder, or state tax officials.**

   In most places, you don't have to pay a state or local transfer tax when you transfer real estate to yourself as trustee. Most real estate transfer taxes are based on the property's sale price and don't apply when no money changes hands. Other places specifically exempt transfers where the real owners don't change — as is the case when you transfer property to yourself as trustee of a revocable living trust.

   Many counties now make this information available online; just type the name of your state and county along with the words "deed" and "record" into a search engine, and your county's website should be at or near the top of the search string.

3. **Record the deed.**

   By recording it, you put a copy of the deed on file in the county office that keeps local property records by taking or mailing the deed, along with a copy of the Certificate of Trust, to the land records office in the county where the property is situated. Depending on where you live, the land records office may be called the county recorder's office, land registry office, or county clerk's office. For a small fee, a clerk will make a copy and put it in the public records. The clerk will also tell you if there are additional requirements for recording a deed, such as a cover page or whether the name and contact information of the deed preparer needs to be written somewhere on the deed.

4. **The land records office returns the original deed to you.**

   The document will be stamped with a reference number to show where the copy can be found in public records.

5. **After you receive your original recorded deed from the land record's office, list it on Schedule A of your trust.**

Simply type the address of the property, along with the deed book and page number and the date it was recorded.

After you have transferred ownership of your real property, be sure to contact your homeowner's insurance to report the change. Doing so shouldn't affect your coverage or the cost of your policy.

Many mortgages contain a due-on-sale clause that permits a bank to *call or accelerate* (demand that you pay the whole thing off immediately) your loan when you transfer property under a mortgage. In the case of transfers to a living trust, federal law prohibits lenders from invoking such a clause. As long as the original borrower (you) is the beneficiary of your own living trust, the law considers the transfer "unrelated to occupancy" of the property. Still, make sure you call your lender before transferring your property into your trust.

If you're the owner of a co-op or condominium, you can't use a deed to transfer your shares in the co-operative community. You need to review the co-op corporation's rules to see if a transfer to a living trust is permitted. The co-op may resist a transfer of ownership from an individual to a trust because the co-op may not recognize the trustee as an appropriate shareholder in the corporation. You may be able to change the co-op board's mind if you explain that you're both the grantor and the trustee, and you aren't actually giving your property to another individual.

Including financial accounts

Retitling financial accounts into your trust is a fairly easy process. Doing so usually involves traveling to the financial institutions (banks or investment firms) where you already have an account and taking the time to sit down with the appropriate person, such as an account manager, financial planner, or customer service representative.

No matter how big a hassle it is to put your financial accounts into your trust, imagine how much more difficult it would be if your partner had to do it for you, especially if someone challenges his or her right to do so.

When you go to each financial institution, make sure to take a copy of your signed, witnessed, and notarized *Certificate of Trust* (an abbreviated version of your trust that we more thoroughly discuss in Chapter 13) as well as your photo ID, account information, and so on.

Depending on the rules of the particular financial institution, you may be required to close your current account and use the funds from that account to open a new one in the name of your trust. On the other hand, the bank may simply change the name on your account from your individual name to the name of your trust.

Repeat this process for every bank or financial account you own. If you're unable to complete the transaction in person, send a letter to your financial institution (be sure to include your account number and a copy of the Certificate of Trust) to let them know you want to transfer the account into your trust. Your financial institution should respond by sending the appropriate paperwork to complete and return in order to accomplish your goal.

On the accompanying CD, we include a sample letter (Form 14-5) that you can modify and send to your financial institution.

If you don't want to fund your trust with an existing financial account, you can still open a new account by taking a copy of your Certificate of Trust, photo ID, and necessary funds to whatever financial institution you choose.

To transfer title to a safe deposit box, you need to reregister its ownership to the trustee of the trust. Doing so is as easy as filling out a form at the bank.

In order to transfer a credit union account to your living trust, you need to ask the credit union (credit unions are membership organizations) for instructions on how to make your trust a member.

After you transfer and retitle existing accounts and/or opened new accounts in the name of your trust, you must list those accounts on Schedule A. To do so, make sure you include the name of the bank as well as the account number. Don't list accounts that haven't been transferred into the trust. *Don't* simply list accounts you own in your name as an individual. Unless the accounts are in the name of the trust, they're subject to probate.

Most financial institutions allow you to designate an account to be paid or transferred on death to a beneficiary — including your trust. These designations are commonly known as *pay on death* (POD) and *transfer on death* (TOD) accounts. A POD/TOD account should prevent the account from being subjected to probate.

One of the main reasons for creating a trust in the first place is because it takes effect when you sign it, and throughout your life you interact with the trust, making it more difficult to challenge it when you die. With a POD/TOD account, you won't be around to defend any challenge made by someone trying to thwart your wishes. Therefore, err on the side of caution and retitle all your accounts to your trust.

Retitling motor vehicles

For vehicles with a legal certificate of title, such as cars, boats, recreational vehicles, and so on, you should first consider whether it is worth your while to retitle them with an outstanding loan. Some lenders don't provide a title until the loan is paid off, and others may not permit a transfer into a trust. Make sure you check with the lender or wait until the loan is paid off.

If you purchase a vehicle after signing your trust, then you should be able to own it as trustee of your trust from the get-go. If you purchase a vehicle at a dealer, present the Certificate of Trust when the dealer is finalizing the paperwork to make sure the vehicle is titled to the trust and not to you as an individual.

If you own a vehicle outright, you can take your title and your Certificate of Trust to the department of motor vehicles and ask them to issue a new title in the name of your trust. Depending on the rules governing the transfer of title to motor vehicles in your state, you should be prepared to pay at least a minimal transfer fee.

You need to add any vehicles that are in the name of the trust to Schedule A by entering the make, model, and year as well as the Vehicle Identification Number (VIN).

Some states treat the transfer of a vehicle into a trust as an actual sale of the vehicle, which means you may be required to pay substantial fees and taxes in order to retitle your vehicle into the name of your trust. Check with your local Department of Motor Vehicles for more information.

Tell your insurance carrier that you transferred ownership to your trust. As a rule, your carrier will add your trust as an additional insured on your policy free of charge.

Transferring your business interests

The way you transfer your interest in your business to your trust depends on how your business was set up. Keep the following in mind, based on the type of business you have:

 ✔ **Sole proprietor:** With this type of business, you transfer your business to your trust the same way you would any other item of valuable property—by listing the name of the business on the *Notice of Assignment of Property.* As we discuss in the earlier section "Property with no proof of ownership," adding the name of your business to this document not only transfers ownership to the trust but also conveys any customer goodwill that your business enjoys.

If you own a business as a sole proprietor and your business has a registered trademark, if you want to protect that trademark, you must reregister it to the name of the trust.

✓ **Partnership interest:** You need to notify your business partners and perhaps modify the partnership agreement to indicate your share of the partnership will be held in your trust. If the partnership agreement limits or forbids transfers to a trustee, you may need to draw up a new partnership agreement.

✓ **Sole owner of stock in a corporation:** Transferring ownership to your trust is simply a matter of filling out the stock transfer form on the back of each stock certificate, marking the certificate as cancelled, and then reissuing new certificates in your name as trustee of your trust. Make a note of the cancellation and reissuance on the stock ledger and be sure to place the cancelled certificates in the back of your corporate records book.

✓ **Closely held corporation:** You should be able to transfer ownership to your trust by following the corporate bylaws and having the stock certificates reissued into the name of the trust. Before going ahead with the transfer, read through the bylaws, articles of incorporation, and any other agreements the corporation may have with shareholders to make sure there are no restrictions on transfers to a trust.

✓ **S Corporation:** You need to make sure the corporation is *qualified* under IRS rules. For more information you should speak to a tax specialist.

✓ **Limited liability company:** You need to get the approval of the other owners, in writing, to effectively transfer your interest to yourself as trustee of your trust.

✓ **Limited partnership:** Because a *limited partnership* interest is a form of investment governed by securities laws, you should contact the partnership's general partner to find out what paperwork is needed to transfer your interest into your trust.

Add any business interest you have funded into the trust by listing the business name and type on Schedule A.

Addressing copyrights and patents

If you want to transfer your interest in a copyright to your trust, list the copyright on the *Notice of Assignment of Property* and then sign and file, with the US Copyright Office, a form transferring all your rights in the copyright to yourself as trustee. Contact the US Copyright office in Washington, DC for a copy of the required form.

Likewise, if you own a patent and want to hold it in trust, you should list the patent on a separate Notice of Assignment of Property, make a copy of the Certificate of Trust, and send both to the Patent and Trademark Office in Washington, DC. You may be required to pay a small recording fee.

Transferring ownership of stocks and bonds

How you transfer stocks, bonds, and other securities to your living trust depends on whether you hold your stocks in a brokerage account or separately. Refer to this list for how to transfer different types of investment accounts:

- ✔ **Brokerage account:** If you hold your investment portfolio in a *brokerage account* (a fund that you entrust to a securities broker), you can rename the account from yourself as an individual to your name as trustee of your trust. Or, you can simply close your account and reopen a new one in the trust's name. If you aren't sure which method is best, contact your broker and ask whether he or she has a form or a set of instructions to guide you. You may need to provide your broker with a copy of the Certificate of Trust along with a letter from you requesting the transfer.

- ✔ **Stocks or bonds:** If you own *stocks or bonds* (financial interest in a corporation or government entity), and the certificates are in your possession, you need to ask your broker (or the transfer agent of the corporation or government agency who issued the original stocks or bonds) to help you obtain new certificates in the name of your trust. You may need to send to the broker or transfer agent the certificates you hold in your own name, along with a copy of the Certificate of Trust and any forms or letters they require you to fill out and sign. Look at the back of your certificate to see whether it has instructions or contact information to help you properly transfer these assets into your trust.

- ✔ **Government securities:** If you're a holder of *government securities* (such as Treasury bills or US bonds, issued by federal, state, or local governments to raise necessary funds), contact your broker or the issuing government agency and ask for instructions on retitling the securities into your trust.

- ✔ **Mutual fund account:** Ask the financial institution what is required to reregister ownership of your account into the name of your trust. More than likely, the firm will send a form for you to complete and send back along with a copy of your Certificate of Trust.

Write on Schedule A the names of any stocks, bonds, or other securities owned by the trust.

Focusing on life insurance, annuity, and retirement accounts

You can name your living trust as the beneficiary of any life insurance policy and your successor trustee will collect and distribute the proceeds to your beneficiaries according to the terms of your trust. The same is true for annuities and retirement accounts, such as IRAs and 401(k)s, which provide for a beneficiary to be named to collect the proceeds after your death.

As the owner of an insurance policy, retirement account, or annuity, you are able to name your trust as the beneficiary. Thus, upon your death, the trust will become entitled to receive the proceeds of your life insurance and the remaining balance of your retirement accounts. All these assets will ultimately be distributed to the beneficiaries you name in your trust.

If you ever change your mind about who you want as your beneficiary, you only need to change your beneficiary to your trust rather than on all your accounts and policies.

When you name your trust as the beneficiary of your life insurance policy, it may be subject to state inheritance taxes. On the contrary, when an individual is named as the beneficiary, the proceeds of the policy are exempt from such taxes. Before naming your trust as beneficiary of your life insurance, check your state's death tax rules. For more information on tax issues, see Chapter 8.

After you change the beneficiary of your accounts and policies to your trust, you need to list them on Schedule A by the name of the agency or company and the policy or account number.

Considering What Happens When You Don't Fund Your Trust

Creating your trust is important, but it's practically worthless until you properly and fully fund it. Remember that any property you leave out of your trust is subject to the probate process. If you want your estate plan to function in the way that you envision, you need to take the time to fund it.

When a trust isn't properly funded, the following can happen:

✔ The successor trustee appointed in the trust will have no authority to manage all the property you own, and, if the successor trustee is your partner, he or she may have no right to inherit that property.

✔ If you become incapacitated — even if you've appointed your partner as successor trustee in your trust — a conservatorship proceeding is required, and your partner has to go to court and ask a judge to be appointed as your *conservator* (someone appointed by the court to take care of the person and/or property of someone who has become incapacitated without adequately making his or her own arrangements in advance) to take care of your money and other assets.

Using a durable power of attorney (DPOA), you can appoint your partner (or someone else) to manage assets outside of your trust. (Refer to the sidebar earlier in this chapter about DPOAs.) Keep in mind, however, the power granted in a DPOA dies with you. Make sure you fully fund your trust and not leave any loose ends.

✔ If your partner is forced to petition the court to be appointed as conservator, the court may reject your partner's request, especially if your state's law doesn't recognize the legality of same-sex relationships. In that case, the judge will likely name a member of your family — even if that relative is a virtual stranger to you — because that relative has superior legal rights over your partner.

In a few states, you can appoint your partner as your conservator in a DPOA and that appointment will be honored by the court.

✔ If a different person is appointed as your conservator, your partner loses control over your care and your assets throughout your incapacity. This process is likely to be very demeaning and frustrating — all at a time when your partner will also be stressing out over your health problems. Petitioning a court to be appointed as conservator can be costly because of court costs and possibly attorney's fees as well. The best way to avoid this all is to fund your trust.

✔ If you own assets outside of your trust when you die, probate is practically guaranteed. If your estate is probated, your beneficiaries may be required to wait months or years to get your assets, and the entire process is played out in public with your personal financial and beneficiary information published at your local courthouse.

Chapter 12 discusses more reasons to avoid probate.

Chapter 15

Passing Along Your Employment Benefits to Your Partner

. . . .

In This Chapter

▶ Understanding employer-based domestic partner benefits

▶ Figuring out how to create a domestic partnership

▶ Getting domestic partner benefits at work

▶ Leaving retirement and pension benefits to your partner

. . . .

*I*n the absence of full and equal marriage equality for same-sex couples, alternatives to marriage have developed in order to make up for the lack of legal protections for the partners and children of gay men and lesbians. Domestic partnership benefits are one of those alternatives.

In 1982, the *Village Voice,* a weekly New York City newspaper, became the first company in the United States to offer domestic partner benefits to its gay and lesbian employees. Since then, an increasing number of public and private employers have been extending to same-sex couples the same or similar benefit packages previously available only to married heterosexual employees.

The term *domestic partnership* describes a committed couple — straight or gay — who isn't married. The three main categories of domestic partnerships are as follows:

✔ **Private and informal:** Created when a committed couple draws up legal documents, such as a last will, living revocable trust, medical and financial powers of attorney, and a living-together or partnership agreement. These documents allow partners to appoint each other to make medical and financial decisions and to leave each other property after death.

✔ **Public and formal:** Several states as well as many cities and towns have set up domestic partnership registries where couples can officially register their partnership. The types of rights and benefits attached to the registered couple vary widely.

> ✔ **Employer-based:** Some private and public employers offer health insurance and/or other benefits to same-sex partners of employees just as they do with spouses of married employees.

Other chapters in this book cover the first two categories of domestic partnerships. In this chapter, we limit our discussion to employer-based domestic partnership benefits, including what they are and how to get them.

Grasping How Domestic Partner Benefits Work

Not all employers offer domestic partner benefits — even when they provide a benefits package to their heterosexual employees. Although some businesses and government entities voluntarily offer domestic partner benefits, others only do so because they're located in a state, county, or city with laws prohibiting discrimination based on sexual orientation.

There are two major categories of employers: public (government) and private. A public employer is obliged to follow its own laws, so, if a state, county, or municipality has a nondiscrimination policy, then as an employer, it probably has a domestic partnership benefits plan for its unmarried gay (and possibly straight) employees.

If you work inside one of the many counties, cities, and towns who provide legal recognition of LGBT folks and especially if you work for the government entity that extended LGBT legal protections, your employer may be required to extend domestic partner benefits. Similarly, if you work for a business that contracts with that government entity, the business also may be obliged to offer such benefits. On the other hand, unless a private employer contracts with a government entity with nondiscrimination policies, that employer isn't required to offer domestic partner benefits to its LGBT employees. Still, lots of private companies voluntarily offer these benefits even though they aren't compelled by law to do so.

So what exactly are domestic partner benefits and why are they important? We're here to explain. These sections explain in greater depth what benefits are at stake, the pros and cons as to why a business may offer them, and how you can qualify for them.

Identifying the types of benefits at stake

Currently no laws specifically protect LGBT employees from being discriminated against in the workplace, although some states and municipalities include sexual orientation in nondiscrimination statutes (refer to Chapter 2 for more information). Likewise no rules compel employers to offer a specific set of benefits in their domestic partner benefit plans. As a result, almost as many varieties of plans exist as employers that offer them.

However, domestic partnership employee benefits can be broken down into two main categories: soft benefits and hard benefits. *Soft benefits,* which tend to be less expensive and easier to implement, include

- ✔ Accident and life insurance
- ✔ Bereavement leave
- ✔ Child care
- ✔ Death benefits
- ✔ Employee discounts
- ✔ Relocation expenses

Hard benefits are those that are more expensive and are likely to involve the need to negotiate with a (potentially reluctant) third-party provider. These benefits may include

- ✔ Medical, dental, and vision insurance
- ✔ Life and accident insurance
- ✔ Long-term care insurance
- ✔ Retirement and/or pension plans

Offering an employee family and sick leave may be easier than trying to negotiate a domestic partner plan that includes health, dental, and vision insurance, especially when an insurance company is reluctant to extend coverage on account of HIV/AIDS and/or fear of fraud.

Unlike heterosexual married employees, LGBT employees can't extend tax-free benefits to their partners. On the contrary, federal law allows married employees to enroll their spouses and children in a benefits plan without having the value of the benefits added to their taxable income. Because the federal Defense of Marriage Act (DOMA) denies federal rights and benefits to same-sex couples, domestic partner benefits are considered taxable income by the Internal Revenue Service. To even things out, some employers reimburse LGBT employees in the amount of the additional tax burden.

Furthermore, employers give hundreds of additional employment benefits to employees on the basis of their marital status. The most prominent of these benefits include

- ✔ **Consolidated Omnibus Budget Reconciliation Act (COBRA):** This benefit allows an employee to maintain his or her health insurance coverage after leaving a job. Some employers have opted to provide a COBRA equivalent benefit to their LGBT employees.

✔ **Family and Medical Leave Act (FMLA):** This benefit requires employers to give qualified employees a leave for up to 12 weeks per year in order to care for an ill or injured spouse or other qualified family member. Again, some employers offer an FMLA equivalent benefit to their LGBT employees.

✔ **Employee Retirement Income Security Act (ERISA) pension protections:** This benefit presumes an employee's legal (heterosexual) spouse to be the beneficiary of the employee's pension and survivor benefits. ERISA further gives the spouse the right to be notified of — and approve — any change to the beneficiary of those benefits. None of these rights are extended to same-sex partners.

✔ **Flexible Spending Accounts (FSA):** An FSA is a financial account that's set up through an employer's benefits plan that lets employees put aside a portion of his or her salary to pay for medical bills as well as for child and/or dependent care and other expenses. Money placed in an FSA isn't subject to federal payroll taxes, which can result in substantial federal income tax savings that aren't available to LGBT partners.

✔ **Health Savings Accounts (HSA):** Similar to an FSA, an HSA allows an employee to put some of his or her income into an HSA to pay for future medical expenses of the employee, his or her spouse, and children without paying federal taxes on the income, which isn't true for same-sex partners.

This list shows that domestic partner benefits don't come close to providing legal rights and protections that are equal to marriage. Still, they've created a less than perfect — but better than nothing — safety net for LGBT families.

Eyeing the pros and cons to why an employer offers these benefits

Employers choose to offer or not to offer domestic partnership benefits for different rationale. They often choose to offer domestic partner benefits to their employees for these reasons:

✔ A state, county, or municipality may require companies that want to do business with or for the government to offer benefits to LGBT employees.

✔ The company has its own nondiscrimination or diversity policy, and the provision of domestic partner benefits is just an extension of their commitment to those policies.

✔ In a tight labor market, companies may want to offer domestic partner benefits to compete for and retain talented employees.

✔ For reasons of equity, a company may offer domestic partner benefits packages because to do otherwise would disadvantage LGBT employees who can't legally marry in order to qualify.

✔ More and more LGBT employees are organizing together as unions and gay and lesbian groups to put pressure on employers to provide domestic partner benefits.

Despite recent progress in the availability of domestic partner benefits, a majority of employers still don't offer them. Some of these companies focus on these deterrents for extending benefits:

✔ **Cost:** Although studies have shown that offering domestic partner benefits is not all that costly, many employers remain reluctant to establish a benefits program because they're simply unaware of the facts. Certain kinds of benefits, such as healthcare and pension benefits, are more expensive, and others, such as leave, travel, and relocation, are less so. As a result, employers sometimes offer the less expensive benefits, even when they don't extend healthcare and pension benefits.

✔ **Health Maintenance Organizations (HMOs):** HMOs have resisted extending benefits to domestic partners for two main reasons:

   • **Fears of fraud:** For instance, an employee may portray a friend as his or her domestic partner just to get healthcare coverage.

   • **HIV/AIDS:** Largely due to ignorance, HMOs may believe a gay person is more likely to contract the disease than a straight employee.

This resistance by HMOs can make it difficult for employers to negotiate a benefits contract that's fair and beneficial to both LGBT and straight employees.

✔ **Bad public relations:** Employers may fear that anti-equality groups may boycott their company (although recent evidence has shown the opposite to be true) or that shareholders may react negatively. Straight employees may also object if adding a domestic partner plan results in an increase in the cost of their own healthcare benefits.

✔ **Religious beliefs:** Some employers refuse to offer domestic partner benefits to same-sex partners on religious grounds. These employers may believe homosexuality is immoral and against God's wishes, or they simply don't feel comfortable offering benefits that create the appearance of a moral equivalency between opposite-sex spouses and LGBT partners.

As employers begin to realize that the negative impact of discriminatory policies on their LBGT employees far outweighs the financial cost of adding a domestic partner benefits package, companies hopefully will be inclined to offer these benefits.

Qualifying for the benefits

Most employers require employees to meet one or more of the following criteria to qualify for enrollment in a domestic partner benefits plan:

- **Must be in a same-sex relationship or otherwise be legally prohibited from marrying:** The rationale for this requirement is that a heterosexual employee has the option to marry his or her partner and thus can enroll under a conventional employee benefits plan.

- **Proof or evidence of the relationship:** Employers may insist that an employee officially register the domestic partnership in his or her home state or municipality. If that isn't an option, the employee may be asked to sign an affidavit or Declaration of Domestic Partnership swearing to the validity of his or her domestic partnership.

- **Proof of specifics about the relationship:** In addition to registering or declaring your domestic partnership, you may also be required to provide proof that you've lived together with your partner for a specific period of time (by presenting a joint lease or some other document showing residency), that it's your intention to continue to cohabitate indefinitely (you may accomplish by a written statement to that effect), that you jointly own property and accounts (prove by producing bank statements), and that you think of yourselves as a married couple (again by issuing a written statement).

You can find a sample Declaration of Domestic Partnership form (Form 15-1) on the accompanying CD.

Asking Your Employer to Provide Domestic Partner Benefits

Just because your employer isn't providing these benefits now doesn't mean it won't in the future. You and your coworkers can always lobby the company to extend domestic partner benefits to unmarried partners. Here are a few guidelines to follow:

- **Work with other coworkers who are supportive of domestic partnership benefits.** Don't act alone. You need support from at least two or three of your coworkers, so organize a meeting with fellow employees to share your idea. The group you assemble doesn't need to be limited to LGBT employees. Heterosexual coworkers who support LGBT equality may be willing to join you. Straight unmarried coworkers who live with their partner also stand to gain from such benefits.

This group can help raise awareness about issues of inequality, and it can also make your employer more aware of the number of employees who favor such a policy. Plus, you won't be sticking your neck out all alone, thus making it harder for a superior to mistreat you for your activism or sexual orientation.

✔ **Do a little research on other companies similar to your employer.** Check out other companies similar in size, location, profitability, number of employees, and so on, who have domestic partnership plans and draft a proposal based on what those plans include.

Your proposal should contain a variety of rationales for why a domestic partnership benefits plan is good for business, including that offering the benefits

- Creates a sense of fairness among employees as it provides equal compensation.

- Attracts and retains high-quality and talented employees. Studies show satisfied and contented employees are more productive and loyal.

- Is consistent with the principle if the employer already has a nondiscrimination policy.

- Earns the support from the LGBT community and its allies, who tend to support companies that support equality.

- Gives the company a progressive appearance. As LGBT equality in the workplace becomes more common, companies that continue to treat gay and lesbian employees differently may appear to be behind the times.

✔ **After you finish the proposal, ask your supportive coworkers to sign it.** The fact that people are willing to sign their names to your proposal indicates to your employer that you have supportive allies and that you shared the plan with coworkers and they received it well. It also helps to ease concerns that the new plan will be unwelcome news to other employees.

✔ **Submit your signed, written proposal and ask for a written response with explanations for any decision made.** Getting your employer's decision in writing is important so there is no misunderstanding — or later misrepresentation — of the reasons your request was accepted or denied. If your employer denies your request, the written response can help you sculpt your next proposal in a manner that addresses and hopefully allays your employer's concerns. Make sure to include your request for a written response, including an explanation, in your initial proposal. If your employer issues an oral response and explanation, make sure you write a letter detailing what was said and send it to your employer by e-mail or US mail with a request that he or she acknowledge your version of the conversation within 10 to 14 days of the date of your letter. If you don't receive a response to your letter within that time period, you can later argue that the employer's silence was an implicit acceptance of your version of the events.

To aid in your lobbying efforts, download *The Domestic Partnership Organizing Manual for Employee Benefits* by Sally Kohn. This comprehensive manual is a bit outdated but nonetheless contains suggestions for making a compelling argument for domestic partnership benefits and how to get coworkers to join your cause. It includes lists of other companies who offer these benefits, sample benefit plans, and so on. The manual is free; you can find it online by typing the title into your favorite search engine.

If your employer doesn't have an antidiscrimination policy, start off by asking your employer to adopt one. This request is smaller than asking for domestic partnership benefits, and even if you fail at getting a benefits package, you may be able to get a policy in place that could act as a springboard for later attempts.

Eyeing Retirement and Pension Benefits

When a heterosexual couple gets married — regardless of their home state — they automatically receive more than a thousand federal and state legal and financial protections, including protections for older couples and surviving partners. However, DOMA blocks an LGBT partner's right to collect his or her deceased partner's Social Security benefits as well as other federally regulated pension and retirement funds.

In order to adequately protect your partner (besides creating wills, trusts, advance directives, and other documents that we discuss throughout this book), you also need to take steps to make sure your partner has the necessary funds to live a reasonably comfortable life after your death. To do so, keep reading these sections.

Designating your partner as beneficiary

If you want your partner to receive your pension benefits, even if you work for a private or public employer that offers ERISA-like benefits to its LGBT employees, you need to check with your employer to make sure you've filled out the proper beneficiary forms naming your partner as the rightful beneficiary of your pension funds.

The federal ERISA governs employee pension plans. Among other things, ERISA protects a surviving spouse's automatic right to receive his or her deceased spouse's pension benefits, even if the employee doesn't purposefully designate a beneficiary. Furthermore, an employee may not change the beneficiary of his or her pension without the spouse's written consent.

Does DOMA prevent employers from offering pension benefits to surviving same-sex spouses?

The federal definition of "spouse" (according to DOMA) is an opposite-sex husband or wife. Therefore, the spousal protections in ERISA don't apply to same-sex partners, even when they're legally married, in a civil union, or registered as domestic partners. Because of DOMA, private and public employers can disregard the rights of an LGBT employee's partner as a legitimate beneficiary of his or her employee's pension funds.

Currently it is unclear whether a private employer is restricted by DOMA's definition of spouse to recognize a same-sex partner's right to a deceased employees benefits. As of this writing, a case involving the private pension benefits of a lesbian employee (who married her partner in Canada but didn't designate her partner as the beneficiary of her pension benefits) is winding its way through the court system. Literally, the night before their daughter died, her parents coerced her into signing a form designating them as the beneficiary of their daughter's pension benefits. Because DOMA restricts ERISA's applicability, the question before the court is whether the employer can recognize their deceased employee's same-sex spouse as the rightful beneficiary with further right to be notified of and authorize a change of beneficiary. A ruling in this case is still pending and is expected to be handed down in the next few months.

Purchasing cross-owned life insurance

Life insurance policies can serve as a great way to supplement the income of a surviving partner and make up for the loss of pension and other benefits currently blocked by DOMA, depending on how the LBGT partners own those policies.

For instance, LGBT couples can purchase cross-owned life insurance policies where each partner is the owner and beneficiary of a life insurance policy on the life of the other partner, and then when the first partner dies, the surviving partner will receive the proceeds of his or her partner's life insurance policy. If the policy's value is substantial enough, the surviving partner can invest the funds, using the interest to help pay for living expenses.

One advantage to owning cross-owned insurance policies is that the insurance proceeds aren't included in the deceased's partner's estate for tax purposes because he or she was neither the owner nor beneficiary of the policy.

Drawing up an ILIT

LGBT couples can also draw up an Irrevocable Life Insurance Trust (ILIT) policy, which acts as a separate entity that both owns and is the beneficiary of one or more life insurance policies.

At the death of the insured partner, the ILIT holds the insurance proceeds and the trustee administers the proceeds, according to the terms of the trust agreement. The ILIT can be written so the funds are used for the benefit of the surviving partner as long as he or she is alive. If any funds are remaining after the surviving spouse dies, they can be distributed to alternate beneficiaries or to a charity. If an ILIT is properly drafted and administered, the proceeds of the life insurance policy aren't subject to estate tax.

Because ILIT's can be expensive to set up and complicated to manage (the IRS requires annual letters be sent to trust beneficiaries and those beneficiaries are required to respond), you should contact an estate planning attorney to assist you.

Designating your partner as a beneficiary of a qualified retirement plan

Qualified retirement plans, such as IRAs and 401(k)s, are probably the most common forms of investment accounts held by American workers today. Often, these accounts are also the most valuable asset owned, sometimes worth more than a home.

Because LGBT couples are denied access to Social Security retirement and other benefits, these accounts are a particularly effective way to financially protect surviving same-sex partners.

Recent changes to the law have made it easier for LGBT employees to designate their partner as the beneficiary of a retirement plan. A designated beneficiary is the person (as opposed to a trust or other non-human entity) you identify on an official beneficiary form as the individual you want to inherit the funds held in your retirement plan after your death.

Check your retirement plan's beneficiary form to make sure your partner is listed as your beneficiary. If you don't designate a beneficiary, your retirement funds will become part of your estate. If you die without a will, the funds may go to your next-of-kin and not to your partner.

Chapter 16

Dealing with the Personal Injury and Death of Your Partner

. . . .

In This Chapter

▶ Comprehending loss of consortium

▶ Understanding emotional distress

▶ Explaining the law of wrongful death

▶ Figuring out whether to file a lawsuit

. . . .

*T*he law of personal injury allows husbands and wives to sue for the harm they suffer when their spouse is physically injured or killed by the negligent or criminal actions of a defendant. In many states, damages can be recovered for two different kinds of damages, broadly speaking:

✔ The financial support that the injured spouse provided

✔ The emotional loss (including sexual relations) that occurs when a spouse is injured or killed

In addition, in some states, spouses can recover for the emotional distress they suffer when witnessing negligently caused physical injuries to immediate family members. For example, when a drunk driver slams into someone's child or spouse, family members who watch the tragedy unfold might have a claim against the motorist because of their own anguish.

These relational torts, though, present an enormous — often insurmountable — hurdle to same-sex couples. That's because most states tie recovery to the legal status of husband and wife. In this chapter, we look at what makes these torts tick and talk about the strategies that are sometimes available to overcome the problems of legal nonrecognition. But this area of the law is particularly challenging for same-sex couples, and in some cases there's no remedy for your loss — yet. We also explore whether or not you should even bring such a lawsuit, even when you can.

Figuring Out Loss of Consortium

Back in medieval days, women were considered the servants of their husbands. So when someone injured a man's wife, the husband was able to sue the wrongdoer for the loss of her services. The idea was that the husband would have to find (and pay) someone to replace those services, and that the person who had caused the loss should bear the cost. The tort was called *loss of consortium,* and only husbands would bring it to court for loss of their wives' services — not the other way around, because wives had no legal claim to their husband's service.

Society thankfully has come a long way from that view of marriage. But loss of consortium didn't go away when women shed their status as servants. Instead, state courts transformed this tort into something else: a legal claim that mostly compensates for the emotional loss that people suffer when their spouses are seriously injured. Of course, wives can now recover for loss of the consortium of their husband, too. As one court memorably stated, "what's sauce for the goose is sauce for the gander."

Today, courts often recite the *s trio* in laying out the kinds of damage for which a person can recover:

- ✔ Society (meaning companionship and support)
- ✔ Sex (which we hope needs no explanation!)
- ✔ Services (still an allowable damage, though rarely an issue)

In short, courts recognize that personal injuries have ripple effects, harming not only the primary victim but also their spouses and their families (some states allow recovery for loss of consortium between parents and children, but some don't). And the law provides the option of seeking monetary damages for these losses.

For same-sex couples, it's unfortunately not so easy. The following sections take a closer look at how state tort law can affect you and what recourse you have to recover damages.

Adding insult: State tort law

Loss of consortium was created to compensate for harm caused within legally recognized families, which is the problem for same-sex couples in many states. And even though the basis of the tort has expanded to reflect the reality that most of the harm is emotional, and that both spouses — not just husbands — are affected, in many states that's as far as it's gotten.

The loss of consortium in the Land of Enchantment

Why the courts are so committed to a rule that only married couples can recover for the loss of consortium they suffer when their spouses are injured is worth questioning. After all, the injury might be no less serious in the case of unmarried, long-term partners. But courts like clear rules, and marriage (and civil unions) provides that — no legal relationship, no claim.

In 2003, the Supreme Court of New Mexico took a different approach. In *Lozoya v. Sanchez,* the court became the first high court of any state to recognize a loss of consortium claim brought by an unmarried cohabitant. The plaintiff was a woman who'd been in a thirty-year relationship with a man who was injured when his vehicle was rear-ended by the defendant. In allowing the claim, the court first noted that the administrative ease of a bright line, spouses-only rule didn't further the aims of justice. It then said:

"We must consider the purpose behind the cause of action for loss of consortium. A person brings this claim to recover for damage to a relational interest, not a legal interest. To use the legal status as a proxy for a significant enough relational interest is not the most precise way to determine to whom a duty is owed. Furthermore, the use of legal status necessarily excludes many persons whose loss of a significant relational interest may be just as devastating as the loss of a legal spouse."

Perhaps this stirring language will inspire other courts faced with a similar situation. In any case, the logic the court used in allowing the claim by a cohabitant in an opposite-sex relationship should also apply to same-sex couples — maybe even more forcefully in states where same-sex couples can't even choose to marry.

In other words, if your relationship to your partner isn't legally recognized, you probably don't have a claim for loss of consortium, no matter how real, deep, and devastating your injury is.

This problem doesn't exist just for same-sex couples. Unmarried opposite sex couples run into the same difficulty. State courts haven't been sympathetic to the argument that the loss of companionship can be just as devastating to those individuals in long-term committed relationships that aren't state-sanctioned as it is to married couples.

The upshot is that you don't even get a chance to show a court how stable your relationship might be — the case will be dismissed right away, just because of its legal (non)status.

To show the practical effects of the law, consider this: An estranged spouse can bring a suit, but you and your partner — no matter how long and how close your relationship — are left out. The *legal stranger* status (which basically means that the law treats you and your partner as if you're in no relationship at all) applies here, just like it does to other rights usually associated with marriage.

As of this writing, the supreme court of only one state (New Mexico) has decided in favor of unmarried cohabitants — although they were of the opposite sex (see the nearby sidebar, "The loss of consortium in the Land of Enchantment"). A few lower court decisions are more sympathetic, but the law is very clearly against you here.

Using marriage or civil union law to recover damages

Until a few years ago, partners in a same-sex relationship had just about no chance in a loss of consortium suit. But here's one area of the law where marriage equality and the virtual equivalents of civil unions and full domestic partnerships have really transformed the landscape — for the better.

Claims for loss of consortium are brought in state courts and apply state common law. The Defense of Marriage Act (DOMA), which deals with the federal rights and benefits of marriage, doesn't come into the equation at all. So if your state gives your relationship the same legal status as a marriage, whether it uses the term "marriage" or not, you have a claim for loss of consortium.

We're only talking here about the right to bring a claim — not about whether you'll actually be able to prove any damages under it. In general, loss of consortium claims only work well in the most tragic cases: where the spouse has suffered a serious, often long-term harm that affects the spousal relationship in a deep way.

Civil union and full domestic partnership laws make clear that couples are to receive all the same rights, benefits, and privileges as married couples, including those that are established through the common law (in other words, by courts). Some laws (like Vermont) even list loss of consortium under the rights conferred by civil union status, but that's not even necessary. Because the right to sue for loss of consortium arises under state law, it's a benefit of civil union status. And in the states that allow opposite-sex couples to enter into civil unions (as of now, only Illinois and Hawaii), the same rule applies.

An increasingly large percentage of same-sex couples have the right to sue for loss of consortium, as the number of states with full marriage equality or some virtual equivalent continues to grow. But it's all or nothing: Either your relationship will be considered a marriage or you're out in the cold.

Although states that recognize same-sex marriages and civil unions will always allow a loss of consortium claim, the situation with other legal statuses — domestic partnerships, reciprocal beneficiaries, and designated beneficiaries — isn't as clear. Some domestic partnership laws are just like civil unions, and some are more limited (some domestic partnerships aren't even statewide, but local). And the other designer statuses each have their own sets of unique rules. So make sure you (or your lawyer) know where your state stands. This area may be unfamiliar even to most personal injury lawyers. (Refer to Chapter 2 for a further discussion on the legal recognition and labeling of same-sex relationships by some states.)

Encountering Potential Emotional Distress from Injury to Your Partner

Loss of consortium claims attempt to compensate for *injury to the relationship* between two people the law recognizes as married (or the equivalent). A closely related claim is for the *emotional distress* that a partner suffers because of the injury to a husband or wife — not for loss of, or damage to, the relationship, but because it can be devastating to witness (or otherwise be affected by) distressing events to one's partner. This area of the law is complex, although it doesn't need to be. We distinguish two kinds of cases in the following sections, because the rules that courts have established are different.

In both kinds of cases, same-sex couples face some of the same challenges we discussed in the earlier section, "Figuring Out Loss of Consortium." But this area of the law is at least somewhat more promising (in some states).

Collecting against the jerk who purposely caused the distress

For more than 100 years, courts have recognized that those who purposely cause emotional distress to others should be liable to them for that distress. But courts are also a bit suspicious of these claims for *intentional infliction of emotional distress*, because they're easy to fake. So courts also require that the defendant's conduct be *extreme and outrageous* and that the distress be *severe*. Often, plaintiffs whose lawsuits succeed are unable to work, or suffer miscarriages or heart attacks — or even death — tied to the distress.

The law of intentional infliction of emotional distress allows recovery for close family members in cases where the defendant's conduct takes place in the presence of those family members. Consider this example:

> Dr. Evil murders Chloe in the presence of her husband, Clark. Clark will be able to recover for his emotional distress, because Evil either intended to cause his distress or knew that it was likely but didn't care (which amounts to the same thing).

Just as with loss of consortium, this *family members'* standard raises the question whether a court would consider unmarried cohabitants — of the same or of opposite sexes — to be eligible to recover. Not much case law on the question exists, probably because not many situations arise under these kinds of facts. So in the very unlikely, and very unfortunate, case that you find yourself in such a situation, you and your attorney might be in uncharted territory.

Collecting for distress for accidental harm

The more typical types of cases are where the defendant acts *negligently* in causing physical injury to one person, which then causes a ripple effect of emotional harm to a third party. Sometimes these cases of *negligent infliction of emotional distress* are the same ones that give rise to loss of consortium claims — you can sue for both in the same lawsuit!

The bad news, though, is that the law is in a very confused state. Sorting it out is a challenge, even for lawyers faced with litigating these claims. To help make sense, we distinguish these two situations:

- ✔ Cases where the bystander suffers emotional distress because of proximity to the harm. In such cases, the plaintiff is said to be in the *zone of danger*. (Our apologies if Kenny Loggins's song from *Top Gun* is now playing in an endless loop in your brain.)

- ✔ Cases where the bystander is at a safe distance and doesn't fear being harmed, but experiences emotional distress at seeing a close family member suffering personal injury (or death).

Some courts allow recovery only in the first kind of case. For example:

> Sally and Bobby, a married couple, are riding their motorcycle on the interstate highway when the rear tire goes flat. Bobby stands to one side while Sally checks out the tire. As she does so, she is struck by a tractor-trailer driven by Hoyt. He had been text-messaging his friend and drove off the road onto the shoulder. Bobby watches in horror as Sally is dragged for hundreds of yards under the truck, and he suffers serious and lasting emotional distress as a result.

This is a classic case of negligent infliction of emotional distress, which most, though not all courts now recognize. Because these cases are much more common, plenty of court-made law is available on the topic.

In those states, the issue of the relationship between the person physically injured (Sally, in this example) and the person suffering emotional distress (Bobby) doesn't really matter. Bobby could recover if, but only if, he was in the zone of danger. Sally could be his wife, his friend, or a complete stranger because his emotional distress claim doesn't come from his relationship, but from his own quite understandable fear.

In fact, we can take Sally out of the picture altogether. If Bobby fears physical injury because he's close to the out-of-control tractor-trailer, in almost all states, he recovers for his emotional distress (assuming he can prove it).

But in some states, courts have gone further and allowed recovery in the second kind of case, too. Seeing why is easy. Consider the lawsuit that led recovery based on the emotional distress caused by harm to a relative. In *Dillon v. Legg*, a mother watched her daughter being hit by a car, but she was found to be just *outside* the zone of danger. No one could say that watching this kind of event wouldn't cause emotional harm, so the California Supreme Court expanded the emotional distress tort to allow recovery to those who witness harm to a close relative of the primary victim (in that case, the daughter struck by the car).

We return to the example with Sally and Bobby. If the tragic accident happened in a state that follows the California rule, Bobby would be able to sue Hoyt for his emotional distress, whether or not he feared for his own safety. That's because Sally and Bobby's marriage will certainly count as a "close" family relationship. (Most courts continue to insist, though, that the plaintiff be *present* at the time of the accident to have a claim. Showing up a few minutes later is enough to get the defendant off the hook.)

Can you see where this is headed? What if Sally and Bobby aren't married, but are in a long-term, intimate relationship? Will that count? The question is really the same one encountered in the loss of consortium cases, but — maybe surprisingly — plaintiffs have more often been able to convince courts to allow emotional distress suits than consortium claims for unmarried partners. At least a few courts have been sympathetic.

Not a lot of case law exists on gay and lesbian couples trying to recover for emotional distress based on the closeness of their relationship. But in the few states (like New Jersey) that have allowed such claims by opposite-sex cohabitants, you can reasonably think that same-sex couples would have as strong a chance of recovery as opposite-sex ones. Maybe the argument is even stronger for gay and lesbian couples, in fact, because marriage isn't an option for them in many states. Yet the odds of recovery are still long, because most courts continue to insist on a close relationship of blood (as in nuclear family) or law (as in legal spouses).

The history of wrongful death actions and survivor statutes

Wrongful death actions are meant to compensate the survivors for the financial, and sometimes the emotional, harm that they suffer as the result of the death of a family member on whom they were dependent. But what happened to the claim of the person killed by the defendant's wrongful conduct? Did they just . . . disappear?

Historically, the answer was yes. The death of a person wasn't actionable under common law. Well, *another* wacky rule was that the death of either party — the plaintiff or the defendant — also ended any right to legal recourse! And that rule applied even if a lawsuit had already been brought.

Just as with wrongful death, state legislatures stepped in to change this situation. So now all states have *survival statutes,* which allow the underlying claim of injured party to survive that party's death, and be passed on to the estate, as a personal asset. This means that whoever is entitled to the personal estate of the deceased will receive whatever damages result from the suit. So anyone, including surviving members of same-sex couples, who are named the beneficiary in a will would receive any damages.

What sorts of damages can be recovered? Whatever damages were suffered by the now-deceased before death: hospital costs; lost wages from the time of injury to death; and, in many (but not all) states, pain and suffering, and where appropriate for egregious conduct, punitive damages.

Of course, the relationship problem is solved in states that recognize same-sex marriages, civil unions, and domestic partnerships. Just as with loss of consortium, emotional distress cases that allow recovery based on the legal status of marriage will also permit claims where a couple is civilly united or in most statewide domestic partnerships.

You can't get *more* than opposite-sex couples! If you're in a state that only allows recovery to those in the zone of danger, then you'll only have a claim if you can show you feared for your own safety.

Handling Wrongful Death Suits

Sometimes someone dies because of a defendant's negligent, or even criminal, conduct. And the law has a complicated response to these *wrongful death* cases, brought by surviving family members.

Historically, the law didn't even allow recovery in these cases. However, this law has changed because state legislatures in all 50 states now recognize a statutory cause of action for wrongful death. (Refer to the nearby sidebar for the history of wrongful death suits.)

Even though a wrongful death suit is brought in state court — just like the other claims we discuss in this chapter — the court has much less discretion in creating the law. Wrongful death statutes are quite specific as to who can file the claim, who can recover, and the kinds of damages that can be awarded. Courts are bound to follow the language of these laws. And, to be blunt, these statutes are *not good for surviving partners in same-sex relationships.*

Before we get into the problems you may face as the surviving member of a gay or lesbian couple, though, we need to explain these laws a bit more.

Grasping the ins and outs of wrongful death claims

Understanding that wrongful death claims differ from personal injury claims in one major respect is important. They're intended to compensate the *survivors* for their loss, not to pay the estate for the underlying death to the primary victim. (If you want to know more about what happens to the deceased's *own* claim, read the nearby sidebar.)

Generally speaking, wrongful death laws allow recovery for:

- ✔ Funeral and burial expenses

- ✔ The value of the wages, other income, and assets that the plaintiff would have been expected to receive from the decedent over his or her remaining lifetime

- ✔ In some states, the emotional distress caused by the death and bereavement (distinguished from emotional harm caused by the *injury* to a loved one)

Wrongful death claims are often much more valuable than loss of consortium and emotional distress claims. When someone's negligence (or worse) kills a family's breadwinner, a wrongful death suit may be the only way to keep that family afloat financially. So surviving partners — whether legally married or not — often have great incentive to bring these claims.

So who can file a wrongful death action? Although states vary, the general rule is that the estate's *executor* or *administrator* (sometimes called the *personal representative*) is the person who has the legal right to file a wrongful death action. (See Chapter 12 for a discussion of the naming and role of executors and administrators. For the possible role of a trustee, see Chapter 13.) But the action is filed on behalf of those who are legally entitled to recover — and the list of qualified beneficiaries under a wrongful death action might or might not include the executor, as the next section explains.

Knowing that recovery is often blocked

If the situation with loss of consortium and emotional distress cases is often grim for same-sex couples, wrongful death is much worse. That's because the statutes state, quite clearly, who's eligible to recover damages. Even though you may expect that anyone who can show a loss might be able to recover, that's not the case in most states. Instead, recovery is limited to a few people. Sometimes these classes of people are specifically named by statute, and sometimes the laws refer to those people who are entitled to recovery where the deceased dies without a will (referred to as *intestate*). In either case, the group usually looks something like this:

- ✔ Legal spouses
- ✔ Children and parents
- ✔ Siblings (in some states)
- ✔ Grandparents/grandchildren (in some states)

Make sure you understand what this means: If your relationship to your partner isn't legally recognized, then in most states you won't even be able to make your case for loss of support.

We can't blame courts here, either. Unlike the consortium and emotional distress cases, wrongful death cases require a court to interpret a statute. Whether they like it or not, they're bound to follow it unless it's unconstitutional.

The problem is that these laws were written a long time ago, when it may have made more sense to assume that the people who would suffer financially and emotionally from another's death would be that person's immediate family members. But now the laws just seem archaic, fencing out anyone — not just same-sex couples — whose relationships don't fit into the boxes these laws create.

Is there any way around this problem? Not much, but at least a few glimmers of hope exist — with an emphasis on *glimmers*.

The Michigan rule

If you don't already live there, you could try moving to Michigan. There, anyone who is a beneficiary under a will (or named under a will as someone entitled to wrongful death recovery) or of a living trust can also recover for any damages they can establish. Michigan law is lousy for gay and lesbian couples in other respects (especially when it comes to relationship recognition) but great here.

The Michigan law won't do you any good if you don't create the legal documents needed to protect yourself and your partner. Gays and lesbians who die without a will or living trust are in no better position in Michigan than they would be in other states that have much narrower laws.

Creative courts

Courts really don't like these restrictive rules, and they understand that denying recovery to the surviving partner in a same-sex relationship can compound personal tragedy with horrendous financial loss. So a few of them have devised ways of getting around the laws:

- ✔ In a California case decided before the state expanded the protections for same-sex couples, the surviving partner of a woman mauled to death by a neighbor's vicious dog was permitted to sue the dog's owners. The court ignored the language of the statute and cited both the impossibility for same-sex couples to contract around this law ("an insurmountable obstacle") and the purpose of the wrongful death law (to provide compensation and deterrence).

- ✔ In a case decided by a court in Washington, DC (again, before the district extended protections to same-sex couples), a judge found that a lesbian qualified as "next of kin" under the wrongful death law and therefore had standing to recover.

- ✔ In New York, a trial judge allowed a wrongful death claim to proceed where the gay couple had entered into a civil union in Vermont — even though New York didn't recognize same-sex marriages or even civil unions at that time. (The case was reversed on appeal, though.)

In a way, it's amazing that same-sex couples have had a bit more success under wrongful death laws than in the loss of consortium and emotional distress cases where they *don't* confront a statute. That might be because courts see the financial ruin that could occur without them, and they also fear that defendants might get off the hook if the one person who can establish economic harm can't recover for it. Although the odds of recovery still aren't in your favor, courts in other states may look to the precedent from these creative courts, especially if the judges are sympathetic to begin with.

Marriage equality to the rescue

Just like with consortium and emotional distress cases, wrongful death suits are magically transformed from likely losers to potential winners by marriage equality. And once again, civil unions and comprehensive domestic partnership laws also do the trick. (If you're in a state with a more limited set of rights for same-sex couples, check whether the law has expanded to cover these cases.)

How does this legal alchemy work in the case of wrongful death? Remember, these suits are different from the other torts we discuss earlier in this chapter, because they're statutory and not court-created. But it's basically the same deal.

After a state recognizes a same-sex union as the legal equivalent of an opposite-sex one (whether it's called marriage or something else), then all the rights of marriage — including the right to bring a statutory claim for wrongful death — come along with it.

In a state that has full marriage equality, such as Massachusetts, the statute's language doesn't even need to be changed. Because the class of persons entitled to recover includes either "spouse" or (in Massachusetts) "wife or husband," legally wed same-sex couples now simply fit within the language of the law.

In states that have civil union laws, the law needs to be amended to include this new class of beneficiary. Here's how Vermont took care of it, back when the state became the first to offer civil union status (they've since moved on to full marriage equality). The law spelled out that parties to a civil union were entitled to all the "legal benefits, protections, and responsibilities" that the law grants spouses, including:

> "causes of action related to or dependent upon spousal status, including an action for wrongful death, emotional distress, loss of consortium."

As with the law of consortium and emotion distress, the same is true for wrongful death. It boils down to the statewide recognition of same-sex relationships. Without that recognition, most of these suits won't get off the ground. With it, many of them will.

Suing for Injury to Your Relationship: Yes or No?

In the tort cases that we discuss in this chapter, calculating whether you should sue for injury is complicated indeed. You (and your partner, if still alive) need to take into account a number of legal, practical, and personal factors before deciding whether to proceed. These sections identify some important points to ponder. If you decide to pursue the claim, we help you find an attorney and explain what to expect during the lawsuit.

Knowing what to consider before you sue

Before you decide to sue or not, you want to think about some practical considerations. When thinking about the practicalities, sort out the claims we discuss throughout this chapter, because they all involve different calculations. Check out the following:

✔ **Loss of consortium claims:** Think twice before pursuing this claim because it depends on the underlying personal injury suit, where the recovery will be much greater than in any secondary suit (which is what a loss of consortium suit really is).

We're not saying that you didn't experience a real loss as the potential loss of consortium plaintiff — where there's a serious injury to your partner. We know you do suffer, but think about whether you want to sue. A jury may possibly be unsympathetic to your same-sex relationship and not want to hear about the *consortium* (sex) you've lost. Jeopardizing the recovery in the underlying personal injury suit may not be worth it, in case the jury would reduce or even deny damages.

Where you live and the likely composition of the jury in that location may also affect your decision to sue. Face it — New York City is more sympathetic than Oklahoma City.

✔ **Emotional distress cases:** Some of the same considerations apply — this claim will be smaller than the personal injury claim, so think about whether it's worth it. You may make a different decision, too, based on whether the claim is one you're bringing based on fear of injury to yourself or based on the distress caused by harm to your partner. Where the harm is based on your relationship, you can run into the same problems that you could with a loss of consortium claim.

✔ **Wrongful death claims:** They often present the strongest practical case for suing. Because your partner has been killed, there's often no other claim to jeopardize. If there *is* another claim (because your partner's right to sue will survive his or her death), it will likely be much smaller than the potential recovery in a wrongful death action — through which the successful same-sex partner stands to recover millions for the loss of a high-wage-earning spouse.

After you sort through these issues and think that a suit may be worth bringing, you want to consult an experienced attorney. The next section helps you as you approach those discussions.

Talking with an attorney

In the case of loss of consortium or emotional distress, you and your partner will likely want to visit the attorney together. Make clear, right away, the nature of your relationship and discuss your interest in suing for both personal injury and one or both of these other torts. Even in a wrongful death case, the attorney needs to know about the nature of your relationship, upfront.

The most obvious benefit of this conversation is that you'll be able to gauge the lawyer's comfort level with what you're presenting. (Where it's possible, of course, you should seek out lawyers who are LGBT-friendly.)

When you talk to an attorney, you also get a legal assessment of both the personal injury claim — just because there's been an accident doesn't mean the claim is strong — and the secondary claim. Any attorney in a state with legal equality for same-sex couples should know that *all* these claims — loss of consortium, the negligent or intentional infliction of emotional distress, and wrongful death — are potentially viable. But lawyers in states with laws not favorable to LGBT equality may have to do some research into the cases and the statutes before letting you know whether the case stands a chance and whether, given the odds, it's worth pursuing.

You and your partner should have a frank discussion with the attorney about this cost-benefit issue. Even if there's some chance of success on a consortium or emotional distress suit, an experienced local lawyer should have some sense of whether the potential judges or jurors might — or might not — be sympathetic to a same-sex couple.

Whatever advice you get from the attorney you visit, the ultimate decision about whether to file a suit is yours. If you feel strongly that you want to pursue it, then try another lawyer if the first one doesn't agree to do so. But if you keep running into a brick wall, rethink your decision — maybe the claim really *isn't* worth it.

Going through the legal stuff

No matter what lawsuit you're thinking of filing, make sure you consider whether filing is the best course of action. For perspective, think of a lawsuit as the last resort only in cases where you feel you have no other choice. Why?

Lawsuits are expensive. They are time-consuming. They force you and your partner to relive experiences you may never want to think about again. (If your partner has been killed, reliving the experience can be even worse.) At some point, they place you and the defendant who caused the harm face to face. Are you ready for all this? Are you sure that this is your best option?

Sometimes, a lawsuit is indeed the way to go. Financial necessity, especially in a wrongful death case, might leave you with little choice but to try suing where other options have failed. Even then, only do so in a state where the law at least affords you some reasonable chance of success. But many times, these suits based on the injury to, or loss of, relationships won't be your best decision. Sometimes, even the underlying personal injury suit isn't well advised. It's all a question of balance, of sober reflection, and of assessing your priorities.

Part IV
Handling Other Relevant Issues

The 5th Wave   By Rich Tennant

Dave used his time well while waiting
for the INS to approve his
partner's green card.

In this part . . .

Some issues don't fit neatly into one of the broad categories we cover in the other parts of this book, but
they're nonetheless important to a large number of same-
sex couples.

This part looks at three of those: immigration, life in the
military after the repeal of the Don't Ask, Don't Tell policy,
and life as an activist. If you're inspired by our
suggestions for activism, you could actually help to
improve the situation for those affected by the federal
laws relating to immigration and the military.

Chapter 17

Wading Through Immigration Issues

*I*magine this situation: On a vacation in Madrid, Spain, you met the love of your life. You extended the vacation for as long as you could, and since returning home, you've spent most of your free time either talking with this special someone on the phone and on Skype, e-mailing him (or her), and anticipating the next time can spend some time together.

This long-distance relationship has gone on for more than a year now. You've been back to Spain a couple of times to visit, and your new partner also has come to the United States twice. Your families and friends have met, and everyone's delighted for the two of you, convinced you've both found that special someone.

You also have some legal mojo on your side: You were recently legally married in your home state of New York, where marriage equality arrived in 2011. And Spain — one of a growing number of European countries to get on board the Equality Train — legally recognizes your marriage. The two of you are ready to do what almost all married couples do: Live together. The question is where.

You love Spain and are fluent in Spanish, but moving there isn't a realistic option for you right now. You've just landed your dream job, and the Spanish economy isn't exactly flourishing. Even so, you may be willing to take your chances — were it not for compelling family reasons. Both of your parents are quite ill, and you're their only reliable caregiver. You're also raising your sister's son, and after a bumpy first couple of years, he's settled in at his school and doing well. Moving him to another country at this time would be a disaster.

Can your new spouse move to the United States? Unfortunately, doing so may not be easy. Although US law usually encourages married folks to stick together as long as at least one of them is a citizen, married same-sex couples are in a much different — and worse — position, all because of the Defense of Marriage Act (DOMA). (Check out Chapter 2 for more about DOMA.)

In this chapter, we explore immigration law as it applies to same-sex couples. Although the option of *sponsoring* a spouse (petitioning the government to grant permanent US resident status to the foreign spouse) under federal immigration law isn't available to a citizen married to a same-sex spouse from another country, you may have some options in certain cases. Understanding these options before you commit yourself to someone else for life is important.

This aspect of immigration is a highly regulated and ever-changing area of the law. The US Immigration and Customs Enforcement (part of the Department of Homeland Security) creates many of the requirements that we discuss in this chapter. This department can change in response to perceived threats to security or just because a new president has different priorities from his or her predecessor. So do your own investigation before proceeding!

Appendix C contains information on the state of same-sex unions throughout the world and what you need to know.

Being Involved with Someone Who Isn't a US Citizen

Before you make a permanent commitment to someone who currently lives in another country and isn't a US citizen, you need to carefully think about the broader practical and personal implications.

In general, these decisions aren't easy. In many cases, one of the two partners will be leaving family and friends behind to settle in a country where he or she has few, if any, roots. For LGBT people, the problems that come from being uprooted — personally and culturally — can be more acute than for others. Whatever strategies you've devised for coping with homophobia may be less useful in a new place, which can be true even if you're moving to a more LGBT-inclusive society, although obviously there would then be enormous advantages, too.

And in many cases, getting to know your partner in the kind of day-to-day way that you'll need to coexist if and when one of you expatriates is difficult. Unless you meet while one of you is working in the other's home country, often your interaction will have been through a series of short visits. Setting up home together — with or without children — is another complexity.

The HIV exclusion: Gone!

In 1987, during the peak of HIV hysteria, Congress passed a law that banned all HIV-positive aliens from gaining entry into the United States. Science didn't support the law; HIV isn't communicable in the same way as other banned diseases, such as tuberculosis. The United States was one of only a very few countries to impose such a ban. (In fact, given the prevalence of HIV infection in the United States compared to other nations that didn't impose such a ban, some speculated that the US was likely an exporter of HIV.)

Although enforcing such a law was difficult (because it largely relied on the honesty of the person seeking admission in stating his or her HIV status), the law obviously had a significant deterrent effect on HIV-positive people who may have wanted to visit or to immigrate to the United States. Public health officials (including the World Health Organization) condemned the policy as furthering the stigmatization of HIV-positive people, while having an overall negative public health impact. Nonetheless, the ban remained in place for more than two decades.

In 2008, Congress finally repealed the law. But administrative action to remove HIV from the list of excludable diseases was still required. Finally, on January 4, 2010, the Department of Health and Human Services and the Centers for Disease Control and Prevention passed a final rule removing HIV from the list.

The good news: If you think HIV is a reason for you or your partner to be prevented from visiting the United States, you're operating with outdated information.

To add to the mix of potential problems, consider the financial issues. If one of you leaves a great job for a less rewarding one — perhaps financially, perhaps personally, or perhaps both — you can expect additional strain on the relationship.

None of this is to say that such relationships can't work. Obviously, quite often they do work, for both same- and opposite-sex couples. But make sure both of your eyes are wide open. One way to keep those lids lifted is to spend some time together, on a trial basis, before making a permanent commitment. Check out the next section for specific considerations your partner needs to look at before visiting the United States.

Visiting the United States

Whether you're legally married or not, visiting the United States on a temporary basis is much easier for your partner than obtaining permanent resident status (much less citizenship). Your partner faces a number of different legal options here. Much of what follows isn't specific to people in same-sex relationships, although a few cautions apply. The following sections explain the visitor visa process and a possible way around it.

Obtaining a Visitor Visa

In most cases, whichever one of you resides in another country needs to apply for a visa in order to visit the United States. (We're not talking about work or student visas here; they're for purposes other than visiting.) The visa most commonly used for a visit is — not surprisingly — the visitor visa. Two types of visitor visas exist:

- ✔ **B-1:** This type is a business visa. The holder of this visa is permitted to enter the United States for up to six months for a variety of business activities (including consulting, attending trade conventions, and so on). The holder isn't permitted to obtain income from a US employer.

  A B-1 visa is different than a work visa, which allows a person to hold employment within the United States. We discuss work and student visas in the "Acquiring a visa or green card" section later in this chapter.

- ✔ **B-2:** This type of visa is more flexible, because it's usually used for fun. These *pleasure visas* (also limited to six months' duration) can be used for tourism, visiting family and friends, plain ol' R&R, and for medical treatment (well, we did say it was *usually* used for fun). Like the B-1 visa, the B-2 doesn't permit the holder to obtain work or income from any US employer.

These visitor visas can be a good fit for LGBT people (or anyone else) seeking temporary entry into the United States. If you or your partner wants one of these types of visa, stride briskly over to the nearest US Consulate in your country of residence or your partner's country of residence and apply for one.

When you apply for one of these two types of visas, you'll be required to do the following:

1. **Fill out a nonimmigrant visa application (currently the DS-160).**

   This form asks for personal, identifying information, and also inquires about the purpose of your visit. The form also requires you to disclose any previous visa applications, requests the name (and status) of all immediate relatives in the United States, and asks additional security-related questions.

2. **Possess a valid passport from your home country.**

   If you don't have a passport, you need one before you can apply for one of these visas.

3. **Present a photograph of yourself (which must measure 2 by 2 inches).**

   The photo is used for identification purposes.

4. **Pay a $160 visa application fee.**

   Acceptable forms of payment vary; check with the relevant embassy (or on its website) for the latest information.

5. **Interview with a consular officer.**

   The officer asks you questions designed to see whether you intend to return to your country of origin. Sometimes the officer will ask hypothetical questions, such as "What would you do if you were offered a high-paying job while visiting the United States?" Be honest, but remember that you have to convince the interviewer that your visit to the United States will be temporary. Translation services are available if the interviewee doesn't speak English — ask about that, if necessary.

   You also need to establish three things during the interview:

   - **That you don't have certain diseases of public health significance.** Among the most significant are active tuberculosis and infectious syphilis.

   - **That you don't have a criminal record.** Criminal convictions for many serious crimes, including drug-related offenses, make you ineligible for a visa. Waivers may be granted under certain limited circumstances, but if you have been convicted of a crime, consult an attorney before even going through the process.

   - **That you don't have the intent to immigrate.** This part can pose special difficulties for gay and lesbian couples, because the interviewer may infer an intent to immigrate from the relationship and the inability to sponsor the partner into the country.

   Much can depend on the specific questions asked during the interview; the consular officer has wide discretion as to what might be asked. To dispel the suspicion of intent to immigrate, the applicant must prove two things that we discuss in the following sections.

Having strong ties abroad

During the interview with the consular officer, you, the applicant, must prove that you have strong ties abroad, which gives you the incentive to return home when the visa expires. Proving may especially be difficult for some same-sex couples.

The ways you can prove that you have strong ties to your home country include

✔ **Showing evidence of a permanent job (or business interest):** Just as with anyone else, if you or your partner (again, whoever's applying for the visa) is unemployed, obtaining a visa may be harder.

✔ **Demonstrating close family relations in your native country:** If you're estranged from your family, perhaps for being gay or lesbian, then establishing strong family ties can be tough.

Another possible minefield in the interview process concerns your relationship itself. What if the consular officer asks you whether you are married? Even if you and your partner *are* married (either in a state that allows same-sex unions or in another country that does) in an important sense, you are *not*. The federal government (because of the DOMA) doesn't recognize your union. Thus, the safest answer would be: "I'm not in a marriage that the US Government recognizes." But that invites the follow-up question:

"Do you have a significant other in the United States?"

This question presents you with two bad choices. If you do the right thing and answer honestly, your application may be denied. But if you're not honest, then your misrepresentation is itself a sufficient ground for denying your application.

Your situation may not come to that, though. A lot depends on the questions you are asked and whether the immigration official is satisfied that you have the intent to return to your home country. And even if your application is denied, you can always reapply.

Having sufficient funds

During the interview, the consular officer will also ask to verify whether you have sufficient funds to afford the visit, so that you won't be induced to take illegal employment while in the United States. For the most part, your same-sex relationship will be treated no differently from an opposite-sex one when it comes to establishing that you have enough money for the visit. To verify you have sufficient funds, all you have to do is show that you have a bank account with sufficient resources for the trip. (Obviously, shorter trips require less of a showing than longer ones.)

Another way to show sufficient funds is to establish that you have a sponsor who is footing the bill for the visit. A *sponsor* is any US citizen or permanent resident, including the applicant's same-sex partner, who can promise to financially support the applicant for the duration of the visit.

Of course, if your partner is your sponsor, follow-up questions about the relationship might ensue. Again, if the consulate official believes that the sponsor is in a relationship with an American citizen, then problems can arise with the intent to return to the home country.

After DOMA falls, the Immediate Relative Immigrant Visa will be your best option

Obtaining the Immediate Relative Immigrant Visa (the IR-1) allows US citizens to sponsor their foreign spouses into the United States for a green card (permanent resident status). Unfortunately this discussion is beside the point (for now) for same-sex couples because DOMA doesn't recognize your marriage. However, you should tuck away this option in case DOMA is either repealed (unlikely, at least in the short term) or declared unconstitutional (much likelier).

The process of obtaining an IR-1 based on marriage begins when the US citizen (of the married couple) files a sponsorship petition with the Department of Homeland Security. If approved, the petition is forwarded to the National Visa Center, which then contacts the foreign applicant and gives that person information about applying for the immigrant visa itself.

This option doesn't apply to same-sex couples who aren't legally married. Consider these cases:

- Neither the US state nor the foreign country in which you and your partner reside recognize same-sex unions at all.

- One of you lives in a state or country that affords *some* relationship status, such as civil union or domestic partnership, to same-sex couples, but not marriage. (For example, France allows same-sex couples to enter into the *pacte civile*, which is a more limited status than marriage.)

Because the Immediate Relative Visa is only available to those who are legally married, for immigration purposes it makes no difference whether you and your partner are legal strangers to each other or whether your relationship is recognized on some level short of marriage. It's not marriage — and that's that, as far as immigration law is concerned.

Even if you're legally married, though, the situation isn't much better. Perhaps your partner is from Canada, and you live in neighboring Vermont. In that case, you have your choice of places to marry, because both Vermont and Canada have adopted full marriage equality. But for immigration purposes, it doesn't matter which of these you choose — because of DOMA. Refer to Chapter 2 for more about DOMA and the different lawsuits seeking to have it overturned.

If and when DOMA disappears, you and your partner may possibly be able to go to a state (or country, like Canada) that recognizes same-sex marriages, enter into a marriage there, and have it federally recognized even if your home state (and nation) doesn't permit same-sex unions. But this is uncharted territory, and you'd both be advised to consult the latest government pronouncements on the matter before assuming your union will qualify!

Going the visa waiver route

Given the problems and complexities of obtaining a visa, you may wish you could just skip the whole process. Well, you may be able to do just that! The Visa Waiver Program was established in 1986 to encourage tourism and to strengthen US international relations.

As its name implies, the Visa Waiver Program allows citizens from the list of approved countries to enter the United States for up to 90 days, as long as they have a valid passport (from their home country) and successfully pass through a customs port of entry. Note: The Visa Waiver Program only allows visits of up to 90 days. So if you're hoping for a longer visit (up to six months), this option won't be available. You still have to obtain a visa.

The program currently includes 36 nations, listed alphabetically: Andorra, Australia, Austria, Belgium, Brunei, Czech Republic, Denmark, Estonia, Finland, France, Germany, Greece, Hungary, Iceland, Ireland, Italy, Japan, Latvia, Liechtenstein, Lithuania, Luxembourg, Malta, Monaco, Netherlands, New Zealand, Norway, Portugal, San Marino, Singapore, Slovakia, Slovenia, South Korea, Spain, Sweden, Switzerland, and the United Kingdom.

The list of countries currently in the Visa Waiver Program is subject to change. Be sure to check the most current list — perhaps your home country (or your partner's) has been added to (or removed from) the list.

Getting *to* the United States and getting *into* the United States can be two different things, because the customs officers have the discretion to deny entry into the country. Being denied entry is highly unlikely, but making a number of visits to the United States within a short period of time may raise red flags, such as the potential for immigrating. This possibility isn't unique to same-sex couples, but it may be more likely to come up with them because of the need to be discreet about the relationship.

Moving to the United States: Your Options

Visits with your same-sex partner are great, but in the long run, you may want more. At some point, you and your partner may actually want to live together — in one country and in one home.

Doing so may be easy, challenging, or downright impossible in another country. It all depends on that nation's laws regarding same-sex marriages, and possibly on the laws regarding homosexual conduct. Given how difficult immigrating into the United States is for those in same-sex relationships, we strongly suggest you look into the possibilities in whatever other country figures into your international relationship. Depending on your situation, you have a few options for seeking to immigrate into the United States, which we discuss in the following sections.

Applying for political asylum

In a small number of cases, you or your partner may possibly be able to seek political asylum in the United States. Applying for *political asylum* (a safe haven from persecution in one's home country) is a very serious process; don't undertake this process unless the applicant (you or your partner) has a legitimate claim.

In that case, asylum may turn out to be the means for the two of you to stay together. If the application is made in good faith, the fact that you're in a same-sex relationship should neither harm nor benefit your chances of being awarded asylum. That said, the desire to stay together should never be the *reason* for seeking asylum.

Obtaining political asylum for you or your partner is very difficult and time-consuming, and you should only undertake it if you have a reasonable chance of success. It's helpful if the partner seeking asylum is from a country, such as Jamaica, where treatment of gay men is known to be so bad that petitions are often granted.

If you believe you have a strong case for political asylum, seek out a lawyer or LGBT-rights group that is familiar with this area of the law. Don't try to navigate all this complexity on your own.

Even if one of you is here illegally, you can still seek asylum. If you or your partner decides to go this route, stick to these steps:

1. **Gain access to a port of entry, or (more likely) already be in the United States.**

   After you're in the country, you, the asylum seeker, have up to one year to file for asylum from the date of entry (longer if you can prove that circumstances have changed since you were last in their home country, making it unsafe to return home).

2. **Fill out Form I-589.**

   The form asks a number of standard questions, but most importantly it requests information about the home country and the reasons for seeking asylum. Through the answers supplied on this form, and the interview that follows, you must establish that:

   > "Race, religion, nationality, membership in a particular social group, or political opinion was or will be at least one central reason for persecuting the applicant."

   The law doesn't define membership in "a particular social group," but it has been described in one proceeding as:

"Persecution . . . directed toward an individual who is a member of a group of persons all of whom share a common, immutable characteristic. The shared one might be an innate one such as sex, color, or kinship ties, or . . . it might be a shared past experience."

This definition has been specifically applied to protect gays and lesbians. In a 1990 immigration hearing, the Board of Immigration Appeals allowed a 40-year-old Cuban man to claim asylum based on his claim of persecution in his home country. A few years later, in 1994, Attorney General Janet Reno designated the decision as precedential, meaning that gays and lesbians can now seek asylum based on sexual orientation, which is now effectively included under the vague umbrella term "particular social group."

If an asylum claim is administratively denied, you can appeal to the federal court.

Don't even think about pursuing an asylum claim without a seasoned immigration attorney in your corner.

Acquiring a visa or green card

You have another avenue to live in the United States. A non-US citizen can use his or her employment to obtain either a more long-term visa or a green card. Not surprisingly, this area of immigration law and policy is complex. Although it doesn't speak directly to the needs of same-sex couples, you can still find some help with it.

Make sure you seek further information before proceeding with a visa or green card. If you're seeking an employment or advance study visa, often the employer or institution of higher learning can help you navigate these choppy waters.

In the "Obtaining a visitor visa" section earlier in this chapter we discuss visas you need to visit the United States for short periods of time. Other visas allow you stay for a longer period. These sections explain your three options.

The CD contains the link to the US Citizenship and Immigration Services site, along with information on other potentially helpful sources of information to help you determine whether a work or student visa is right for you.

Getting a work visa

A *work visa* allows workers to remain in the country as long as they're performing work for their employers. Although these visas are for limited periods of time, they can often be renewed, as needed. Several different types of work visas exist, and the requirements for obtaining them vary. Some of these visas also have annual caps on the number of people who may hold them, so check with your employer (if appropriate), or do some further research.

For many same-sex couples, a work visa may be a way to remain in the United States for an extended period of time, perhaps until DOMA is finally put to rest, and the two of you can have your marriage federally recognized.

Going the student visa route

Student visas are what they sound like — visas that allow students to spend time studying in the United States. They're available in several different categories (academic, vocational, and exchange). Many colleges and other educational institutions are expert at working with foreign nationals on obtaining these visas and then making sure that the rules are followed.

Applying for a green card

If you or your partner wants to remain in the country permanently, you have another significant possibility. You can apply for a *green card*, based on your employment. The green card grants permanent residency to its holder — not citizenship, which you must apply for separately. Several categories of people may apply for a green card through employment, or even based on a job offer. The categories are

- ✔ An offer of permanent employment
- ✔ An entrepreneurial plan that will result in significant investment and employment in the United States
- ✔ A self-petition, but only if you're Superman (or Woman) (an alien of extraordinary ability, listing such qualifications as being a Nobel prize winner or a notable athlete)
- ✔ A job falling into a very specific list (such as, currently "Panama Canal Employee")

Falling within one of the categories just makes one eligible to apply for a green card; it by no means guarantees that one will be issued to you. The government has caps on the number of people who may immigrate in any given year (and sometimes caps on specific categories, as well).

Green cards based on work, rather than on family unification considerations, are relatively rarer. Government policy favors family solidarity over employment, but that policy doesn't extend to same-sex couples, because of DOMA. Nonetheless, many same-sex couples have been able to remain together because of green cards (or work visas). Although a work visa may be your best option, it's always contingent and may add to your on-going stress about how you're going to find a way to live together. The green card, if you can get it, is the way to go, at least until DOMA is repealed or declared unconstitutional by the Supreme Court.

Marrying a member of the opposite sex: Don't do it

Driven to desperation by their inability to marry someone of the same-sex, some gay and lesbian foreign nationals have sought to get around the law that prohibits their spouses from sponsoring them into the United States by entering into a marriage with someone of the opposite sex. This step is very perilous, and we don't recommend doing so. Why not?

In part because of national security concerns, the penalties for marriage fraud are extremely severe. Either party to what's determined to be the "sham marriage" can face up to five years in prison and a financial penalty of up to $250,000. In addition, the foreign national will be barred, for life, from ever again obtaining a visa to enter the United States.

Estimates of sham marriages range as high as one-third of all marriages between US citizens and foreign nationals. Therefore, the government is extremely vigilant and couples are unlikely to get away with a sham marriage. In short, a sham marriage just isn't worth the risk. Find another option, if you can.

Generally, the government doesn't much care about the content of your marriage. Some people live apart from their spouses, don't raise their kids together, don't mingle their assets, and don't even like each other. In most cases, the government leaves the content of the marriage to the couple.

But that's not so when it comes to immigration and to sponsoring one's spouse into the country. In that case, the government is much nosier. That's because the right to sponsor a spouse into the country is the only way to create a family for immigration purposes, and the US Immigration and Customs Enforcement wants to make sure that people aren't taking advantage of the law to bring in unqualified people. The marriage must be *bona fide*, which translates to: Done for the purpose of entering into a real marital relationship and not to commit immigration fraud.

An immigration officer will interview the couple. This officer will be on the lookout for discrepancies between the stories that each tells about the relationship. In addition, the government considers certain facts as bearing on the genuineness of the marriage:

✔ Whether the couple is living together

✔ Whether the couple is mingling its assets

✔ The statements of others who know the couple

That's not to say, though, that the government is always right. In that case, the government's decision to term a marriage "sham" can be appealed to federal court. But this situation is unlikely to affect many same-sex couples, at least as long as DOMA remains on the books.

Chapter 18

After Don't Ask, Don't Tell: Living in the Military as LGB (not T)

From late 1993 until September 20, 2011, gays and lesbians in the military operated under the peculiar rule that became known as *Don't Ask, Don't Tell* (DADT). Congress enacted DADT as a compromise during the early days of the Clinton administration between those who wanted gays and lesbians to serve openly — including then-President Bill Clinton — and those who didn't believe that those with a "homosexual orientation" should be in military service at all.

When the Obama administration took office, military leaders began to voice the view that DADT was more corrosive to "morale" and "unit cohesion" than the presence of those individuals with a same-sex orientation could ever have been. Soldiers need to rely on each other in every way, and being deployed with troops who are forced — by law — to lie about their fundamental nature got in the way of that reliance. The military lost many thousands of soldiers who were discharged under DADT but who were otherwise ready, willing, and able to serve their country.

In 2010 Congress repealed the policy, contingent upon certification from President Obama, Secretary of State Hillary Rodham Clinton, and Chairman of the Joint Chiefs of Staff Admiral Mullen that repeal wouldn't harm military readiness. That certification took place on July 22, 2011, and the repeal became official on September 20, 2011, after a further 60-day waiting period that had been specified in the legislation.

Today, being attracted to someone of the same sex (or even being attracted to members of both sexes!) isn't grounds to keep you or your partner out of the military, nor to discharge you if your sexual orientation comes to light later.

A brief history of gays in the military (including DADT)

Many people think that the military always excluded homosexuals from service. But that's not true. In fact, the armed services have been changing their policies on same-sex orientation and conduct ever since the United States has had a military.

In the early days, the military didn't even have a distinction between homosexual and heterosexual people. The concept of sexual identity as such didn't exist until the very end of the 19th century, and the military was therefore concerned only about specific acts that it thought detrimental to military order. For example, in 1778, a Lieutenant Enslin was booted out of the military for engaging in sodomy (then defined as "unnatural acts," but most often used to describe men having sex with other men) with a private.

Not until the 20th century did the effort to root out those seen as *being* homosexual (as opposed to engaging in certain acts) come into full force. An effort to purge the Navy of gay men shortly after World War I led to disgust at the tactics used (which amounted to entrapment and enticement), but also marked the beginning of the move from same-sex conduct to a ban on homosexual people.

By World War II, this newer approach led to a widespread effort to keep out of military service not just men who were perceived to have a homosexual orientation, but also men and women who didn't exhibit stereotypical behavior of their gender. Even career choices were seen as evidence of such nonconformity, with (for example) males who worked in interior design excluded on that basis.

In 1949, the exclusion of "homosexual personnel" became official Department of Defense policy, and that policy was clarified in early 1981 by a directive that declared homosexuality to be "incompatible with military service" and required the discharge of anyone who either engaged in homosexual activity or stated that he or she were homosexual. An exception,

popularly known as the "Queen for a Day" rule, permitted anyone found to have engaged in homosexual activity to remain in the military if he or she could show that his or her actions didn't reflect their sexual orientation and that he or she would never do this again! The 1981 directive was in place when President Clinton was elected in 1992.

In 1993, President Clinton signed the Don't Ask, Don't Tell (DADT) policy, which was seen as a compromise. DADT was therefore one step up and one step back. On the one hand, it did allow gays, lesbians, and bisexuals (but not transgendered people, who continue to be excluded from military service to this day) to serve — as long as they didn't reveal their sexual orientation ("tell"). On the other hand, DADT put into Congressional law what had previously been only a Department of Defense directive, which any president could have revoked. In fact, that's what President Clinton had tried to do, before senior military officers outmaneuvered him.

Whether the resulting compromise of DADT was an improvement is best left to historians. It's clear, though, that the policy was improperly understood and inconsistently applied. Many gays and lesbians served in the military during the period of time when DADT applied, but others were discharged on scanty evidence. Moreover, service members weren't sure what constituted "telling" about their sexual orientation. Gay and lesbian former service members have told their stories about having letters discovered (in one case, a letter in a different language that a fellow soldier was able to translate, and then report), taste in music used as evidence of sexual orientation, and other absurdities. Others have reported that the military tended to overlook sexual orientation during war, when it couldn't afford to ship anyone out — but then the service member suspected of being gay would be discharged as soon as the conflict was resolved or stabilized.

That doesn't mean, though, that being gay, lesbian, or bisexual in the military is a walk in the park. This chapter discusses some of the continuing problems that you may face and steps for solving them. Although the repeal of DADT was a hugely important step, there's a long way to go before your relationship will be considered the equivalent of your straight fellow soldiers'. You may face harassment. You may be separated from your spouse (or partner). And you won't be eligible for many of the most important benefits that your straight, married counterparts receive — again, because of the Defense of Marriage Act (DOMA).

Knowing What Being Out in the Military Really Means

The repeal of DADT means that every gay and lesbian person can, legally speaking, be out and open about his or her sexual orientation. For many people, especially people in a serious relationship, being out is the best choice. But military culture continues to be different from civilian life, so you seriously want to think about whether you want to come out, how you do come out, and how to express yourself.

If you do come out, be aware of a few pitfalls, such as harassment. These sections help you determine if coming out is the best choice for you (and what you need to consider). If you decide to come out, we also explain how you can handle harassment and other pitfalls you may encounter.

Knowing if coming out is right for you

For some people, coming out is a no-brainer. You can talk to your fellow soldiers about your life and relationship, as they talk about theirs. You can dismantle the scaffold of lies, half-truths, and misdirections that you needed to get by in the DADT world. Heck, you can even introduce your partner to your friends on base or talk about the ups and downs of dating (a subject on which straights and gays can both hold forth, at length).

But for some people, coming out is a trickier proposition. Although military leaders lately have been training troops about the need to accept and work with all soldiers (even the LGB ones), on a particular base, or during a particular deployment, the reality is probably more complex. Some of your fellow soldiers may hold misconceptions about gays and lesbians that make working with them tougher, at least for a while. And if your commanding officers are homophobic, they can make your life difficult in spite of the law. Although that's also true in civilian life, the deliberately autocratic structure of the military can make dealing with hostility more difficult.

So how do you know if you need to come out? Ask yourself these questions as you figure out what's right for you:

- ✔ **Are you single or in a relationship?** As a practical matter, remaining closeted will be more difficult if you're in a serious relationship. Doing so is also likely to place a strain on your relationship.

- ✔ **What is the climate on your particular base?** Are other people are out? If so, how are they treated? If not, how close are you to your fellow soldiers? Does your commanding officer strike you as fair-minded? Your legal rights are one thing; your comfort level is another.

- ✔ **How important is coming out to your identity?** You may find this entire discussion silly, because you don't have a choice. You can only function as a fully out person. But other people are more cautious, preferring to establish themselves in a particular context before revealing themselves as a gay, lesbian, or bisexual person.

Coming out is a process. You may feel comfortable in coming out to a few close friends on base, or you may feel telling anyone is unnecessary until you become more established with your group. Just know, it's a personal decision. Do what makes you feel comfortable.

Dealing with harassment

To its substantial credit, the military lately has done a much better job than it once did in changing the culture in which women were harassed and in which gays and lesbians were spoken of disparagingly (when they were known to be in the military, but not permitted to be open about their sexual orientation). But harassment continues, and thinking it's going to stop is naïve, even in an era of heightened sensitivity and awareness of the importance of diversity in the military.

That doesn't mean you have to put up with harassment. If you're being harassed for being gay or lesbian (or for any other reason), you can address this behavior in several manners.

You do need to know something up front. The repeal of DADT wasn't accompanied by an expansion of the antidiscrimination and antiharassment policies to include sexual orientation or gender identity. And as of this writing, no law or policy covers these categories. However, if you're being harassed, you can still take action.

Before taking any action, make sure to carefully document your case to protect yourself:

✔ Note incidents of harassment, in writing, as soon as possible.

✔ If you can, speak to witnesses of the harassment and see whether they'll commit to backing you up by testifying about what they saw.

✔ If the harassment is in writing or involves property damage, keep documents and take photos. In other words, get busy building your case, just like anyone else victimized by harassment.

✔ If you fear imminent danger to your person, report your concern immediately to the Military Police (MP). Although the MP may not be able to provide help for a hostile environment situation, the MP can handle this kind of threat.

✔ You may also want to turn to a military chaplain for a safe harbor.

In general, you should report harassment up through the chain of command. The chain of command can discipline anyone or begin any investigation. But this step won't help if the chain of command is itself the problem. In that case, proceed directly to one of the following ways to handle harassment.

Making an Equal Opportunity complaint

Each branch of the military has a Military Equal Opportunity (MEO) office that handles complaints of harassment and discrimination. Submitting a complaint to this office is a good step to take if your chain of command complaint is unproductive. The MEO can investigate and decide how the complaint should be handled. This method of proceeding has benefits and drawbacks, though:

✔ You may not only get relief from the harassment or discrimination you're experiencing, but you may be instrumental in creating policy change, too. The MEO creates procedures to prevent future harassment, so by directing your complaint there, you're helping to ensure that office is receiving accurate information on the incidence of harassment, which may then show up in policy recommendations.

✔ Just because sexual orientation isn't a protected class doesn't mean you shouldn't report the harassment. You just want to form your complaint in a way that will be recognized. So be sure to state your complaint in a generic way (just that you're being harassed, with details provided about the nature of the harassment) or to state that you're being harassed based on failure to conform to stereotypical roles of your sex. (That's harassment based on *sex*, which *is* recognized!)

Going the Article 138 complaint route

The Uniform Code of Military Justice in Article 138 allows any service member to seek redress against a commanding officer. You can use this approach to redress any wrong that you may feel has been done to you, even if no specific law or regulation has been violated. If your commanding officer is harassing you, follow these steps:

1. **Address a letter to the commander with whom you have a problem.**

2. **If the redress is denied, complain to any senior commissioned officer, who can then forward the complaint to the officer exercising court-martial convening authority over the offending officer.**

3. **The officer in turn reports the complaint to the Secretary of the Service.**

4. **The office of the Secretary of the Service then looks into the complaint.**

Complaining to the Inspector General

You can also consider reporting harassment to the Inspector General (of the base, of the service, or of the Department of Defense). After you make this complaint, the IG will investigate and make recommendations. The IG can't take any action on its own but can put pressure on those in command in order to induce action.

Considering other avenues to pursue

In some cases, you may not get the results you want, or you may simply want to vault yourself out of military procedures entirely. If so, you may choose these other options. *Remember:* We suggest you pursue them only if attempting to gain redress through established channels hasn't been helpful:

- ✔ **Congressional inquiry:** In rare cases, you may want to seek help from your Congressional Representative in resolving the problem. The law protects such communications, but whether or not they're successful depends on whether your representative is sympathetic to your complaint. If so, he or she may communicate with a liaison officer at the service branch's headquarters.

- ✔ **Alert the media:** If all else fails, you might (might!) consider contacting the media to draw attention to the situation. This really is a measure of last resort, because it can lead to more harassment. If you're considering taking this step, think about retaining an attorney to advise you on how to proceed.

You may also consider seeking advice from an organization called the Servicemembers Legal Defense Network (SLDN) at www.sldn.org. Another advocacy group for gay, lesbian, and bisexual soldier is Servicemembers United, a group that proudly and accurately bills itself as America's Gay Military Organization. You can discover more information on the group at www.servicemembersunited.org.

Grasping the Uniform Code of Military Justice: Not necessarily your friend!

When Congress repealed DADT, it made one serious oversight. It "forgot" to repeal Section 125 of the Uniform Code of Military Justice (UCMJ). (The UCMJ is essentially the criminal code for the military, violations of which can result in serious penalties, including discharge and imprisonment.)

Section 125 criminalizes *sodomy,* which is defined to include both anal and oral sex between members of the same or the opposite sex. The law includes both consensual and nonconsensual conduct and isn't even restricted to conduct that takes place in connection with one's military service. In other words, in theory you or your partner in the military could be prosecuted under this section just for expressing sexual intimacy with each other.

Prosecution isn't likely to happen, and it's not even clear that a prosecution for consensual sex would be constitutionally permissible unless it were somehow detrimental to the military (for example, sexual relations between a commanding officer and a subordinate).

Section 125 will probably be repealed soon; an effort to do so in 2011 passed in the Senate, but stalled in the House of Representatives. Several other sections of the UCMJ can be used against gays, lesbians, and same-sex couples. These sections briefly discuss them.

Sexual misconduct under Article 120:

The UCMJ uses this term to cover two different kinds of behavior:

- ✔ **Wrongful sexual contact:** This is sexual contact without "legal justification" or "lawful authorization." *Sexual contact,* in turn, is defined as an "intentional touching" (even through clothing) of personal areas of the body. The potential problem with this term is one of perception: a homophobic fellow soldier can misinterpret (or even misrepresent) an accidental collision with another service member as intentional sexual contact.

- ✔ **Indecent conduct:** This term is defined very broadly, as immorality "relating to sexual impurity that is grossly vulgar, obscene, and repugnant to common propriety, and [that] tends to excite sexual desire or deprave morals with respect to sexual relations."

  What on earth does that mean? Well, it includes violations of privacy, such as "observing" another person without his or her consent in situations that they would reasonably find offensive. As a result, a homophobic service member can allege a violation of this provision against a gay or lesbian fellow soldier for eyeing them in the shower or even for watching them change.

Conduct unbecoming and general provisions: Articles 133 and 134

These two quite broad articles are scary catch-all provisions that deal with actions the military wants to punish but that aren't otherwise covered by other articles.

- ✔ Article 133 outlaws "conduct unbecoming an officer and a gentleman." (Never mind that the military is no longer restricted to "gentlemen"!)

- ✔ Article 134 waves a vague prohibition at conduct that results in "prejudice of good order and discipline in the armed forced" and conduct that "brings discredit upon the armed forces."

Although some of the conduct covered by these articles is relatively clear (such as fraternization between those of different ranks and adultery), the language of both is broad and can be used against gay, lesbian, and bisexual service members to prosecute for virtually any physical act shown to have a sexual — or even a romantic purpose. When DADT was in force, prosecutions under these sections weren't common — authorities would just use DADT to get gays out of the service. But people have actually done prison time for homosexual conduct found to be in violation of these provisions, and the worry is that the repeal of DADT will lead to an increase of such prosecutions.

We aren't including this information to scare you back into the military closet. In fact, being out can help because it normalizes you and your partner, at least in the long run. In the near term, though, predicting what may happen under these criminal provisions isn't easy. And these provisions may even help you, by providing incentive for a commanding officer or fellow soldier who may be less than sympathetic to your presence in the military to avoid prosecution by acting like "an officer and a gentleman."

Living in the Military as a Same-Sex Couple: Your Benefits and Realities

The repeal of DADT was a huge accomplishment, freeing gays, lesbians, and bisexuals from serving with the constant shadow of being investigated, discovered, and discharged. Repeal has also encouraged the enlistment of many who would otherwise have self-selected out of the military, unwilling to live a shrouded lie. But in addition to the problems of harassment and continued persecution we discuss in the previous sections, same-gender couples face other challenges when at least one of them is in the military. (When both members of the couple are in the military, they also face challenges.)

Some problems simply relate to assimilating your same-sex relationship into a culture that has no experience with other gay and lesbian couples. This problem isn't unique to the military; you and your partner have almost certainly had experiences as a couple moving within the larger straight society that have been painful. But in civil society you often have a greater degree of choice about whom you associate with and can steer your families in and out of wavy surf, as needed. The military's forced intimacy makes this kind of navigation more challenging. In other words, sometimes there's no way to avoid the unpleasantness.

Part of your job is to transform any discomfort that other soldiers and their military families may feel around your family into acceptance. The military isn't the place for dramatic challenges to the status quo. You'll do better by getting a sense of the culture — not just in the military generally, but also in your particular posting — and then fitting in. (If you're not a fitter-inner, the military probably isn't your best bet in the first place!) If you're the non-military spouse, get involved in whatever social or charitable activities the other spouses are doing. Be confident that familiarity will breed comfort.

Unfortunately, you and your partner won't be able to fully integrate into military life even if you want. That's because the law places big obstacles in your path — and by the law, we mean (once again) the Defense of Marriage Act (DOMA). Because federal law governs the military, Section 3 of DOMA applies, which means that whether or not your state of residence recognizes your union, the military does *not*. It's as though you were single. Given the substantial benefits that the law affords married couples in the military, this is no small problem.

The news isn't all bad, though. You can protect your partner and family in a few ways, even in the face of DOMA.

Benefits available to same-sex couples

The repeal of DADT has opened the door for same-sex couples to receive benefits that they wouldn't have received otherwise. Some of the benefits available to military personnel and their families depend on the *affirmative designation* (the person you choose) of the soldier. Here's where the repeal of DADT has had a positive effect. When that policy was in effect, naming your partner as the designated beneficiary of a particular benefit may have aroused suspicion and triggered an investigation into your sexual orientation (because DADT wasn't consistently applied as it was intended).

Now, you needn't fear such a designation — unless you're still trying to live in the closet, in which case you're going to get people's attention by doing so. Many of the benefits available to soldiers go to these designated persons. Here are some of the most significant benefits:

- ✔ Beneficiary of Servicemembers' Group Life Insurance and Veterans' Group Life Insurance payments

- ✔ Recipient of unused contributions from Post Vietnam-Era Assistance Program and the Montgomery G.I. Bill Death benefits

- ✔ Beneficiary of the thrift-savings plan

- ✔ Recipient of the retirement annuity under the survivor benefit plan (as long as the service member doesn't have a dependent child)

- ✔ Beneficiary for death gratuity and beneficiary for unpaid pay/allowances

- ✔ Appointment as the designated caregiver of a wounded service member during recovery, under the Wounded Warrior Act

- ✔ If the service member is deployed, appointment as the caregiver of the service member's child(ren) on a Family Care Plan

Beyond these benefits, you can make sure your relationship is recognized when it most matters in a couple of other ways.

Emergencies and hospital stays

A gay or lesbian soldier can name his or her same-sex partner as the one to be notified in the event of an emergency (if the service member is injured, killed, or is missing in action). The service member can name the same-sex partner as a *designated person* (DP) to receive notification if the soldier is injured. Your partner won't be considered primary next of kin (PNOK), though, because legally, they're not. (*Primary next of kin* is the term the military uses to identify one person who will receive notification of the service member's death. There is only one such person, and that person's identity is determined according to a list ranking that begins with the service member's spouse.)

The DP will be contacted very quickly in the event of an emergency, but because the PNOK will often be contacted first, we suggest you and your partner arrange with the PNOK to contact your partner immediately when notification of an emergency is received, and to designate a PNOK who knows about, and who supports, your relationship.

And if you're both the legal parents of the child, that child can be the PNOK — meaning that, if the child is a minor, the parent will be contacted. So in effect your partner is the PNOK.

Another way for your nonmilitary spouse to notify his or her soldier-partner in case of emergency is through the Red Cross. The Red Cross is the best way of making contact with the soldier, while deployed, because

- ✔ The Red Cross is good at doing it.

- ✔ Getting notified by the Red Cross can serve as verification of the emergency in case the service member seeks emergency leave to deal with the situation.

If you do have an emergency, will the military grant the leave? Everything gets complicated here (thanks again, DOMA). Such leaves are granted, or not, at the discretion of the commanding officer. You should provide whatever documentation of the emergency you have, including the Red Cross notification. If granted, the leave will last for 30 days.

Even if you do provide good documentation, it's not clear that leave will be granted. If the emergency involves a dependent child of whom the service member is a legal parent, then the relationship is one of immediate family, and the leave should be granted. But if the emergency relates to the partner, it's more complicated.

In the DADT-era, the non-service member was referred to as a close friend. Now that need for covering up is gone, but because there's no new guidance on how to deal with same-sex couples, the Red Cross may possibly still refer to the partner as a close friend. Because the commanders haven't provided more guidance to grant leave to service members on the basis of a same-sex relationship, the safest course may still be to go the close friend route.

The good news: Hospital visitation is much less complicated. A service member patient can receive as a visitor any person he or she designated. So your partner should have no problems visiting you in the hospital, if that situation arises.

What about the kids?

As long as the gay or lesbian military member of the couple is the legal parent of the couple's children, all the benefits available to dependent military children are available to those children. If you're not the legal parent of your partner's child, though, consider adopting that child if your state law allows you to do so. (Otherwise, that child won't be eligible for the benefits that other kids receive.) These benefits are substantial:

- ✔ **Medical and dental healthcare and insurance:** In order to receive these benefits, the service member must register the child in the Defense Enrollment Eligibility Reporting System. After it's done, the soldier may enroll the child in any qualified health plan.

- ✔ **Emergency notification:** See the previous section.

- ✔ **Housing:** If you and your partner have a dependent child, you are eligible for military family housing at the dependent-rate basic allowance.

In addition, all service members with dependent children must set up a Family Care Plan before being deployed. You need this plan in order to plan for the child's care if the service member is killed or seriously injured while deployed. When creating this plan, the service member may designate whomever he or she chooses, including a same-sex partner, as the dependent's caregiver (regardless of whether that partner is the child's legal parent).

To make sure your partner is able to make all the decisions affecting your child's health and welfare, set up a comprehensive power of attorney as part of the Family Care Plan.

Benefits unavailable to same-sex couples

Many of the most important benefits that military families and couples enjoy aren't available to same-sex couples. You can't designate your way into these benefits. And you can't use your marriage, civil union, or domestic partnership, either: Federal law, which applies to the military, doesn't recognize them.

Before we cover a list of what you can't get for your nonmilitary, same-sex partner, an important note is in order. Some of the items on the following list are written into law, thereby triggering DOMA. Others, though, are Department of Defense regulations that may be repealed without action by Congress. In other words, the benefits covered by these regulations could be extended to same-sex couples (or even unmarried opposite-sex couples in committed relationships). But as of this writing, here are the benefits that aren't available:

- ✔ Basic allowance for housing at the dependent rate (unless the soldier in your family has a dependent child)
- ✔ Military family housing (again, unless a dependent child is involved)
- ✔ Shopping privileges at base commissaries
- ✔ Free legal services
- ✔ Spousal testimonial privilege in courts martial
- ✔ Mental and dental insurance
- ✔ Morale, welfare, and recreation programs (leisure activities and programs otherwise available to military dependents)
- ✔ Relocation and transportation expenses for same-sex spouses when the service member is assigned to a new base
- ✔ Employment assistance during a permanent station change
- ✔ Education subsidies

✔ Family separation allowances covering travel expenses associated with visiting service members deployed to bases where your partner can't relocate

✔ Surviving spouse benefits, other than those previously mentioned (which may be allocated to a designated beneficiary)

✔ Family advocacy services, such as new parent support and assistance for abused or mistreated spouses

✔ The right to be buried in a military cemetery alongside the military member

There's another problem: If both partners are members of the military, they're ineligible for special consideration for joint duty assignments. These assignments are usually given to opposite-sex couples both serving in the military, for obvious reasons. But couples in same-sex relationships may seek a *hardship*-based request for a joint assignment, which may or may not be granted. It might help if the couple has one or more kids, but, again, there's no guarantee. The military defines hardship narrowly, to include only cases involving extreme family problems that are temporary in nature, and where there is no other way to resolve the family's difficulties.

You may have noticed how extensive these benefits are, compared to those available to people in the civilian population. The very existence of these benefits reflects at least three important considerations.

✔ Life in the military is challenging and often poses difficulties greater than (or even unknown to) those in civil society. These challenges strain families in many ways, and the government responds to this reality with a number of programs designed to mitigate the harshness of military life.

✔ Recruiting talented people into the military is an on-going priority, and one way to encourage more to join is to offer these kinds of benefits and support.

✔ Society wants to support (and thank) the military and the families that support them. These programs help us do just that.

The flipside is that none of these rational reasons for providing this extensive group of benefits are seen as applying to same-sex couples — even those who have taken whatever legal steps they can to have their union recognized. The continued existence of DOMA sends the message that, even in the post-DADT world, same-sex couples don't have the same challenges, don't merit society's support, and don't need to be recruited. In a sense, this message is a legal echo of the infamous booing of the gay soldier by the audience at the 2011 Republican primary debate.

And the message continues even after the soldier has died, perhaps in the line of duty, by the rule that same-sex couples can't be buried together.

Chapter 19

Becoming an Activist for LGBT Equality

. . . .

In This Chapter

▶ Explaining the importance of activism

▶ Accessing the political process

▶ Using your strengths to get involved

. . . .

*H*ow much of an activist do you want to be? Whether you realize it
or not, if you're part of a couple, you and your partner are already
activists — at least in one sense of that word. Unless you're willing to go to
extraordinary lengths to remain in the closet, you're making a public statement about the value of LGBT people and their families simply by being
involved in a same-sex relationship. If you're single, you probably have more
room to maneuver in figuring out just how open you want to be.

For some people, living openly is enough. Just by doing so, you're exposing
the majority, straight population to your reality. Whether you're in relationship or not, have kids or not, and whether you're politically involved or not,
you're providing a model that educates and informs others. An act as simple
as placing a photograph of your family on your desk at work is, for same-sex
couples, activism — more so in a workplace where this is unusual, or even
unprecedented. Talking about your partner with your fellow employees and
your family is another way to spread the word.

Of course, for some people even these simple acts of affirmation are dangerous. In some places, you can still lose your job for being gay or lesbian. You
may also suffer the disapproval, or even the loss, of your family when you
introduce or even discuss your partner. As you're doubtless painfully aware,
even the simple act of holding hands in public can result in a same-sex couple's safety being put at risk.

But every small thing that you can do to present your life as a member of the LGBT community in a way that feels safe, you should. And look for ways to press further, little by little. By doing so, you're helping yourself and the progress toward dignity and equality at the same time.

If that's not enough for you, consider getting involved in other ways that are more obviously activism. The rest of this chapter offers some suggestions on how to become an activist and provides information on organizations that work on LGBT and family equality issues.

Doing Your Part in the Struggle for LGBT Equality

The work of LGBT equality is far, far from finished. In most states, you can still be fired for being gay, lesbian, bisexual, or transgendered. Places of public accommodation can discriminate against you, no matter if you're single or in a relationship. You can marry in just a few states. Even in those states, your union doesn't count for much, because of the Defense of Marriage Act (DOMA) that declares your marriage a nullity for federal law purposes. You may not be able to adopt a child or your partner's child, and you may be denied custody or visitation rights just because of your sexual orientation.

And the law isn't the only thing that creates problems for LGBT people. In many other ways, such as disapproving and nasty looks and not-always veiled comments, and living in a society that often reminds you in many ways that you're lesser or different (and not in a good way!) — the LGBT community faces an on-going challenge.

So what are you going to do about it? The following sections give you some ideas.

Being an activist is easier than you think

Perhaps because of the way the media focuses on big events, you can easily get the idea that activism involves very public efforts, such as marching, petitioning, speaking out, attending rallies, and so on.

Being an activist isn't that complicated. Many people contribute in many different ways to the cause. In fact, you can take a couple steps if you're thinking of being an activist:

✔ **Figure out which issues are most important to you.** Are you affected by your inability to marry your partner? Has discrimination cost you a job or a promotion? Have you been the victim of a hate crime directed against you just because you're LGBT? Have your kids suffered because of your sexual orientation? Do you just feel more education is needed around issues important to gay and lesbian couples? You can think of issues that you want to address.

✔ **Think about your own skill set.** Are you a writer, a blogger, a social media type? Are you someone who enjoys large public demonstrations (and affirmations)? Are you the organizational type — maybe with leadership potential, but perhaps as someone who prefers working behind the scenes? There are phone calls to be made, publications to be worked on, offices in need of volunteers, and so on. Just do something.

Getting involved with a LGBT organization

To become an activist, investigate LGBT organizations and see where you can participate. Plenty of well-known and effective LGBT-rights organizations do advocacy, litigation, and policy work on the national level. A few groups work on the state level, while others are local. Most often, the primary way people support these organizations is by donating money. If you're particularly interested in what a particular group is doing, you can arrange for a monthly sum to be deducted from your bank account.

Investigate what these groups do: Some are mostly involved in high-impact litigation, while others work the corridors of political power in Washington, DC. Some emphasize family issues, while others concern themselves with federal legislation to protect LGBTs in their relationships and in the workplace. If you want to support these broad-based efforts, you won't have trouble finding an organization that speaks to you.

The CD contains a list of several of the most prominent national organizations, with URLs and very brief descriptions of their focus and mission.

If you're in a relationship, you and your partner may get more satisfaction from involvement with a local organization. Several obvious advantages to supporting a local LGBT organization include

✔ Local groups are closer to the problems that many people are experiencing. Whatever the national climate as to a particular issue, there will be significant differences on the ground, close to where the issues are happening.

✔ You likely have greater opportunities for hands-on work. Local organizations are chronically underfunded and often understaffed. Volunteers are often welcomed with open arms (and perhaps even tears of gratitude)!

✔ Some local groups serve groups that work for broader issues of social justice and public health, not just for the LGBT community, but beyond. If those concerns mirror your own, you may find great personal satisfaction in working for a local HIV testing site, getting trained to work a phone help line, working at a local LGBT youth center, and so on.

✔ Your kids (if you have any) can get to see you in action. You'll be showing them the importance of activism, rather than just talking about it, which can be hard for younger kids to understand, anyway.

If you live in or near a major metropolitan area, there will be no shortage of organizations, and you should easily be able to find information about them. If you live in more rural or remote areas though, you may have more difficulty in finding an organization that speaks to your interests. If so, be flexible! If you're blessed with time, energy, and ambition, start your own organization.

Think about what you want to do and how much time you have to give. Don't make commitments that are overly optimistic, and know that you have the flexibility to adjust your commitments upward or downward as your life changes. Just be sure to communicate with others in the organization so that no one's counting on you for something you can't realistically do.

No matter what organization you get involved with, you are a volunteer. Be clear about what you're willing to do. And whatever it is, it deserves to be appreciated.

Using social media to tell your story

With about *one billion* Facebook users as of this writing, can you imagine a more effective tool for getting your voice out there? Other social media sites, such as Twitter, LinkedIn, Google Plus, and so on, means you have many opportunities to share your message online.

Of course, you can only send stuff to those individuals who choose to connect to you. Some choose to connect to only a few people, while others have hundreds, even thousands, of connections. Whatever the number, you have an audience for telling your story.

You have a couple decisions to make: how much you want to disclose about your life and to how broad a circle of people. For some people, social media can be a way of getting out the word about their lives to those who may otherwise not know much about the LGBT community.

Just as with openly living your life, using social media in an open way can be a powerful educational tool, exposing the non-gay majority to the everyday facts about your life. Most of your life, they will discover, isn't too different from their own lives. And that sort of familiarity can breed understanding and empathy, which they need for those times when you choose to share information about some of the challenges you're facing just because you're LGBT. If a doctor treats you poorly or a neighbor's kids can't play with yours just because your son has two moms, or the local swim club won't recognize your family *as a family*, letting others know about what's going on can be a release for you and educational for them. You'll even get some expressions of support, which can be helpful. (Those people who don't like what you're sharing aren't likely to be nasty about it; they'll probably just dump you as a contact.)

Some people post news stories about the LGBT community. Sometimes these stories are funny, sometimes celebratory, but often they're noting some discrimination, clueless comment, or downright outrageous action against members of the LGBT community. If you're inclined to do this, remember that not everyone shares your sense of outrage. Too much posting of this sort can cause at least some people to pass right over what you're sending them. Use good judgment.

Countering anti-equality arguments

Hearing or reading homophobic, or simply uninformed, assertions about the LGBT community can be infuriating. Countering these misperceptions is essential, but doing so can be difficult if you're confronted with a statement you believe, or know, to be wrong, but are unprepared to answer. Figuring out how to talk back in these cases is an important part of activism. You're educating people, empowering yourself, and advancing the whole movement, one conversation at a time.

To do so, start by taking a deep breath (literally), and reminding yourself that every one of the arguments that's been made against equality has a good answer, and that many of the debates that people want to engage in have already been answered. If you're not already knowledgeable about LGBT rights, educate yourself. There are a number of excellent accounts of some of the legal and social disabilities that have historically confronted the community, and that continue to do so, even today. Read, talk, attend a conference — in short, become a sponge for information that you can use to talk back to ignorance.

Then, try out these responses to the parade of clueless comments (and develop your own!):

✔ *Comment:* Passing antidiscrimination laws to protect LGBT people is providing special rights to these groups.

✔ *Response:* Antidiscrimination laws are simply intended to place the protected group on the same footing as everyone else. When a group is added to the list, it's because there's a documented history of discrimination against that group. That's why there are protections for race, sex, national origin, religion, and disability. And that's also why gays, lesbians, bisexuals, and transgendered folks need to be protected.

✔ *Comment:* You can't compare the treatment of African-Americans, or women — who couldn't even vote until about 90 years ago — to the treatment of the LGBT community.

✔ *Response:* Well, it's true that the experiences of those in the LGBT community are different from the ones you've mentioned. But it's not a contest to determine who's had it the worst, and plenty of documentation exists of the horrendous treatment of the LGBT community. [You can follow up with specific examples of how LGBT people have been beaten, forbidden from congregating in public, denied rights to custody of their children, treated as criminals for even their private sexual intimacy, denied the right to marry or serve in the military, and so on. The list is long.]

✔ *Comment:* Kids need a mother and a father. Allowing same-sex couples to marry or to adopt children is sending the message that this isn't important.

✔ *Response:* The social science research shows that kids do just as well with lesbian parents, and that the emerging research suggests the same outcomes for gay dads, too. So many kids are in need of adoption that would otherwise not find permanent homes, and that almost all states agree — that's why most allow same-sex couples (or gay and lesbian individuals) to foster and adopt kids. And after that's permitted, it makes little sense not to allow the parents of those kids to marry.

✔ *Comment:* We should draw the line at marriage. It just *means* the union of a man and a woman, and for good reason. That's the only form of association that can create new, human life. (One version of this argument would allow civil unions or domestic partnerships. This makes the speaker seem more reasonable, because the benefits of marriage are offered, just not the social status.)

✔ *Response:* We allow opposite-sex couples to marry no matter whether they're too old to reproduce or infertile even in obvious ways (as where they're unable to have sexual intercourse). Marriage isn't really about tying marriage rights to reproduction; that's just a convenient way to rule out same-sex couples. Although only opposite-sex couples can reproduce without outside help, that's no reason to exclude same-sex couples, any more than it would be to exclude similar opposite-sex couples.

This list obviously isn't complete. You may hear other comments or need to create other responses that we offer. As with any sincere disagreement among fair-minded people, listen to what the other person is saying and respond in a way that is complexly personal, analytical, and practical. On these issues, many people are persuadable.

But some people are just hostile and aren't willing to listen to what you're saying. At some point, the smartest thing to do is simply to walk away.

Lobbying for Equality

Are you a political animal or do you have aspirations to become one? If so, you can realize your goal in several different ways. You can run for office and make changes firsthand. Although the idea of a member of the LGBT community being both out and successful may have been scoffed at until quite recently (except in a few very gay-friendly precincts, such as San Francisco and New York), now it's not necessarily front-page news. Gays and lesbians are mayors of major cities, Congress members, and untold state and local politicians and judges who have been successful. Of course, some walls haven't been breached, notably the Senate (as of this writing, anyway), the Supreme Court, and, most notably, the office of president. But today, you can find plenty of examples of successful LGB (and even a few transgendered) politicians to infuse you with hope.

Short of running for office yourself, there are plenty of things you can do. Here are some suggestions.

Locating your federal, state, and local representatives

You can educate yourself about the positions that your local, state, and federal politicians have taken on issues that matter to you. Often, though, their websites don't include the gay-related stuff, although more than likely they have taken positions on these issues. You may be able to find their positions on LGBT issues through a quick web search, but maybe not. If you find nothing on these issues, it's generally not a good sign. You should take additional steps to find out where they stand, and then engage them on these issues. But how? Check out these suggestions:

✔ **Expand your Internet search.** For federal and state lawmakers, you can usually find their record on LGBT issues if you're willing to dig a bit more deeply. Just because they don't want to emphasize that record doesn't mean they haven't voted. Check out the sites of LGBT advocacy and other progressive groups, which often track such information.

✔ **Call or e-mail their offices.** Especially if you're a constituent of a certain politician, he or she (more likely, a staff member) can often get back to you. Sometimes you may just get a form letter explaining a position on the issue you've inquired about. Still, this information is often recorded, and at least the politician knows that you (and others) have a concern. To the extent you can personalize the issue, you should.

✔ **If possible, go a step further and try to set up an appointment to actually visit your local state or federal representative.** At least for some, meeting them isn't impossible. For others, getting an appointment and meeting them can take a lot of time and patience that you may not have. If you do manage to get in, recognize that your time to speak is very limited. Tell your story and let him or her know what you want them to do (if anything). Even if you're fairly certain there's no chance that the course of action you're suggesting will be followed, at least you have put a face on an issue that the politician might safely have been dismissing with thoughtless sloganeering.

Discussing the "hot button" issues: The how-to

Knowing how to bring up and discuss the issues yourself is also important. Doing so with grace and gentle humor is essential (or no one will listen to you), but not easy. You need to identify opportunities to speak out and make the most of them. If you can figure out how to do so deftly, you can advance the cause by creating allies who may not otherwise have realized that your family suffers from inequality that has a real effect.

For example, lots of people like to complain about their taxes. Next time that happens, mention that you and your partner can't even file a joint return. (And if you're married in your state, you have an opportunity to talk about DOMA and how it overrides state law on marriage.) Even "better" (in this sense only) if your inability to file that joint return required your family to pay more than another, otherwise identical family — and better yet if you happen to know by how much!

You can also find broader lessons in the tax example:

✔ You can discuss how the law (mis)treats your family. That doesn't mean you need to bring up the unfairness every single time it remotely presents itself (no one wants to hear constant complaining), but that even well-meaning straight people can be comfortably clueless about your life.

✔ Many people respond to unfairness if you can show them concrete results. Yes, not being able to marry is fair, but why? Tell them, and give them examples of how you're affected.

✔ The more specific you can be, the better. Putting numbers and concrete results to the discussion can make it stick better with your audience.

Finding your voice: Blogging and writing letters to the editor

Some people do their best work from the privacy of their own homes. If you're a writer, use your skill to engage the public on LGBT issues that matter to you. Maybe a particular news story has infuriated or encouraged you. Perhaps you've had a personal experience that speaks to some broader issue that you're uniquely positioned to discuss. Or maybe you just like to write, and LGBT issues are a natural fit for you.

The good news is that getting your stuff noticed is easier than it used to be. Before the Internet, your options really were only your local newspaper. You could write letters to the editor or an op-ed piece. But in the print era, the amount of space was relatively small and crowded. Few could get noticed.

Today, magazines and newspapers have web presences that greatly expand the amount of text they can publish. Some publications are entirely online. You have many, many opportunities to get your voice out there, so find a way to do so.

You can also just take to the Internet yourself and create your own blog. Several good software programs are available. They're easy to figure out and use, and many of them are free, which enables you to launch your own blog. The upside is that you get to write what you want to establish your own voice. The downside? Getting noticed among the throngs of other bloggers isn't easy. Here are some suggestions for would-be bloggers out there:

✔ **Commit to a regular schedule.** Sticking to a schedule is more difficult that you may think, especially after your initial enthusiasm begins to wane. But if you want to build an audience, they'll start to check in with you. And if you don't have anything to read, they'll drift away. The Internet is a crowded place, and readers have options, so make sure you post regularly to keep them coming back for more.

✔ **Pick something that you're interested enough to stick with.** For most people, having a specific focus is a good idea. Are you a lesbian living in City X? A transgendered man dealing with the constant ignorance of those around you? Do you see the amusing side of LGBT life? Are you a sports nut or an opera buff? You have some interest that you can write passionately about. (Some people find this approach too constricting and prefer to blog about various and sundry things; perhaps not even a majority of the posts will be about LGBT issues.)

✔ **Get the word out in any way you can.** Comment on other sites by link-ing back to something you've written on yours (but only if it's relevant!). Tweet. Post to Facebook and other social media sites. Be creative. Be consistent. Be insistent. And keep plugging away.

One possible side benefit of blogging is that, as you become more confident doing so, you may feel more inclined to reach out and write opinion pieces for other publications.

Making your own kind of music

Figure out who you are and how you want to get involved. Activism can be frustrating and painful, but in the long run it can be quite powerful. All the years of living as an LGBT person in a society that has a complex and not-always positive view of you has provided you with the material you need to engage your activist self. Tap into that well of experience. As this book dem-onstrates, there's a great deal of work to be done.

Part V
The Part of Tens

The 5th Wave   By Rich Tennant

"I've been working more than 80 hours a week for the past two years preparing for retirement, and it hasn't bothered me or my husband, what's-his-name."

In this part . . .

The Part of Tens is one of the most popular features of *For Dummies* books because it provides lots of valuable information in a quick-read format. If you think of the other parts in this book as main courses, the Part of Tens is like a dessert.

In this part, you can discover some reliable tricks for dealing with relatives who may be less than supportive of your relationship. And we also remind you of ten ways that the law works against you, your partner, and your family — and therefore why you need this book!

Chapter 20

Ten (Or So) Keys to Dealing with Disgruntled Relatives

In This Chapter

▶ Coping with difficult relatives

▶ Protecting yourself and your partner in times of crisis

*W*ith the advent of the Internet and the success of the LGBT equality movement, things are getting better. But despite the success of the LGBT civil rights movement at changing hearts and minds, opponents of equality are pushing back against that progress. The opposition has made many accusations.

The result of these allegations is that no matter how much progress is made, lots of gay men and lesbians have family members who buy into the antigay propaganda. To deal with them, you have a few options:

✔ Avoid those family members altogether.

✔ Figure out how to deal with them.

✔ Help them see the error of their ways.

For people choosing the second and third options, this chapter provides tips on how best to interact with angry or hurt family members — yours or your partner's — who are in mourning (because the idea of who they wanted you to be is gone) or in the midst of a crisis. We hope these tips help your family members understand you and your relationship (if you're in one) and eventually accept you.

Coming Out to Your Family

Coming out of the closet, no matter your age, can be frightening. Not too long ago, a majority of gay and lesbian youth and adults were in the closet about their sexual orientation — and for good reason. Even today, LGBT folks, especially teens, who dare to come out are rebuked and sometimes shunned by friends and family. The fear of rejection is so great that some gay men and lesbians have spent decades keeping their relationships a secret, never telling family members or coworkers the truth about their home life.

If you're in a relationship, you owe it to yourself and your partner to inform your family about your relationship status. Even if you're not in a relationship, disclosing your sexuality is important to be truthful to yourself.

Why is coming out important, particularly when you're in a relationship? Imagine a scenario where you suffer a sudden illness or injury (or worse) and you've made legal documents appointing your partner as your agent to make healthcare and other decisions for you and to inherit your property. Now picture your partner and your family members all together in your hospital room (with you being unable to speak for yourself) when the doctor walks in and asks "Who here is authorized to consent to emergency surgery?"

If you've been telling your family your partner is merely your friend or roommate, he or she is now in the awkward position of either lying, being evasive, or outing you. These options are all bad, especially because everyone in the room is already feeling concerned about your ailments.

Coming out to your family is difficult, and you may suffer some sort of emotional trauma, but hearing from you that you're gay is better than from your partner or from a stranger. Besides, a majority of families who've dealt with the coming out issue have been able to get beyond the negative feelings after they've had time to get accustomed to the idea.

If you're absolutely adamant about not coming out to your family, at least tell them you've appointed your "roommate" or "best friend" to make your medical and financial decisions and also named him or her as executor of your will and sole beneficiary.

Establishing the Best Way to Talk to Your Partner's Relatives

If your partner is the one who has suffered a serious injury or illness, you may have to talk to his or her family about what's really going on. Depending on your own relationship with your partner's family (and your understanding of the likelihood of a loud or violent reaction), you can choose to reveal the truth about the status of your relationship face to face, through a friend or supportive family member, or in a letter that they can read outside of your presence.

If your partner isn't likely to recover and the conflict between your partner and his or her family was never resolved, those relatives more than likely will experience guilt, fear, and/or frustration that they may express toward you. If that happens, try to keep in mind that they're suffering. Try to be patient and don't exacerbate the situation by voicing your feelings about their past actions. Your partner's best interest is to be surrounded by loved ones, so tread carefully.

If your partner is likely to recover, just continuing the ruse and leaving the coming out story for later may be easier. Your partner knows his or her family better than you do, so trust your partner's judgment about why he or she's never bothered to come out to them.

If you do decide to out your partner, don't act surprised or offended if the family reacts badly. Unless they start getting verbally or physically abusive, just let them go through all the natural phases one would expect to see after getting shocking and unwelcome news.

If the family already knows your partner's sexual orientation and disapproves of your relationship, you can avoid them. If that's not possible, for your partner's sake, be polite. Obviously, if one or more of them is verbally or physically abusive, taking turns with the family visiting your partner part of the day and you visiting at a different time may be the best solution.

Making Sure You're Safe

Very few people are able to go through their entire lives without having to confront their own or their partner's family. And when relations with kinfolk are strained, family gatherings tend to happen only when someone is sick, gets married, or dies — in other words, during times of increased stress.

Whatever the motive, if you must be in the presence of relatives — yours or your partner's — who say or do things to hurt you, make sure you're physically and emotionally safe and have moral support. Perhaps you have relatives who will rally to your side if someone acts inappropriately. If not, have a friend or two sit with you to act as a buffer or as a shoulder to lean on.

If all else fails and you're in a medical facility or funeral home and you feel physically or emotionally harassed by a relative, ask the relative to leave. If the person doesn't, ask someone in charge to remove the relative from the premises.

Using Healthy Communication

If you have some difficult family members, you may feel frustrated because you can't communicate with them. Believe it or not, there really is a way to communicate with relatives — or anyone, for that matter — that's more likely to diffuse a potentially volatile situation.

To communicate with a difficult person, try these three basic steps:

1. **Echo back what the person said.**

   When you do, try not to sound angry, sarcastic, or otherwise judgmental. With no added emotion and in your own words, repeat back what you heard the person say. If his words were abusive or cruel, perhaps he can hear it and immediately take a step back. If you heard him wrong and he insists that's not what he meant, ask him to repeat it, and when he does, echo his words back again.

2. **After you show you understood what was said, try letting the person know his feelings are valid.**

   You don't need to agree that he is right. Just simply note he is entitled to those feelings.

3. **Try to empathize with what he is going through and let him know you can see where he's coming from.**

Practicing this kind of communication isn't easy, but it really works if you make the effort. There is a chance the other person won't want to play along or cooperate. If all else fails, stop trying to communicate, and don't get dragged into an argument.

Backing Up Your Decision-Making Authority with Written Proof

If your partner has authorized you to make medical and financial decisions or put you in charge of his or her funeral arrangements or memorial service plans, be prepared for potential blow-back from your partner's hostile family members when they're told about it.

To prevent any extra craziness, make your decisions official by creating the necessary paperwork (check out the chapters in Part III). If possible, have on hand a copy of the legal documents granting you the authorization to make decisions. Make sure you give copies to the hospital, funeral director, your partner's doctor, and so on. If you have a living will setting out your partner's wishes for medical treatment at the end of his or her life, make sure the family is aware that your decisions merely reflect your partner's wishes.

Nothing triggers a guilt-ridden or hurt relative more than discovering she has no decision-making power or authority over her sick or deceased family member. No matter what happens, try to remember you're only doing what you promised your partner you would do.

Deflecting Religious Attacks

Oftentimes opponents of LGBT relationships use their religious beliefs as a rationale for denying rights to same-sex partners. Family members aren't above using this tactic, and some have successfully convinced hospital personnel and others to ignore legal documents and side with them in overriding their relative's wishes on religious grounds.

One of the best ways to overcome this ploy is to fight fire with fire by bringing in an LGBT-affirming clergy member to present a counter argument also based on religious teachings. If you're unable to find someone to make your case in person, ask her to call or write a letter to whoever is blocking your authority to act under your partner's legal documents. After she sees two (or more) sides to the argument, she ideally will back down.

Establishing Legal Parenting Rights

As an LGBT parent, more than likely you have a lopsided legal relationship with your partner's child. As a result, making sure you have legal parenting rights for both partners is imperative.

Because same-sex couples can't have children the "natural" way, the law usually considers only one of them to be the legal parent — at least until the co-parent has a chance to adopt their child as a second parent.

During that time (between birth and adoption and second-parent adoption) the nonlegal parent has no right to custody of his or her own child. Thus, if something were to happen to the parent with legal rights (injury, illness, or death), the co-parent would have no right to raise his or her child. That's why creating parenting rights via legal documents and adoption is so important. You want to do these things sooner than later. We provide insight on what to do in Chapters 7, 12, and 13.

Especially if the legal parent's family is hostile to the relationship, you have a good chance that the nonlegal parent will lose custody of the child if you don't create the necessary paperwork. And with no state or federal law to back up the co-parent's rights, unless the legal parent put in writing his or her preference for guardian of the child, those rights may be lost forever.

If something happens to a legal parent and the co-parent has not been officially appointed as guardian, *do not* let the legal parent's family take the child away, unless you're absolutely certain they won't try to usurp your right to raise the child as your own!

Maintaining Your Dignity

Society treats LGBT people as second-class citizens. The government and many religious leaders make harmful and inaccurate statements that the family may not realize are false. When so many people in positions of authority say hurtful things, trying to convince anyone, even relatives, that these authority figures are wrong may be difficult. No matter how relatives treat you, you need to maintain your dignity.

Unlike a majority of other oppressed minorities who were raised in families where everyone shares traits that set them apart from the majority (race, color, religion, creed, ethnicity, and so on), most LGBT individuals are the only gay or lesbian person in their immediate family. The mean parents and siblings can't relate to being gay or lesbian, which can exacerbate feelings of being different. Being completely isolated from others who can relate to what they're experiencing, especially in a crisis, is bad for any person.

One of the best ways to cope is to get support from others. Thanks to the Internet, finding a community is now easier than ever. We hope you can find members of a gay- and lesbian-affirming organization, church, or local LGBT center who can support you in your time of need.

Taking a Break

If dealing with difficult and hostile family members becomes too much, take a break. You may not be able to do anything except wait it out. And often, time is all that's needed for hurt feelings to mend and tempers to cool. You won't be helping anyone, least of all your partner, if you're not physically, mentally, and emotionally fit.

Chapter 21

Ten Ways the Law Harms the LGBT Community

. . . .

In This Chapter

▶ Connecting the effects of the law to everyday lives of the LGBT community

▶ Spelling out specific legal disabilities

. . . .

*G*ays and lesbians face many legal hurdles in their daily lives. Unfortunately these laws also serve as a societal backdrop for enabling homophobia in its many odious forms. This chapter deals with specific laws that harm various members of the community in different ways. But the most important effect of these laws is the pervasive homophobia that they recognize, support, and enable.

We hate to be the bearers of such bad news, but knowing how the law hurts you is important because you can then take action to effect change. (Check out Chapter 19 where we discuss how you can become an activist.) This chapter points out ten ways the law hurts same-sex couples, their families, and every single person who identifies as a member of the LGBT community. The takeaway? All LGBT folks and their allies still have a great deal of work to do before equality is achieved.

LGBT Youth (and the Children of Same-Sex Parents) Are Harmed

More than likely, you understood from a young age what the law had to say about being gay and about same-sex unions. The law itself supports a culture and set of expectations from which you instinctively felt excluded. And marriage laws are only the most obvious signal that the majority, straight society sends to LGBT and questioning youth that their lives have less value. Every single law and practice that either excludes LGBT people or discriminates against them directly contributes to a culture in which homophobia is the accepted norm.

Children in gay- and lesbian-headed households also suffer from this societal attitude. They often suffer ridicule or exclusion just because of the sexual orientation of their parents.

Just as antigay laws help create a culture of homophobia, so too do positive changes in the law contribute to a better atmosphere for LGBT families. Not everyone thinks these changes are for the better, though. For example, in his dissent from the Supreme Court's decision in *Lawrence v. Texas,* Justice Antonin Scalia pined over what he saw as the Court's role in changing this environment. The Court held that states had no business criminalizing the way that same-sex couples express private sexual intimacy for each other. But Scalia would have upheld the law, exactly *because* it expressed broader moral disapproval of gays and lesbians! Many Americans, he wrote, didn't want members of the gay community as business partners, teachers of their children, and so on. And that was okay by him.

The flip side, of course, is that the law *was* struck down. And with more and more states offering marriage equality, with antidiscrimination laws being enacted, with the repeal of Don't Ask, Don't Tell, and so on, clearly the legal problems that the community face are easing — although not fast enough. And the societal homophobia is falling right along with it.

Antigay Measures Validate Bullies

Anti-marriage equality measures go into state constitutions. State legislatures introduce bills to ban discussing homosexuality in schools, no matter the subject or context. A state governor revokes the health benefits that gay and lesbian partners of state employees had been previously been able to receive.

Sometimes these measures pass, and sometimes they don't. But their very presence and the publicity they generate lead to a climate in which those who are inclined to bully or intimidate members of the LGBT community — and other gender nonconformers — are empowered. You probably think of schools as the site of bullying, but this kind of treatment isn't limited to that setting. Employees are harassed and bullied by coworkers and bosses, gay and lesbian couples are taunted and sometimes physically assaulted, and even homophobic family members can draw strength from a climate in which their views are supported.

Your Boss Can Fire You for Being LGBT

The lack of employment antidiscrimination protection is one of the most important practical problems facing the LGBT community. In many places, an employer can legally discriminate in hiring, promoting, or retaining an employee just for being gay or lesbian — and state law protection for transgendered people is even rarer. Many companies, large and small, have their own nondiscrimination policies, but some still don't. And those policies aren't law (unless they're also in a contract, in which case the can be enforced by a court).

If you or your partner can get fired — or not hired in the first place, or not promoted — just because of your sexual orientation, you'll undoubtedly experience stress. If you're in the process of coming out of the closet, more than likely, you'll stall. Even if you're already out, you may try to hide or downplay your sexual orientation.

Federal workplace protection is needed, but the Employment Nondiscrimination Act (ENDA), which would protect gays, lesbians, bisexuals, and the transgendered, has been stalled in Congress for years. So for now, members of the LGBT community have to rely on state or local law. (A recent ruling by the Equal Employment Opportunity Commission ruled that discrimination against transgendered employees is prohibited under federal law, but this ruling doesn't have the force of a statute and may be challenged in court.)

LGBT Parents Are Denied Legal Rights and Financial Benefits

One of the strongest arguments for full marriage equality is that when the law doesn't recognize the relationship between gay and lesbian couples raising children, that lack of recognition harms their children in measurable ways:

- One parent may not be recognized as the child's legal parent.
- When a child is denied a second legal parent, that child is likelier to end up without a stable and secure environment.
- When the parents are unable to access financial benefits that accrue to legally married people, this inequality harms the whole family, including their children.

Partners Are Denied Access to their Deceased Partner's Home and Property

The law throws more than a few bones the way of married couples, and nowhere is this in greater evidence than in how property rights and taxes are treated. When one member of a legally married couple dies, the surviving partner is protected in ways designed to increase the odds that he or she will be able to hang on to the deceased partner's estate. LGBT couples lose out on these rights unless they sign a will and/or trust (refer to Part III for how to establish a will or trust) that leaves all their belongings to their surviving spouse. Even if they take these smart steps, they must pay inheritance and estate taxes that legally married couples don't have to pay.

LGBT couples are denied access in these ways:

- ✔ If they don't have a will, the surviving LGBT partner is left out in the cold when it comes to the estate. In the case of a married couple, the surviving spouse takes a substantial share of the estate under the law of intestacy.

- ✔ If estate taxes need to be paid, a surviving legal spouse is exempt from it, but not the survivor of an unmarried, same-sex couple.

- ✔ In about half the states, married couples hold property through *tenancy by the entirety,* which provides the best protection of the surviving spouse's interest in the property when the other one dies. Tenancy by the entirety isn't available to same-sex couples who can't marry. (Refer to Chapter 5 for more information.)

Couples Have to Spend Money on Documents to Protect Their Rights

Marriage creates many rights and assumptions in favor of couples, freeing them from the necessity of drawing up contracts to deal with their personal affairs and their financial relationship. LBGT couples must spend hundreds, sometimes even thousands, of dollars to protect themselves, as best they can, by drawing up the documents — primarily wills and trusts — which we discuss in Part III of this book.

Because same-sex couples must rely on documents they draw up to try to establish their rights, those documents are often challenged by disgruntled relatives or invalidated (or read unsympathetically) by judges who don't approve of same-sex couples.

LGBT Tenants Can Be Evicted Because of Sexual Orientation

In 1968, the US Congress passed the Fair Housing Act (FHA) as Title VIII of the Civil Rights Act. The law prohibits discrimination in housing if that discrimination was based on a person's race, religion, handicap, familial status, or thanks to a recently enacted regulation by the Department of Housing and Urban Development, sexual orientation or gender identity. Unfortunately, the exemptions to the FHA are big enough to drive a tank through!

So even though discrimination for LBGT folks is illegal with HUD properties, the law isn't foolproof. For instance, if the property you want to buy or rent has one of the following, then you can be denied the right to purchase or lease the property with no legal recourse, unless you're fortunate enough to live in a state or city with its own nondiscrimination statute that also covers sexual orientation and/or gender identify:

- ✔ The building has fewer than five apartments.
- ✔ The building is being sold or leased by the owner (without a real estate broker).
- ✔ Your landlord lives in one of the units.

And keep in mind that HUD, like all federal agencies, is part of the executive branch of government, which means that a new president can rescind these regulations.

Older Couples Don't Have Rights to Spend Their Final Days Together

Social Security death benefits go to surviving members of married opposite-sex couples, but not to same-sex couple survivors — even if they're married in a state that recognizes their marriage — because of DOMA. The same is true under any pension plan covered by the federal ERISA law, at least if the pension goes to the "spouse." (But an employer may be able to set up a pension plan to enable you to leave your pension to your partner if you expressly so designate him or her.)

And unless all your documents are in order, including your living revocable will and durable power of attorney (refer to Chapter 9 for more information), you and your partner may not be able to spend your final days together, make decisions for each other, or even visit each other in the hospital.

Immigration Laws Prevent Bi-National Couples from Being Together

Immigrating into the United States is difficult. The government allows only a limited number of slots each year, and getting one of them requires meeting specific requirements. For example, highly skilled workers have an advantage over others. But one exception to this rule is for married couples. Recognizing the value and importance of intact families, the law allows US citizens to sponsor their spouses, making them eligible for so-called green cards, which allow them to live and work in the United States permanently.

Not so for same-sex couples. In most states, same-sex couples aren't permitted to marry. But even in states where full marriage equality has been achieved, the "immediate family member" option isn't available as a way of (re)uniting same-sex couples — because, again, thanks (no thanks) to DOMA. Because immigration law is federal, DOMA applies, and it declares same-sex marriages null and void.

LGBT Families Bear an Increased Tax Burden

Generally, married couples get to file their federal income taxes jointly. Although being married can create a *marriage penalty* (additional tax liability) in cases of higher wage earners, it can also *decrease* the tax burden for others (most typically, in situations with one high wage earner and another who earns little or no income).

This tax advantage isn't available to same-sex couples, though. Why? As you might have guessed by now, it's because of DOMA. For federal purposes, even legally married same-sex couples aren't . . . legally married.

Appendix A

About the CD

*U*sing the CD that accompanies this book couldn't be easier. You can pop it into pretty much any Mac or Windows computer made in the last ten years as long as that computer has an optical drive capable of playing good, old-fashioned CDs. If you're the hesitant type, check out the following system requirements.

System Requirements

Make sure that your computer meets the minimum system requirements shown in the following list. If your computer doesn't match up to most of these requirements, you may have problems using the software and files on the CD. For the latest and greatest information, please refer to the ReadMe file located at the root of the CD-ROM.

✔ A PC running Microsoft Windows or Linux with kernel 2.4 or later

✔ A Macintosh running Apple OS X or later

✔ An Internet connection

✔ A CD-ROM drive

If you need more information on the basics, check out these books published by John Wiley & Sons, Inc.: *PCs For Dummies* by Dan Gookin; *Macs For Dummies* by Edward C. Baig; *iMacs For Dummies* by Mark L. Chambers; *Windows XP For Dummies* and *Windows Vista For Dummies,* both by Andy Rathbone.

Using the CD

To install the items from the CD to your hard drive, follow these steps.

1. **Insert the CD into your computer's CD-ROM drive.**

   The license agreement appears.

   Strike the following Note if your CD will not support Windows OS.

   Note to Windows users: The interface won't launch if you have autorun disabled. In that case, choose Start➪Run. (For Windows Vista, choose Start➪All Programs➪Accessories➪Run.) In the dialog box that appears, type *D:\Start.exe*. (Replace *D* with the proper letter if your CD drive uses a different letter. If you don't know the letter, see how your CD drive is listed under My Computer.) Click OK.

   Notes for Mac Users: When the CD icon appears on your desktop, double-click the icon to open the CD and double-click the Start icon. Also, note that the content menus may not function as expected in newer versions of Safari and Firefox; however, the documents are available by navigating to the Contents folder.

2. **Read through the license agreement and then click the Accept button if you want to use the CD.**

   The CD interface appears. The interface allows you to browse the contents and install the programs with just a click of a button (or two).

What You'll Find on the CD

The following sections are arranged by category and provide a summary of the software and other goodies you'll find on the CD. If you need help with installing the items provided on the CD, refer back to the installing instructions in the preceding section.

The following lists materials referred to in chapters and for numerous additional resources related to the chapter topic. Each form is available to you as a PDF file. You need Adobe Acrobat Reader (available on this CD) to view, print, and edit the PDF files. You can use your favorite word processing program to view, print, and edit the .rtf files.

Chapter 2

Appendix B contains a list of state marriage recognition laws

Chapter 4

Form 4-1: Sample Nondiscrimination/Diversity Statement

Chapter 5

Form 5-1: Sample Co-Tenant Agreement

Form 5-2: Sample Living Together Agreement

Form 5-3: Sample Quit Claim Deed Creating a Joint Tenancy with Rights of Survivorship (JTWROS)

Form 5-4: Sample Quit Claim Deed Creating a Tenancy in Common

Form 5-5: Sample Sweat Equity Agreement

Chapter 7

Appendix B: State-by-State Adoption Laws and Surrogacy Laws

Form 7-1: Sample Co-Parenting Agreement

Form 7-2: Sample Nomination of Guardian

Form 7-3: Sample Authorization to Consent to Medical Treatment

Chapter 9

Form 9-1: Sample Medical Advance Directives

Form 9-2: Sample Generic Living Will

Form 9-3: Sample Medical Power of Attorney

Form 9-4: Title of Each State's Medical Advance Directives

Form 9-5: Sample Stand-Alone Hospital Visitation

Form 9-6: Example Hospital Visitation Clause

Form 9-7: Sample Health Insurance Portability and Accountability Act (HIPAA)

Form 9-8: Sample Durable Power of Attorney for Finances (DPOA)

Form 9-9: Health and Human Services (HHS) hospital visitation rule

Form 9-10: Sample Irrevocable Medicaid Trust

Chapter 10

Form 10-1: State-By-State List of Domestic Partnership Statutes

Form 10-2: Sample Living Together Agreement

Chapter 11

Form 11-1: Sample Asset and Property Inventory Form

Form 11-2: Estate-Planning (List-Making) Worksheet

Form 11-3: Signing Requirements for DPOA in All 50 States

Form 11-4: Signing Requirements for Medical Advance Directives in All 50 States

Chapter 12

Form 12-1: Blank Asset and Property Inventory Form

Form 12-2: Sample Last Will and Testament

Form 12-3: Sample Self-Proving Affidavit

Form 12-4: Sample Separate Writing

Form 12-5: Sample Disposition of Remains

Form 12-6: Example Information for Executor Form

Form 12-7: Sample Pour-Over Will

Chapter 13

Form 13-1: Sample Living Revocable Trust

Form 13-2: Sample First Amendment to Living Revocable Trust

Form 13-3: Sample Revocation of Living Revocable Trust

Form 13-4: Sample Certification of Trust

Form 13-5: Estate-Planning Worksheet

Form 13-6: Sample Blank Asset and Property Inventory Form

Form 13-7: Sample Acceptance as Trustee of Living Revocable Trust

Form 13-8: Resignation as Trustee of Living Revocable Trust

Form 13-9: Example Trust Clauses

Form 13-10: Detailed List of Duties of Trustee

Form 13-11: Sample Letter Requesting a Death Certificate

Form 13-12: Sample Letter from Successor Trustee to Financial Institutions

Form 13-13: Sample-Letter-from-Successor-Trustee-to-Insurance-Agency

IRS Form 56 Notice of Fiduciary Relationship

IRS Forms SS-4

IRS Instructions for Obtaining a Federal Tax Identification Number (FEIN)

Chapter 14

Form 14-1: Sample Schedule A

Form 14-2: Sample Notice of Assignment of Property

Form 14-3: Sample Grant Deed

Form 14-4: Sample Quit-Claim Deed

Form 14-5: Letter to Send to Financial Institution to Fund Trust

Chapter 15

Form 15-1: Domestic-Partnership Declaration

Chapter 17

Appendix C: International Marriage Equality Recognition

Troubleshooting

We tried our best to compile programs that work on most computers with the minimum system requirements. Alas, your computer may differ, and some programs may not work properly for some reason.

The two likeliest problems are they don't have enough memory (RAM) for the programs you want to use or you have other programs running that are affecting installation or running out of a program. If you get an error message such as *Not enough memory* or *Setup cannot continue,* try one or more of the following suggestions and then try using the software again:

- ✔ **Turn off any antivirus software running on your computer.** Installation programs sometimes mimic virus activity and may make your computer incorrectly believe that it's being infected by a virus.

- ✔ **Close all running programs.** The more programs you have running, the less memory is available to other programs. Installation programs typically update files and programs, so if you keep other programs running, installation may not work properly.

- ✔ **Have your local computer store add more RAM to your computer.** This is, admittedly, a drastic and somewhat expensive step. However, adding more memory can really help to speed of your computer and allow more programs to run at the same time.

Customer Care

If you have trouble with the CD–ROM, please call the Wiley Product Technical Support phone number at 877-762 -2974. Outside the United States, call 1-317-572-3994. You can also contact Wiley product technical support at `http://support.wiley.com`. John Wiley & Sons, Inc. will provide technical support only for installation and other general quality control items. For technical support on the applications themselves, consult the program's vendor or author.

To place additional orders or to request information about other Wiley products, please call 877-762-2974.

Index

• Z •

John Wiley & Sons, Inc.
End-User License Agreement

READ THIS. You should carefully read these terms and conditions before opening the software packet(s) included with this book "Book". This is a license agreement "Agreement" between you and John Wiley & Sons, Inc. "WILEY". By opening the accompanying software packet(s), you acknowledge that you have read and accept the following terms and conditions. If you do not agree and do not want to be bound by such terms and conditions, promptly return the Book and the unopened software packet(s) to the place you obtained them for a full refund.

1. **License Grant.** WILEY grants to you (either an individual or entity) a nonexclusive license to use one copy of the enclosed software program(s) (collectively, the "Software") solely for your own personal or business purposes on a single computer (whether a standard computer or a workstation component of a multi-user network). The Software is in use on a computer when it is loaded into temporary memory (RAM) or installed into permanent memory (hard disk, CD-ROM, or other storage device). WILEY reserves all rights not expressly granted herein.

2. **Ownership.** WILEY is the owner of all right, title, and interest, including copyright, in and to the compilation of the Software recorded on the physical packet included with this Book "Software Media". Copyright to the individual programs recorded on the Software Media is owned by the author or other authorized copyright owner of each program. Ownership of the Software and all proprietary rights relating thereto remain with WILEY and its licensers.

3. **Restrictions on Use and Transfer.**

    (a) You may only (i) make one copy of the Software for backup or archival purposes, or (ii) transfer the Software to a single hard disk, provided that you keep the original for backup or archival purposes. You may not (i) rent or lease the Software, (ii) copy or reproduce the Software through a LAN or other network system or through any computer subscriber system or bulletin-board system, or (iii) modify, adapt, or create derivative works based on the Software.

    (b) You may not reverse engineer, decompile, or disassemble the Software. You may transfer the Software and user documentation on a permanent basis, provided that the transferee agrees to accept the terms and conditions of this Agreement and you retain no copies. If the Software is an update or has been updated, any transfer must include the most recent update and all prior versions.

4. **Restrictions on Use of Individual Programs.** You must follow the individual requirements and restrictions detailed for each individual program in the "About the CD" appendix of this Book or on the Software Media. These limitations are also contained in the individual license agreements recorded on the Software Media. These limitations may include a requirement that after using the program for a specified period of time, the user must pay a registration fee or discontinue use. By opening the Software packet(s), you agree to abide by the licenses and restrictions for these individual programs that are detailed in the "About the CD" appendix and/or on the Software Media. None of the material on this Software Media or listed in this Book may ever be redistributed, in original or modified form, for commercial purposes.

5. **Limited Warranty.**

   (a) WILEY warrants that the Software and Software Media are free from defects in materials and workmanship under normal use for a period of sixty (60) days from the date of purchase of this Book. If WILEY receives notification within the warranty period of defects in materials or workmanship, WILEY will replace the defective Software Media.

   (b) **WILEY AND THE AUTHOR(S) OF THE BOOK DISCLAIM ALL OTHER WARRANTIES, EXPRESS OR IMPLIED, INCLUDING WITHOUT LIMITATION IMPLIED WARRANTIES OF MERCHANTABILITY AND FITNESS FOR A PARTICULAR PURPOSE, WITH RESPECT TO THE SOFTWARE, THE PROGRAMS, THE SOURCE CODE CONTAINED THEREIN, AND/ OR THE TECHNIQUES DESCRIBED IN THIS BOOK. WILEY DOES NOT WARRANT THAT THE FUNCTIONS CONTAINED IN THE SOFTWARE WILL MEET YOUR REQUIREMENTS OR THAT THE OPERATION OF THE SOFTWARE WILL BE ERROR FREE.**

   (c) This limited warranty gives you specific legal rights, and you may have other rights that vary from jurisdiction to jurisdiction.

6. **Remedies.**

   (a) WILEY's entire liability and your exclusive remedy for defects in materials and workmanship shall be limited to replacement of the Software Media, which may be returned to WILEY with a copy of your receipt at the following address: Software Media Fulfillment Department, Attn.: *Same-Sex Legal Kit For Dummies,* John Wiley & Sons, Inc., 10475 Crosspoint Blvd., Indianapolis, IN 46256, or call 1-877-762-2974. Please allow four to six weeks for delivery. This Limited Warranty is void if failure of the Software Media has resulted from accident, abuse, or misapplication. Any replacement Software Media will be warranted for the remainder of the original warranty period or thirty (30) days, whichever is longer.

   (b) In no event shall WILEY or the author be liable for any damages whatsoever (including without limitation damages for loss of business profits, business interruption, loss of business information, or any other pecuniary loss) arising from the use of or inability to use the Book or the Software, even if WILEY has been advised of the possibility of such damages.

   (c) Because some jurisdictions do not allow the exclusion or limitation of liability for consequential or incidental damages, the above limitation or exclusion may not apply to you.

7. **U.S. Government Restricted Rights.** Use, duplication, or disclosure of the Software for or on behalf of the United States of America, its agencies and/or instrumentalities "U.S. Government" is subject to restrictions as stated in paragraph (c)(1)(ii) of the Rights in Technical Data and Computer Software clause of DFARS 252.227-7013, or subparagraphs (c) (1) and (2) of the Commercial Computer Software - Restricted Rights clause at FAR 52.227-19, and in similar clauses in the NASA FAR supplement, as applicable.

8. **General.** This Agreement constitutes the entire understanding of the parties and revokes and supersedes all prior agreements, oral or written, between them and may not be modified or amended except in a writing signed by both parties hereto that specifically refers to this Agreement. This Agreement shall take precedence over any other documents that may be in conflict herewith. If any one or more provisions contained in this Agreement are held by any court or tribunal to be invalid, illegal, or otherwise unenforceable, each and every other provision shall remain in full force and effect.